The Emergence of Civilizational Consciousness in Early China

This book provides a conceptual history of the emergence of civilizational consciousness in early China. Focusing on how words are used in pre-Qín (before 221 BCE) texts to construct identities and negotiate relationships between a 'civilized self' and 'uncivilized others,' it provides a re-examination of the origins and development of these ideas.

By adopting a novel approach to determining when civilizational consciousness emerged in pre-Qín China, this book analyzes this question in ways that establish a fresh hermeneutical dialogue between Chinese and modern European understandings of 'civilization.' Whereas previous studies have used archaeological data to place its origin somewhere between 3000 BCE and 1000 BCE, this book explores changes in word meanings in texts from the pre-Qín period to reject this view. Instead, this book dates the emergence of civilizational consciousness in China to around 2,500 years ago. In the process, new chronologies of the coining of Old Chinese terms such as 'customs,' 'barbarians,' and 'the Great ones' are proposed, which challenge anachronistic assumptions about these terms in earlier studies.

Examining important Chinese classics, such as the *Analects*, the *Mencius*, and the *Mòzǐ*, as well as key historical periods and figures in the context of the concept of 'civilization,' this book will useful to students and scholars of Chinese and Asian history.

Uffe Bergeton is Assistant Professor of Pre-Tang Chinese Language, Culture, and History in the Department of Asian Studies at University of North Carolina at Chapel Hill, USA. Having a background in both linguistics and ancient Chinese history, he specializes in the study of pre-Qín China.

Routledge Studies in the Early History of Asia

Marco Polo's China
A Venetian in the realm of Khubilai Khan
Stephen G Haw

The Diary of a Manchu Soldier in Seventeenth-Century China
"My service in the army," by Dzengeo
Introduction, Translation and Notes by Nicola Di Cosmo

Past Human Migrations in East Asia
Matching archaeology, linguistics and genetics
Edited by Alicia Sanchez-Mazas, Roger Blench, Malcolm D. Ross, Ilia Peiros and Marie Lin

Rethinking the Prehistory of Japan
Language, genes and civilisation
Ann Kumar

Ancient Chinese Encyclopedia of Technology
Jun Wenren

Women and the Literary World in Early Modern China, 1580–1700
Daria Berg

Asian Expansions
The historical experiences of polity expansion in Asia
Edited by Geoff Wade

The Emergence of Civilizational Consciousness in Early China
History Word by Word
Uffe Bergeton

The Emergence of Civilizational Consciousness in Early China

History Word by Word

Uffe Bergeton

LONDON AND NEW YORK

First published 2019
by Routledge
2 Park Square, Milton Park, Abingdon, Oxon OX14 4RN

and by Routledge
52 Vanderbilt Avenue, New York, NY 10017

Routledge is an imprint of the Taylor & Francis Group, an informa business

© 2019 Uffe Bergeton

The right of Uffe Bergeton to be identified as author of this work has been asserted by him in accordance with sections 77 and 78 of the Copyright, Designs and Patents Act 1988.

All rights reserved. No part of this book may be reprinted or reproduced or utilised in any form or by any electronic, mechanical, or other means, now known or hereafter invented, including photocopying and recording, or in any information storage or retrieval system, without permission in writing from the publishers.

Trademark notice: Product or corporate names may be trademarks or registered trademarks, and are used only for identification and explanation without intent to infringe.

British Library Cataloguing-in-Publication Data
A catalogue record for this book is available from the British Library

Library of Congress Cataloging-in-Publication Data
Names: Bergeton, Uffe, author.
Title: The emergence of civilizational consciousness in early
    China : history word by word / Uffe Bergeton.
Description: New York ; London : Routledge, 2019. | Series: Routledge
    studies in the early history of Asia ; 10 | Includes bibliographical
    references and index.
Identifiers: LCCN 2018029325 | ISBN 9781138344099 (hardback) |
    ISBN 9780429438721 (ebook) | ISBN 9780429797859 (epub) |
    ISBN 9780429797842 (mobipocket encrypted)
Subjects: LCSH: China—Civilization—To 221 B.C. | Group identity—
    China—History—To 1500. | Language and culture—China—History—
    To 1500. | Chinese language—Etymology—History—To 1500. |
    Comparative civilization. | Europe—Civilization.
Classification: LCC DS741.65 .B47 2019 | DDC 931—dc23
LC record available at https://lccn.loc.gov/2018029325

ISBN: 978-1-138-34409-9 (hbk)
ISBN: 978-0-429-43872-1 (ebk)

Typeset in Times
by Apex CoVantage, LLC

Every effort has been made to contact copyright holders for their permission to reprint material in this book. The publishers would be grateful to hear from any copyright holder who is not here acknowledged and will undertake to rectify any errors or omissions in future editions of this book.

This book is dedicated to 小秧

Contents

List of figures	viii
List of tables	ix
Acknowledgments	x
Introduction	1
1 The coining of civilizational consciousness in modern Western Europe	8
2 From 'awe-inspiringly beautiful' to 'morally refined': the coining of 'civility' in pre-Qín China	49
3 Coiners and critics of 'civility/civilization' (*wén*)	95
4 Inventing the 'barbarian': from 'belligerent others' to 'civilizationally inferior others'	135
5 Ethnographic vocabulary of civilizational otherness: the 'elegant' 'rites' of the 'Great ones' versus the 'vulgar' 'customs' of the 'barbarians'	172
Conclusion	196
Index	214

Figures

1.1	Conventions for talking about different aspects of words.	10
1.2	1500–1760s: combinations of words from (a) and (b) expressing the concept '*civilization*.'	21
1.3	1500–1760s: nonce occurrence of *civilization* in the verbal meaning 'civilization.'	22
1.4	Conceptual structure of the universal concept of 'civilization.'	24
1.5	Illustration appearing in editorial entitled "Civilisation" in the satirical magazine *Punch*, July–December 1841.	27
1.6	Lexicalizing *civilization* (1780s–1830s): from universal to ethnographic concept of 'civilization.'	29
1.7	Criteria for the archaeological concept of 'civilization.'	30
1.8	Conceptual structure of the archaeological concept of 'civilization.'	31
2.1	*Wén* 文 in oracle bone and bronze inscriptions.	57
2.2	Warring States period jade *bì* disc.	72
2.3	Tracing the history of the meaning changes of the word *wén*.	75
3.1	Tracing the history of the meaning changes of the word *wén* (same as Figure 2.3)	108
3.2	Comparing the modern European and pre-Qín universal concepts of 'civilization.'	110
4.1	Directional associations of *mán, yí, róng*, and *dí*.	141
4.2	Coining of words for the concept of 'civilizationally inferior others.'	156
4.3	Tracing the history of the meaning changes of the word *yí*.	157
5.1	Tracing the history of the meaning changes of the words *xià* and *yǎ*.	174
5.2	Tracing the history of the meaning changes of the words *yù* and *sú*.	180
5.3	Key terms articulating pre-Qín civilizational consciousness.	183
6.1	Pre-Qín 'wén' and the eighteenth-century European universal concept 'civilization.'	198
6.2	Is dialogue between the coiners of *wén* and *civilization* possible?	202

Tables

1.1	Lexicalization of civilizational consciousness in modern Western Europe.	35
4.1	Relative frequency of different types of ethnonyms.	160
4.2	Ethnonym compounds.	164
6.1	Language-specific concepts of 'civilization' in three different traditions/horizons.	207

Acknowledgments

This book ties together several research projects spanning several years. It could not have been written without the encouragement, feedback, and mentorship of countless people. As a student at University of Southern California, I was fortunate to be introduced to the fascinating world of early China by Bettine Birge, Erica Brindley, George Hayden, and Edward Slingerland. At the University of Michigan, my faculty advisor, William Baxter, safely guided me through the PhD program. Many of the ideas in this book were honed through conversations with him. My debt to him cannot be overstated. I am also grateful to my other faculty mentors and members of my PhD committee, Miranda Brown, Pär Cassel, Christian de Pee, and Norman Yoffee, for their feedback and support. Edward Shaughnessy's untiring efforts to help young scholars by organizing paleography workshops at the University of Chicago and archaeology trips to China also have played an important part in my formation as a scholar of early Chinese texts.

My colleagues in the Department of Asian Studies at the University of North Carolina at Chapel Hill have made it possible for me to write this book by creating a truly inspiring work environment. The feedback that I received from two faculty colloquia at which I presented parts of my book manuscript has been of great help. For that I would like to thank Jan Bardsley, Mark Driscoll, Zeina Halabi, Li-Ling Hsiao, Wendan Li, Pamela Lothspeich, Morgan Pitelka, Yaron Schmer, Afroz Taj, Robin Visser, Nadia Yaqub, and Gang Yue.

Numerous people have read and commented on earlier versions of the book manuscript (or parts thereof): Jan Bardsley, William Baxter, Miranda Brown, Pär Cassel, Christian de Pee, Mark Driscoll, Jon Felt, Royce Grubic, Zeina Halabi, Eric Henry, Ash Henson, Jens-André Herbener, Maria Khayutina, Pamela Lothspeich, Dirk Meyer, Molly Mullin, Morgan Pitelka, Stacy Moser, Yaron Schmer, Aaron Sonnenschein, Michael Tsin, Ignacio Villagran, Robin Visser, and Norman Yoffee, and Gang Yue.

I am grateful to Harvard Art Museums for granting permission to reprint the high-resolution photograph of the Warring States jade disc (located in the Arthur M. Sackler Museum) in Figure 2.2 and to *Punch* Magazine Cartoon Archive for allowing me to include the image in Figure 1.5.

Several parts of the book manuscript have been presented at conferences and as invited talks. I am particularly grateful to Chen Jian and Liu Zhao at the Center for Chinese Paleography at the Fudan University in Shanghai, China, for inviting me to present my work on the concept of '*wén.*' I am also indebted to Dirk Meyer at Oxford University for giving me the opportunity to present my work on the concept of the 'barbarian' there. Finally, I am indebted to Lee-moi Pham 范麗梅 for inviting me to present my analysis of the concept of 'customs' (*sú* 俗) at the Institute of Chinese Literature and Philosophy, Academia Sinica, Taipei, Taiwan. The feedback I have received from audiences at these events has been invaluable. All these people, as well as many others not mentioned here, deserve credit for the book's strengths; the remaining shortcomings and flaws are mine alone.

Finally, I owe my biggest debt of gratitude to my wife, Iris Yim. Without her companionship, love, and patience, I would never have been able to write this book.

Introduction

When did Chinese civilization begin? This is an old question with new relevance. Curiosity about China has surged as the country takes on new roles and more extensive power internationally. The Chinese government itself has turned to the history of Chinese civilization as it refashions national identity in the post-Mao era. Dates proposed for the origin of Chinese civilization can vary by several millennia. According to ancient mythological accounts that still inform the popular idea that China has five thousand years of history, civilization was first created by the sage–kings in the Golden Age of the Yellow Emperor. Inspired by traditional historiography, many Chinese archaeologists trace the emergence of Chinese civilization to the third or second millennium BCE. In contrast, Western scholars tend to place it in the second or first millennium BCE. I propose rephrasing the question altogether.

The lack of a single definition of the word *civilization* on which all archaeologists can agree has generated a wide range of different dates for the "origin of Chinese civilization." For example, when interpreting the material finds from a particular excavation site dating back to the third millennium BCE, some archaeologists may argue that the social formation they represent meets the criteria of a "civilization" if it bears witness to the presence of monumental architecture, metallurgy, and so forth. Others may disagree because there is no evidence of writing. Given the variation in concepts of 'civilization,' it is perhaps not surprising that the proposed dates of the origin of Chinese civilization differ so much.[1]

Instead of entering the often politicized debates on how old "Chinese civilization" is, which often involves quibbling over definitions of "Chineseness" and the various modern concepts of 'civilization' still used by most Chinese and some Western scholars, I take the different approach of asking instead when what I call "civilizational consciousness" first emerged in China.[2] The word-by-word approach to changes in thought proposed here is based on the assumption that the history of ideas can be explored through studies of historical changes in the words referring to those ideas. Ideas, like word meanings, are context-dependent; they emerge and continue to evolve through complex interactions of a group of individuals among themselves, with other groups, the sociopolitical environment itself, and other aspects of the ever-changing historical settings. The question I ask is therefore "How is the emergence of a collective civilizational consciousness

2   Introduction

reflected in changes in the words used to express an emergent concept of 'civilization'?" Rather than using the modern Western archaeological definitions of 'civilization' to determine when early societies in the area that is now China became a "civilization," I shall explore how lexical changes in word meanings over time can be used to date the birth of an indigenous early Chinese language-specific concept of 'civilization.' What ancient Old Chinese words were used to conceptualize and articulate a language-specific concept of 'civilization'? When, why, and how were they coined?

Numerous studies of early Chinese texts implicitly assume the existence of an early Chinese concept of 'civilization.' Roel Sterckx, for example, provides an insightful analysis of Chinese narratives of the "primitive origins of *civilization*" from the Warring States period (481–221 BCE) in which "*civilization* is presented as a course of successive cultural transitions." According to Sterckx, "several sources account how sages from antiquity engaged in acts of cultural creation or revealed to humankind feats of a *civilizing* potentiality that was embedded in the structures of nature and the cosmos. . . . *Civilization* brought a change in the habitat of both the living and the dead."

Here Sterckx uses the Modern English word *civilization* to discuss how early Chinese texts "present" "civilization" or describe the "histories of civilization" or the "civilizing endeavors of the sages."[3] Similar uses of the term *civilization* (and its Modern Chinese counterpart *wénmíng* 文明 'civilization') can be found in other studies of early Chinese history and thought.[4] Such uses of the English word *civilization* imply that the authors of early Chinese texts had a concept of 'civilization.' However, the nature of this language-specific ancient Chinese concept is rarely explicitly addressed in any depth.[5]

Poo Mu-chou's *Enemies of Civilization* (2005) is a notable exception, in that it contains a comparative analysis of how "cultural consciousness" in ancient Egypt, Mesopotamia, and China was expressed in each tradition's relationship with 'others' as "enemies of civilization." Poo defines "cultural consciousness" as "the characteristics of a culture commonly shared and employed by its people to distinguish themselves from people of other cultures" and argues that it is a "forceful factor in the formation and development of individual *civilizations*."[6] Poo focuses on the concepts for 'self' and 'other' and argues that a 'self–other' dichotomy is a key formative element of "cultural consciousness."[7] Beyond brief discussion of terms for 'self,' 'other,' and a few other concepts, however, he does not provide a comprehensive study of a broader range of terms used to articulate early Chinese concepts of 'culture' or 'civilization.' Furthermore, his proposed date of the emergence of "cultural consciousness" differs from the onset of civilizational consciousness proposed here by a few centuries.[8,9]

Existing studies imply that a collective consciousness of belonging to a coherent "civilization" existed at some point in early China, but there is still no consensus on when or how such a consciousness emerged. While it is possible to refer to this civilizational consciousness loosely using the English terms *culture* or *civilization*, as Sterckx and Poo do, it is important to remember that many of

Introduction 3

the language-specific meanings and connotations of these Modern English words are not found in the pre-Qín period—that is, the period before the unification of the Qín dynasty in 221 BCE. We therefore need an explicit theoretical framework for analyzing how this civilizational consciousness was conceptualized and communicated in language-specific Old Chinese terms.

The present study provides a novel theoretical framework for the study of collective civilizational consciousness and uses it to argue that a collectively shared awareness of belonging to a 'civilization' (defined by shared practices and values) emerged among a small group of masters of statecraft and moral philosophy in China around the middle of the first millennium BCE. It uncovers which Old Chinese words were used to articulate this early Chinese concept of 'civilization' and how the language-specific meanings of this concept differ from Modern English concepts of 'civilization.'

One of the central claims I put forth is that it is possible to trace and date the emergence of ancient Chinese conceptions of 'civilization' by determining when the words used to articulate these concepts were coined. In this sense, I study the emergence of a collective civilizational consciousness word by word. When I refer to ancient Chinese conceptions of 'civilization,' I am not using the English term *civilization* as a universally applicable metalinguistic category that we can discover in other languages and traditions. Rather, what I am saying is that early Chinese texts bear witness to the existence of a different, but still kindred, concept of 'civilization.' At a certain level of abstraction, this language-specific pre-Qín concept consists of meaning components similar to the key semantic components of a specific Modern English concept of 'civilization' that emerged in the sixteenth to the eighteenth centuries.

It follows that much of this project takes a comparative approach. I explore the emergence of collective civilizational consciousness in ancient China by comparing it with the concept of 'civilization' that emerged in late Renaissance and Enlightenment Europe. Some readers might find this comparison between early modern and pre-modern concepts problematic. However, this approach has been adopted by hermeneutic necessity rather than by choice. If I had written this book in Arabic rather than English, then I would have had to engage in a similar preliminary study of the language-specific meanings of the Arabic word 'urbanism/civilization' *ḥaḍāra* (حَضَارَة) in order to clarify what is meant by saying that a form of *ḥaḍāra*-consciousness emerged at a certain point in pre-Qín China. Therefore, if we are to use the phrase *civilizational consciousness*, then we have to understand the historical origins of the many different layers of meaning of the English term *civilization*. Otherwise, we may end up unconsciously imposing these language-specific modern meanings onto language-specific words and concepts of 'civilization' (or kindred concepts) in pre-Qín texts.

In other words, while my focus is on determining when civilizational consciousness first emerged in ancient China, I explore this question as a hermeneutic dialogue between language-specific ancient Chinese and modern European concepts. Beyond cross-linguistic conceptual comparison, I also explore similarities

4   *Introduction*

in the sociopolitical contexts in which the emergence of civilizational consciousness took place in pre-Qín China and early modern Europe.

Chapter 1 presents the word-by-word approach to intellectual history in general
and epistemic changes in collective civilizational consciousness in particular.[10] It
provides a theoretical framework for exploring the emergence of civilizational
consciousness through historical studies of the coining of the key semantic building blocks of early modern European concepts of 'civilization.' It also proposes
a definition of collective consciousness that links language to society: collective
civilizational consciousness emerged when a critical mass of people felt the need
to coin the words used to articulate it. This approach is used to analyze and map
the semantic structures of the different modern Anglophone concepts of 'civilization' since they first emerged in the sixteenth to twentieth centuries.

Chapter 2 traces the early stages in the evolution of the Old Chinese word *wén*
文 from the original meaning of '(decorative) pattern' to the later acquired meanings of 'moral refinement' or 'civility' and links these lexical changes to larger
sociopolitical and epistemic changes.[11] By the late second millennium BCE, the
word *wén* had acquired the meaning 'awe-inspiringly beautiful' ('commandingly
beautiful,' 'having an imposing/noble appearance') and was used to describe the
charismatic power of the king and members of the high aristocracy. In the Warring
States period *wén* also began to refer to the 'moral refinement' or 'civility' of a
morally superior or noble man, regardless of birth. The dating of these chronological changes in the meaning of the word *wén* is important for understanding the
shift that occurred from the aesthetically interpreted charismatic power in the pre-
Warring States period to the emphasis on ethically interpreted charismatic virtue
of the king and the ruling elites introduced by certain moral philosophers around
the beginning of the Warring States period. According to this proposed chronology of semantic changes, existing translations of *wén* in pre–Warring States texts
as 'civil,' 'civilized,' or 'culture' are anachronistic.

In Chapter 3, I show how the word 'civility' (*wén*) eventually came to be used
in extended meanings to refer to an indigenous concept of 'civilization' that, at
a certain level of abstraction, can be shown to contain similar semantic building
blocks to the concept of 'civilization' which emerged in sixteenth- to eighteenth-
century Europe. The chapter also analyzes the timeline of semantic changes for a
handful of other terms (e.g., 'the realm under Heaven' [*tiānxià* 天下] and 'rites'
[*lǐ* 禮]) that played a role in the articulation of the indigenous pre-Qín concept
of 'civilization.' While the concept of 'civility/civilization' (*wén*) was popular
among its coiners and promoters, it also had its critics. By exploring the fierce
debates on the concept of *wén* in the Warring States period, this chapter provides
new insight into the complex fragmentation of the Zhōu elite's understanding and
evaluation of its own traditions and mores as a 'civilization.' When I discuss "the
concept of 'civility/civilization' (*wén*)" in the pre-Qín period, I do not imply that
'civility/civilization' is the definitive English translation or gloss of the Old Chinese term *wén*. *Wén* does not mean 'civilization' in the Modern English sense(s)
of the word. As discussed in Chapters 2 and 3 and the conclusion chapter, *wén*
is a language-specific concept with meanings that differ considerably from the

Introduction 5

English word *civilization*. That is, I use 'civility/civilization' only as a convenient placeholder for the longer understanding of *wén* discussed below.

In Chapter 4, I propose a new take on the much studied and controversial topic of the concept of 'others' in pre-Qín texts and argue that the narrative of otherness changed from warfare to culture around the beginning of the Warring States period. The new set of terms referring to non-Zhōu others as 'civilizationally inferior others' or 'barbarians' that emerged in the Warring States period became a central component of the ruling elite's burgeoning understanding of itself as a 'civility/civilization' (*wén*). Analyzing structural changes in paradigms of ethnonyms (rather than focusing on semantic changes in individual terms), I show the term *yí* 夷 emerged as the default term for 'civilizationally inferior others' or 'barbarians.'

In Chapter 5, I argue that a new ethnographic vocabulary of civilizational otherness emerged in tandem with the Zhōu–barbarian dichotomy. The concept of 'barbarians' as 'civilizationally inferior others' emerged as a foil for the understanding of the autonym *Xià* 夏 'Great ones' that the Zhōu elites used to refer to themselves. Likewise, the coining of the new words 'customs' (*sú* 俗), 'vulgar' (*sú* 俗), and 'elegant/proper, *Xià*-like' (*yǎ* 雅) made it possible to describe the 'vulgar' (*sú*) 'customs' (*sú*) of the 'barbarians' (*yí*) and contrast them with the (allegedly) universally valid and 'elegant/proper/*Xià*-like' 'rites' (*lǐ*) of the civilized 'Great ones' (*Xià*).

While the Old Chinese terms studied in Chapters 2–5 have been the subject of previous studies, there is still no generally accepted consensus of when they acquired the meanings they have in Warring States texts. Based on readings in the Chinese commentarial tradition, some dating back two millennia, Warring States meanings of these terms are often projected anachronistically onto pre-Warring States texts. I therefore seek to provide a comprehensive chronology of these terms as an interconnected set of concepts that enabled and informed the emergence of a particular form of civilizational consciousness around the middle of the first millennium BCE.

This book is not about something called "Chinese civilization," understood as a materially manifested entity whose physical remains can be dug out of the ground; it is rather about the origins and development of language-specific pre-Qín concepts of 'civilization.' It is about ideas as conveyed through language, not material manifestations. Existing studies of "Chinese civilization" tend to place its "origin" sometime in the Neolithic or Bronze Age, that is, sometime in the period from 4000 BCE to 1000 BCE. In contrast, I argue that an indigenous language-specific form of civilizational consciousness first emerged in China around 600–400 BCE, much later than is typically claimed for the origin of "Chinese civilization" in the archaeological sense of the word.

The civilizational consciousness which was first explicitly formulated among a sub-group of thinkers during the Warring States period did not stay fixed but instead continued to change in response to complex epistemic and sociopolitical changes. It was further developed and gained broader currency when it was incorporated into the ideology of empire during the Hàn Dynasty (206 BCE–220 CE).

6 *Introduction*

Since all the words used by Warring States thinkers to articulate civilizational consciousness continued to change (by developing new meanings, or becoming obsolete, and so forth), the exact nature of the collective consciousness of belonging to a 'civilization' also changed over time. Complex political developments (the collapse of the Hàn Dynasty, and the ensuing coexistence of multiple "dynasties," and so forth) triggered the emergence of a complex set of identities that informed the creation of new collective consciousnesses in different areas. It would be impossible to go into all of this in a single book. The present study is therefore limited to the pre-Qín period.

Notes

1 Italics are used to indicate that I am referring to words. Single quotation marks ' ' indicate concepts or meanings of words.
2 The words *China* and *Chinese* are anachronistic when discussing the pre-Qín period, that is, the period before the unification of the Qín dynasty in 221 BCE. At that time, the word *Zhōngguó* (which refers to China in modern Mandarin) referred to the 'Central States' in the plural sense, that is, the states of the Warring States period. The term *China* is used here for convenience to refer roughly to the 'area which is now China.' In the pre-Qín period, the ruling elite of this area identified themselves as belonging to a group called the *Xià* or the *Huá*. Since the period studied here overlaps to a large extent with the Zhōu dynasty (1045–256 BCE), I use the term *Zhōu* to refer to the Xià or Huá elites of the Zhōu realm rather than the anachronistic term *Chinese*. See the analysis of the term *Xià* in chapter 5.
3 Sterckx (2002: 93–6, italics added).
4 Di Cosmo (2002) uses the word *civilization* in an interesting discussion of how "civilizations" arise in tandem with the construction of distinctions between a self and other: "It seems a shared human experience that the malleable substance at the origin of *'civilizations'* – a sense of cultural cohesion, shared destiny, and common origin – coagulates into a harder and stronger matter when peoples who belong to it are confronted, at times in a threatening way, by other peoples who are seen as being different and 'beyond the pale.' . . . [T]he antagonism between those who are 'in' and those who are 'out,' and the criteria the community adopts to demarcate not only its territory but also the characteristics that are assumed to be the very basis of its raison d'être (a faith, a race, a code of behavior, a shared set of values) are at the foundation of how a *'civilization'* defines itself" (Di Cosmo 2002: 1–2, italics added).
5 Wang (1991: 2–3) briefly mentions that the emergence of a kind of "self-awareness as a distinct civilization" dates it to the time of "the writings of Confucius and his contemporaries (sixth to fifth centuries BC)." But he does not flesh out the details of this "self-awareness as a civilization" or analyze how and why it came about and why it did not emerge earlier.
6 Poo (2005: 2–3, italics added). See also Poo (2005: 67): "All three *civilizations* . . . considered the cultural characteristics of the inhabitants of the peripheral world 'not only different but inferior . . . The culture of the foreigners is viewed either as lacking the basic requirements of the civilized world or else as opposite to the normal (i.e., correct) behavior' [(Liverani 1990: 36–7)]."
7 According to Poo (2005: 47), it is unlikely that "the Shang people had already developed a strong Sino-centric perspective that considered the Shang state as the center of the world, the unquestionable leader of civilization." This observation is similar to my claim that civilizational consciousness had not yet emerged in the Shāng (ca. 1570–1045 BCE). However, Poo does not propose any accounts of why "cultural consciousness" did not develop in the Shāng.

Introduction 7

8 Poo's discussion of pre-Warring States texts suggests that they bear evidence of the existence of a form of "cultural consciousness" as early as the ninth or eighth century BCE. He discusses a "vessel from 823 BCE" that mentions "the northwestern barbarian tribe Xianyun and the southern barbarian Huai Yi" (Poo 2005: 78) and concludes that the "Western Zhou had trouble with the barbarian neighbors" (Poo 2005: 78). Poo's use of the term *barbarian* implies that by the ninth century BCE the Zhōu had a concept of "barbarians." In contrast, as I argue in chapter 4, there are compelling reasons why the pre-Qín concept of 'barbarians' or 'civilizationally inferior others' did not develop until the eve of Warring States period (481–221 BCE), several centuries after the end of the Western Zhōu (1045 BCE–771 BCE).

9 Pines' (2002, 2005, 2009) analysis of the emergence of the concept of *tiānxià* as a "regime of value" as well as his analysis of the emergence of the Zhōu–barbarian dichotomy and the notion of a unified 'empire' has also served as inspiration for the analysis of civilizational consciousness proposed here.

10 I use the word *epistemic* in the Foucauldian sense. As observed by Naugle (2002: 181), Foucault's concept of *épistème* bears "a family resemblance to worldview." According to Foucault (1972: 15), an "episteme may be suspected of being something like a worldview, a slice of history common to all branches of knowledge, which imposes on each one the same norms and postulates, a general stage of reason, a certain structure of thought that the men of a particular period cannot escape."

11 My claim is not that pre-Qín word *wén* was semantically equivalent to the modern English word *civility*, but rather that at a certain level of abstraction it shared some of the key semantic components of the English word *civility*. The pre-Qín and modern English concepts of 'civility' are different language-specific constructions with idiosyncratic meanings and uses. As discussed in chapters 2–3, no single English word adequately captures the meanings and connotations of the pre-Qín concept of 'civility/civilization' (*wén*).

References

Di Cosmo, Nicola. 2002. *Ancient China and Its Enemies: The Rise of Nomadic Power in East Asian History* (Cambridge University Press: Cambridge).

Foucault, Michel. 1972. *The Archaeology of Knowledge*. Translated by A. M. Sheridan Smith (Random House: New York).

Liverani, Mario. 1990. *Prestige and Interest: International Relations in the Near East ca. 1600–1100 BCE* (Sargon SRL: Padova).

Naugle, David, K. 2002. *Worldview: The History of a Concept* (Eerdmans: Grand Rapids).

Nylan, Michael, and Thomas A. Wilson. 2010. *Lives of Confucius: Civilization's Greatest Sage Through the Ages* (Doubleday: New York).

Pines, Yuri. 2002. 'Changing Views of Tianxia in Pre-Imperial Discourse', *Oriens Extremus*, 43: 101–16.

———. 2005. 'Beasts or Humans: Pre-Imperial Origins of Sino-Barbarian Dichotomy', in Reuven Amitai and Michal Biran (eds.), *Mongols, Turks, and Others: Eurasian Nomads and the Sedentary World* (Brill: Leiden), pp. 59–102.

———. 2009. *Envisioning Eternal Empire: Chinese Political Thought of the Warring States Era* (University of Hawaii Press: Honolulu).

Poo, Mu-chou. 2005. *Enemies of Civilization: Attitudes Toward Foreigners in Ancient Mesopotamia, Egypt, and China* (SUNY Press: Albany).

Sterckx, Roel. 2002. *The Animal and the Daemon in Early China* (SUNY Press: Albany).

Wang, Gungwu. 1991. *The Chineseness of China: Selected Essays* (Oxford University Press: Hong Kong & New York).

1 The coining of civilizational consciousness in modern Western Europe

As leaves in the woods are changed with the fleeting years;
the earliest fall off first: in this manner words perish with old age,
and those lately invented flourish and thrive, like men in the time of youth.
—Horace, *Ars Poetica*[1]

At 9:40 pm on November 13, 2015, three armed men entered a theatre in Paris and began shooting at the concert audience. Eighty-nine people were killed and hundreds more wounded. Elsewhere in Paris, coordinated bombing and shooting attacks brought the death toll to 130. The so-called Islamic State of Iraq and Syria (ISIS) later claimed responsibility for the killings. In response, many state leaders and politicians were quick to use the term *civilization* in their condemnations of these heinous acts.

In the United States, hawkish politicians described the Paris attacks as a "clash of civilizations," drawing upon the language of political scientist Samuel Huntington.[2] Even before the Paris attacks, Republican presidential candidate Mike Huckabee had stated that the fight against ISIS was "about the survival of Western civilization."[3] As observed by *Washington Post* writer Michael Gerson, one of the goals of the attacks was to encourage a "perception of a civilizational struggle between Islam and the West."[4] Sadly, they were quite successful in this regard.[5] Even statesmen who explicitly reject incendiary "clash of civilizations" rhetoric often draw upon a concept of 'civilization.' President Obama, for example, declared the events in Paris an "attack on the civilized world."[6] Obama's statement evokes the existence of a singular "civilized world" characterized by allegedly universally accepted values and practices, which is threatened by "uncivilized" others. The concept of 'civilization' invoked in these passages, which we can call a universal concept of 'civilization,' is prescriptive: it defines how people and societies should be in order to be "civilized," rather than simply describing how they are. It is an ideological concept that has been constructed by people inside particular social formations to cast themselves as "civilized" groups or "civilizations." In their ethnocentric smugness, people using this concept in their

The coining of civilizational consciousness 9

discourse often assume it to be universally valid and applicable. This is why I refer to it as the "universal concept of 'civilization.'" This, of course, does not mean that I share any assumption of universality.

As eloquently stated by the German sociologist Norbert Elias (1897–1990), the "concept of civilization . . . expresses the self-consciousness of the West. . . . It sums up everything in which Western society of the last two or three centuries believes itself superior to earlier societies of 'more primitive' contemporary ones."[7]

The term *civilization* itself is thus a key element of the engine that keeps the wheels of contemporary "Western" civilizational consciousness spinning. This chapter explores the emergence and development of this particular civilizational consciousness. What were the sociopolitical developments that paved the way for the emergence of the universal concept of 'civilization' in early modern Europe, and which terms were used to articulate this concept? What role did the coining of the English term *civilization* in the eighteenth century play in the crystallization of this language-specific Anglophone civilizational consciousness?

Since the word *civilization* continues to be used to express the self-consciousness of "the West," it is not a neutral term which can be used unproblematically as an analytical category in the study of other "civilizations."[8] Modern European civilizational consciousness is very different from pre-Qín civilizational consciousness. To what extent is it then still possible to talk about the emergence of civilizational consciousness in pre-Qín China? A study of the emergence of the terms that articulated civilizational consciousness in modern Europe will help address this question and set the stage for the study of the coining of civilizational consciousness in pre-Qín China. Mapping the history and meanings of the semantic components of the English word *civilization* provides us with a metalanguage to explore the meanings of the Old Chinese words that were used in pre-Qín sources to articulate a language-specific form of civilizational consciousness. It is the first and necessary step in our approach to the cross-linguistic comparison of language-specific 'universal' concepts of 'civilization' in modern Europe and pre-Qín China as a hermeneutical dialogue between different traditions anchored in historical contexts millennia apart.

Before embarking on the comparative historical study of the various stages in the emergence and evolution of civilizational consciousness in modern Western Europe and pre-Qín China, we need to clarify a number of theoretical questions. What is collective consciousness? How can the coining of new words (or old words in new meanings) be used as source material in the historical study of changes in collective consciousness? How can we link changes in word meanings and thought to the larger sociopolitical context? What are the hermeneutical challenges faced in this kind of word-by-word approach to intellectual history? It is to these questions that I turn next before returning to the study of the coining and evolution of civilizational consciousness in early modern Europe.

10 *The coining of civilizational consciousness*

The history-word-by-word approach to changes in thought

Historical research is typically conducted with *texts* as primary source documents. In contrast, I focus on the *word* as the basic unit. I am interested in how we can use lexical changes in word meanings to study historical changes in collective consciousness and social structure. This approach allows us to study the question of when civilizational consciousness emerged by looking at when the key conceptual components of language-specific concepts of 'civilization' were coined (or lexicalized, in linguistic jargon) as single terms.

What's in a word?

To use words as source material in historical studies, we must be able to talk unambiguously about their different components. Words are complex, multi-layered entities consisting of bundles of phonological, semantic, and syntactic features.[9] Figure 1.1 uses the word *cat* to illustrate the conventions for talking about different aspects of words. First, as shown in row (a), italics are used to indicate that we are talking about the word *cat*. As indicated by the oval, three different constituent feature bundles make up the word *cat*: (b) the sound image, or phonological representation, /kæt/, which is represented as a sequence of the speech sounds /k/ /æ/ /t/ bracketed by slanted lines; (c) the concept or meaning 'cat' 🐱, i.e., the semantic representation of the meaning 'cat,' is indicated by single quotes as 'cat'; and (d) the syntactic features of being a count noun (as opposed to a mass noun, a verb, or an adjective, and so forth).[10] Beyond the three linguistic feature bundles in (b), (c), and (d), which make up a word as it is stored in the mental dictionary in the minds of speakers of English, the word *cat* may also have extra-linguistic aspects such as (e) referents and (f) written forms.

Word meanings, or concepts, are highly malleable and context-sensitive. A four-year-old probably does not think of her beloved Felix as a 'domesticated, feline mammal.' Not having learned biological taxonomy, she may instead think of a 'furry animal that purrs when stroked, and which brings in mice from the yard.'[11] As discussed below, the malleability and context-sensitivity of meanings facilitate the emergence of new meanings of the word *civilization* in response to changes in sociopolitical context.

Linguistic aspects:
    a.   Word, term, linguistic expression: *cat*
    b.   Sound-image   /kæt/
    c.   Meaning, concept, idea, notion   'cat'
    d.   Syntactic features   count noun

Extra-linguistic aspects:
    e.   Referent(s)   CAT
    f.   Written form(s)   <cat>

Figure 1.1 Conventions for talking about different aspects of words.

The coining of civilizational consciousness 11

Syntactic features tell us how words combine to form larger phrases and sentences. For example, in addition to the meaning 'civilization' and the sound-image /sɪvɪlaɪzeɪʃən/, the word *civilization* has syntactic features characterizing it as a noun. These syntactic features tell us that the word *civilization* can form a noun phrase by combining with the adjective *Chinese* (as in *Chinese civilization*). Various concepts of 'civilization' can also be lexicalized in adjectival and verbal forms as witnessed by the adjectives *civilized*, *civilizational*, and the verb *to civilize*.

The concept 'cat' associated with the sound-image /kæt/ should not be confused with the specific physically existing CAT which the noun phrase *the cat* may refer to when someone utters the sentence *Mary is holding the cat* in a specific context. As shown in (e) in Figure 1.1, small caps are used to indicate that we are talking about the referent of a word, i.e., an entity in the world referred to by the word. The concept 'cat' understood as 'domesticated, feline, mammal' is not identical to the particular white Siamese CAT with blue eyes called Felix that 4-year-old Mary can hold in her lap. Similarly, the archaeological concept of 'civilization' is not the same as the set of physical remains that some archaeologists view as a particular CIVILIZATION located in the Central Plains of China in the mid-second millennium BCE.

Finally, it is important not to confuse the ways words are written with the words themselves. Words can, and most often do, exist without writing. As shown in (f) in Figure 1.1, angled brackets < > are used to indicate the written form of a word. The string of three letters <cat> is the product of a writing system that has adapted Latin letters to write English. It is not part of the linguistic features making up the word *cat*. Distinguishing between writing and words is particularly important when studying the history of Chinese words. The meanings 'pattern,' 'stripe(s),' and 'decoration' were among the meanings of the Old Chinese word *wén* 文 which, as will be argued in Chapters 2–3, also in some contexts referred to a language-specific pre-Qín concept of 'civility/civilization.' According to the orthographic conventions of modern Mandarin, the meanings 'pattern,' 'stripe(s),' and 'decoration,' which used to be written with the graph <文>, are now written with the graph <紋> which is also pronounced *wén*. Thus, for example, the word *hǔ wén* 'tiger stripes,' which used to be written <虎文>, is now written <虎紋>. This does not mean that the graph <紋> in <虎紋> writes a completely different word from the one written as <文> in <虎文>. It simply means that the meanings 'pattern, stripes' of the polysemous word *wén* eventually came to be written with a graph different from the one writing other meanings. Since Chinese dictionaries are organized by graphs, this creates the illusion that the graphs *wén* <文> and *wén* <紋> write unrelated words.

The lexicon as historical source

Studying history word by word involves using the lexicon to trace epistemic changes through changes in word meanings. A lexicon is the shared vocabulary of a group of individuals communicating in the same language. It changes over time in response to changes in the historical context. New words may enter the lexicon as loan words from other languages when new products (e.g., *tobacco*, first

12   *The coining of civilizational consciousness*

attested in English in 1588), technologies, or ideas (e.g., *feng-shui*, first attested in English in 1797) are introduced from other linguistic communities. New terms may also be coined by native speakers themselves to express new concepts reflecting changes in different aspects of their world, such as changes in administrative institutions or social hierarchies (e.g., *corporatization*, first attested in 1958).[12] As we shall see below, the English noun *civilization* was derived from the verb *civilize* in the eighteenth century to refer to an emergent concept of 'civilization.' Diachronic changes in the lexicon such as these reflect changes in worldview or collectively shared conceptual frameworks. Hence, the lexicon is a valuable source in historical studies of changes in thought.

Coining, or lexicalization, is the process of adopting new words into the lexicon, or of giving existing words new meanings through metaphorical extension or other derivational processes. People constantly make up terms in response to changes in their physical or intellectual environments. Recent neologisms such as *selfie* and *texting*, for example, did not exist before the invention of cell phones. Lexicalization functions as an umbilical cord linking language to society. Exploring how and why lexicalization takes place therefore helps us contextualize the lexicon as a historical source.

Lexicalization always takes place in specific historical contexts; it is a highly context-sensitive process that pre-packages perceived reality into discrete language-specific concepts associated with language-specific terms in order to enable members of the linguistic community to communicate more efficiently.[13] Lexicalization does not take place until a significant number of people have begun to exchange ideas about a concept and thus come to need an efficient way to express it. Since lexicalization tends to be a relatively slow process, determining when a certain word appears for the first time in a comprehensive text corpus spanning several centuries is often a reliable way to study epistemic changes in a linguistic community's shared worldview, or collective consciousness. When a linguistic community agrees on coining and using a new word, then the new concept has become part of the group's collective consciousness.

Yuri Pines uses an apt comparison to archaeology to illustrate the differences between the traditional historian's approach of doing close readings of a few selected texts and a "distant reading," corpus-based approach to history more like the one adopted here.[14] As Pines explains, archaeologists can either do meticulous excavations of single excavation sites in order to obtain information that is rich in descriptive details, or they can perform regional surveys (of burial types, decorations on pottery shards, etc.) comprising a large number of sample excavations in order to study larger patterns synchronically or diachronically.[15] The corpus-based, word-by-word approach to history employed here is a "regional survey" in Pines' sense. It illustrates how much historians and linguists "can gain from crossing the boundaries of their disciplines and venturing out into the domains of the other."[16] It aims to "detect synchronic patterns as well as diachronic processes"[17] in the crystallization of concepts of 'civilization' and 'identity' through diachronic survey studies of the uses and meanings of a few key terms that played a central role in the emergence of collective civilizational consciousness in pre-Qín China.

The coining of civilizational consciousness 13

The word-based, phonological, definition of consciousness proposed by Ray Jackendoff allows us to articulate the role lexicalization plays in the formation of collective consciousness. For Jackendoff, "what we experience as conscious thought gets its form not from meaning, but from the inner voice, the verbal images of pronunciation" that are generated in the mind.[18] Being conscious of an idea depends on the ability to articulate it verbally and thus "hear" it in one's mind. To be sure, the term *consciousness* is frequently used in colloquial speech and other theoretical frameworks to refer to ineffable intuitions or qualia-like embodied experiences, such as, for example, the awareness of physical pain, hunger, or the taste of pineapples. However, these more inclusive definitions of consciousness (which may include non-verbal, ineffable embodied experiences) are not very helpful for the purposes of defining what we mean when we talk about the collective consciousness of a group of individuals.[19] That is, unless these experiences or thoughts are matched with verbal images by the inner voice in the mind, they are not conscious, according to Jackendoff's definition. This does not mean that all cognitive processes are matched to verbal images; on the contrary, most cognitive processes are unconscious—that is, not hooked up to the inner voice or verbalized Joycean stream of consciousness in the mind.[20]

Jackendoff's definition of consciousness applies to single individuals. Extending it to groups of people allows us to define collective consciousness more precisely: the collective consciousness of a linguistic community is the shared worldview that is verbally articulated in their lexicon, shared myths, and historical narratives. It is an intersubjective form of consciousness that crucially relies on verbalization and is passed down from one generation to the next through verbal transmission. In a linguistic community as geographically dispersed as the literate elite in pre-Qín China, the medium of writing was crucial for the sharing of ideas.[21] In the case of a dead language such as Old Chinese, the lexicon can therefore be understood as the repository of words in the corpus of extant written texts. It is the core of the collective consciousness of the group of people communicating in Old Chinese. Metaphorically speaking, the lexicon is a manifestation of a central part of the 'mind' of their speech community. Collectively shared ideas can thus be studied through the pre-packaged chunks of 'perceived reality' (meanings) associated with sound images that we refer to as words stored in the lexicon.

Extending Jackendoff's verbal definition of consciousness to linguistic communities enables us to use changes in the lexicon to study changes in collective consciousness. All members of a linguistic community may or may not share longer narratives and phrasal expressions of complex concepts (e.g., the expression of the concept that is lexicalized in the word *corporatization* through paraphrases such as "to make an entity corporate by introducing or imposing the structures, practices, or values associated with a large business corporation"[22]). However, once a concept has been lexicalized in a single word (e.g., *corporatization*), then it is, per definition, part of the shared lexicon of a particular group or sub-group. The emergence of a new word in the language signifies a recently but solidly established idea. Lexicalization can therefore be used as a reliable indication that a concept has entered collective consciousness.

14   The coining of civilizational consciousness

Most linguistic communities are highly heterogeneous groups of individuals. Different subsets are likely to have different collectively shared lexica. Words such as *selfie* and *texting* are used by most English speakers under a certain age but may be absent from the shared vocabulary of many nonagenarians. Similarly, words such as *lexicalization* and *corporatization* tend to be used mostly by specialists such as linguists and lawyers. Words are usually first coined by (or introduced into) a sub-group of a larger linguistic community. Whether or not they become part of the lexicon of the majority of speakers in the linguistic community depends on various historical and sociological factors. When it emerged in the 1760s, the word *civilization* was part of the specialized vocabulary of economists and political thinkers in France and Scotland. Today it is a key word shared by the majority of adult speakers of English. Similarly, as will be explored in Chapters 2–3, the word *wén* 文 was first used in the new meaning 'civility/civilization' in small groups of thinkers and their followers around the middle of the first millennium BCE and only later became part of the shared vocabulary of the literate elite.

To be sure, using vocabulary changes as a way to study changes in thought is not a new idea.[23] The German sociologist Norbert Elias (1897–1990) opens his seminal 1939 study on the concept of the "civilizing process" in Western European thought with an eloquent formulation of the importance of *historical* analyses of word meanings in the study of epistemic change:

> Mathematical concepts can be separated from the group which uses them. . . . Concepts such as *civilization* [cannot]. . . . The collective history has crystallized in them and resonates in them. The individual . . . makes use of them because it seems a matter of course, because from childhood he learns to see the world through the lens of these concepts. The social process of their genesis may long be forgotten. One generation hands them on to another without being aware of the process as a whole, and the concepts live as long as this crystallization of past experiences and situations retains an existential value, a function in the actual being of society—that is, as long as succeeding generations can hear their own experiences in the meaning of the words. The terms gradually die when the functions and experiences in the actual life of society cease to be bound up with them.[24]

Elias makes several important points. First, the study of word meanings is highly relevant to historical research. Rather than being left to linguists, the study of lexical change ought to be considered an important tool in the historian's toolkit. Second, the meanings and uses of key terms in collective consciousness are informed by the needs of the people who coined them and the exigencies of the social formations in which they lived. Thus, the "collective history" of a community "has crystallized" and "resonates" in words such as *civilization*. Third, Elias notes that people have a tendency to believe that the words through which they conceptualize the world are universally given and immutable. It is easy to forget that key words in contemporary Western thought, such as *civilization*, are

The coining of civilizational consciousness 15

parochial constructs which have not always existed. That is, analytical categories like 'civilization,' 'culture,' and 'identity' that form the backbone of theories in contemporary academic disciplines from the social sciences to the humanities are language- and context-specific contingent historical entities and must be studied as such.[25] Fourth, words are liable to change and even become obsolete over time as they either disappear for good or are replaced with other words that better capture and communicate the linguistic community's understanding of the world.

The conceptual history (Ger. *Begriffsgeschichte*) developed by the German historian and linguist Reinhart Koselleck (1923–2006) further develops the idea, introduced by earlier historians such as Norbert Elias and Lucien Febvre (1878–1956), that historical studies of sociopolitical changes should be informed by careful attention to the semantic history of key concepts and the terms used to refer to them.[26] Koselleck's project of tracing the history of key political and social concepts resulted in the monumental, multi-volume *Geschichtliche Grundbegriffe. Historisches Lexikon zur politisch-sozialen Sprache in Deutschland* co-edited with the Austrian historian Otto Brunner (1898–1982) and the German historian Werner Conze (1910–1986).[27] This project aimed to transcend the limitations of traditional word-based lexicography by focusing on concepts rather than words. This was done by paying attention to synonyms and paraphrases referring to kindred or related concepts in a semantic field.[28] This type of approach is similar to the historical study of lexicalization developed in this book in that they both enable tracing the history of the different terms (and paraphrases) used at different periods to refer to a concept or semantic field. Koselleck's insistence on the profound interconnections between social history and conceptual history (*Begriffsgeschichte*) also resembles the emphasis adopted here on situating the process of lexicalization in a specific historical context.[29]

The German philosopher Hans-Georg Gadamer's (1900–2002) philosophical hermeneutics also informs the history-word-by-word approach outlined here and provides it with a hermeneutical framework. Gadamer (1975) criticizes the widespread assumption that meaning is an object which can be discovered in texts by application of a specific method.[30] In contrast, Gadamer views meaning as a dynamic phenomenon that emerges through a dialogical process of interpretation in which the "prejudices" of the tradition of the interpreter engage the resistance of the tradition or "horizon" of the text or object being interpreted. Meanings of words and texts are not objects to be discovered but rather processes involving the "fusion of horizons."[31] A dialogical meeting of "prejudices" is central to interpretive understanding. Keen awareness of the historical nature of the "prejudices" of each tradition or horizon is therefore indispensable. Because words and concepts are language-specific, pre-packaged chunks of perceived reality, they also have tradition-specific "prejudices" of whose historical nature we must be aware. As observed by Gadamer, "if we are not to accept language automatically, but to strive for a reasoned historical understanding, we must face a whole host of questions of verbal and conceptual history."[32] According to Gadamer, "common expressions [i.e., words] are . . . the heritage of a *common spirit*, and if we only understand rightly and penetrate their covert richness of meaning, then

16   *The coining of civilizational consciousness*

we can make this *common spirit* perceivable again."[33] In other words, collective consciousness—Gadamer's "common spirit"—resides in the lexicon.

Through Gadamer's dialogical hermeneutics, we can begin to make sense of the pre-Qín linguistic community's tradition-specific terms and concepts of 'civilization' by approaching them with heightened awareness of the historical nature of the "prejudices" of our own modern Anglophone terms and concepts of 'civilization.' Because we are situated in a particular historical context that has shaped our "prejudices," we have a "historically-effected consciousness" of the world.[34] As interpretive agents, we must therefore be aware of the historical nature of our own collective consciousness as it is crystallized in the pre-packaged chunks of reality lexicalized in words through which we make sense of the world. In order to better our chances of a successful "fusion of horizons," we must undertake comparative historical studies of the language-specific terms and concepts of 'civilization' that are used to lexicalize civilizational consciousness in both the Western European and the pre-Qín tradition.

Comparing concepts across languages and historical contexts

Some sort of metalanguage is necessary to analyze and compare terms and concepts across languages and historical contexts. We need to use language to talk about language. As described in the introduction, scholars of early China writing in English often use the modern Anglophone word *civilization* more or less uncritically in discussions of early Chinese concepts. This can be problematic. First, when using English words as metalanguage to analyze pre-Qín concepts, one runs the risk of imposing modern Anglophone concepts onto pre-Qín texts. Second, this approach invites the problematic assumption that English words such as *civilization, culture, identity*, and so forth—and the modern concepts that they refer to—are universally applicable. To mitigate both problems, I adopt elements of the so-called Natural Semantic Metalanguage framework for cross-linguistic comparison developed by Anna Wierzbicka.

The central idea of Wierzbicka's approach is that in cross-linguistic studies any of the languages being compared can serve as the metalanguage in which the study is articulated. The key for successful cross-linguistic comparison of complex concepts is to break these down into the smaller semantic molecules and atoms of which they are composed. The assumption is that all human languages have lexicalized terms for a core set of semantically irreducible conceptual primes. Wierzbicka has identified 60 some such semantic primes or atoms. They include substantives (*I, you, someone/person, something/thing, people, body*), evaluators (*good, bad*), logical concepts (*not, maybe, can, because, if*), and so forth. In contrast to these basic concepts, which are coined as words (or parts of words, grammatical affixes, etc.) in all human languages, many words are not universally lexicalized. For example, Old Chinese obviously lacks lexicalized counterparts to the English words *selfie* and *corporatization*. However, in Wierzbicka's framework such language-specific concepts can be broken down into semantic atoms or molecules which are lexicalized in all the languages being compared, thereby

The coining of civilizational consciousness 17

facilitating cross-linguistic conceptual comparison. In principle, the lexicalized semantic atoms and molecules of any human language can be used to paraphrase complex concepts in any other language. English is therefore not any more privileged as metalanguage than any other of the 6,000 languages now spoken.[35]

The status of English as global lingua franca of science and academic research sometimes leads to the potentially problematic assumption that the concepts referred to by words which by historical accident happen to be lexicalized in English are universal concepts readily accessible to speakers of all human languages. As Wierzbicka puts it, "linguists, and also anthropologists, often behave as if they believed that English is indeed the fittest [language]. They do so by absolutizing some concepts which are lexically encoded in English and giving them a fundamental status in human cognition."[36] Wierzbicka argues that only heightened attention to language-specific lexicalizations of concepts will allow us break free from this insidious ethnocentric legacy of Orientalism and modern Western epistemic hegemony that takes the universality of many modern Anglophone analytical categories for granted. That is, we need to pay more attention to variations in how different languages pre-package reality differently through lexicalization. For example, as observed by Wierzbicka, a word referring to a concept similar to the concept referred to by the English word *color* is not part of the lexicon of some pre-colonial, aboriginal Australian languages. Hence, speakers of these languages do not have at their immediate disposal a pre-packaged chunk of perceived reality corresponding to the English concept of 'color.'[37] It is therefore misguided to assume that the Anglophone concept of 'color' is universal.

Like *color*, the English word *civilization* is also often assumed to be a universally applicable analytical category. But since modern European concepts of 'civilization' are language-specific constructs that arose in response to the communicative needs of particular groups in specific historical contexts, there is of course no reason to assume that they are universal.[38] However, this does not mean that it is impossible to compare concepts of 'civilization' across languages and historical contexts. A decompositional approach to conceptual analysis can help us overcome the problems related to cross-linguistic comparison of complex concepts such as 'civilization' by breaking them down into semantic molecules and/or atoms that have lexicalized counterparts in other languages. Thus, as discussed below, using this approach we can paraphrase the early modern European universal concept of 'civilization' as 'the idea of a universal process of progress operating on the civility of individuals and the laws and government institutions of larger social formations (states, empires, etc.), resulting in the establishment of value-laden distinctions between self (i.e., the civilized) and others (i.e., the uncivilized) and between a primitive past and an advanced present.'[39]

This decompositional approach to cross-linguistic conceptual comparison can be employed to demonstrate that, at a certain level of abstraction, a language-specific concept of 'civilization' occasionally referred to in pre-Qín texts with the word *wén* shares some of the conceptual components—or semantic molecules—of the modern European universal concept of 'civilization.' The risk of imposing language-specific meanings of the metalanguage (e.g., English) onto the language

18   *The coining of civilizational consciousness*

studied (e.g., Old Chinese) can be further mitigated by switching roles; that is, using the language studied (e.g., Old Chinese) in a new role as metalanguage to study language that was formerly the metalanguage (e.g., English).[40] This bi-directional approach to cross-linguistic studies provides a hermeneutic framework in which a Gadamerian "fusion of horizons" can take place.[41] It enables us not only to use early modern European concepts of 'civilization' to explore kindred pre-Qín concepts of 'civilization,' but also to let the "prejudices" of pre-Qín concepts inform a fresh take on early modern European civilizational consciousness.

The invention of the modern European universal concept of 'civilization' and the coining of the word *civilization*

The approach to the study of epistemic changes outlined above enables us to link the coining of the early modern European concept of 'civilization' and the emergence of a language-specific collective civilizational consciousness to the sociopolitical and intellectual contexts in which they occurred. By studying the historical context of lexicalization, we can identify the coiners of new terms and formulate hypotheses about the changes in their environments and intellectual milieus that led them to feel the need to pre-package new chunks of their per-ceived reality into more readily communicable words such as *civilization*. Since the modern European concept of 'civilization' appears to have been articulated and lexicalized first in English and French, the following study is limited to these two languages.[42]

The modern European concept of 'civilization' that emerged in the sixteenth to eighteenth centuries can be broken down into five core conceptual components, or semantic molecules. Foremost is the notion of 'progress' from an inferior, ear-lier stage of 'barbarity' to later, more advanced stages of 'civilization.' Second, when viewed as taking place within an individual, 'progress' was conceived of as an improvement in the 'refinement of behavior' referred to as *civility* or *polite-ness*. Third, when viewed as taking place in social formations, 'progress' was conceived of as an improvement in laws and government institutions regulating interpersonal behavior referred to as *police*—see, for example, T. Carte's 1747 *General History of England*: "Having established an admirable order and *police* throughout his territories."[43] This now obsolete use of *police* refers to the state of affairs that should prevail in a well-ordered polity. It does not refer narrowly to the 'police force,' understood as the 'body of people employed by a state to ensure law and order.' Fourth, humanity was divided into the 'civilized' (who had more refined *civility* and *police*) and the 'barbarians' (who either lacked or had insuf-ficiently developed *civility* and *police*).[44] By the temporal logic of 'progress,' the idea that the ancient forefathers of the civilized peoples of Europe had started out at a similarly primitive stage as contemporary savages of the new world also led to the creation of a distinction between a 'barbaric' past versus a (more) 'civilized' present, which then became part of the core conceptual components of the early notion of 'civilization.' Fifth, although the normative values according to which 'progress' along the dimensions of 'civility' and 'police' were judged were clearly

The coining of civilizational consciousness 19

grounded in ethnocentric European values, they were nevertheless assumed to be universally valid. This language-specific modern European universal concept of 'civilization' as a process of moral and societal improvement that separates both a primitive past from an advanced present and barbarian 'others' from a civilized 'self' was invented in Western Europe in the sixteenth to the eighteenth centuries. By the 1770s, it entered the shared vocabulary of a large segment of the English-speaking population in the word *civilization*.

Historical context of the emergence of the universal concept of 'civilization'

Early forms of the universal concept of 'civilization' began to emerge in Europe in the sixteenth century in response to a number of sociopolitical developments related to what Weber (1864–1920) analyzed as a shift from traditional and charismatic authority to bureaucratic modes of power.[45] The gradual bureaucratization of power accompanying the social and intellectual developments that led to the creation of the modern nation-states in Europe played a key role. Before the emergence of centralized nation-states, aristocratic families extracted wealth directly from their land and subjects. Although the vassals and landed aristocracy owed loyalty to the king (in varying degrees), they were in essence miniature kings themselves. Like the king, they ruled through a combination of traditional and charismatic authority, and they had legal jurisdiction inside their respective domains, which they protected externally with their own armies.[46] Also like the monarch, heads of aristocratic families inherited their charismatic and traditional power dynastically through a system of primogeniture.

It was to a large extent the efforts of the royal families to curb the landed nobility's financial and military power that eventually led to the creation of more centralized states. As noted by Thomas Patterson, "by the early 1500s, the rulers of Spain, France, and England had begun to consolidate their political power in order to acquire revenues so that they could conduct wars, diplomacy, trade, and colonization."[47] Rather than depending exclusively on the fealty of vassals and the loyalty of the landed aristocracy, the kings of the increasingly centralized states (England, Spain, France, etc.) began to employ trained government officials to manage tax collection, legal administration, and so forth. With the expanding bureaucratization of the centralized kingdoms, qualifications for office-holding gradually became less exclusively based on hereditary succession.

Alongside the older system of hereditary succession to landed domains loyal to the king, a new system of recruitment for government bureaucracies based more on technical and moral qualifications emerged. In this new system, the moral refinement (expressed in manners and behavior, or 'civility') of the officials and their grasp of the intricacies of the increasingly complex legal systems and other government institutions ('police') grew in importance. To borrow Pierre Bourdieu's terminology, *acquired* cultural capital emerged as an alternative means to create social distinctions.[48] In principle (if not necessarily in practice), candidates for official positions, noble and non-noble alike, could acquire the

20 *The coining of civilizational consciousness*

necessary qualifications through their own efforts. If they made enough 'progress' in the self-cultivation of their manners ('civility'), and if they acquired specialized knowledge of legal systems and government institutions ('police'), then they could potentially qualify to wield bureaucratic power as officials on behalf of the king and the nation. These developments contributed to the fusion of the key sub-components of the idea of 'civilization' ('progress,' 'civility,' 'police,' etc.) into a single concept. It is no coincidence that it was state-employed, university-trained jurists—such as the political philosopher Jean Bodin (1530–1596) and Loys Le Roy (1510–1577), a historian and translator of Aristotle and Plato—who, in the late sixteenth century, were among the first to expand the meanings of the words *civility* and *police* to include the emergent idea of 'civilization.'[49] Theories of 'civilization' were part of the cultural capital through which the coiners of early modern European civilizational consciousness gained access to office in the expanding state bureaucracies.[50]

Another important sociopolitical development contributing to the emergence of the idea of 'civilization' was the exploration of overseas territories, which had begun in the late fifteenth century but assumed grand proportions in the sixteenth century. European explorers encountered peoples who had radically different modes of social organization ('police') and conventions for interpersonal interaction ('civility'). Eurocentric descriptions of such peoples served as a foil to the European civilizational consciousness that was crystallizing at the time and re-activated the classical vocabulary of the 'barbarian' other.[51] Here were peoples who, from the point of view of European thinkers, were deficient in both 'civility' and 'police.' Since they were assumed to have made little or no 'progress' in these two dimensions and still seemed to live in nature—like the ancestors of the Europeans had done in a "primitive past" before the onset of 'civilization'—they were often referred to as *savages* or *barbarians*. This classification of the overseas 'others' as 'civilizationally inferior' or 'uncivilized' served to justify religious proselytizing and economic exploitation and gave Europeans the notion that their colonial empires had a moral duty to spread the blessings of 'civilization' across the globe.

In sum, the emergence of the idea of 'civilization' is linked to increased bureaucratization, an encroachment of bureaucratic authority on charismatic and traditional authority, and the emergence of a market of acquired cultural capital. As shown in Chapters 2–5, a similar process of sociopolitical reorganization and bureaucratization triggered by the centralization of state government paved the way for the emergence of an indigenous concept of 'civilization' in China during the Warring States period (481–221 BCE).

1500–1760s: multiple ways of expressing the universal concept of 'civilization'

The lexical developments leading to the coining of the English and French term *civilization* to refer to the universal concept of 'civilization' can be divided into two periods: 1500–1760s, and 1760s onward.[52] During the early stage, the emergent concept of 'civilization' could be expressed in three different ways: with phrasal combinations of words referring to the semantic molecules 'progress,'

The coining of civilizational consciousness 21

'police,' 'civility,' and so forth; with one of the words *civility* or *police* in extended meanings; and, extremely rarely, with the word *civilization* as a nonce word (that is, a word spontaneously created by isolated individuals in specific situations) in a verbal sense referring to the 'process of civilizing.'[53]

Voltaire's (1740) *Philosophie de l'Histoire* uses a phrasal combination of the participles *civilized* (Fr. *civilisés*) and *policed* (Fr. *policés*)[54] to express the universal concept of 'civilization': "the Egyptians . . . could not have joined together, become *civilized, policed*, industrious and powerful, until long after all the other peoples which I have considered."[55] As summarized in Figure 1.2, various combinations of words referring to the semantic molecules 'police' and 'civility' could be used to express the emergent concept of 'civilization':

a. *police, policed*   (terms for laws, government institutions, order)
b. *civilize, civilized, civility* (terms for refinements of behavior, politeness)

Figure 1.2 1500–1760s: combinations of words from (a) and (b) expressing the concept 'civilization.'

During the period from the sixteenth to the eighteenth century, the need to be able to express the emergent concept of 'civilization' expediently in a single word was felt more and more strongly. As argued by George Huppert, in both English and French, the word *police* was commonly used to refer to a high degree of development of a society's "politics, laws, administration, military and fiscal organization."[56] However, it appears to have been used only occasionally in the extended meaning of 'civilization.' In Furetiere's *Dictionnaire Universel* (1732), *police* is defined as "the laws, order and behavior to observe for the subsistence and maintenance of states and societies. . . . In general, it is the opposite of barbarity. The savages of America had neither laws nor police, when they were discovered. The different states have different kinds of police for their manners and for their government."[57] In his 1791 *Letter to a Member of the National Assembly*, Edmund Burke (1729–1797) referred to the Turks as "a barbarous nation, with a barbarous neglect of police, fatal to the human race."[58] In sum, as also pointed out above, the word *police* was occasionally used to refer to an early concept of 'civilization.'[59]

The word *civility* could also occasionally be used to refer to an emergent concept of 'civilization.' According to the *Oxford English Dictionary* (*OED*), passages in which "barbarous peoples" are contrasted with those who have "civility" can be found in English as far back as the sixteenth century.[60] In his description of the Irish, Nisbet (1722) stated, "one of their Progenitors assisted St. Patrick to propagate the Christian faith in Ireland, and to reduce the barbarous People there, to *Civility* and Christianity."[61] Although it is possible that *civility* should be understood here narrowly as 'refinement of manners' rather than 'civilization,' the contrast with 'barbarous People' suggests that the latter reading is at least plausible.[62] However, the meaning 'civilization' does not occur in any dictionary definitions of the word *civility* from the sixteenth to the nineteenth century.[63] So despite sporadic attestations in the extended meaning 'civilization,' *civility* never seems to have become a generally accepted word for the concept of 'civilization.'

22 *The coining of civilizational consciousness*

The use of the word *civility* to refer to the new concept of 'civilization' was derived by semantic extension from its earlier use denoting 'politeness' and 'urbanity' and the process of making someone 'polite,' 'courteous,' or 'refined.' As will be argued in Chapter 3, this semantic extension is similar to the extended use of the pre-Qín Chinese term 'civility/moral refinement' (*wén*) to refer to an indigenous Old Chinese concept of 'civility/civilization' (*wén*).

According to the *OED*, the earliest attestation of the English word *civilization* to refer to a 'civilizing process' is from 1656: "The divine curiosity of Philosophers, and good wits . . . hath taught us more morality, *civility, policy*, and what is usefull [sic] to the *civilization* of our lives."[64] This use of *civilization* appears to combine the elements of 'civility' and 'police,' as indicated in Figure 1.3.

a. *civility* 'refined behavior, manners'   [concept operating on individual]
      \

      civilization   [combined progress in both *police* and *civilité*]
      /

b. *police* 'laws, government institutions' [concept operating on society/institutions]

Figure 1.3 1500–1760s: nonce occurrence of *civilization* in the verbal meaning 'civilization.'

The universal scope of this process of 'civilization' is highlighted by a 1706 reference to the "Beginning" of the "civilization of Mankind," which is also quoted in the *OED* entry for the word *civilization*.[65] However, these two early instances of the word *civilization* referring to the concept of 'civilization' appear to have been sporadic nonce words that failed to gain wider currency. Furthermore, they refer narrowly to a *process* rather than a *state* of 'civilization' and focus on the dimension of 'civility.'

In sum, from 1500 to the 1760s the idea of 'civilization' could be expressed through combinations of words for the semantic molecules of 'civility' and 'police.' Semantic extensions of the words *civility* and *police* to denote the concept 'civilization' may also have been used. During this period there was no widely accepted single word for the emergent concept of 'civilization.'

1760s onward: civilization *as default term for the universal concept of 'civilization'*

To understand how the word *civilization* came to refer to the universal concept of 'civilization,' we need to identify the group of individuals who coined it and explore their motivations for doing so. According to the *OED*, the use of the word *civilization* to refer to a "progressive *state* of human social, cultural and intellectual development" first appears in the mid-eighteenth century.[66] This marks the beginning of the second stage in the coining of civilizational consciousness in modern Europe, which coincides with the height of the Enlightenment period. Many eighteenth-century philosophers saw the word *civilization* as a weapon

The coining of civilizational consciousness 23

against critics of the idea of 'civilization' such as Rousseau. The word's embodiment of the concept of 'progress' along the dimensions of 'civility' (individual) and 'police' (society) gave it great appeal among Enlightenment thinkers, who believed in the ability of Reason to free humankind from enslavement to nature, superstition, and primitive customs. Hence, from the 1760s onward, *civilization* became the default term for the universal concept of 'civilization.'

In English the word *civilization* begins to be attested regularly in the 1760s, as illustrated by the following case from 1761: "If all mankind arrived at an equal, or even a tolerable degree of *civilization* . . . what would it signify, where one was born, or of what particular district one became a citizen?"[67] In spite of the growing popularity of the word *civilization* in the 1760s and 1770s, it also had its critics, as witnessed by Boswell's (1740–1795) record of his discussions with Samuel Johnson (1709–1784) in 1772, the famous author of the *Dictionary of the English Language*:

> On Monday, March 23, I found him [Johnson] busy, preparing a fourth edition of his folio Dictionary. . . . He would not admit *civilization*, but only *civility*. With great deference to him, I thought *civilization*, from to *civilize*, better in the sense opposed to *barbarity*, than *civility*, as it is better to have a distinct word for each sense, than one with two senses, which *civility* is, in his way of using it.[68]

Despite Johnson's reservations, the word *civilization* quickly gained popularity.[69] Boswell and Johnson's different attitudes toward the relatively new word may thus very well reflect a generational difference in linguistic usage. In 1772, Boswell was only 32 while Johnson was already 63. As observed by Febvre, late eighteenth-century Enlightenment thinkers found in *civilization* a "word with which to designate . . . the triumph and spread of reason not only in the constitutional, political and administrative field [as expressed by the word *police*] but also in the moral, religious and intellectual field [as expressed by the word *civility*]."[70]

Semantic molecules of the universal concept of 'civilization'

The five key semantic molecules ('progress,' 'civility,' 'police,' 'distinctions,' and 'universality') are all explicitly spelled out in early definitions of the universal concept of 'civilization' whose semantic structure is mapped in Figure 1.4. The central conceptual component was the idea of 'progress,' as shown in line 1. In his *The History of Civilization in Europe* (1828), French statesman and historian François Guizot (1787–1874) stated that "the idea of progress and development [is] the fundamental idea contained in the word civilization."[71] 'Progress' takes places along the two dimensions of 'civility' and 'police.' More dimensions could (and for completeness probably should) be included, such as, for example, Humboldt's notion of *Bildung* (the language-specific German concept of self-cultivation or personal development through education in the arts). Advances in arts, sciences, religion, and technology within their concept of 'civilization' could also be included.[72] However, the dimensions of 'civility' and 'police'—operating

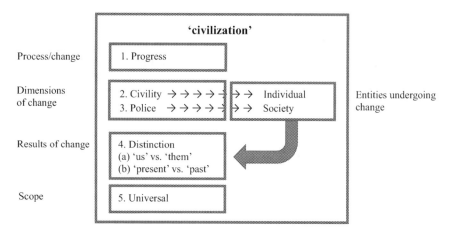

Figure 1.4 Conceptual structure of the universal concept of 'civilization.'

on the individual and on society, respectively—were the most fundamental. Guizot explicitly defined the concept of 'civilization' as consisting "of two key elements: the development of human society and the development of man himself. On the one hand, a social and political development, on the other, an inner, moral development."[73] Progress in the first dimension of 'civility' (i.e., the semantic molecule 2 in Figure 1.4) usually takes the form of moral education or self-cultivation that leads to the refinement of an individual. The second dimension of change—that of 'police' (i.e., the semantic molecule 3 in Figure 1.4)—consists of improvements in legal systems and government institutions, creating more ordered and well-organized societies.

These changes in individuals and social formations result in various 'distinctions' that make up the fourth conceptual component of the concept of 'civilization.' One such 'distinction' is between, on one hand, individuals and societies that have undergone improvements and become 'civilized,' and, on the other, individuals and societies that have remained in a state of 'barbarity.' A second distinction, between an 'advanced present' and a 'primitive past,' follows from the temporal logic inherent in the idea of 'progress.' Both distinctions are based on a set of normative values assumed to be universally valid, even though they were ostensibly grounded in the European tradition.

The universality of the concept of 'civilization,' its fifth key semantic molecule, was also formulated by Guizot, who assumed that "there is such a thing as one *universal civilization* of the human race."[74] The coiners of the term *civilization* used it in the singular to refer to the 'progress' that elevated humankind from a state of barbarity to more advanced stages of 'civilization.' In their ethnocentric smugness, they naturally assumed that this universal process had reached its pinnacle in Western Europe. As astutely observed by by the French diplomat–scholar Chrétien-Louis-Joseph de Guignes (1759–1845) in the *Edinburgh Review*

The coining of civilizational consciousness 25

in 1809, "It is to be lamented that philosophers have not yet laid down any very distinct canons for ascertaining the principal stages of civilization. . . . All they do is to fix on one or two of the principal nations of Europe as at the highest point of civilization."[75]

The European coiners of the term *civilization* helped facilitate the exploitation of the overseas colonies by casting their inhabitants as 'civilizationally inferior others' or 'barbarians,'[76] who should become 'civilized' by adopting ethnocentrically defined European ideas of 'civility' and 'police.' Similarly, within the centralized states in whose service many of them worked, the early European promoters of 'civilization' placed themselves at the top of a civilizational hierarchy, at the bottom of which were the illiterate, uneducated peasants and workers who were viewed with the same disdain and pity as the 'barbarians' and 'savages' encountered in Europe's overseas explorations. By placing themselves at the top of the civilizational hierarchy, which they themselves had formulated, the coiners of the term *civilization* gave the Eurocentric market of cultural capital global reach. The quality and "market value" of different forms of cultural capital (manifested in different values and practices) were thus assessed by the ethnocentric standards of the European universal concept of 'civilization.'

In the history-word-by-word approach adopted here, the coining of the words *civility*, *police*, and *civilization* to refer to a universal concept of 'civilization' can be used to determine when collective civilizational consciousness emerged in modern Western Europe. European thinkers writing in French and English began to develop civilizational consciousness in the sixteenth century when they started using the terms *civility* and *police*, as well as combinations of words for 'civility' and 'police,' to refer to early forms of the universal concept of 'civilization.' However, this civilizational consciousness only fully crystallized and reached a larger community of thinkers (and readers of their works) in the late eighteenth century after the word *civilization* had become a convenient and widespread way to refer to the idea of 'civilization.'

The rapid rise of the word *civilization* as the default word for the universal concept of 'civilization' took place in the mid-seventeenth century, when the European world economy began to expand rapidly after a century of stagnation. The British victory at the Battle of Plassey in 1757, which gave the British East Asia Company a foothold in Bengal, can be seen as a turning point in Europe's increasing economic and political dominance over the rest of the world.[77] The crystallization of the early modern European idea of 'progress' in the seventeenth and eighteenth centuries also appears to have contributed to the appeal of the idea of 'civilization.'[78] As observed by Elias, the concept of 'civilization' reflected "the rise of the bourgeoisie" and the growing influence of the "middle-class intelligentsia" on the sociopolitical scene.[79] It is easy to understand why the concept of 'civilization' was popular among economic thinkers such as Adam Smith (1723–1790), who saw it as an important element in the ideological justification of European world dominance and deployed it in the global enforcement of the protection of private property and free commerce. At the same time, Enlightenment philosophers embraced the idea of 'progress' embodied in the concept of 'civilization' as a sign

26 *The coining of civilizational consciousness*

of confidence in the power of Reason to break free from enslavement to nature and backward customs through progress in the 'civility' of people and the 'police' of their governmental institutions.

The visualization of the conceptual structure of the early modern European universal concept of 'civilization' in Figure 1.4 provides a framework by which we can determine the onset of particular forms of civilizational consciousness in other traditions through studies of the lexicalization of the language-specific terms used to articulate (the semantic molecules of) the concept of 'civilization.' Although I use the phrase *civilizational consciousness*, I do not rely on ethnographic or archaeological concepts of 'civilization' as an analytical category to study the emergence of indigenous concepts of 'civilization' in early China. Instead, I employ a decompositional approach to engage in cross-cultural comparison of the different language-specific universal concepts of 'civilization' that evolved in modern Europe and pre-Qín China.

The word *civilization* and the concepts to which it refers are part of eighteenth-century English and French usage patterns that I compare to the meanings and uses of kindred terms and concepts in the Old Chinese language of the pre-Qín period. When I do use the term *civilization*, as in *civilizational consciousness*, it should therefore be understood as shorthand for a longer phrasal expression containing all the semantic components of the eighteenth-century universal concept of 'civilization,' as schematically analyzed in Figure 1.4. That is, *civilizational consciousness* is shorthand for 'a collective consciousness based on the idea of a universal process of progress operating on individuals and social formations along the dimensions of civility (refinement of manners, behavior, etc.) and police (laws, government institutions), which results in the establishments of value-laden distinctions between self (the civilized) and others (barbarians) and between a primitive past and an advanced present or future.' As I show in Chapters 2–5, a particular language-specific civilizational consciousness which can be paraphrased in such terms can be identified in pre-Qín texts from the Warring States period. However, since all its semantic molecules have language-specific Old Chinese meanings, this pre-Qín civilizational consciousness is also very different from the civilizational consciousness that emerged in eighteenth-century Europe.

Critics of the universal concept of 'civilization'

Ever since the emergence of the idea of 'civilization' in the sixteenth century, critics have been pointing out (as they still do) that it legitimized unequal distribution of wealth, cynical exploitation of the "uncivilized," alienation, and deprivation of freedom.[80] Many of those ills could be cured, some believed, by returning to the original ways of life that were still practiced by the indigenous peoples whom the proponents of 'civilization' called 'barbarians' and tried to 'civilize.' And so the idea of the 'noble savage' (Fr. *bon sauvage*) was born.[81] According to such notions, which began to be promoted in the sixteenth century by thinkers such as Michel de Montaigne (1533–1592), living in nature was not a crude state of barbarism but rather a more authentic human condition that satisfied true needs and led to greater individual freedom in simple societies with little or no social

The coining of civilizational consciousness 27

hierarchy.[82] In contrast, the idea of 'civilization' was considered to be a cynical ideology designed to justify the exploitation of peoples who were stipulated not to have attained a sufficiently high degree of 'civilization'—be they overseas 'barbarians' or 'savages,' or domestic lower classes. Some critics of 'civilization' viewed the protection of private property and free market exchange by the rule of law in highly 'civilized' and 'policed' societies as elements of an exploitative ideology concocted by an elite minority in order to enslave the rest of the world.

The French philosopher Jean-Jacques Rousseau (1712–1778) is perhaps the best known eighteenth-century critic of 'civilization.' Although he never used the term *civilization* (using instead phrases like *civilized peoples*),[83] his criticism of the idea was so influential that the term *civilization* itself may have been coined and popularized partly as a defensive reaction to thinkers like him.[84] Writing in the early 1770s, the Scottish philosopher John Millar (1735–1801) targeted critics of 'civilization' like Montaigne and Rousseau when he stated that "many writers appear to take pleasure in remarking, that as the love of liberty is natural to man, it is to be found in the greatest perfection among barbarians, and is apt to be impaired according as a people make progress in *civilization* and in the arts of life."[85]

In defense of 'civilization,' Millar, in the Hobbesian tradition, acknowledged that it limits certain liberties, but only out of necessity in order to bring security, order, and prosperity by liberating people from the state of chaos and "constant hostilities which are natural to independent tribes of barbarians" unacquainted "with arts and *civilization*."[86]

Beyond Rousseau, numerous others have criticized the concept of 'civilization.' Figure 1.5 offers a colorful description of the dangers of being "disfigured

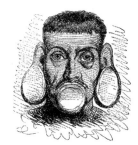

[Head of a Botecudo previous to disfigurement.]

[Head of a Botecudo disfigured by chin and ear pendants.]

[Head of a Botecudo disfigured by civilisation.]

Figure 1.5 Illustration appearing in editorial entitled "Civilisation" in the satirical magazine *Punch*, July–December 1841. According to the author, "the popular advocates of civilisation certainly are not the most civilised of individuals. . . . To them, nothing can show a more degraded state of nature than a New Zealand chief, with his distinctive coat of arms emblazoned on the skin of his face; nor anything of greater social elevation than an English peer, with the glittering label of his 'nobility' tacked to his breast. To the rational mind, the one is not more barbarous than the other; they being . . . the real barbarians who, like these *soi disant* civilisers, would look upon their own monstrosities as the sole standard of excellence."[87]

Credit: PUNCH Magazine Cartoon Archive.

28 *The coining of civilizational consciousness*

by civilization" from 1841. As discussed in Chapters 2–5, there are numerous parallels between the debates between pre-Qín coiners and critics of *wén* 'civilization' and those between European coiners and critics of *civilization*.

From *civilization* in the singular to *civilizations* in the plural: birth of the ethnographic and archaeological concepts of 'civilization'

The semantic evolution of the modern Anglophone term *civilization* did not stop in the eighteenth century. Since then it has acquired numerous other meanings. Here I focus on two of these that have played pivotal roles both in shaping modern European civilizational consciousness and in how European scholars have articulated the question of the origin and nature of "Chinese civilization": the ethnographic and archaeological concepts of 'civilization.'

Emergence of the ethnographic concept of 'civilization' 1800–1850

Sometime between 1800 and the 1830s, the term *civilization* began to be used to denote what the Italian sociologist Alfredo Niceforo (1876–1960) fittingly dubbed the ethnographic concept of 'civilization.'[88] According to Niceforo, the word *civilization* in the ethnographic sense refers to "the totality of characteristics (states or conditions) of the collective life [of a group], that is, the material, intellectual and moral aspects of life, as well as the political and social organization of a population group or of a [historical] period." It is "a simple enumeration of facts"—that is, a list of descriptive characteristics that do not include value judgments.[89]

Whereas the universal concept of 'civilization' was a single universal process, the ethnographic notion of 'civilization' made it possible to identify and compare different *civilizations* (in the plural) as entities *sui generis*. In Burnouf and Lassen's (1826: 2) *Essai sur le Pali*, the plural *civilizations* clearly refers to different traditions with particular characteristics. According to Burnouf and Lassen, the Pali language "joins together in a sort of unity peoples who belong to such diverse civilizations as the heavy and coarse mountain-dwellers of Arakan and the more 'policed' inhabitants of Siam."[90] As shown in Figure 1.6, while the universal concept of 'civilization' is assumed to apply to humankind at all times and in all locations, the ethnographic concept is bounded in both time and space.

The coining of *civilization* in the ethnographic sense coincided with the shift from the universalism of Enlightenment thinkers to the particularism of the emergent ideology of nationalism around the turn of the nineteenth century. The German thinker Johann Gottfried Herder's (1744–1803) idea that each nation and people has its own particular *culture* (Ger. *Kultur*) and national identity helped pave the way for envisioning multiple *cultures*.[91] That is, while the Anglo-French concept of 'civilization' was universalistic, the late

a 'Universal civilization' ⇨	b 'Ethnographic civilization'
• *civilization* (singular)	• *civilizations* (plural)
• scope: universal	• scope: local, specific region and/or period
• process of progress	• value-neutral description of the "material, intellectual
• see figure 1.4 above	and moral aspects of life, as well as the political and social organization of a population group or of a [historical] period"; limited to "a simple enumeration of facts" (Niceforo 1921: 30)

Figure 1.6. Lexicalizing *civilization* (1780s–1830s): from universal to ethnographic concept of 'civilization.'

eighteenth-century German concept of 'Kultur' was particularistic.[92] Beginning around the turn of the nineteenth century, the German word *Kultur* was often translated as *civilization* in French and English.[93] This may have contributed to the emergence of particularistic ethnographic concepts of 'civilization' in both languages. The equation between a 'nation' and 'its people' that gained popularity around the turn of the nineteenth century appears to have stimulated use of the word *civilization* in the ethnographic sense to discuss and compare *European civilization, Egyptian civilization, Chinese civilization*, and so forth. In the first few decades of the nineteenth century, the idea that different groups in different parts of the world could have their own particular ethnographically defined "civilizations" became widespread. Various forms of the ethnographic concept of 'civilization' remain at the heart of many current uses of the term.

Emergence of the archaeological concept of 'civilization'

The development of the discipline of archaeology in Europe in the late nineteenth and early twentieth century was driven in part by nationalist agendas of rooting national identity in the past.[94] Scholars began explicitly articulating questions such as "How old is Egyptian civilization?" and "When did Chinese civilization begin?" With increasing interest in such questions, scholars began to pay more attention to the definition of the ethnographic concept of 'civilization.' Scholars began to debate what criteria archaeological finds from a specific place and time had to meet to be considered a 'civilization.' Is the existence of a writing system necessary? What about state formation? Monumental architecture? Many different sets of criteria have been proposed, and so far no general consensus has been reached. Thus, as illustrated in Figure 1.7, the ethnographic concept of 'civilization' has branched into various lists of criteria used by archaeologists working in different theoretical frameworks:

30   *The coining of civilizational consciousness*

(a) Childe (1950) & Maisels (1999)

1   Urban centers
2   Full-time specialists (craftsmen, merchants, officials, priests, etc.) supported by surpluses from farming
3   Primary producers paying surpluses to a deity or divine ruler
4   Monumental architecture
5   Ruling class exempt from manual labor
6   Systems for recording information (writing, numerical notation)
7   Development of exact practical sciences
8   Monumental art
9   The regular importation of raw materials both as luxuries and as industrial materials
10   Peasants, craftsmen, and rulers form a community
11   The social solidarity of the community is represented (or misrepresented) by the preeminence of temples and funerary cults
12   A state organization is dominant and permanent

(b) Renfrew (1972)

1   Social stratification
2   Highly developed handicraft specialization
3   Town
4   Written language
5   Monumental construction

Figure 1.7 Criteria for the archaeological concept of 'civilization.'[95]

Using Childe's (1950) and Maisels' (1999) 12 criteria, or Renfrew's (1972) five, or one of the many other such lists proposed, yields widely different chronologies of the emergence of "early civilizations." Based on the criteria in Figure 1.7(b), Renfrew (1980: 14) proposes that the Egyptian and Mesopotamian civilizations both emerged around 3000 BCE, the Indus Valley civilization after 2700 BCE, the civilization of Shāng China around 1500 BCE, the Minoan Crete civilization around 2000 BCE, the Olmec civilization of Mexico around 1000 BCE, and the Chavin civilization of Peru around 900 BCE. However, many different dates have been proposed for the emergence of each of these "early civilizations." Using different thresholds of 'civilization,' scholars have dated the beginning of "Chinese civilization" anywhere from 4000 BCE to the first millennium BCE.

The conceptual structure of the archaeological concept of 'civilization' can be mapped as shown in Figure 1.8.[96] Many definitions of the archaeological concept of 'civilization' involve a notion of change. However, the absence from the archaeological concept of 'civilization' of the moralizing component of 'civility' (which played a key role in the universal concept of 'civilization') means that the set of entities undergoing change no longer includes individuals but only social formations (groups, cultures, states, etc.). The archaeological concept of 'civilization' thus lacks the moralizing, prescriptive dimension of the universal concept of 'civilization' that tells people how they should be as individuals to become more

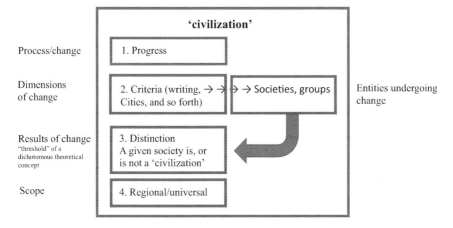

Figure 1.8 Conceptual structure of the archaeological concept of 'civilization.'

'civilized.' Consequently, the distinctions resulting from the change in social formations are usually no longer necessarily viewed normatively as 'progress' from 'barbaric' to 'civilized' stages. Instead, change can now be viewed in value-neutral, descriptive terms as a transition from one type of social formation (e.g., a hunter–gatherer, or foraging, society) that does not meet the criteria for being considered a 'civilization,' to another type of social formation (e.g., an early state or 'empire') that does.[97]

Invention and transformations of "Chinese civilization"

Since it was first coined in the 1760s, the word *civilization* has served as a kaleidoscopic lens through which Anglophone China observers have constructed different conceptualizations of "Chinese civilization." The phrases *civilization of China* and *Chinese civilization* can have widely different and even contradictory meanings depending on whether *civilization* is understood in the universal, ethnographic, or archaeological sense. Tracing the historical development of the many different meanings of the phrase *Chinese civilization* allows us to see how the complex semantic development of the English word *civilization* has generated a wide array of different perceptions of "Chinese civilization." It also illustrates how all these definitions of "Chinese civilization" differ from the study of the onset of civilizational consciousness in pre-Qín texts undertaken in Chapters 2–5.

In the eighteenth century, the word *civilization* was used to invoke a universal concept of 'civilization' which was grounded solidly in ethnocentric European values (see Figure 1.4). In 1770, the French economist Nicholas Baudeau (1730–1792) used the word *civilization* in this sense in discussions of China. Baudeau

32 *The coining of civilizational consciousness*

praises "the efforts made by. . . [the ancient Chinese sage–kings, Fú Xī, Shén Nóng, and Huáng Dì who, according to tradition, ruled China in the third millennium BCE] for the *civilization of China*."[98] Here, the word *civilization* clearly refers to the universal process of 'civilization,' that is, the 'civilizing of China.' For Baudeau, the ancient Chinese historical records were reliable proof that in the age of the sage–kings Yáo, Shùn, and Yǔ, "the Empire of China, was *policed*, cultivated, *civilized*, enriched, and decorated by the arts."[99]

An early sinophobe use of the word *civilization* in discussions of China can be found in the French philosopher Constantin-François Volney's (1757–1820) harsh dismissal of China from 1789: "The Chinese, governed by an insolent despotism, . . . restrained by an immutable code of gestures, and by the radical vices of an ill-constructed language, appear to be in their *abortive civilization* nothing but a race of automatons."[100] Volney uses the word *civilization* to refer to a universal process of progress in which the Chinese had allegedly failed to move beyond an early stage. This imagined lack of 'progress' was repulsive to many eighteenth-century European thinkers. Thus, in the late eighteenth century the universal concept of 'civilization' allowed sinophobe thinkers to place "Chinese civilization" at a low level of development while sinophile thinkers could extol "Chinese civilization" as a model to emulate.

The first occurrence of the phrase *Chinese civilization* in English I have been able to find appears in a travel report by Chrétien-Louis-Joseph de Guignes published in the *Edinburgh Review* in 1809. Describing a certain M. Vanbraam's frustration over the mendacity of the mandarins, the author finds it amusing that M. Vanbraam nevertheless struggles to "think highly of the *Chinese civilization*."[101] Read in isolation, this may appear to be a use of the ethnographic sense of the word *civilization*. But a closer look at the immediate context quickly undermines this interpretation. When discussing "the state of civilization among the Chinese," the author states that "the information we now have concerning China, however defective in marking the particular aspect which, among them, a particular stage of civilization exhibits, is yet abundantly sufficient to prove, that they are in the very infancy, or very little advanced."[102]

In other words, the author understands and uses the phrase *Chinese civilization* to refer to China's stage in a universal progress of 'civilization.' In sum, the phrase *Chinese civilization* is only attested in a handful of texts from 1800 to the early 1820s and is used mostly, if not exclusively, in the 'universal' sense.[103]

The emergence of the ethnographic concept of 'civilization' in the early nineteenth century allowed European scholars to use the phrase *Chinese civilization* to refer to an entity *sui generis* with its own idiosyncratic traditions and characteristics (see Figure 1.6). Uses of the English phrase *Chinese civilization* in the ethnographic sense, to refer to a distinct tradition with its own particular practices and values, first appeared in the 1820s and 1830s. In 1824 the author of a magazine article wrote that the "historical chasm among the Hindoos, may be equally applied to all the nations who have embraced their religion, unless where its effects were counteracted by *Chinese civilization*."[104] An early ethnographic use of *civilization* is also present in an anonymous article from 1831 in *Asiatic Journal*. "Chinese literature and philosophy," the author states, were not imported

The coining of civilizational consciousness 33

to Japan "till 284, in the reign of the Daïri Ozin-teno, when this prince sent an embassy to the kingdom of Fiak-sae (Pe-tse), in Corea, in quest of educated men, who were capable of diffusing *Chinese civilization . . .* throughout this empire."[105] In these two instances, *Chinese civilization* refers to a particular entity, defined by idiosyncratic features, that is capable of "counteracting" other religions and of being "diffused" into a different country. Both uses of the term *civilization* are thus ethnographic.[106]

In the late nineteenth century, racially informed uses of the word *civilization* became a powerful weapon in Western denigrations of "Chinese civilization." The Scottish anatomist Robert Knox (1791–1862) explicitly linked the concept of race to the ethnographic concept of 'civilization.'[107] In his *Races of Men* (1862), he stated that "the results of the physical and mental qualities of a *race* are naturally manifested in its *civilization*, for every *race* has its own form of *civilization . . .* as it has its own language and arts."[108] Subsuming the Chinese under "Oriental races," he added, "It is not merely the savage races . . . which seem incapable of *civilization*; the *Oriental races* have made no progress since Alexander the Great. The ultimate cause of this, no doubt, is race."[109] Racialized concepts of 'civilization' enabled Western critics of China to introduce a separation between "civilized" Europe and the "semi-civilized," or even "barbarian," Chinese that was grounded in what was assumed to be innate differences between the "White" and "Yellow" races.[110]

Finally, the advent of archaeological definitions of 'civilization' in the late nineteenth and early twentieth century generated yet another set of conceptualizations of *Chinese civilization*.[111] K. C. Chang, arguably the twentieth century's most influential archaeologist who wrote in English, uses the phrase *Chinese civilization* to refer to the particular beginning of human civilization in China as it is characterized by tradition-specific traits unique to China, such as bronze vessels, jade carvings, tiger and dragon motifs, and so forth.[112] Different archaeologists have used different variants of the archaeological concept of 'civilization' (that is, different criteria for the threshold of civilization) to propose dates for the origin of "Chinese civilization" as a physically manifested entity (excavated ruins of ancient cities, pottery shards, etc.) that range from 4000 BCE to the first millennium BCE.

The very existence of the phrase *Chinese civilization* may lead (and often has led) to the essentializing assumption that an entity *sui generis* called "Chinese civilization" has existed in some form or other for millennia. If "Chinese civilization" is said to be five thousand years old, then one may be tempted to say that a millet farmer living in a small Neolithic village in North China in the year 3000 BCE and a stockbroker living in twenty-first century Shanghai both somehow belong to the same "Chinese civilization." But this obscures the fact that these two individuals and the lives they live have little, if anything, in common. Indeed, the Shanghainese stockbroker (despite allegedly belonging to "Chinese civilization") has much more in common with stockbrokers or other professionals in Europe, India, Africa, or the United States, than with the Neolithic millet farmer. Similarly, the Neolithic millet farmer (despite allegedly belonging to "Chinese civilization") had much more in common with people who lived in Neolithic village settlements elsewhere in the world than he does with the present-day Shanghainese stockbroker.[113]

34 *The coining of civilizational consciousness*

Conclusion

The history-word-by-word approach to the study of epistemic changes enables us to link the coining and evolution of collective civilizational consciousness to sociopolitical and intellectual history. The process of lexicalization connects the history of linguistic expressions to the history of collectively shared ideas. By studying the historical context of the lexicalization of the concept of 'civilization,' we can identify the coiners of new terms and of new meanings of old terms. We can then formulate hypotheses about the changes in their environments and intellectual milieus that led them to feel the need to pre-package new chunks of their perceived reality into more readily communicable words such as *civilization*. Semantic changes in meanings of the English word *civilization* can thereby be used to trace the emergence of and transformation of civilizational consciousness in the Anglophone "West."

The modern European concept of 'civilization' emerged and was coined in the period from the sixteenth to the eighteenth century. The stages in the coining of modern European civilizational consciousness are summarized in Table 1.1 on page: 35. Solid lines indicate periods in which the linguistic expressions (a)–(g) in the first column are attested to in the meanings given in the rightmost column. Dotted lines indicate transition periods of sporadic attestations or intermediate meanings.

A number of sociopolitical changes contributed to the birth of the early modern concept of 'civilization' in the sixteenth century. The emergence of increasingly centralized nation-states led to a bureaucratization or routinization of power and the waning of traditional and charismatic authority. The growing need for professionally trained administrators created an institutionalized market of acquired cultural capital, which both enabled and motivated state-employed officials to produce and circulate theories about 'civilization.' Rows (a)–(d) indicate that, until the 1750s, the emergent idea of 'civilization' could be expressed through (a) a combination of words for 'police' and 'civility,' or by the words (b) *police* and (c) *civility*, or (d) nonce occurrences of *civilization*. In this period, none of the three words in (b)–(d) became widely used to refer to an early form of the universal concept of 'civilization.'

As shown in (e) in Table 1.1, in the 1770s, the word *civilization* became the default word for the universal concept of 'civilization' among political philosophers and Enlightenment thinkers. Energized by Europe's recent ascent to economic and political world dominance and spurred on by the rise of the bourgeoisie, many thinkers and economists saw the universal concept of 'civilization,' coined in the word *civilization*, as a powerful tool in their attempts to legitimize European colonialism and global commerce as a beneficial process in which Reason moves humankind from "barbarity" to "civilization." The word *civilization* became a convenient way to refer to the complex idea of 'a universal process of progress operating on individuals and social formations along the dimensions of civility (i.e., the refinement of manners, behavior, etc.) and police (i.e., laws, government institutions), which results in the establishment of value-laden distinctions between self (the civilized) and others (barbarians) and between a primitive past and an advanced present or future.' The coining of the word *civilization* around

Table 1.1 Lexicalization of civilizational consciousness in modern Western Europe.

Linguistic expression	1550 1600	1600 1650	1650 1700	1700 1750	1750 1800	1800 1850	1850 1900	1900 2015	Concept of 'civilization'
(a) *civility + police* (figure 1.2)	■■■■	■■■	■■■	■■■	■■ ■				Universal
(b) *civility*	■ ■	■■■	■■■	■■■	■■ ■				Universal
(c) *police*		■ ■ ■■■	■■■	■■■	■■ ■				Universal
(d) *civilization* (figure 1.3)			■ ■ ■ ■ ■ ■ ■	■ ■ ■ ■ ■					Universal (nonce word, process only)
(e) *civilization* (figure 1.4)					■ ■ ■ ■■■	■■■	■■■	■■■	Universal (process & state)
(f) *civilization* (figure 1.6)						■ ■ ■ ■■	■■■	■■■	Ethnographic
(g) *civilization* (figures 1.7, 1.8)							■ ■ ■ ■	■■■■	Archaeological

36 *The coining of civilizational consciousness*

1760 thus crystalized a language-specific form of European collective civilizational consciousness, whose onset is indicated by the partially transparent vertical line in Table 1.1.

As indicated in (f), with the rise of nationalism, the ethnographic concept of 'civilization' developed over the first two or three decades of the nineteenth century and was used to refer to idiosyncratic features of particular 'civilizations' *sui generis* limited in time and space. Finally, as shown in (g), with the development of modern archaeology over the course of the nineteenth and twentieth centuries, the concept of 'civilization' further splintered into numerous different lists of criteria for the threshold of 'civilization.'

This survey of the lexicalization of the different concepts of 'civilization' in early modern Europe provides a framework with which to study the lexicalization of civilizational consciousness in pre-Qín China. Having made explicit the historical nature of the tradition-specific "prejudices" inherent in European concepts of 'civilization,' we can use these to engage in a hermeneutical dialogue or "fusion of horizons," in Gadamer's sense of the word—with the "prejudices" of the language-specific terms used in the lexicalization of civilizational consciousness in pre-Qín China. This should establish a clear sense of what a history-word-by-word approach to the study of collective civilizational consciousness in pre-Qín China involves. First, one must look through pre-Qín texts for expressions corresponding to the various conceptual components of a universal concept of 'civilization' as they are schematically outlined in Figure 1.4. Once indigenous pre-Qín ideas for the conceptual components ('progress,' 'civility,' 'police,' 'distinctions,' and 'universality') can be identified (either in lexicalized form as single terms or in phrasal constructions), then it is theoretically possible for a form of civilizational consciousness (akin to the one in Figure 1.4) to be explicitly articulated. As we shall see in Chapters 2–5, a shift from charismatic authority to more bureaucratic modes of power, as well as the introduction of a market of acquired cultural capital that informed the lexicalization of civilizational consciousness in early modern Europe, also played a role in the coining of civilizational consciousness in pre-Qín China.

Notes

1 Horace, *Ars Poetica*, tr. Smart (1863: 302).
2 Huntington (1996). See also Patterson's (1997: 9–14; 54–5) analysis of Newt Gingrich's use of the term *civilization*.
3 Ishaan Tharoor. "GOP debate: Some Republican Candidates Want a Clash of Civilizations," *The Washington Post*, 17 September 2015. www.washingtonpost.com/news/worldviews/wp/2015/09/17/on-foreign-policy-some-republican-candidates-embrace-a-clash-of-civilizations/ (Accessed 15 December 2015).
4 Michael Gerson. "America's Politicians Are Feeding the Islamic State Narrative," *The Washington Post*, 16 November 2015. www.washingtonpost.com/opinions/dont-feed-the-islamic-state-narrative/2015/11/16/e41dbcf6–8c90–11e5-ae1f-af46b7df8483_story.html?hpid=hp_no-name_opinion-card-e%3Ahomepage%2Fstory (Accessed 15 December 2015).
5 For analysis of how the events of September 11, 2001, rekindled rhetoric of a conflict between a "civilized world" and "barbarians," see Bowden (2009: 161–88; 208–11).

The coining of civilizational consciousness 37

6 Michael D. Shear and Peter Baker. "Supporting France, Obama Loath to Add Troops to ISIS Fight," *New York Times*, 16 November 2015. www.nytimes.com/2015/11/16/world/europe/obama-g20-turkey.html (Accessed 15 December 2016).

7 Elias (1994: 3).

8 I use the expression "the West" heuristically as a shorthand for modern Europe, the United States, and other countries (e.g., Australia) whose values were fundamentally shaped by the ideas of the Enlightenment period and who self-identify with "the West" as a "realm of value." This does not mean that I adopt the essentializing dichotomies between "West" and "East," or the "West and the rest," which are a legacy of Western imperialism and colonialism. For the invention of the concept of the "West," see GoGwilt (1995).

9 I use the words *expression, word*, and *term* interchangeably.

10 Beyond parts of speech, *syntactic features* also refer to case and agreement features; see Chomsky (1995).

11 Linguists disagree on how to represent meanings. For a survey of semantic theories of word meanings, see Geeraerts (2010).

12 For these attestations of *tobacco, feng-shui*, and *corporatization*, see *Oxford English Dictionary* (*OED*). www.oed.com/ (Accessed 15 December 2016).

13 The study of the emergence of new words received attention from the compilers of large dictionaries of the European languages in the nineteenth and early twentieth centuries. Computational approaches to the study of text corpora have given it a renaissance in the twenty-first century, as discussed in Geeraerts (2010). For the present study I have drawn on the theories of diachronic semantics proposed in Geeraerts (1997) and Geeraerts (2006).

14 The phrase "distant reading," coined by Moretti (2013), refers to data-centered methods of studying quantitative patterns in large collections of texts.

15 Pines (2009: 41).

16 Lackner, Amelung, and Kurtz (2001: 4).

17 Pines (2009: 41).

18 Jackendoff (2012: 103).

19 This does not mean that other definitions of 'consciousness' may not be useful for other purposes.

20 Jackendoff (2012: 81ff).

21 For the role played by writing in the production and dissemination of ideas in pre-Qín China, see Meyer (2012).

22 *Oxford English Dictionary*. www.oed.com/ (Accessed15 December 2016).

23 The French historian Lucien Febvre (1878–1956) emphasized the importance of the studying meaning changes in key terms:

> It is never a waste of time to study the history of a word. Such journeys, whether short or long, monotonous or varied, are always instructive. But in every major language there are a dozen or so terms, never more, often less, whose past is no food for the scholar. But it is for the historian if we give the word historian all its due force.
>
> Such terms, whose meanings are more or less crudely defined in dictionaries, never cease to evolve under the influence of human experience and they reach us pregnant, one might say, with all the history through which they have passed. They alone can enable us to follow and measure, perhaps rather slowly but very precisely (language is not a very rapid recording instrument), the transformations which took place in a group of those governing ideas which man is pleased to think of as being immobile because their immobility seems to be a guarantee of his security.
>
> (Febvre 1973: 219)

24 Elias (1994: 6–7, italics added).

25 For key words of Western modernity, see Knobloch (1961), Williams (1976), Taylor (1998), and Bennett et al. (2005).

38 *The coining of civilizational consciousness*

26 Koselleck (1979); Koselleck (2002); Koselleck (2004).

27 Brunner, Conze, and Koselleck (1972–1979).

28 Hampsher-Monk, Tilmans, and van Vree (1998: 1–2).

29 Koselleck (1998: 23–35).

30 This assumption is often associated with the hermeneutical theory of the German theologian and philosopher Friedrich Schleiermacher (1768–1834); see Schleiermacher, Wojcik, and Roland (1978: 5; 10).

31 Gadamer (1975: 269) defines horizon as "the range of vision that includes everything that can be seen from a particular vantage point. . . [W]orking out of the hermeneutical situation means the achievement of the right horizon of enquiry for the questions evoked by the encounter with tradition."

32 Gadamer (1975: 11).

33 Gadamer (1976: 72, italics added).

34 Other translations of Gadamer's original German term *wirkungsgeschichtliches Bewußtsein* include: "effective-historical consciousness," "consciousness effected by history," or "consciousness of the effects of history" (Schrift 2014: 257, n.7).

35 For an introduction to Wierzbicka's Natural Semantics Metalanguage theory and full list of semantic atoms or primes, see Wierzbicka (2006a: 16–19). For criticism of Wierzbicka's approach, see Geeraerts (2010: 127–37).

36 Wierzbicka (2008: 407). See also Wierzbicka (2006b).

37 Instead of specialized color terms, the Australian language Warlpiri uses more concrete visual descriptors such as *yalyu-yalyu*, 'blood-blood'; *yukuri-yukuri* 'grass-grass'; and *kunjuru-kunjuru* 'smoke-smoke' (Wierzbicka 2008: 410). These are not one-to-one equivalents of the English color terms *red, green, gray*; rather, they constitute a different way of conceptualizing the external appearance of things. Warlpiri also lacks a word for the abstract concept 'color.' Consequently, to assume "that speakers of . . . languages [such as Warlpiri] none the less 'think' in terms of 'colour' (although they never speak about 'colour') is to impose on those languages a conceptual grid alien to them" (Wierzbicka 2008: 408). Wierzbicka explains the absence of color terminology in pre-colonial Warlpiri by suggesting that the Warlpiri were known not to engage in the practice of dyeing. Her hypothesis is that lexicalized color terms such as *yala-wana* meaning 'yellow[-one]' entered the language (as loan words from English) with the introduction of mass-produced objects brought by the European settlers and the changes in lifestyle this implied. Fully understanding diachronic lexical changes requires linking them to sociopolitical changes.

38 See also Jenco (2015).

39 I do not strictly follow Wierzbicka's analytical procedure of breaking down all complex concepts into her list of 60 some semantic primes, or atoms. Many of the terms in the paraphrase of the universal concept of 'civilization' are themselves complex 'molecules' rather than 'atoms,' e.g., *progress, civility*, and so forth. However, these molecules can be broken down into smaller atoms if necessary for cross-linguistic comparison.

40 The relationship between language and thought is controversial. It may therefore be useful to state the position adopted here. I assume that all human languages are equally well-equipped to perform the same basic functions: describing situations, interacting with others, and so forth. Languages may appear to be structurally very different (e.g., Spanish and modern Chinese). But grammatical and morphological differences do not make certain languages unable to express certain thoughts that can be readily expressed in other languages. Some basic concepts are universal or nearly so ('up,' 'down,' 'move,' etc.). In Wierzbicka's framework, these universally lexicalized concepts are the semantic atoms which facilitate cross-linguistic understanding. But many concepts are tradition-specific and are therefore harder (but not impossible) to translate. The Modern English words *deflation, selfie*, and *democracy* are difficult to translate into Old Chinese. Similarly, it is hard to translate Old Chinese *xiào* 孝

The coining of civilizational consciousness 39

'filial piety,' *lǐ* 禮 'rites; moral decorum' and *wén* 文 'pattern; civility/civilization' into English. Does this mean that people in pre-Qín China thought differently from speakers of Modern English? The answer is no, in the sense that Old Chinese drew on the same syntactic and morphological toolkit as all other human languages. However, since they had lexicalized a whole array of complex tradition-specific concepts that are unfamiliar to us, they tended to conceptualize the world somewhat differently. To understand early Chinese terms, it is not enough to look for one-to-one Modern English translation equivalents (which are often impossible to find anyway). We must try to understand the semantic structure of these complex language-specific concepts. In sum, I do not advocate the strong linguistic relativism of the so-called Sapir–Whorf hypothesis, which assumes that language largely determines thought. However, I do agree with Wierzbicka that language-specific terms predispose native speakers to conceptualize the world in certain ways. In Foucauldian terms, language-specific terms affect the epistemic parameters of our worldview and our collectively shared consciousness. For the Sapir–Whorf hypothesis, see Lucy (1992).

41 While Wierzbicka's framework enables such a bi-directional approach, in practice she tends to use English as metalanguage.

42 The French word *civilisation* and the English word *civilization* have language-specific meanings and are not always used in the same ways. For example, in contemporary twenty-first-century French the word *civilisation* is used in many instances where English would use *culture*. However, during the eighteenth century the word *civilization* seems to have referred to the same universal concept of 'civilization' in both languages. It appeared about the same time in the works of French and Scottish philosophers and economists, some of whom were in direct contact. Adam Smith, one of the first to use the word *civilization* in English, is known to have visited the Paris salon of the German–French philosopher Baron d'Holbach (1723–1789); see Blom (2005: 124) and Durant and Durant (1965: 149). D'Holbach used the word *civilisation* as early as 1774; see Elias (1994: 38). According to Stocking (1987: 14), "[d]uring the winter of 1750–1751, Adam Smith in Edinburgh and Baron Turgot at the Sorbonne each gave lectures attempting a more general or scientific formulation of the idea of progress in civilization." In the following, I only use French example for the early stages of the evolution of coining of the term *civilization*.

43 Carte (1747: 380, italics added). The *Oxford English Dictionary* quotes this sentence as to illustrate the use of the word *police* to refer to "social or communal organization; civilization," see www.oed.com (Accessed 15 December 2016).

44 The English word *barbarian* derives from classical Greek word βάρβαρος (*bárbaros*). During and after the Persian Wars (499–449 BCE), this term began to be used as a derogative way to refer to non-Greek peoples as 'civilizationally inferior others'; see Edith Hall (1989) and Jonathan Hall (1997). Through translations of Classical Greek and Roman texts, this term made its way into European vernaculars by the Renaissance. As observed by Patterson (1997: 88), "long dead authorities, writing about their own societies, provided the modern boosters [of civilization] with a pool of ideas, images, and metaphors they could draw upon and recycle."

45 For Weber's notion of bureaucratization, see Weber (1991: 196–244). For Weber's study of charismatic authority, see Weber (1968: 18–27).

46 Weber distinguished three types of authority: (i) charismatic, (ii) traditional, and (iii) rational–legal or bureaucratic; see Camic, Gorski, and Trubek (2005: 144) and Treviño (2001: 168–74). Medieval European "feudalism" is often seen as a form of traditional authority.

47 Patterson (1997: 28).

48 For concept of 'cultural capital' and its role in the creation of social distinctions, see Bourdieu (1984).

49 Huppert (1971) and Patterson (1997).

50 See also Patterson (1997: 28–9).

40   *The coining of civilizational consciousness*

51 See Patterson (1997: 57–85).
52 The present analysis of the lexicalization of the European concepts of 'civilization' draws on Moras (1930), Pflaum (1961), Knobloch (1961), Banuls (1969), Elias (1994), Febvre (1973), Benveniste (1953), Dampierre (1961), Huppert (1971), Fisch (1978), and Stocking (1987: 8–45). Certain observations in these studies are outdated. I have therefore supplemented their research on early attestations of these words by reading through early sources and searching databases such as Google's books.google.com.
53 Crystal (1995: 132) provides a useful definition of a nonce word: "A nonce word (from the sixteenth-century phrase *for the nonce*, meaning 'for the once') is a [word] created for temporary use, to solve an immediate problem of communication. Someone attempting to describe the excess water on a road after a storm was heard to call it a *fluddle* – she meant something bigger than a puddle but smaller than a flood. The newborn [word] was forgotten (except by the passing linguist) almost as soon as it was spoken . . . There was no intention to propose it for inclusion in a dictionary."
54 Rather than continuing to write both the French and English forms, e.g., *civilized* (Fr. *civilisés*) and *policed* (Fr. *policés*), I henceforth use the English forms *civilized, civility, policed*, and so forth, as stand-ins for the French counterparts.
55 As translated in Febvre (1973: 229). French: "Les Égyptiens ne purent être rassemblés en corps, civilisés, policés, industrieux, puissants, que très longtemps apres tous les peuples que je viens de passer en revue."
56 Huppert (1971: 759).
57 Furetière (1732: 951). French: "Loix, ordre & conduite à observer pour la subsistence & l'entretient des États & des Sociétez . . . En général il est opposé à la barbarie. Les Sauvages de l'Amérique n'avoient ni loix, ni *police*, quand on en fit la découverte. Les États différents ont divérses sortes de *police* pour leurs mœurs & pour leur gouvernèment."
58 Burke (1791: 22). The Oxford English Dictionary (OED) lists this passage by Burke to illustrate the use of the word *police* to refer to "[s]ocial or communal organization; civilization," The OED has examples of *police* in this meaning going back to the sixteenth century.
59 According to Svogun (2013: 37), in "Burke's day, the word 'police' was synonymous with civilization." While I do not agree that *police* was synonymous with *civilization*, it evidently did refer to 'civilization' in some contexts.
60 See, for example, the following passage quoted in the *OED* entry for *civility*: "From them the Greekes, then barbarous, receiued *Ciuilitie*" (W. Raleigh 1614, *Hist. World* i. ii. viii. §1. 361), www.oed.com/, italics added.
61 Nisbet, A. (1722, *Syst. Heraldry* I. ii. iii. 268), as quoted in the *OED* entry for *civility*, www.oed.com/, italics added.
62 For a study of the use of the word *civility, civilize, civilized* to refer to an emergent concept of 'civilization' in the sixteenth to eighteenth century, see Huppert (1971) and Patterson (1997: 29).
63 Huppert (1971: 761).
64 Du Bosc and Montagu (1656: 83, italics added), as quoted in the *OED* entry for *civilization*. No previous studies of *civilization* discuss this early occurrence.
65 A. Snape (1706, *Serm. preach'd Before Princess Sophia*, p. 18), as quoted in the *OED* entry for *civilization*.
66 Febvre (1930), Moras (1930), Benveniste (1953).
67 Gordon (1761: 87, italics added), also cited in the *OED* entry for the word *civilization*.
68 Boswell (1910 [1791]: 414); see also Benveniste (1953: 51) and Febvre (1973: 223).
69 As observed by Moras (1930: 50), the 1770s was the decade when the word *civilization* was adopted by many thinkers.
70 Febvre (1973: 228).
71 Guizot (1911 [1828]: 11). French: "L'idée du progrès, du développement me paraît être l'idée fondamentale contenue sous le mot de civilisation" (Guizot 1878 [1828]: 15). Also quoted in Febvre (1973: 241).

The coining of civilizational consciousness 41

72 Elias (1994: 3–4).
73 Guizot (1878 [1828]: 408). French: "La civilisation m'a paru consister dans deux faits principaux: le développement de la société humaine et celui de l'homme lui-même; d'une part, le développement politique et social, de l'autre, le développement intérieur, moral."
74 Guizot (1878 [1828]: 9, italics added). English translation is from Febvre (1973: 241).
75 *De Guignes* (1809: 414).
76 Patterson (1997:54).
77 See Hung (2003: 263).
78 Bernal (1987: 177).
79 Elias (1994: 40).
80 For an overview of critics of 'civilization,' see Patterson (1997: 56–85).
81 For the concept of the "noble savage" in the French Enlightenment, see Harvey (2012: 69–95).
82 Patterson (1997: 62–5; 94).
83 For Rousseau, "the arts, literature, and the sciences" developed by 'civilization' insidiously entered people's minds and made them slaves to ideas of progress, industry, hard work, and respect for social hierarchies. These trappings of 'civilization' are "chains" that "stifle in men's breasts that sense of original liberty. . . [and] make of them what is called a *civilized people*" (tr. by C.D.H. Cole in Rousseau (1973 [1750]: 4–6, italics added), also quoted in Patterson (1997: 68–9)).
84 As observed by Patterson (1997: 41), "French and Scottish political economists coined the word *civilization* in the 1760s and 1770s to refute Jean Jacques Rousseau's charge that people were morally corrupted by life in civilized society and that neither greater learning nor the desire to be better than other people had improved the human condition."
85 Millar (1773 [1771]: 228, italics added).
86 Millar (1773 [1771]: 65, italics added).
87 *Punch* ('Civilization' 1841: 27, images resized and captions and title retyped for clarity). The Botocudo (spelled *Botecudo* in *Punch*) is an early name given to the Brazilian groups now also called the Aimoré. As explained in the *Encyclopædia Britannica* (1911: vol. 4: 304), the name Botocudo (from Portuguese *botoque* 'plug') alludes to the wooden disks the Aimoré apply to piercings of the lips and ears.
88 According to Febvre, the stage during which people began to talk about "*civilisations* which were more or less heterogeneous and autonomous and conceived of as the attributes of so many distinct historical or ethnic groups . . . was arrived at between 1780 and 1830" (Febvre 1973: 234, italics added). However, the clearest examples of the word *civilization* used to refer to the ethnographic concept date from the early decades of the nineteenth century.
89 Niceforo (1921: 30). French: "le mot civilisation indique . . . l'ensemble des characters (état ou conditions) de la vie collective: vie *matérielle, intellectuelle, morale*, et organisation politique et sociale d'un groupe de population ou d'une époque . . . une simple énumeration de faits."
90 Burnouf and Lassen (1826: 2). French: "il [=le Pali] resserre le lien puissant qui, aux yeux du philosophe, ramène sous une sorte d'unité des peoples de civilisations aussi diverses que le montagnard lourd et grossier de l'Arakan, et l'habitant plus policé de Siam." English tr. from Febvre (1973: 236). For early English uses of the phase *Chinese civilization* to refer to the ethnographic concept of 'civilization,' see the subsection titled Invention and transformations of "Chinese Civilization" below,
91 Barnard (1965). For a summary of Herder's views on 'civilization' and 'culture,' see also Patterson (1997: 71–5).
92 Stocking (1987: 20–5) provides a succinct survey of the early concept of 'culture' (German *Kultur*) in Germany. As summarized by Stocking (1987: 20), "During the period when 'civilization' took on its modern meaning in France and Scotland. . . [t]he characteristically German term for the development and cumulative achievement of human capacity was not 'civilization' but 'culture' – a more concretely metaphorical word, with an already long traditional reference to the process of personal cultivation.

42   *The coining of civilizational consciousness*

'Civilization' was also incorporated into German usage, but the German reaction against the cultural imperialism of the French Enlightenment, and a growing sense of economic and political backwardness to France and England, were expressed in a complex historical tension between the two terms. At times synonymous, often overlapping, but in general somewhat antithetical in meaning, 'civilization' came to connote the universal 'external' phenomena of material progress and social organization; 'culture,' the varied 'inward' moral and aesthetic manifestations of the human spirit."

93 Young (1995: 37). For the differences between German *Kultur* and Anglo-French *civilization*, see also Elias (1994: 3–41).

94 Champion and Díaz-Andreu García (1996).

95 This list is adapted from Trigger (2003: 43). See also Maisels (1999: 25–6). Both Maisels (1999) and Trigger (2003) provide more recent interpretations of the criteria suggested by Childe (1950). Maisels (1999: 329–41) applies this list to ancient China.

96 Many different definitions of 'civilization' have been used by archaeologists. The schematic analysis of what I call "the archaeological concepts of 'civilization'" cannot capture this complexity. However, it is useful for understanding the common conceptual core of way the term *civilization* has been used in archaeology. However, it should also be noted that some archaeologists have proposed definitions of 'civilization' which do not fit into the mold of Figure 1.8. Yoffee (2005) differs from most other frameworks, which provide criteria that social formations have to meet to be called *civilizations*. Instead, he defines his non-evolutionary concept of 'civilization' as "the larger social order and set of shared values in which states are culturally embedded" (Yoffee 2005: 17). Yoffee links his notion of 'civilization' to a " 'civilizational' ideology, namely that there should be a state," or a "central authority, whose leaders have privileged access to wealth and to the gods" (Yoffee 2005: 17). In this respect, Yoffee's notion of 'civilization' is akin to the concept of civilizational consciousness developed here in that it consists of a set of indigenous concepts and values constructed by people inside the ancient social formation being studied, rather than of a list of criteria defined by modern archaeological theory.

97 Many scholars to argue that the term *civilization* should be abandoned. Lists of criteria that a society must have to be sufficiently "complex" to qualify as a 'civilization' may lead to the implication (intended or not) that societies lacking these features are somehow less complex and therefore further back on an evolutionary scale. According to Wagner and Tarasov (2008: 83–4), we should abandon the use of the term *civilization* in the study of the early history and pre-history of humankind in order to end what they call "the colonialization of the past."

98 Baudeau (1770: 95, italics added). According to Daire (1846: 652–3) and Herencia (2014: 128), the author of this anonymous review of Guignes' edition of the *Book of History* was Nicholas Baudeau.

99 Baudeau (1770: 95, italics added). In a review of a large Jesuit work on Chinese history, Baudeau observed that in the early Chinese historical records, one can "follow the progress of civilization in a great people" (Baudeau 1776: 121). French: "on y suit les progress de la civilization chez un grand Peuple."

100 Volney (1820 [1789]: 102, italics added). French: "Le Chinois, avili par le despotism du bamboo, aveuglé par la superstition astrologique, entravé par un code immutable de gestes, par le vice radical d'un langue et surtout d'une écriture mal construites, ne m'offre, dans sa *civilisation* avortée, qu'un people automate."

101 De Guignes (1809: 413).

102 De Guignes (1809: 412–13).

103 Attestations of the phrase *Chinese civilization* from 1811 to 1821 include: (i) "astonishment at the progress of Chinese civilization" (Patrick 1811: 19); and "eulogisms on Chinese civilization and philosophy" ("Alphabetic Studies, and Chinese Imitations" 1821: 47). There are no indications that these occurrences of *civilization* are used in an ethnographic sense.

The coining of civilizational consciousness   43

104 *The Monthly Magazine: Or, British Register* ("Mr. Klaproth's Appreciation of the Asiatic Historians," 1824: 513, italics added here).
105 *Asiatic Journal* ('Account of Japan. Extracted from Japanese Works, by M. Klaproth' 1831: 206, italics added).
106 The English translation of the German philosopher and philologist Karl Wilhelm Friedrich Schlegel's (1772–1829) *Philosophy of History,* published in 1835, appears to be one of the first texts to explicitly link the phrase *Chinese civilization* to the *Chinese nation*: "All researches into the *origin of the Chinese nation and Chinese civilization* ever conduct the enquirer to the north-west, where the province of Shensee is situated, and to the countries lying beyond" (Schlegel 1835: 194, italics added). The original German phrase is "chinesischen Nation und Cultur" (Schlegel 1829: 182). *Cultur* is an old spelling of the word *Kultur*. As mentioned above, German *Kultur* was often translated into English as *civilization*.
107 Gobineau (1855), translated into English by Adrian Collins in (1915), also uses a racialized concept of 'civilization': "no spontaneous civilization is to be found among the yellow races" (Gobineau 1915: 212).
108 Knox (1862: 56–7, italics added).
109 Knox (1862: 599, italics added).
110 Racially informed uses of the word *civilization* can be found in both the "universal" "ethnographic" senses in discussions of the Chinese. According to the French zoologist Georges Cuvier (1769–1832), while the "Mongolian or yellow race . . . formed great empires in China and Japan" its "*civilization* has always remained stationary" (Cuvier 1817: 95, italics added). Here Cuvier uses the word *civilization* to refer to the stage that he assumed the "Yellow race" to have reached in a universal process of 'civilization' ethnocentrically grounded in the Western European tradition and values. For a brief historical overview of the influence of Cuvier's racial theories on the concept of 'civilization,' see Stocking (1968: 35–41).

 Uses of the word *civilization* in a racialized ethnographic sense in discussions of "Chinese civilization" and the "Yellow race" emerged somewhat later in the nineteenth century. In an 1880 essay arguing that "civilisation" in China derived from Mesopotamia, the French sinologist Albert Terrien de Lacouperie (1845–1894) stated that "the discovery of a foreign origin in the rudiments of their [the Chinese] *civilisation*, oddly enough, confirms the opinion asserted so many times that want of originality and of imagination is one of the characteristics of the *Yellow race*" (Lacouperie 1880: 34, italics added). In other words, Lacouperie explained the allegedly derivative character of "Chinese civilization" (in the ethnographic sense) as following directly from a supposedly racially determined inability to innovate.
111 Terrien de Lacouperie's (1966 [1894]) *Western Origin of the Early Chinese Civilization from 2,300 BC to 200 AD* exemplifies nineteenth-century use of the ethnographic concept of 'civilization' in discussions of 'the origin of Chinese civilization.'
112 See Chang (1999: 55). Many other definitions of 'civilization' have been proposed by archaeologists. See, for example, Yoffee's (2005) definition of 'civilization,' discussed in note 96 above. See also Allan's (2007) concept of cultural hegemony.
113 As observed by Shelach (2015: 159), one of the major themes in Chinese research on the origin of "Chinese civilization" is the problematic idea of an "unbroken continuation of Chinese identity from the Neolithic all the way through to the late imperial period." See also the discussion of the influence of contemporary national politics on archaeology in Shelach (2004: 20–3).

References

'Account of Japan: Extracted from Japanese Works, by M. Klaproth'. 1831. *The Asiatic Journal, and Monthly Register for British and Foreign India, China and Australia*, 6: 192–207.

44   *The coining of civilizational consciousness*

Allan, Sarah. 2007. 'Erlitou and the Formation of Chinese Civilization: Toward a New Paradigm', *The Journal of Asian Studies*, 66: 461–96.

'Alphabetic Studies, and Chinese Imitations', in 1821. *The London Magazine*, 47–8. London: Baldwin, Cradock, and Joy.

Banuls, A. 1969. 'Les Mots "Culture" et "Civilisation" en Francais et Allemand', *Études germaniques*, 24: 171–80.

Barnard, F. M. 1965. *Herder's Social and Political Thought: From Enlightenment to Nationalism* (Clarendon Press: Oxford).

Baudeau, Nicholas. 1770. 'Le Chou-king des chinois', *Ephémérides du citoyen, ou Chronique de l'Esprit National*, 9.

———. 1776. 'Histoire générale de la Chine, ou lest Grandes Annales de cet Empire, traduit du texte chinois par le feu Pere Joseoph-Anne-Marie de Moyriac de Mailla, Jésuite François, Missionaire à Pékin; publiées par M. l'Abbé Grosier', *Ephémérides du citoyen, ou Chronique de l'Esprit National*, troisieme: 121–68.

Bennett, Tony, Lawrence Grossberg, Meaghan Morris, and Raymond Williams. 2005. *New Keywords: A Revised Vocabulary of Culture and Society* (Blackwell Publishers: Malden, MA).

Benveniste, Émile. 1953. 'Civilisation', in *Éventail de l'histoire vivante, hommage à Lucien Febvre offert à l'occasion de son 75e anniversaire* (A. Colin: Paris).

Bernal, Martin. 1987. *Black Athena: The Afroasiatic Roots of Classical Civilization* (Free Association Books: London).

Blom, Philipp. 2005. *Enlightening the World: Encyclopédie, the Book That Changed the Course of History* (Palgrave Macmillan: New York).

Boswell, James. 1910 [1791]. *The Life of Samuel Johnson: Together with a Journal of a Tour to the Hebrides*. In three volumes. Vol. 1 (Swann Sonnenschein and Co: London).

Bourdieu, Pierre. 1984. *Distinction: A Social Critique of the Judgement of Taste* (Harvard University Press: Cambridge, MA).

Bowden, Brett. 2009. *The Empire of Civilization: The Evolution of an Imperial Idea* (University of Chicago Press: Chicago).

Brunner, Otto, Werner Conze, and Reinhart Koselleck (eds.). 1972–1979. *Geschichtliche Grundbegriffe: Historisches Lexikon zur politisch-sozialen Sprache in Deutschland* (E. Klett: Stuttgart).

Burke, E. 1791. *Letter to a Member of the National Assembly* (Printed for J. Dodsley: Paris).

Burnouf, Eugène, and Christian Lassen. 1826. *Essai sur le Pali, ou Langue sacrée de la presque 'île au delà du Gange* (Librarie Orientale de Dondey-Dupré Père et fils: Paris).

Camic, C., P. S. Gorski, and D. M. Trubek. 2005. *Max Weber's Economy and Society: A Critical Companion* (Stanford University Press: Palo Alto).

Carte, T. 1747. *A General History of England* (J. Hodges: London).

Champion, Timothy, and Margarita Díaz-Andreu García. 1996. 'Introduction', in Timothy Champion and Margarita Díaz-Andreu García (eds.), *Nationalism and Archaeology in Europe* (Westview Press: Boulder).

Chang, Kwang-Chih. 1999. 'China on the Eve of the Historical Period', in Michael Loewe and L. Edward Shaughnessy (eds.), *The Cambridge History of Ancient China: From the Origins of Civilization to 221 B.C.* (Cambridge University Press: Cambridge), pp. 37–73.

Childe, V. Gordon. 1950. 'The Urban Revolution', *Town Planning Review*, 21: 3–17.

Chomsky, Noam. 1995. *The Minimalist Program* (MIT Press: Cambridge, MA).

'Civilization'. 1841. *Punch, or the London Charivari*, 1: 27.

Crystal, David. 1995. *The Cambridge Encyclopedia of the English Language* (Cambridge University Press: Cambridge).

The coining of civilizational consciousness   45

Cuvier, Georges. 1817. *Le règne animal distribué d'après son organization* (Déterville: Paris).

Daire, E. 1846. *Physiocrates* (Guillaumin: Paris).

Dampierre, E. de. 1961. 'Note sur Culture et Civilisation', *Comparative Studies in Society and History*, 3: 328–40.

De Guignes, Chrétien-Louis-Joseph. 1809. 'Voyages à Peking', *The Edinburgh Review*, No. XXVIII: 407–29.

Du Bosc, J., and W. Montagu. 1656. *The Accomplish'd Woman* (Bedell and Collins: London).

Durant, Will, and Ariel Durant. 1965. *The Age of Voltaire: A History of Civilization in Western Europe from 1715 to 1756 with Special Emphasis on the Conflict Between Religion and Philosophy* (Simon & Schuster: New York).

Elias, Norbert. 1994. *The Civilizing Process* (Blackwell Publishers: Oxford).

Febvre, Lucien. 1930. *Première semaine internationale de synthèse. Deuxième fascicule. Civilisation, le mot et l'idée* (Renaissance du livre: Paris).

———. 1973. *A New Kind of History: From the Writings of Febvre* (Harper & Row: New York).

Fisch, Jörg. 1978. 'Zivilisation, Kultur', in Otto Brunner, Werner Conze, and Reinhart Koselleck (eds.), *Geschichtliche Grundbegriffe: Historisches Lexikon zur politisch-sozialen Sprache in Deutschland* (Band 7) (E. Klett: Stuttgart).

Furetière, Antoine. 1732. *Dictionnaire universel françois & latin* (Pierre-François Giffart: La Haye).

Gadamer, Hans-Georg. 1975. *Truth and Method* (Seabury: New York).

———. 1976. *Philosophical Hermeneutics* (University of California Press: Berkeley, CA).

Geeraerts, Dirk. 1997. *Diachronic Prototype Semantics: A Contribution to Historical Lexicology* (Clarendon Press: Oxford).

———. 2006. *Words and Other Wonders: Papers on Lexical and Semantic Topics* (Mouton de Gruyter: Berlin & New York).

———. 2010. *Theories of Lexical Semantics* (Oxford University Press: Oxford).

Gobineau, Joseph Arthur, Comte de. 1855. *Essai sur l'inégalité des races humaines* (Firmin Didot: Paris).

———. 1915. *The Inequality of Human Races* (G.P. Putnam's Sons: New York).

GoGwilt, Christopher Lloyd. 1995. *The Invention of the West: Joseph Conrad and the Double-Mapping of Europe and Empire* (Stanford University Press: Stanford, CA).

Gordon, John. 1761. *A New Estimate of Manners and Principles: Or a Comparison Between Ancient and Modern Times, in the Three Great Articles of Knowledge, Happiness, and Virtue. Part III. Of Happiness: In Which Some Principles of Mr. Rousseau Are Examined* (J. Bentham: Cambridge).

Guizot, François. 1878 [1828]. *Histoire de la civilisation en Europe depuis la chute de l'empire romain jusqu'à la revolution française* (Librairie Académique Didier: Paris).

———. 1911 [1828]. *The History of Civilization in Europe* (Cassell and Company: London, New York, Toronto & Melbourne).

Hall, Edith. 1989. *Inventing the Barbarian: Greek Self-Definition Through Tragedy* (Clarendon Press: Oxford).

Hall, Jonathan M. 1997. *Ethnic Identity in Greek Antiquity* (Cambridge University Press: Cambridge).

Hampsher-Monk, Iain, Karin Tilmans, and Frank van Vree (eds.). 1998. *History of Concepts: Comparative Perspectives* (Amsterdam University Press: Amsterdam).

Harvey, David Allen. 2012. *The French Enlightenment and Its Others: The Mandarin, the Savage, and the Invention of the Human Sciences* (Palgrave Macmillan: New York).

46   *The coining of civilizational consciousness*

Herencia, Bernard. 2014. *Les Éphémérides du citoyen et les Nouvelles Éphémérides économiques 1765–1788 Documents et table complète* (Centre international d'étude du xviiie siècle ferney-voltaire: Paris).

Hung, Ho-Fung. 2003. 'Orientalist Knowledge and Social Theories: China and the European Concepts of East-West Differences from 1600 to 1900', *Sociological Theory*, 21: 254–80.

Huntington, Samuel P. 1996. *The Clash of Civilizations and the Remaking of World Order* (Simon & Schuster: New York).

Huppert, George. 1971. 'The Idea of Civilization in the Sixteenth Century', in Anthony Molho and John A. Tedeschi (eds.), *Studies in Honor of Hans Baron* (Northern Illinois University Press: Dekalb, IL).

Jackendoff, Ray. 2012. *A User's Guide to Thought and Meaning* (Oxford University Press: New York).

Jenco, Leigh. 2015. *Changing Referents: Learning Across Space and Time in China and the West* (Oxford University Press: Oxford).

Knobloch, Johann. 1961. *Europäische Schlüsselwörter: Kultur und Zivilisation* (Hueber: Munich).

Knox, Robert. 1862. *The Races of Men a Philosophical Enquiry into the Influence of Race Over the Destinies of Nations* (Henry Renshaw: London).

Koselleck, Reinhart. 1979. *Historische Semantik und Begriffsgeschichte* (E. Klett: Stuttgart).

———. 1998. 'Social History and Begriffsgeschichte', in Iain Hampsher-Monk, Karin Tilmans, and Frank van Vree (eds.), *History of Concepts: Comparative Perspectives* (Amsterdam University Press: Amsterdam).

———. 2002. *The Practice of Conceptual History: Timing History, Spacing Concepts* (Stanford University Press: Stanford, CA).

———. 2004. *Futures Past: On the Semantics of Historical Time* (Columbia University Press: New York).

Lackner, Michael, Iwo Amelung, and Joachim Kurtz. 2001. 'Introduction', in *New Terms for New Ideas: Western Knowledge and Lexical Change in Late Imperial China* (Brill: Leiden & Boston), pp. 1–12.

Lacouperie, Terrien de. 1880. *Early History of the Chinese Civilisation* (E. Vaton: London).

———. 1966 [1894]. *Western Origin of the Early Chinese Civilization from 2,300 B.C. to 200 A.D.* (Zeller: Osnabrück).

Lucy, John Arthur. 1992. *Language Diversity and Thought: A Reformulation of the Linguistic Relativity Hypothesis* (Cambridge University Press: Cambridge & New York).

Maisels, C. K. 1999. *Early Civilizations of the Old World: The Formative Histories of Egypt, the Levant, Mesopotamia, India, and China* (Routledge: London).

Meyer, Dirk. 2012. *Philosophy on Bamboo: Text and the Production of Meaning in Early China* (Brill: Leiden).

Millar, John. 1773 [1771]. *Observations Concerning the Distinction of Ranks in Society* (J. Murray: London).

Moras, Joachim. 1930. *Ursprung und Entwicklung des Begriffs der Zivilisation in Frankreich (1756–1830)* (Seminar für Romanische Sprachen und Kultur: Hamburg).

Moretti, Franco. 2013. *Distant Reading* (Verso: London).

Niceforo, Alfredo. 1921. *Les indices numériques de la civilisation et du progrès* (E. Flammarion: Paris).

Patrick, A.M. 1811. 'The Chinese World', *The Classical Journal*, 3: 16–23.

The coining of civilizational consciousness 47

Patterson, Thomas C. 1997. *Inventing Western Civilization* (Monthly Review Press: New York).

Pflaum, G. M. 1961. *Geschichte des Wortes Zivilisation* (Inaugural Dissertation, Munich University).

Pines, Yuri. 2009. *Envisioning Eternal Empire: Chinese Political Thought of the Warring States Era* (University of Hawaii Press: Honolulu).

"Mr. Klaproth's Appreciation of the Asiatic Historians," in 1824. *The Monthly Magazine: Or, British Register*. Vol. LVIII, Part 2: 511–31.

Renfrew, Colin. 1972. *The Emergence of Civilisation: The Cyclades and the Aegean in the Third Millennium BC* (Methuen: London).

———. 1980. 'The Emergence of Civilization', in Arthur Cotterell (ed.), *The Encyclopedia of Ancient Civilizations* (Mayflower Books: New York), pp. 12–20.

Rousseau, Jean Jacques. 1973 [1750]. *A Discourse on the Arts and Sciences in the Social Contract and the Discourses*. Translated by C. D. H. Cole (J.M. Dent: London).

Schlegel, Friedrich von. 1829. *Philosophie der Geschichte* (Schaumburg: Wien).

———. 1835. *The Philosophy of History*. Translated by James Burton Robertson (Saunders & Otley: London).

Schleiermacher, F. D. E., Jan Wojcik, and Haas Roland. 1978. 'The Hermeneutics: Outline of the 1819 Lectures', *New Literary History*, 10: 1–16.

Schrift, A. D. 2014. *Poststructuralism and Critical Theory's Second Generation* (Routledge: London & New York)

Shelach, Gideon. 2004. 'Marxist and Post-Marxist Paradigms for the Neolithic', in K. M. Linduff and Yan Sun (eds.), *Gender and Chinese Archaeology* (Altamira: Walnut Creek), pp. 11–27.

———. 2015. *The Archaeology of Early China: From Prehistory to the Han Dynasty* (Cambridge University Press: Cambridge).

Smart, C. 1863. *Works of Horace: Translated Literally into English Prose* (Harper & Brothers: New York).

Stocking, George W. 1968. Race, Culture, and Evolution; Essays in the History of Anthropology (Free Press: New York).

———. 1987. *Victorian Anthropology* (Free Press & Collier Macmillan: New York & London).

Svogun, T. V. 2013. *The Jurisprudence of Police: Toward a General Unified Theory of Law* (Palgrave Macmillan: New York).

Taylor, Mark C. 1998. *Critical Terms for Religious Studies* (University of Chicago Press: Chicago).

Treviño, A. J. 2001. *The Sociology of Law: Classical and Contemporary Perspectives* (Transaction Publishers: New Jersey).

Trigger, Bruce G. 2003. *Understanding Early Civilizations: A Comparative Study* (Cambridge University Press: Cambridge & New York).

Volney, Constantin-François. 1820 [1789]. *Les ruines ou Meditation sur les révolutions des Empires* (Baudouin Frères: Paris).

Wagner, Mayke, and Pavel Tarasov. 2008. 'The Present Perception of the Origin of Chinese Civilization', in Dieter Kuhn and Helga Stuhl (eds.), *Perceptions of Antiquity in Chinese Civilization* (Edition Forum: Heidelberg).

Weber, Max. 1968. *Max Weber on Charisma and Institution Building: Selected Papers* (Chicago University Press: Chicago).

———. 1991. *From Max Weber: Essays in Sociology* (Routledge: London & New York).

48　*The coining of civilizational consciousness*

Wierzbicka, Anna. 2006a. *English: Meaning and Culture* (Oxford University Press: Oxford).

———. 2006b. 'The Semantics of Colour: A New Paradigm', in Carole P. Biggam and Christian Kay (eds.), *Language and culture* (J. Benjamins: Philadelphia).

———. 2008. 'Why There Are No "Colour Universals" in Language and Thought', *Journal of the Royal Anthropological Institute*, 14: 407–25.

Williams, Raymond. 1976. *Keywords: A Vocabulary of Culture and Society* (Oxford University Press: New York).

Yoffee, Norman. 2005. *Myths of the Archaic State: Evolution of the Earliest Cities, States and Civilizations* (Cambridge University Press: Cambridge).

Young, Robert. 1995. *Colonial Desire: Hybridity in Theory, Culture, and Race* (Routledge: London & New York).

2 From 'awe-inspiringly beautiful' to 'morally refined'

The coining of 'civility' in pre-Qín China

*Zǐgòng [a disciple of Confucius] said, 'What do you think of a poor man who yet does not flatter, or a rich man who is not proud?' The Master [Confucius] replied, 'They will do; but they are not equal to him, who, though poor, is yet cheerful, and to him, who, though rich, loves the rules of propriety.' Zǐgòng replied, 'It is said in the Book of Songs, 'As you cut and then file, as you carve and then **polish**.' Is this [line from the Songs] not a definition of that [Confucius's statement above]?'*
—*Analects*, 1.15[1]

*To civilize: to **polish** one's manners.*
—Furetière, *Dictionnaire Universel*[2]

It was late summer of the year 1057 BCE. The Zhōu army was aligned in perfect battle formation on the flat plain, ready to engage the marauding troops of the restive Quǎn-róng people facing them to the northwest. Horse-drawn chariots—each manned by a driver and an aristocratic warrior in colorful, shining battle armor wielding ornately decorated bronze weapons—were supported by groups of lightly armed foot soldiers. Chāng, the ruler of the Zhōu domain, had been bestowed the right to conduct military campaigns to the West of the Shāng realm by Dì Xīn (r. 1086–1045 BCE), the last ruler of the Shāng dynasty (ca. 1570–1045 BCE).[3] Standing majestically in his elegantly adorned war chariot as his driver drove slowly in front of his battle-ready army, he spoke to his commanders and foot soldiers, stirring in them feelings of loyalty to his cause and to himself. Wearing the full armor and decorations that signaled his status as king and military commander, he was as stunningly beautiful and awe-inspiring in appearance and demeanor as a Homeric hero or Arjuna, the warrior–hero of the *Bhagavad-Gītā*. Firmly under the spell of Chāng's charismatic power, the Zhōu troops felt proud to have such an imposing and valiant leader and were resolved to follow him to death if called upon to do so. After leading numerous successful military campaigns, Chāng would be called Chāng the 'awe-inspiringly beautiful' (文 *wén*).

Although the details are largely fictional, this battle description is intended to be as realistic as possible. Based on late Shāng and early Zhōu written records and material culture, we know that Shāng and Zhōu rulers were warrior aristocrats

50   *From 'awe-inspiringly beautiful' to 'morally refined'*

who accompanied their troops in battle riding in horse-drawn chariots. While evidence about Chāng's life and actions is scarce, the above description of his appearance on the battlefield offers a plausible explanation for why and how he eventually became known as King Wén (r. 1099/56–1050 BCE).[4]

In the Shāng and Western Zhōu (1045–771 BCE), the charismatic authority of the ruler and the members of the ruling elite was expressed predominantly in aesthetic terms. A person's social standing could be decoded by his or her dress and accouterments, such as jade and turquoise ornaments. Being 'awe-inspiringly beautiful' (*wén*) in this sense was the visual expression of King Wén's charismatic power and authority.

This pre-Warring States use of *wén* can also be translated 'imperiously beautiful,' 'commandingly beautiful,' 'imposingly beautiful,' or 'having a noble/awe-inspiring/commanding appearance and presence.' That is, I do not assume that 'awe-inspiringly beautiful' is the definite English translation or gloss of *wén*. I use 'awe-inspiringly beautiful' as a placeholder for a language-specific early Chinese concept of 'having a noble/awe-inspiring/commanding appearance and presence' for which there is no direct translation into Modern English.

Around 600–400 BCE, about half a millennium after the death of King Wén, the term *wén* began to be reinterpreted in ethical terms to refer to an individual's 'patterned civility' or 'moral refinement.' Subsequently, people began to think about King Wén more as the 'morally refined' king than as the 'awe-inspiringly beautiful' king. Over the course of the Warring States period (481–221 BCE), the new meaning of *wén* as 'ritualized/patterned civility' won out over the older meaning, which eventually became obsolete. The understanding of *wén* as 'morally refined' (or 'cultured,' 'civil,' and so forth) came to dominate the Chinese commentarial tradition in imperial China. As a consequence, it has often been applied anachronistically to pre-Warring States texts and still informs the way many modern scholars understand the term *wén*.

In this chapter, I explore the earliest chronological stages in the coining of civilizational consciousness in pre-Qín China.[5] How did the word *wén*, which appears to have originally meant 'pattern,' come to mean 'awe-inspiringly beautiful,' and how was that meaning later reinterpreted as 'morally refined'? The theory of lexicalization outlined in Chapter 1 enables us to explore the sociopolitical changes that accompanied the emergence of these new meanings of the word *wén*. Who were the coiners of these new meanings, and what changes in collective consciousness motivated them to create a concept of 'ritualized civility'? What specific features of the word *wén* made it suitable to express this new idea?[6]

Aesthetically grounded charismatic authority: from 'pattern' to 'beautiful'

In the Shāng and Western Zhōu dynasties, visual displays of social rank and wealth played an important role in establishing social hierarchies and legitimizing the charismatic authority of the ruling elite. Evidence of this can be found in the material remains from that period and in the earliest extant writings in Chinese,

From 'awe-inspiringly beautiful' to 'morally refined' 51

which date back to about 1300–1100 BCE. Archaeologists interpret the presence of monumental architecture and luxury objects as evidence of social stratification. That the Shāng and kings and royal family occupied the top of the hierarchy is evident in the enormous size of the royal tomb complexes and palaces, and the lavish resources spent on tomb goods such as bronze vessels (some weighing several hundred pounds), costly jade discs and ornaments, chariots, sacrificial victims sometimes numbering in the hundreds, and other trappings of wealth and power. While smaller than the largest Shāng royal tombs, richly furnished tombs of Western Zhōu rulers and members of the hereditary noble lineages nevertheless also bear witness to steep social stratification. Specialized artisans producing prestige items appear to have occupied a position between the aristocratic elite at the top of the hierarchy and the laborers and slaves at the bottom.[7] Procuring raw materials such as copper and tin, jade, turquoise, and ivory to transform them into prestige objects required huge amounts of resources to which only the aristocratic elite had access.[8] Consequently, using and wearing such objects was both a hereditary prerogative and a conspicuous marker of elite status, which enhanced a person's aesthetically expressed charismatic authority.

The hypothesis that the word *wén* is used as a descriptive epithet meaning 'awe-inspiringly beautiful' (or 'having a noble/commanding appearance and presence') in names such as King Wén is supported by archaeological finds which indicate that during the Shāng and Western Zhōu the charismatic authority of the king and members of the ruling elite was to a large extent expressed and communicated through the visual display of prestige objects. Max Weber defined "charismatic authority" as a

> certain quality of an individual personality, by virtue of which he is set apart from ordinary men and treated as endowed with supernatural, superhuman, or at least specifically exceptional powers or qualities. These are such as are not accessible to the ordinary person, but are regarded as of divine origin or as exemplary, and on the basis of them the individual concerned is treated as a leader.[9]

I am using Weber's concept of charismatic authority heuristically, in an extended sense that applies not only to the person of the king but also to the members of the royal family and high nobility who served as his military commanders and who ruled parts of his realm on his behalf and in various official positions. The Shāng kings united political and religious authority in one person. In the dynastic system of primogeniture, their charismatic power was an inherited prerogative that was expressed and communicated visually through dress, jade pendants, and use of lavishly decorated objects. Similarly, the leaders of the aristocratic lineages also ruled their domains through aesthetically expressed, inherited charismatic power.[10]

The 'beautiful' (kalós) heroes of pre-Classical Greece

In many respects, the prominent role played by 'awe-inspiring beauty' (*wén*) in the construction of social hierarchies and charismatic authority in the Western

52 *From 'awe-inspiringly beautiful' to 'morally refined'*

Zhōu can be compared to the role played by being *kalós* (Gr. καλός) 'beautiful' in pre-Classical Greek society. In Homeric society, a person's appearance could generally be taken as a good indication of his worth and social standing.[11] Being *kalós* 'beautiful' was an outward manifestation of one's *areté* (Gr. ἀρετή) 'excellence/power,' which was a concept often used in reference to the courage and military prowess of heroes and nobles.[12] In contrast, physical ugliness was often viewed as an indication of weakness and social inferiority.[13] A passage in the *Odyssey* describing the scene just after Odysseus has taken out the single eye of the Cyclops bears witness to an assumed connection between physical appearance and social importance and power. Surprised at having been defeated by Odysseus, the Cyclops says:

(1) I had always expected it would be some big, ['awe-inspiringly beautiful' (*kalós*)] man who would come here, someone clothed in great courage; but it turned out to be a puny, insignificant, weakling who deprived me of my sight, after overpowering me with wine.[14]

A soothsayer had already forewarned the Cyclops that Odysseus of Ithaca would one day destroy his eye. Consequently, the Cyclops imagined Odysseus to be 'great, tall,' 'awe-inspiringly beautiful' (*kalós*), and possessing 'great authority.' He was therefore surprised and disappointed to discover that Odysseus was 'small (of stature),' 'worthless,' and 'weak.' Simply by looking at Odysseus, the Cyclops did not consider him to be a worthy adversary in terms of martial prowess, strength, or natural authority.

The pre-Warring States word *wén* referred to a concept of '(awe-inspiring) beauty' akin to the concept of 'beauty' referred to by the Greek word *kalós* in the Homeric period. That is, *wén* referred not just to the physical features of an individual but more broadly to his or her overall appearance and presence, which included dress and various accouterments worn or used (armor, decorated weapons, chariots, etc.), as well as bearing and demeanor. The Western Zhōu and Homeric notions of 'awe-inspiring beauty' are thus very different from the concepts of 'beauty' referred to by the word *beautiful* in Modern English. Again, the Cyclops had not been anticipating with trepidation the arrival of a hero who was merely 'beautiful' or 'pretty' in the modern sense of the English word *beautiful*. No, he was expecting someone whose immense power and martial prowess were manifested in his being 'awe-inspiringly beautiful' (*kalós*). Similarly, King Wén was a strong leader whose charismatic power was communicated visually through his 'awe-inspiring beauty'/'commanding/imposing/noble appearance' (*wén*).

Physically manifested 'awe-inspiring beauty' as marker of inherited status and rank

The quality that gives someone charismatic authority can, as observed by Weber, be "judged from an ethical, aesthetic, or other such point of view."[15]

From 'awe-inspiringly beautiful' to 'morally refined' 53

Ultimately, what matters is how the charismatic power is interpreted by those ruled by a charismatic leader. During the period from the end of the Western Zhōu to the beginning of the Warring States period, the structure and justification of political power changed. Increasingly, power became routinized in bureaucracies and delegated to professional administrators. This led to a shift from the earlier system, in which charismatic authority was grounded predominantly in aesthetic terms, to a system where it was grounded increasingly in ethical terms. Weber does not dwell on the distinction between aesthetically and ethically grounded charismatic power; however, such a distinction neatly captures how the pre-Warring States understanding of the 'awe-inspiring beauty' (*wén*) of the 'Lord' or aristocratic 'nobleman' (*jūnzǐ*) in texts such as the *Book of Songs* became reinterpreted in moral terms, as the 'moral refinement' (*wén*) of the '(morally) noble man' (*jūnzǐ*) in Warring States texts such as the *Zuǒzhuàn* and the *Analects*.[16]

Shāng and Western Zhōu period texts contain numerous indications that the word *wén* was interpreted aesthetically rather than ethically. Although attested occurrences are sparse, the core meaning of *wén* appears to have been 'pattern,' referring to either naturally occurring patterns (such as tiger stripes) or decorative patterns applied to physical objects (like carvings or tattoos). The word *wén* was also used to refer to rank-indicating embroidered 'emblems' on garments and flags. But by far the most frequently attested use of *wén* is as a positive epithet meaning 'awe-inspiringly beautiful.' No occurrences of the term *wén* referring to concepts of 'civility/civilization' or 'moral refinement' are found in pre-Warring States texts.[17]

Reconstructing semantic developments in the earliest attestations of the word *wén* enables us to explain of how the new meaning of 'awe-inspiringly beautiful' derived from the basic meaning 'pattern.' *Wén* occurs in the meaning 'decorative pattern' in a few passages in the pre-Warring States corpus. The poem "Xiǎo Róng" (Máo 128) in the *Book of Songs* (*Shījīng*) contains a description of war chariots that, among other attributes, have "patterned-decorated (*wén*) floor-mats" (*wén yīn* 文茵).[18] In the *Shìmíng* 釋名, a collection of dictionary-like descriptions of words from the Eastern Hàn, *wényīn* 文茵 is defined as "being made from tiger skin and having patterned colorings" (*wén cǎi* 文采).[19]

The use of the word *wén* to refer to rank-indicating emblems—which included 'embroidered patterns'—derives from the basic meaning of 'decorative pattern.' Máo 177 contains a description of woven (*zhī* 織) 'patterned markings [of rank]' (*wén*) on flags: "[the flags] have woven pattern-emblems (*wén*) and bird insignia and the white banners were brilliant" (織文鳥章，白旆央央).[20] Thus, in the *Songs*, 'emblems' (*wén*) were simply a special kind of institutionalized embroidered 'decorative pattern' (*wén*).[21]

This use of *wén* to refer to rank-marking decorative patterns on emblems gave rise to its use to refer to people of high rank—who would have carried 'status-indicating emblems' (*wén*) on their robes and used 'decorated' (*wén*) accouterments—as 'awe-inspiringly beautiful' (*wén*) by metaphorical extension.

54 *From 'awe-inspiringly beautiful' to 'morally refined'*

A similar metaphorical extension, from a word referring to physical decorations to a more abstract term referring to high rank, is exemplified by the English term *decorated*, as in *MacArthur is a highly decorated officer*. Máo 299 contains a passage that supports the reading of *wén* as 'awe-inspiringly beautiful' in the pre-Warring States period:

(2) Solemn, solemn is the Marquis of Lǔ, respectfully bright [is] his charismatic power. Respectful and careful, having 'awe-inspiring dignity' (*wēi* 威) and deportment, he is a model to the people. Truly 'awe-inspiringly beautiful' (*wén*)! Truly warrior-like! He shines upon his resplendent ancestors. (穆穆魯侯、敬明其德。敬慎威儀、維民之則。允文允武、昭假烈祖)[22]

Here the ruler of Lǔ is described as having "awe-inspiring dignity (*wēi*) and deportment" in parallel with his attributes of being "truly awe-inspiringly beautiful (*wén*) and truly warrior-like." This juxtaposition of *wén* and *wēi* ('dignified, imposing, awe-inspiring') indicates that these terms have compatible and potentially overlapping meanings.

In addition to being 'awe-inspiring' (*wēi*), members of the royal family or high nobility were often described as having a beautiful external appearance, dressed in beautiful robes and equipped with beautifully fashioned and decorated objects. The following passage from Máo 55 illustrates the impressively beautiful external appearance of the 'lord' (*jūnzǐ*) that indicates his social status and authority, and that inspires awe and respect in the beholder:

(3) Elegant is **the lord**, he is as if cut, as if polished; as if carved, as if ground. How bright, how beautiful, how majestic, how splendid! Elegant is **the lord**, his ears are [decorated with] jewels and precious stones. His fastened cap is bright like stars. . . . Elegant is **the lord**, like bronze, like tin, like a jade tablet, like a jade disc. How magnanimous, how generous! (有匪君子，如切如磋，如琢如磨。瑟兮僩兮，赫兮咺兮。有匪君子，充耳琇瑩。會弁如星 ... 有匪君子，如金如錫，如圭如璧。寬兮綽兮)[23]

By describing the physical appearance of the lord and his accessories as imposingly beautiful and by comparing him to precious artifacts of metal and jade, this passage illustrates that physical appearance played an important role in constructing social hierarchies in the pre-Warring States period in ways that may seem alien from a modern perspective. The beholder knows that the lord is the lord because he is as physically beautiful as a carved and polished piece of jade, he wears robes with 'emblems' (*wén*), and he is equipped with rank-indicating accouterments. These features make him 'awe-inspiringly beautiful' (*wén*). The preoccupation with physical beauty and the social importance of being 'awe-inspiringly beautiful' in pre-Warring States Zhōu society seems to have been largely overlooked in previous studies of the term *wén*.

When *wén* appears in the meaning 'awe-inspiringly beautiful' in pre-Warring states texts, it is frequently in expressions referring to ancestors—for example, 'awe-inspiring [late] father' (*wén kǎo* 文考) and 'awe-inspiring ancestor' (*wén*

From 'awe-inspiringly beautiful' to 'morally refined' 55

zǔ 文祖)—and posthumous titles, which are name-like appellations given to high-status individuals after their death.[24] They are composed of a descriptive term (such as 'awe-inspiringly beautiful' [*wén* 文], 'courageous, warrior-like' [*wǔ* 武], 'successful/accomplished' [*chéng* 成], and so forth) modifying an expression referring to either (i) a title, e.g., 'king' (*wáng* 王) or 'ruler/duke/lord' (*gōng* 公); (ii) a noun indicating family seniority, e.g., *bó* 伯 'senior (uncle),' *shū* 叔 'junior (uncle)'; or (iii) the term *zǐ* 子 'son, prince, master.'[25] As observed by Lothar von Falkenhausen, the context in which these expressions occur in bronze inscriptions—which seldom amount to more than a laconic dedication "to our awe-inspiring [late] father"—do not allow us to determine the exact meaning of *wén*. Falkenhausen tentatively adopts *accomplished* as a stopgap translation.[26]

Translating wén *in pre-Warring States texts*

Although I agree with Falkenhausen that we should be careful not to presume to know exactly what *wén* means in pre-Warring States inscriptions, I argue that *awe-inspiringly beautiful* is a better translation than *accomplished*.[27] The translation *accomplished* obscures the semantic link between the basic meaning of *wén* as 'externally visible decorative pattern' and its derived uses to describe the externally visible 'decorative patterns' (on the emblems [*wén*], on garments, and on decorated [*wén*] accouterments) of a high status, 'awe-inspiringly beautiful' (*wén*) ancestor or deceased ruler. As mentioned above, this metaphorical use of *wén* is akin to the Modern English use of the adjective *decorated* to refer to military rank. That is, just as the medals and honors physically carried by a 'decorated soldier' indicate his rank and status, so too does the physical appearance of a Zhōu king or aristocrat (with embroidered clothes, carved jade objects, etc.) constitute the external 'decoration' (*wén*) that indicates his 'awe-inspiring dignity' (*wēi*) and authority. Unlike a 'decorated soldier,' however, the high status of the Zhōu royal family and high nobility derived more from birthrights than from accomplishments. The quality of being 'awe-inspiringly beautiful' (*wén*) was not due to an accumulation of deeds and accomplishments (and even less the result of a long process of moral edification) but rather was a function of who one *was*—that is, one's exalted social status by birth, which could be manifested in visible markers of status and wealth.

Another reason it is problematic to render *wén* as *accomplished* is that this translation appears to derive from the tendency in much of the Chinese exegetical tradition to project Warring States-era 'moralizing' interpretations of *wén* as 'morally refined' onto pre-Warring States texts. Falkenhausen (1996) has made an important contribution by establishing that the uses of *wén* in pre-Warring States posthumous names and expressions referring to ancestors did not have the "moralizing dimension" that they began to acquire in later texts such as the *Analects* (a collection of sayings attributed to Confucius and his followers composed in the period from the fifth century BCE to the third or second century BCE).[28]

Accomplished is one of the expressions used by James Legge to translate adjectival *wén* in the sense 'morally refined' in the *Analects* and other early Chinese

56 *From 'awe-inspiringly beautiful' to 'morally refined'*

texts. Since Legge produced his translations with the help of Chinese scholars, it is highly plausible that his translation of *wén* was shaped by the Chinese commentarial tradition, in which *wén* is often assumed to mean acquired 'moral refinement.' As I argue below, this was indeed one of the meanings of the term in texts from the Warring States period such as the *Analects* and the *Xúnzǐ*. Translating *wén* as (morally) *accomplished*—as Legge occasionally does—is thus justified in these texts. However, as a translation of *wén* in pre-Warring States texts *accomplished* is anachronistic.

Although little or no evidence in pre-Warring States texts supports interpreting *wén* to mean 'civilized,' 'cultured,' or 'morally refined,' such anachronistic interpretations still abound. Let us first consider the occurrence of the expression *wén dé* 文德 'awe-inspiring charismatic power' in the last stanza of Máo 262: "Bright, bright is the Son of Heaven. His good reputation is endless. By displaying his 'awe-inspiring' (*wén*) 'charismatic power' (*dé*), he ruled the states of the four (quarters)" 明明天子、令聞不已、矢其文德、洽此四國.[29] From the preceding stanzas of this poem, which describe the Son of Heaven's military might and his successes in suppressing enemies and securing his domain, we learn about a military official Hǔ, who was rewarded for his efforts on the battlefield. In return, as described in the stanza quoted above, he extols the 'awe-inspiring charismatic power' (*wén dé*) of the Son of Heaven. Given the poem's emphasis on military exploits, Karlgren's translation of *wén dé* as "fine virtue" is somewhat awkward.[30] Legge's translation of *wén dé* as "civil virtue" seems to bear a heavy imprint of the traditional Chinese commentarial tradition that projects abstract Warring States-period meanings of *wén* (such as 'civility/civilization') into the pre-Warring States period.[31] In contrast, the translation of *wén* as 'awe-inspiringly beautiful' (or 'imposingly/commandingly beautiful,' 'having a noble/imposing/ awe-inspiring appearance and presence') proposed here is grounded in an analysis of the social importance of external appearance in Western Zhōu times.

The definition of *wén dé* in Xiàng's (1986) *Dictionary of the Books of Songs* is a typical example of the Chinese commentarial tradition imposing later abstract meanings of *wén dé* onto pre-Warring States texts. The entry states, "*wén dé* refers to using the transformative teachings of rites and music to engage in the governing of the state. It is used in contrast to 'military accomplishments.'"[32] The problem with this definition is that there is no evidence before the Warring States period for interpreting the expression *wén dé* to refer to 'ruling through charismatic virtue and moral education.'[33] Although he does not list his sources, the editor of the *Dictionary of the Book of Songs* likely got the inspiration for this anachronistic definition of *wén dé* from the Chinese commentarial tradition, in which commentators often projected concepts from the Hàn and post-Hàn periods into the pre-Qín and pre-Warring States periods.

The term *wén* in pre-Warring States texts has often been translated as 'civil' or 'cultured.' Consider, for example, the translation of the phrase *sī wén Hòu Jì* 思 文后稷 in Máo 275 as "that cultured *Hòu Jì*."[34] *Wén* has also been translated as *cultured* in bronze inscriptions from the Western Zhōu. The expressions 'awe-inspiring [late] father' (*wén kǎo* 文考) and 'awe-inspiring ancestor' (*wén zǔ* 文祖)

From 'awe-inspiringly beautiful' to 'morally refined' 57

as they occur in mid–Western Zhōu bronze inscription, for example, have recently been translated as "cultured father" and "cultured ancestor," respectively.[35] Such translation may be problematic since pre-Warring States texts do not contain any evidence for moral/ethical interpretations of *wén*. Furthermore, as argued above, it is possible to link pre-Warring States uses of *wén* to early Zhōu assumptions of a connection between social status and having an external appearance that is 'awe-inspiringly beautiful' (*wén*). Hence, I suggest that the occurrence of *wén* in this passage describes *Hòu Jì* as 'awe-inspiringly beautiful' in his majestic appearance.[36]

Further indications that in pre-Warring States times the word *wén* was interpreted in aesthetic rather than ethical terms may be found in the earliest forms of the graph <文> used to write this word. The literature on early Chinese paleography contains numerous attempts at reconstructing the 'etymology' of the word *wén* by identifying semantic components in the early forms of the graph <文> in oracle bone inscriptions (OBI) and bronze inscriptions (BI)—see (a)–(c) and (d)–(e), respectively, in Figure 2.1.[37]

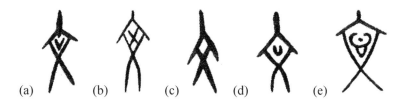

Figure 2.1 Wén 文 in oracle bone and bronze inscriptions.[38]

The basic meaning of the word *wén*, as it is used in later texts from the *Book of Songs* through the end of the Warring States period, is '(decorative) pattern,' so it is not surprising that many paleographic accounts of the meaning of the graph <文> involve the meaning 'pattern' in one way or another. The *Shuōwén* suggests that <文> means 'crisscrossed lines' (*cuò huà* 錯畫).[39] Based on the assumption that early forms of the graph look like a 'big person/man' with something added on the torso, Jì Xùshēng (2010: 732) suggests that the original meaning of the graph is "a human body with intercrossing patterns" and that "tattoo, tattooed (lit. 'decorated body')" (*wén shēn* 紋身) may have been an early meaning of this word.[40]

While widespread, the idea that *wén* originally referred to tattoos may be problematic. In texts from the first millennium BCE, tattooing is often described as a vulgar custom of non-Zhōu groups. It is therefore difficult to imagine that the Shāng, who developed the early forms of the graph <文>, engaged in the practice of tattooing bodies. This would entail that the Zhōu elite, who otherwise adopted (or already shared) many Shāng practices and aspects of material culture, would slowly forget about the practice of tattooing and eventually end up associating it with civilizationally inferior groups.[41] It therefore seems more plausible that the crisscrossing lines or heart-shaped patterns in the graphs in Figure 2.1 originally

58 *From 'awe-inspiringly beautiful' to 'morally refined'*

depicted decorations on clothing or chest-accouterments, rather than tattoos. Again, the basic meaning of word *wén* was probably '(pattern) decoration,' not tattoo.[42]

While paleographic studies of the graphs may sometimes be useful, in many cases they still provide little more than qualified guesses about how the shape and structure of graphs may inform hypotheses about the meanings the words they were used to write. Nevertheless, the idea that the early forms of the graph <文> shown in Figure 2.1 resemble a 'pattern-decorated person' is compatible with the lexicalization process proposed in this chapter. The analysis of *wén* as meaning 'awe-inspiringly beautiful' when used as an epithet also finds support in the entry for the term in Xú Zhōngshū's 徐中舒 (2006) *Dictionary of Oracle Bone Inscriptions*, which defines *wén* as meaning 'beautiful' (*měi* 美) and states that "it is used as a positive appellation when prefixed to royal names."[43]

In sum, *wén* in pre-Warring States texts meant something quite different from the English words *cultured, civil,* and *accomplished.* First, it was only applied to noblemen (or noblewomen),[44] either during their lifetimes or posthumously, in expressions such as 'awe-inspiringly beautiful [late] father' (*wén kǎo*) and posthumous titles such as 'Awe-inspiringly beautiful [late] Duke' (*Wén Gōng*). Reserved for people of aristocratic descent, *wén* was not so much an acquired feature as an inherited privilege. In this respect it differs from the English words *cultured* and *civil(ized)*, which refer to traits acquired through long years of edification or training. Second, the word *wén*—which, in its most basic meaning, refers to 'decorative patterns'—is much more grounded in the physical appearance and presence of the person described (his clothes, accouterments, etc.) than the English word *cultured*, which derives from the basic meaning of 'culturing' or 'growing.' Third, the meaning 'awe-inspiringly beautiful' is certainly not readily associated with the English word *culture(d)*. While one might be in awe over someone's culture—in the nineteenth century, senses of refinement of thought and manners (which may include the way a person dresses)—this is still quite different from the awe that a Western Zhōu ruler or noble man, wearing 'emblems' (*wén*) and standing on his beautifully 'decorated' (*wén*) chariot, would inspire in someone at the bottom of the social hierarchy.

Sociopolitical changes from the Western Zhōu to the Warring States period

The epistemic changes that led to the crystallization of civilizational consciousness around the middle of the first millennium BCE took place in tandem with significant sociopolitical changes in the Zhōu realm. In the period from the eighth to the third century BCE, the Western Zhōu lineage-based social hierarchy, which centered on the royal family and a mostly hereditary system of government officials, was slowly replaced with a multi-state political system of increasingly ruler-centered states run by salaried government officials recruited and promoted based on a combination of family background and acquired personal qualifications. This new system led to the creation of an economy of cultural capital in which theories of statecraft, military strategy, and moral philosophy began to circulate.[45] A number of factors contributed to these changes.

From 'awe-inspiringly beautiful' to 'morally refined' 59

Breakdown of ritualized lineage-based government

The breakdown of lineage-based social hierarchies began during the mid–Western Zhōu period with the gradual erosion of the Zhōu kings' political power. Before the conquest of the Shāng in 1045 BCE, the Zhōu had controlled a relatively small area. In order to manage their vastly increased post-conquest domain, the early Western Zhōu rulers established a number of garrison states that they placed under the hereditary rule of Zhōu princes and noble families.[46] Over time, these states grew in strength and size and became increasingly independent from the Zhōu center. Eventually, in the Spring and Autumn period (771–481 BCE), the leaders of the powerful states of the Zhōu realm began to vie for role of de facto political and military leader.[47] Thus, while the Zhōu king was still in principle the highest political authority, his position had become largely ceremonial—in some ways similar to the pope in Medieval Europe[48]—while real-political power was held by the leaders of the strongest states in the multi-state system.[49]

The old government system, based on a ritualized hierarchy of noble ranks, received a further blow during the Spring and Autumn period (771–481 BCE), when the ministerial lineages of the various states began to usurp the political authority and ritual prerogatives of the local rulers. At the time of Confucius (551–479 BCE), the ruler of the state of Lǔ had been reduced to a largely ceremonial role, while the real power lay with the head of the Jì family, whose official position was that of minister.[50]

As the old Western Zhōu kinship-based rule by members of the royal family and high nobility eroded, the ritual system on which their power was built slowly began to disintegrate. In the old system, different ranks in the hierarchy had different ritual prerogatives and duties determining what people of different standing could and should do.[51] For example, according to the *Zuǒzhuàn*, the number of rows of feather-decorated dancers that one was allowed to employ in ritual ceremonies was determined by rank: "The Son of Heaven uses eight [rows], the lords of the various states use six, high officers use four, and the 'retainer-officials' two."[52] In *Analects* 3.1, Confucius is described as criticizing the Jì family for overstepping ritual decorum by employing more rows of dancers than the four ritually allowed for high officers: "Eight rows [of performers] are dancing in [their] courtyard. If this can be tolerated, then what cannot be tolerated?"[53] By using eight instead of four rows of dancers, the Jì family was usurping the ritual prerogatives of the Zhōu king himself. For Confucius—as portrayed by the authors of the *Analects*—this kind of behavior represented a serious threat to the ritual fabric that maintained social order and cohesion.[54] Thus, at the eve of the Warring States period, the early Zhōu ritualized, lineage-based system of rank and office-holding was gradually being replaced by a new social order; while acquired wealth and power became more important, the importance of inherited social rank was increasingly challenged.[55]

Due to population growth triggered by technological advances in agriculture and metallurgy, the administrations of the various states of the Zhōu realm needed more skilled administrators than could be furnished through hereditary

60 *From 'awe-inspiringly beautiful' to 'morally refined'*

office alone.[56] As a consequence, rulers of the Central States began to recruit talented individuals of various backgrounds to serve as officials. Rather than being given land, these non-hereditary officials began to receive salaries. During this period of sociopolitical restructuring, the economic system of the Zhōu realm underwent a profound transformation, from an economy based on manorial management to a more currency-based market economy.[57] Changes contributing to this development included the introduction of peasant land tenure, direct taxation, and the expansion of currency systems.[58] Improvements in road infrastructure and riverine transport also contributed to expanding inter-state trade and communication.[59] Beyond increasing the exchange of goods, these changes also facilitated the movement of individuals and ideas between the states of the Zhōu realm.[60]

Changes in the nature of warfare also spurred the creation of non-hereditary positions for military specialists. In the Western Zhōu, warfare had largely been the domain of the hereditary nobility. Armies were relatively small and were composed mainly of high-status chariot-riding warrior aristocrats accompanied by foot soldiers of lower ranks. In contrast, systems of mass conscription of peasants, established during the Warring States period, could mobilize armies that "may have numbered in the hundreds of thousands."[61] Wars could now last several years and were no longer geographically confined to battlefields. As wars evolved into highly complicated strategic and logistic undertakings, a growing need developed for various kinds of military specialists. Thus, in the Warring States period, military treatises, some of which were attributed to masters of military strategy from earlier periods, began to be composed.[62] In order to ensure military success, rulers slowly began to recruit military specialists and advisors based on their qualifications rather than on their kinship background and noble rank.[63]

The different states varied with respect to the extent to which they institutionalized the changes that undermined the hereditary privileges of the nobility. The process started in earnest with the reforms implemented by Shāng Yāng (390–338 BCE) in the state of Qín in the mid-fourth century BCE and culminated in the establishment of the Qín dynasty in 221 BCE.[64] Productive labor, such as farming and weaving, was rewarded by exemptions from taxes and corvée. Military rank was determined by concrete achievements—enemy soldiers killed, number of successful battles, etc.—as defined by a rigidly enforced promotion system. One consequence of these changes was the fading in importance of lineage-ruled city-states. As observed by Mark E. Lewis, once defeated, city-states were often "absorbed by their conquerors, who redistributed the land to their own population in exchange for military service and taxes. . . . In place of the [city-based] nobility, the state was increasingly dominated by a single autocratic ruler, whose agents registered the peasants and mobilized them into state service and collected taxes to support the ruler's military ambitions."[65]

It follows that in the Warring States period, the old political system institutionalized in the kinship system of patrilineal succession to hereditary office-holding

From 'awe-inspiringly beautiful' to 'morally refined' 61

was under assault by an increasing bureaucratization of power and the rise of a group of 'retainer-officials' or 'men of service' (*shì* 士) vying for position and power in the rapidly growing state bureaucracies.[66]

The sociopolitical changes that led to the increasing routinization of power and the accompanying shift from aesthetically grounded charismatic authority to ethically grounded charismatic power were linked through a "reciprocal dialectic" to changes in cosmological theories.[67] The ruling lineage of the Shāng (ca. 1570–1045 BCE) had viewed themselves as inhabiting the center of the world, referred to as the 'central Shāng' *zhōng shāng* 中商, or the 'central land' *zhōng tǔ* 中土. Surrounding this center were the 'four quarters' (lit. 'four sides' [*sì fāng* 四方] or 'four lands' [*sì tǔ* 四土]) inhabited by non-Shāng 'others.'[68] Politically, this cosmology contrasted the 'central Shāng' with a various non-Shāng groups.[69] Beyond the political dimension, the expression *sì fāng* also referred to the cardinal directions in ritual and cosmological terms. The *sì fāng* were associated with different 'winds' (*fēng* 風), which were mentioned in divination records concerning meteorological phenomena. Other inscriptions also mention the 'sides' (*fāng*) in connection with sacrifices to the cardinal directions.[70] Being at the top of political and religious hierarchies, the Shāng king served as the central spirit medium, or shaman, connecting the human and the spiritual realms. The *sì fāng* cosmology corroborated the king's charismatic authority, both politically and religiously, by placing him at the center of humanity and the universe.

As observed by Wang Aihe (2000), the old *sì fāng* cosmology structured around a static center–periphery contrast gave way during the second half of the first millennium BCE to a more dynamic cosmological system of the so-called 'five interactive phases' (*wǔ xíng* 五行).[71] This new symbolic order of the universe introduced a separation of knowledge of the divine realm from the ancestral cult of the king. In the words of Wang Aihe, the five-phases cosmology "formed a body of knowledge that was no longer monopolized by the king, but instead was possessed and reproduced by the rising political groups—including religious and natural experts, the rising ministers and bureaucratic officials, military professionals, and the emerging cultural elite or scholars."[72]

These new groups used the discourse of the new cosmology to construct theories of statecraft and frame political arguments. By doing so, they "usurped the hereditary king's monopolized divine authority and distributed it among themselves, eventually changing the nature of rulership altogether" by separating "divine knowledge from political power."[73] The 'charismatic power' of the Shāng kings was an inherited prerogative. The Shāng royal and aristocratic lord inherited the charismatic power that made him 'awe-inspiringly beautiful' (*wén*) in the eyes of his subjects. As witnessed by certain passages in the *Book of Songs*, by the time of the Spring and Autumn period the term *jūnzǐ* was used to refer to 'noblemen' in an aristocratic sense. At this time the term *wén* continued to refer to the 'awe-inspiringly beautiful' appearance of members of the hereditary high nobility, who could now be referred to as *jūnzǐ*. In contrast, in the Warring States period, the acquired qualities necessary for being considered a 'morally refined' (*wén*) 'noble

62 *From 'awe-inspiringly beautiful' to 'morally refined'*

man' (*jūnzǐ*) were determined by moral philosophers such as the composers of the *Analects* and the *Xúnzǐ*. Furthermore, in these emerging moral philosophies the criteria for 'true kingship' were formulated mainly in 'moral' or 'ethical' terms. Thus, while the rulers of the various states still held political power, in the moral realm they were reduced to receiving instructions from these masters of moral philosophy.

Emergence of an economy of cultural capital

The coining of civilizational consciousness first became possible when a group of specialists in statecraft and moral philosophy began to emerge around the middle of the first millennium BCE. These specialists had vested interests in discussing concepts such as 'civility/moral refinement,' 'rites,' 'customs,' and 'civilization' that were central to their theories of statecraft. Consequently, they needed a specialized vocabulary with which to circulate their ideas more conveniently. As alluded to in Chapter 1, this situation parallels the circumstances surrounding the coining of civilizational consciousness in Modern Western Europe between the sixteenth and eighteenth centuries.[74] To a large extent, the composers of the various theories of statecraft and moral philosophy that began to emerge in the sixth and fifth centuries BCE similarly came from the groups of people vying for employment in the state administrations of increasingly ruler-centered states.

The Warring States period literature is replete with examples of skilled specialists traveling from state to state peddling their special knowledge of ritual ceremonies, military strategy, or theories of statecraft in order to become gainfully employed.[75] Some of these specialists, when presenting themselves to local rulers in hopes of employment, engaged in debates about the value of past traditions in solving contemporary social problems. In this way, the lexicalization of the key semantic molecules of an emergent language-specific pre-Qín concept of 'civility/ civilization' (*wén*) was by its very nature intimately linked to the existence of a particular economy of cultural capital, which provided the social infrastructure necessary for the production and circulation of theories of statecraft and moral philosophy. The following passage from the *Hánfēizǐ* shows that the exchange of intellectual expertise for rank and remuneration was conceived of in economic terms:

(4) The rulers **sell** offices and noble rank; the ministers **sell** their knowledge and physical strength. Thus, one must rely on oneself, not on other people! (主賣官爵，臣賣智力，故自恃無恃人)[76]

The basic meaning of the word *mài* 賣 is 'to sell goods in return for money,' and it is used in this manner elsewhere in the *Hánfēizǐ* and in other late Warring States texts. The use of the word 'sell' (*mài*) in the passage in (4) clearly shows that the various moral philosophies and theories of statecraft from the Warring States period relied on the existence of a 'market' for such intellectual

From 'awe-inspiringly beautiful' to 'morally refined' 63

products.[77] The comparatively rigid aristocratic rank-based system of promotion in place during the Shāng and Western Zhōu did not allow much leeway for such an economy of cultural capital to develop. Hence, there was little or no institutionalized support for itinerant retainer–officials looking for employment based on their skill and knowledge. As observed by Collins (1998: 380), "political and economic changes bring ascendancy or decline of the material institutions which support intellectuals," such as monasteries and universities, in the European context.[78] Similarly, the emergence of centralized governments in which specialized administrators were needed provided the institutional support that allowed pre-Qín masters of statecraft and moral philosophy to produce and circulate theories of how to run a state. The existence of a community of political thinkers triggered the coining of terms for abstract concepts—such as 'civility/civilization' (*wén*)—which were needed to articulate new theories of statecraft. Had there been such communities of thinkers and masters of statecraft supported by markets of cultural capital in the Shāng and Western Zhōu, it seems fair to assume that late Warring States thinkers would have known their works and referred to them in their own theory-building.[79]

From 'beautiful' (*wén*) 'nobleman' (*jūnzǐ*) to 'morally refined' (*wén*) 'noble man' (*jūnzǐ*): ethical reinterpretation of aesthetic *wén*

Over the five centuries of the Spring and Autumn and Warring States periods (from 771 to 221 BCE), the Zhōu realm underwent many important social, political, and economic changes as well as the introduction of a new cosmology, which articulated a new relationship between the human realm and the divine. It was within this new sociopolitical system and cosmology that a new concept of 'civility' was coined in the word *wén*.

In the pre-Warring States corpus, *wén* was used literally to refer to 'decorative patterns' on physical objects or metaphorically to refer to 'decorated' people who bore the externally observable marks of high rank and authority, making them appear 'awe-inspiringly beautiful.' While these older uses continued down into the Warring States period and later, the *aesthetically* grounded *wén* meaning 'awe-inspiringly beautiful' underwent a reinterpretation in *ethical* terms and was increasingly used to refer to externally observable patterns in the appearance and behavior of a 'morally refined' individual. The pre-Warring States uses of *wén* to mean 'awe-inspiringly beautiful' referred to the externally observable, charismatic appearance of the people at the top of the *social* hierarchy. In contrast, Warring States uses of *wén* in the meaning 'morally perfected' referred to the charismatic qualities and appearance of the people at the top of a *moral* hierarchy.[80]

This shift from aesthetic to ethical charismatic authority occurred in parallel with changing use of the term *jūnzǐ* 君子 'lord.' The term *jūnzǐ* is composed of the words 'lord' (*jūn* 君) and 'son' (*zǐ* 子) and literally means 'the lord's son.' In a

64 *From 'awe-inspiringly beautiful' to 'morally refined'*

more extended meaning, it refers to 'noblemen' as members of the ruling elite and hereditary nobility in general. In the passage from Máo 55 in (3) above, the word *jūnzǐ* clearly refers to 'my lord' in the aristocratic sense. Around the beginning of the Warring States period, the term also came to be used in an extended meaning to refer to 'noble men' in the sense of people who are morally superior, regardless of whether they were of noble birth. The word *jūnzǐ* is used in the *Analects* almost exclusively in a moral sense, to refer to '(morally) noble men.'[81] A typical example is *Analects* 4.16: "The Master said, The 'noble man' (*jūnzǐ*) is alert to what is 'right' (*yì* 義). The petty man is alert to what is profitable."[82] In the *Analects*, the ethical distinction between morally 'petty' and 'noble' men was more important than the social distinction between 'noblemen' and people of non-aristocratic background. In the virtue ethics presented in the *Analects*, the term *jūnzǐ* therefore referred to an individual whose moral character had been refined through a long process of education and self-cultivation.[83,84]

I argue that abstract uses of *wén* as a noun referring to a concept of 'civility/civilization,' understood as 'ideal patterns of conventionalized behavior,' emerged around the same time as (or slightly after) the reinterpretation of adjectival *wén* from 'awe-inspiringly beautiful' to 'morally refined'; this was also when the term *jūnzǐ* was reinterpreted from 'nobleman' to 'noble man.' This development can first be traced in the oldest layers of the *Zuǒzhuàn* and the *Analects*, composed sometime in the period from the late fifth century to the mid-fourth century BCE, where both meanings are equally present. In the *Analects*, the moral readings of *wén* are more prominent than in the *Zuǒzhuàn*. By the time of the composition of the *Xúnzǐ* in the third century BCE, the term *wén* had clearly entered the collectively shared vocabulary (lexicon) of the literary Zhōu elite, both in the adjectival meaning of 'morally refined' and in the nominal meaning of 'civility/civilization.'

Transition from aesthetical to ethical understanding of wén

The *Zuǒzhuàn* contains some of the earliest evidence of a reinterpretation of aesthetic *wén* in ethical terms.[85] Adjectival uses of *wén* in the *Zuǒzhuàn* retained the older pre-Warring States meanings of 'awe-inspiringly beautiful' while at the same time developing new interpretations in moral terms. That *wén* could still mean something akin to 'beautiful' at the time of the *Zuǒzhuàn* is supported by passages that juxtapose *wén* and expressions meaning 'elegant' and 'beautiful.' Xiāng 31.10 describes abilities and qualities that qualified people for government offices. In a list of individuals selected, someone called Feng Jianzi is mentioned as being "able to execute important affairs" (能斷大事), and a person called Zǐ-Tàishū is described as being employed because he was "beautiful, gracious, and 'refined' (*wén*)" (美秀而文).[86] This indicates that the new ethical property of being *wén* was compatible, and potentially overlapped, with the property of being 'beautiful' (*měi* 美). Thus, at the time of the composition of the *Zuǒzhuàn* in the fifth century BCE, the word *wén* retained the ability to refer to a 'beautiful' external appearance that it had in the pre-Warring States period. This archaic

From 'awe-inspiringly beautiful' to 'morally refined' 65

meaning of *wén* appears to have become somewhat obsolete by the end of the third century BCE.

In the *Xúnzǐ*, most of which is generally assumed to have been composed in the third century BCE,[87] the ethical reinterpretation of *wén* is complete. Consequently, as discussed below, *wén* is used almost exclusively to refer to the 'moral refinement' of the 'noble man' (*jūnzǐ*). In spite of that, the authors still acknowledged the important social function of the 'awe-inspiringly beautiful' appearance of the ruler, especially in reference to the 'former kings' (*xiān wáng* 先王) of old:

(5) The former kings and sages . . . knew that if those who were rulers of men and superiors did not make [themselves] 'beautiful' (*měi* 美) and did not 'decorate' (*shì* 飾) [themselves], then they would not be able to unify the people . . . that if they were not 'awe-inspiring' (*wēi* 威) and strong, then they would not be able to prevent aggression and conquer ferocious enemies. Hence. . . [one] must chisel and polish [stones], [and one] must carve and engrave, and 'emblems' (**wén**) and insignia must have noble designs[88] in order to fill the eyes [of their subjects]. (先王聖人 . . . 知夫為人主上者，不美不飾之不足以一民也 . . . 不威不強之不足以禁暴勝悍也。故 . . . 必將鋼琢刻鏤，黼黻文章，以塞其目)[89]

The description of the ruler as 'imperious' or 'awe-inspiring' (*wēi* 威) and 'beautiful' (*měi* 美) seems very close to the use of *wén* in the *Zuǒzhuàn* passage from Xiāng 31.10, discussed above. Only by 'decorating' (*shì* 飾) and making himself 'beautiful' (*měi*) can the ruler unify the people. The ruler's impressive 'emblems' (*wén*), embroidered onto his ceremonial robes, play a central role in this process by 'filling the eyes [of his subjects].' Although the word *wén* is used to refer to status-signaling '(decorated) emblems,' the word 'beautiful' (*měi*) is used instead of the word *wén* to refer to the 'awe-inspiring beauty' of the ancient rulers, indicating that by the third century BCE, the use of *wén* to denote 'awe-inspiring beauty' was becoming obsolete.

The *Zuǒzhuàn* also contains support for the hypothesis that *wén* could mean 'awe-inspiringly beautiful.' In Xiāng 31.13, we learn that during a visit to the state of Chǔ, Běigōng Wénzǐ 北宮文子 observed that the chief minister of Chǔ was beginning to behave like the ruler of a state. Nevertheless, Běigōng Wénzǐ concluded from the chief minister's lack of 'dignity and deportment' (*wēi yí* 威儀) that he would not succeed in his schemes. To prove his point, Běigōng Wénzǐ expounds on the qualities necessary for being the ruler of a state. To give his arguments scriptural support, he quotes a passage from Máo 299, also discussed in (2) above, which describes the ruler of Lǔ as "respectful and careful about maintaining his awe-inspiring dignity and deportment (*wēi yí*), a model to the people." Although he quotes only this line, other lines in Máo 299 describe the ruler of Lǔ as being "truly awe-inspiringly beautiful (*wén*) and truly warrior-like." By citing Máo 299, which juxtaposes *wén* and *wēi*, Běigōng Wénzǐ is thus implying that he assumes both 'dignity and deportment' (*wēi yí*) and *wén* to be necessary attributes of a true ruler. In the remainder of Xiāng 31.13, Běigōng Wénzǐ elaborates on

66 *From 'awe-inspiringly beautiful' to 'morally refined'*

these attributes in a way that connects *wén* even more explicitly to the properties of having 'awe-inspiring dignity' (*wēi*) and being 'held in awe' (*wèi* 畏):

(6) King **Wén** attacked against Chóng . . . the *Mán-yí*[90] peoples led each other to submit. This can be called [them] standing in awe (*wèi* 畏) of him. . . . To this day the acts of King **Wén** are a 'model' (*fǎ* 法): this is what is called emulating him. King Wén had 'awe-inspiring dignity and deportment' (*wēi yí*). Thus, a 'nobleman'/'noble man'(*jūnzǐ*), while in office, is 'held in awe' (*wèi*). . . . His gestures have 'refinement' (***wén***) and his speeches are elegant. He uses these things to oversee his underlings, this is called to have awe-inspiring dignity and deportment (*wēi yí*). (文王伐崇 . . . 蠻夷帥服，可謂畏之 . . . 文王之行，至今為法，可謂象之。有威儀也。故君子在位可畏 . . . 動作有文，言語有章，以臨其下，謂之有威儀也)[91]

In Běigōng Wénzǐ's description of the 'awe-inspiring dignity and deportment'(*wēi yí*) of the ruler, the words *wèi* 'awe, fear' and *wēi* 'awe-inspiring dignity' are connected to *wén* in two respects.[92] First, King Wén's actions are held up as a 'model' (*fǎ* 法) for awe-inspiring behavior (e.g., subjugating the restive Mán-Yí groups). Běigōng Wénzǐ thus mentions King Wén to illustrate that his actions that inspired 'awe' (*wèi*) are examples of him being 'awe-inspiringly beautiful' (*wén*), both in a moral sense and in his physical appearance and actions. Second, Běigōng Wénzǐ's summary of the behavior and attributes of 'nobleman/noble man' (*jūnzǐ*)[93] begins by saying that "the *jūnzǐ*, when in office, is 'held in awe' (*wèi*)." Toward the end of the list of the *jūnzǐ*'s attributes, Běigōng Wénzǐ includes a description of his movements and stirrings as having *wén*. Běigōng Wénzǐ concludes by stating that these attributes are "that by which he oversees his underlings" and thus amount to what "is called having awe-inspiring dignity (*wēi*) and deportment." The passage makes one of the most explicit connections between being *wén* and being 'awe-inspiringly dignified' (*wēi*) that is found in the pre-Qín corpus.

In addition to the older meaning 'awe-inspiringly beautiful,' other *Zuǒzhuàn* passages show that *wén* can refer to both external appearance *and* moral attributes. In the passage from Huán 2.2 quoted in (7), Zāng Āibó, a Lǔ official, remonstrates with Duke Huán (r. 711–694 BCE) for transgressing ritual propriety by looting the ritual vessels of the state of Gào and placing them in the Grand Temple of the state of Lǔ. Zāng Āibó uses the opportunity to lecture Duke Huán on the proper behavior and appearance of a ruler and the importance of him 'displaying his charismatic power/moral virtue' (*zhāo dé* 昭德). In Zāng Āibó's description of the ideal ruler, he links the ruler's property of inspiring apprehension and fear to his 'awe-inspiring beauty' (*wén*), as displayed by his emblems, and to his virtues as recorded in his 'decorated' (*wén*) objects:

(7) He who rules people displays his 'charismatic power/moral virtue' (*dé*) and blocks transgressions so that he may thereby shine on the hundred officers from above. . . . Hence, he displays his great 'charismatic power'/'moral virtues' (*dé*) in order to show it to his sons and grandsons. . . . As for the

From 'awe-inspiringly beautiful' to 'morally refined'   67

weaves of fire, of dragons, of black and white axes, and of blue and black undulations, these display his 'patterned refinement' (***wén***). . . . As for his 'charismatic power/virtue' (*dé*), and his property of being frugal and measured. . . **'decorated'** (*wén*) objects are used to record them. [These properties] are manifested in sound and brightly displayed so that they shine on the 100 officers from above. Consequently, the 100 officers are struck with apprehension and fear, and do not dare to transgress the rules and statutes. (君人者將昭德塞違，以臨照百官 . . . 故昭令德以示子孫 . . . 火龍黼黻昭其文也 . . . 夫德儉而有度 . . . 文物以紀之，聲明以發之，以臨照百官。百官於是乎戒懼而不敢易紀律)[94]

The first occurrence of *wén* in (7) refers to the 'awe-inspiring beauty' of the ruler, expressed by the embroidered emblems of status and rank, specifically the 'flame and dragon patterns' (*huǒ lóng* 火龍) and the noble designs found on his garments, flags, and banners. This occurrence of *wén* is thus comparable to when it is used to refer to 'woven patterns and bird insignia' (*zhī wén niǎo zhāng*) in Máo 177 discussed above. Note also the similarities between Zāng Āibó's description of the ideal ruler and the description found in Máo 55 (see [3] above); both passages emphasize the stunning external appearance of the ruler, detailing his garments and various accouterments on himself and his chariots and horses. Thus, this *Zuǒzhuàn* passage reflects a society in which physical appearance is still closely connected to status and authority.

Unlike the passage from Máo 55, Zāng Āibó does interpret some of the physical objects and qualities as signs of 'moral virtue' (*dé* 德). In contrast, in Máo 55, the 'lord' (*jūnzǐ*) simply **is** 'beautiful' and 'awe-inspiring.' The end of the *Zuǒzhuàn* passage in (7) above summarizes the link between 'moral virtue' (*dé*) and virtues of 'frugality' (*jiǎn*) and 'measure' (*dù*) by stating that they are externally manifested/expressed in his 'patterned accouterments' (*wén wù* 文物). In the *Zuǒzhuàn*, the ruler's external appearance thus serves the double purpose of being visually 'awe-inspiringly beautiful' and at the same time indicating his 'moral virtues' (*dé*) of 'frugality' (*jiǎn* 儉) and appropriate sense of 'measure' (*dù* 度).[95]

Although *wén* began to refer to moral virtue in the fifth century BCE, it still retained connotations of its basic meaning of '(externally visible) decorative pattern.' In the passage in (7) discussed above, *wén* refers to the fire and dragon emblems (*wén*) on garments, and 'decorated accouterments' (*wén wù*). In Xiāng 31.13, also discussed above, *wén* describes the 'movements and stirrings' (*dòng zuò*) of the *jūnzǐ* as well as his property of having awe-inspiring 'dignity and deportment' (*wēi yí*). Xī 24.1 adds to this picture by describing words as the 'external decoration' of a person: "Utterances are the decoration (*wén*) of oneself. When a one is about to go into reclusion, what is the use of decorating (*wén*) oneself? That would be seeking ostentatious display."[96] This statement, uttered by Jiè Zhī Tuī to explain why he would not plead his case with Duke Wén of Jin—who had neglected to reward him for his loyal service during the long years of the duke's exile—indicates that in the *Zuǒzhuàn*, *wén* was the externally observable expression "in clothing,

68　*From 'awe-inspiringly beautiful' to 'morally refined'*

accouterments, gestures, and words" of a person's inner worth and dignity.[97] The use of *wén* to describe people in the *Zuǒzhuàn* retained the earlier pre-Warring States meanings of 'awe-inspiringly beautiful' display of external marks of social status and authority. To these older meanings, the author(s) of the *Zuǒzhuàn* also began to add moral interpretations of *wén* as the externally manifested signs of moral virtues.

Wén *referring to the 'moral refinement' or 'civility' of an individual*

The *Analects* discusses the moral interpretation of *wén* more explicitly than the *Zuǒzhuàn*, and it is in the *Analects* that adjectival *wén*, understood as 'morally refined,' is first viewed as an **acquired** attribute of the 'noble man' (*jūnzǐ*).[98] In it, we also find the first uses of *wén* as an abstract noun referring to a language-specific concept of 'civility/civilization,' conceived of as 'ideal *patterns* of conventionalized behaviors.' Since the term *jūnzǐ* came to refer to non-aristocratic individuals (i.e., 'noble men' in the moral sense of the term), the property of being *wén* is no longer a prerogative of the hereditary nobility but can be acquired even by non-nobles, provided that they engage in the proper moral edification process, which consists in imitating the 'ideal patterns of conventionalized behavior' (*wén*). In the *Analects*, *wén* is therefore no longer understood exclusively in terms of the 'awe-inspiring beauty' of a person's appearance as in the pre-Warring States period but is increasingly conceptualized in moral terms. In *Analects* 5.15, Confucius and his followers are described by the Warring States composers of the *Analects* as explicitly discussing the motivation for the use of *wén* in posthumous titles:[99]

(8) Zǐgòng 子貢 asked, "What is the reason Kǒng **Wén**zǐ is [posthumously] called **Wén**?" The Master replied, "He was diligent and fond of learning. And he did not consider it shameful to ask those below him. This is the reason why he is [posthumously] called **Wén**." (子貢問曰孔文子何以謂之文也?子曰 敏而好學，不恥下問，是以謂之文也)[100]

After his death around 484 BCE, Kǒng Yǔ 孔圉, a minister at the Wei court, was given the posthumous title Kǒng Wénzǐ 孔文子. Zǐgòng's question of why Kǒng Yǔ was honored posthumously with the title *Wén* was probably motivated by his knowledge of Kǒng Yǔ's rather mixed record during his lifetime.[101] Confucius justified Kǒng Yǔ's posthumous title by citing positive traits such as being hardworking, humble, and studious.[102] Although Confucius likely knew that Kǒng Yǔ may have been far from perfect, at least he possessed enough positive traits for Confucius to call him 'morally decorated/refined' (*wén*). *Analects* 5.15 thus illustrates a new use of *wén* to mean 'morally refined,' a meaning not seen before the middle of the first millennium BCE.[103]

The clearest examples of *wén* being used to refer purely to moral attributes are found in the *Xúnzǐ*. In many ways, the *Xúnzǐ* represents third century BCE

From 'awe-inspiringly beautiful' to 'morally refined' 69

developments of earlier uses of *wén* found in the *Analects* and the *Zuŏzhuàn*. First, the *Xúnzĭ* defines the 'moral refinement' (*wén*) of the 'noble man' (*jūnzĭ*) in more explicitly moral terms than these two earlier works:

(9) The **noble man** (*jūnzĭ*) . . . debates, but does not compete. . . . He is hard and strong, but not violent. . . . He is respectful, reverent, attentive and cautious, but still generous. Indeed, this is what is called [being] utmost **wén**.
(君子 . . . 辯而不爭 . . . 堅彊而不暴 . . . 恭敬謹慎而容。夫是之謂至文)[104]

Unlike the laconic passages from the *Analects* discussed above, this passage from the *Xúnzĭ* leaves no doubt that the *wén* of the 'noble man' (*jūnzĭ*) consists in having a set of moral qualities that are observable in his behavior and demeanor. In the virtue ethics of the *Xúnzĭ*, a person's moral qualities are inseparable from his character. Hence, although "referent, attentive and cautious" may not qualify as "ethical" properties in a narrow definition of the term, in Xúnzĭan virtue ethics, such character traits are the embodiment of a truly moral character, found in someone who consistently acts ethically. In contrast to the *Book of Songs* and the *Zuŏzhuàn*, having a 'beautiful' (*mĕi*) or 'awe-inspiring' (*wēi*) external appearance is no longer necessary for being a 'morally refined' (*wén*) 'noble man' (*jūnzĭ*).

The word 'charismatic power/virtue' (*dé*) underwent a reinterpretation similar to the words 'awe-inspiringly beautiful/morally refined' (*wén*) ['awe-inspiringly beautiful' → 'morally refined'] and 'nobleman/noble man' (*jūnzĭ*) ['aristocratic nobleman' → 'morally refined noble man (regardless of birth)']. In the pre-Warring States period, the ruler possessed an inherited religio-political 'charismatic power' (*dé*).[105] Having powerful royal ancestors and the capacity to communicate with the gods through divination, the Shāng ruler wielded charismatic power to change the world. Divination enabled him to see into the future, and he could harness the support of gods and ancestors to win battles and change the weather. While the term *dé* may have been given ethical meanings in certain contexts in some pre-Warring States texts, Warring States thinkers predominantly define the 'virtue/power' (*dé*) of the ruler in moral terms.[106] From 'charismatic power,' it began to be reinterpreted as 'charismatic (moral) virtue.' Again, with Xúnzĭ, the reinterpretation of *dé* in moral terms was complete. Unlike Confucius, who is portrayed in the *Analects* as believing in Heaven as a normative deity, Xúnzĭ (as portrayed by the authors of the *Xúnzĭ*) lacked this kind of religious belief.[107] For him, sacrifices to gods and ancestors had a purely social function. While the rationally thinking 'noble man' (*jūnzĭ*) knows there are no Gods, he can still support religious practices (e.g., ancestor worship) among the people as a morally edifying practice that also has psychological benefits (venting and regulating emotions). So, when Xúnzĭ talked about the 'charismatic virtue' (*dé*) of the 'noble man,' it was understood in non-religious moral terms. The compound expression *wén dé* thus means 'awe-inspiringly imposing' (*wén*) 'charismatic power' (*dé*) in the pre-Warring States period.[108] In contrast, in *Analects* 16.1, composed in the Warring States period, *xiū wéndé* 修文德 refers to 'cultivating morally refined virtue.'[109]

70   *From 'awe-inspiringly beautiful' to 'morally refined'*

'As if carved, as if polished': 'wén' as acquired cultural capital

In the Warring States period, being *wén* in the moral sense began to be considered an acquired rather than an inborn quality. In this respect, this use of *wén* is similar to sixteenth- to eighteenth-century uses of the Franglophone words *civilize* and *civilized* to refer to the acquisition of civility through a slow process of 'polishing one's manners.' *Analects* 1.15 contains a metaphorical interpretation of the line "as if cut, as if polished, as if carved, as if ground" from Máo 55 in the *Book of Songs*. This carving and polishing metaphor implies that the 'moral decoration/refinement' of a noble man is acquired through a slow process of moral edification:

(10) Zǐgòng asked, 'being poor but not fawning, wealthy but not arrogant. What do you think of this?' The Master said, 'That is acceptable, but it is not as good as being poor but still finding joy in the Way, or being wealthy but still being fond of the rites.' Zǐgòng said, 'A poem says, **as if cut, as if polished; as if carved, as if ground**. Is what you just said not an example of what is expressed in this line?' (子貢問曰貧而無諂，富而無驕，何如？子曰可也。未若貧而樂道、富而好禮者也。子貢曰《詩》云『如切如磋，如琢如磨』其斯之謂與？)[110]

The main purpose of *Analects* 1.15 is to describe the 'moral refinement' of the '(morally) noble man' (*jūnzǐ*) as consisting in having acquired certain moral traits such as being "observant of the rites" and "delighting in the Way," rather than being "obsequious" and "arrogant." The fact that *Analects* 1.15 quotes from Máo 55 provides us with an opportunity to compare the semantic shift of *wén* from 'awe-inspiringly beautiful' in pre-Warring States times (as illustrated by Máo 55 in (3) discussed above) to 'morally refined' in the Warring States period (as illustrated in *Analects* 1.15). The passage from Máo 55—"as if cut, as if polished; as if carved, as if ground"—is used metaphorically in *Analects* 1.15 to refer to the process of edification.[111] Just as the decorative patterns (*wén*) on a jade vessel are applied externally, so is also the 'decoration/moral refinement' (*wén*) of the 'noble man' (*jūnzǐ*) acquired through imitation of an external tradition of 'ideal patterns of conventionalized behavior.'[112]

Further support for the analysis of *wén* as an acquired attribute is found in *Analects* 14.12, where *wén* is used as a transitive verb meaning 'to pattern' or 'to decorate': "If someone who possesses Zāng Wǔzhòng's wisdom, Gōngchuò's freedom from desire, and Zhuāngzǐ of Biàn's courage . . . is *wén*-ed ('morally refined') through ritual and music, then he can be considered a perfected person."[113] Here, Confucius describes the 'perfected man' (*chéng rén* 成人). In addition to possessing certain inner qualities (i.e., wisdom, freedom from desires, courage) as raw material, he also needs to undergo further 'refinement or decoration' (*wén*) through 'rites and music' (*lǐ yuè* 禮樂). Only then will he achieve the balance of 'moral refinement' (*wén*) and 'native substance' (*zhì* 質), which is required of the 'noble man' in *Analects* 6.18.[114]

From 'awe-inspiringly beautiful' to 'morally refined'   71

By opening up the possibility that 'moral refinement' (*wén*) can be acquired, *Analects* 1.15 and 14.12 also imply that it is possible for persons of non-noble background to become 'morally refined' (*wén*) through the proper edification process. Thus, for example, the passage from *Analects* 14.12 quoted above does not assume that the 'perfected person' has to be of noble birth. Furthermore, since *wén* is explicitly mentioned as part of the curriculum taught by Confucius[115]—and since several of his students, such as Yán Huí,[116] were of non-noble origin—it is clear that the edification process through which one acquires *wén* was not confined to nobles.[117]

While the *Analects* does not formulate its theory of moral education explicitly, the *Xúnzǐ* spells out the implications of using crafts metaphors[118] to describe the process of acquiring *wén*:

(11) **'Pattern'** (*wén*) 'imitation' (*xué*) is to a person what polishing and grinding are to jade. A poem says, **As if cut, as if polished; as if carved, as if ground**. This refers to imitating and inquiring. As for Hé's jade disc and the Jǐnglǐ stone, after jade specialists polished them, then they became treasures of all under Heaven. As for Zǐgòng and Jì Lù—who were men of lowly backgrounds—donned **pattern** (*wén*) imitation and dressed in the rites and duty, then they became illustrious retainer-officials[119] for all under Heaven. (人之於文學也，猶玉之於琢磨也。《詩》曰「如切如磋，如琢如磨」謂學問也。和之璧，井里之厥也，玉人琢之，為天子寶。子贛、季路，故鄙人也，被文學，服禮義，為天下列士)[120]

This crafts metaphor shows that the *Xúnzǐ* viewed the edification process as a gradual fashioning of the moral mettle of the individual through 'imitation of the ideal patterns of conventionalized behavior' (*wénxué* 文學)[121] [polite studies], which were preserved in the tradition of government institutions and social mores from the early Zhōu.

Lakoff and Johnson's theory of conceptual metaphor can be used to map the implications of this jade carving metaphor.[123] Conceptual metaphors are grounded in embodied experiences. For example, the use of the word *up* when we say *The prices are going up* is a conceptual metaphor. When pouring liquid into a container, *up* usually indicates more. In Lakoff and Johnson's terminology, our concrete experiences with liquids moving up when poured into containers is the source domain of embodied experience that structures the abstract idea (in the target domain) of an increase in mathematical quantity or price.

Similarly, in the jade carving metaphor, the physical process of carving hard stones, provides the structuring source domain for the conceptualization of moral edification. First, just as raw jade does not have the teleological potential to turn into beautifully carved objects on its own, the implication is that human beings also do not have innate knowledge of normative values that would allow them to turn into sages on their own. Second, in the same way that raw rocks containing jade appear crude and unappealing at first glance, the potential worth of people of humble origins (such as Zǐgòng and Jì Lù) also cannot easily be judged from

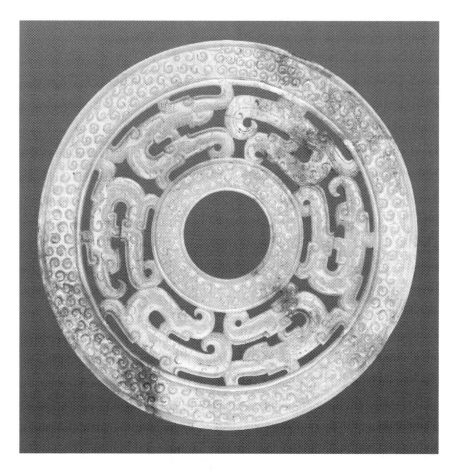

Figure 2.2 Warring States period jade *bì* disc. This disc is similar to the legendary jade disc of Mr. Hé mentioned in *Xúnzǐ*'s jade carving metaphor in (11). The disk is in openwork with decoration of dragons and birds similar. It is 11.4 cm in diameter and 0.6 cm thick and is located in the Arthur M. Sackler Museum.[122]

Credit: Harvard Art Museums and the Arthur M. Sackler Museum.

appearances. Third, by cutting and carving, the jade carver can turn an unassuming rock into a treasured gem; similarly, since (as assumed in *Xúnzǐ*) people do not have the innate normative values needed to transform themselves on their own, the implication is that they need to learn about the 'ideal patterns of normative values' (*wén*) from an external tradition under the guidance of a teacher or mentor. Through this process, even 'lowly people' (*bǐ rén*) are able to become skilled and morally refined retainer–officials, known everywhere under Heaven. The implications furnished by the source domain (i.e., jade carving), although not spelled out in the original passage, then allow us to infer that the authors assumed the carved

From 'awe-inspiringly beautiful' to 'morally refined' 73

patterns on the jade object to correspond to the 'moral refinement' (*wén*) of the 'noble man' (*jūnzǐ*).[124]

In sum, the acquisition of 'moral refinement' (*wén*) through a long edification process based on the imitation of the 'ideal patterns of conventionalized behavior' (*wén*) of the early Zhōu was as a prerequisite for office-holding in both the *Analects* and the *Xúnzǐ*. By using the exact same phrase 'as if cut, as if polished; as if carved, as if ground' from Máo 55 as the one also quoted by Zǐgòng in *Analects* 1.15, the *Xúnzǐ* explicitly anchors its theory of moral education in the tradition of the *Analects* and its exegetical tradition of the *Songs*; see (3) and (10). As in *Analects*, the 'moral refinement' (*wén*) of the 'noble man' (*jūnzǐ*) is an acquired trait accessible to anyone willing to undergo the necessary edification process.

The development of an exegetical tradition around texts such as the *Songs* and *Shàngshū* increased historical awareness of how contemporary practices differed from those of the idealized past.[125] Many Warring States texts contain explicit discussion of the interpretation of these textual traditions. Widespread interest in expounding meanings of passages from these revered scriptures led many to speculate about traditional institutions and the social mores embodied in them. In order to communicate their interpretations of these foundational texts more efficiently, the Warring States exegetes felt a need to coin new terms for abstract concepts, such as 'customs' (*sú*) and 'civility/civilization' (*wén*). It is therefore not surprising that uses of *wén* to express concepts such as 'moral refinement' and 'civility' emerged in the theories of conservative thinkers such as Confucius (as portrayed in the *Analects*), who considered the Classics to be a repository of valuable insight about the ideal organization of human society.[126] The *Songs* and the *Shàngshū*, which were known as 'ancient' texts even during the Warring States period, constituted the core of a relatively small body of texts serving as the backbone of an elite education.[127] The exegetical debates over the meaning and importance of these texts created an environment conducive to the development of a heightened civilizational consciousness.[128]

The often quite contrived interpretations of the *Songs* from the Warring States period onward frequently imposed later Warring States meanings of *wén* and other terms onto the pre-Warring States period. As discussed above, in Máo 55 the phrase "as if cut, as if polished; as if carved, as if ground" was used as a metaphor to state that the aristocratic lord (*jūnzǐ*) is as 'beautiful' as a jade disc; see (3). There is no indication that in that context the passage should be understood to refer to the 'moral refinement' of a 'noble man' (*jūnzǐ*). This did not, however, prevent the composers of the *Analects* and the *Xúnzǐ* from reading this passage as a reference to the 'moral refinement' of the morally 'noble man' (*jūnzǐ*), regardless of his aristocratic rank, as shown in (10) and (11). Thus, although the traditional commentaries to the Classics are a valuable tool, they must be used with the awareness that they may contain millennia-old anachronistic readings, such as reading *wén* in pre-Warring States texts to refer to 'acquired moral refinement.'

Both the coiners of the modern Western European universal concept of 'civilization' and the Warring States coiners of the concept of '*wén*' endorsed moralizing philosophies in which individuals have the duty to engage in self-cultivation

74 *From 'awe-inspiringly beautiful' to 'morally refined'*

practices aimed at improving their 'civility' or 'moral refinement.' Interestingly, both traditions also used carving and polishing metaphors. As discussed in Chapter 1 and highlighted in the second epigraph at the beginning of this chapter, French dictionaries from the seventeenth and eighteenth centuries defined the meaning of the verb *to civilize* (Fr. *civiliser*) as 'to polish one's manners' (Fr. *polir les mœurs*). In 1770, the French Enlightenment thinker Guillaume Raynal (1713–1796) wrote, "The people who have *polished* all others were merchants."[129] As observed by Febvre (1973: 222–24, 32–3), the preceding context—in which Raynal asked, "What gathered these people together, clothed them and *civilized* them? It was trade"[130]—allows us to determine that he used the verb *polir* 'to polish' and *civiliser* 'to civilize' interchangeably to refer to the process of civilization. While the English word *polite* is no longer readily associated with its original metaphorical source domain of being 'polished,' in French the words *poli* 'polite' and *poli* 'polished' are still homophones. Hence, when one says in French that someone is *poli* 'polite,' the listener's understanding of this utterance and her conceptualization of 'politeness' may very well be informed metaphorically by the concept of 'polishing.'[131]

Similarly, as indicated by the carving metaphor for self-cultivation and learning in (11), the concept of 'moral refinement' (*wén*) in the *Xúnzǐ* is also likely to be informed metaphorically by the use of the word *wén* to refer to 'decorative patterns' carved onto artifacts, such as carved jade discs. That the carving metaphor implied in the word *wén* is a live metaphor is clearly demonstrated by the explicit carving simile in (11), as well as by the passage from the *Analects* in (10). To preserve *wén*'s metaphorical associations with pattern-carving, a better translation of the phrase 'pattern-imitation' (*wén-xué*) in (11) may therefore be the phrase *polite studies*, which, according to Shapin, in eighteenth-century English referred to the study of "civil history, belles-lettres, rhetoric, ancient and modern languages, genealogy, antiquarianism, [and] geography."[132]

Conclusion

In this chapter, I have traced the early chronological stages in the coining of civilizational consciousness in pre-Qín China by mapping the diachronic polysemy of the word *wén*, as shown in rows (I) to (IV) in Figure 2.3. The basic meaning of *wén* was 'pattern'; see row (I) in Figure 2.3.[133] By the earliest attested writing on oracle bones from the late Shāng dynasty, from about 1300 to 1045 BCE, the meanings (II) 'decoration'/'decorated' and (III) 'awe-inspiringly beautiful' appear to have already been derived by regular processes of metaphorical extension.[134] 'Awe-inspiringly beautiful' is the meaning of *wén* in the name King Wén and in similar uses of *wén* as a positive epithet in names and posthumous titles in the pre-Warring States period. After this aesthetically interpreted descriptor was reanalyzed in ethical terms to mean (IV) 'morally refined,' around the middle of the first millennium BCE, the older meaning '(awe-inspiringly) beautiful' appears to have lingered on for a while before slowly becoming obsolete by the end of the Warring States period (as indicated by the dotted line in Figure 2.3). The obsolescence

From 'awe-inspiringly beautiful' to 'morally refined' 75

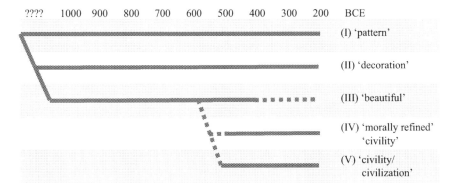

Figure 2.3 Tracing the history of the meaning changes of the word *wén*.[135]

of the older aesthetic *wén* and the introduction of anachronistic Warring States-period ethical interpretations of pre-Warring States instances of *wén* eventually led to the persistent anachronistic readings of King Wén as the 'civil' or 'cultured' king in pre-Warring States texts.

The mapping of the ethnocentric 'prejudices' inherent in the modern English words *civility* and *civility* in Chapter 1 has allowed us to avoid some of the hermeneutical pitfalls of imposing the meaning of modern Anglophone concepts and words onto pre-Qín words and concepts. It is of course impossible to achieve "objective" reconstruction of the "original meaning" of words in pre-Qín texts. But by letting the "prejudices" of the language-specific words of *civility* and *civilization* in our own modern Western tradition engage in a hermeneutical dialogue with the "prejudices" of the language-specific terms for 'civility' (*wén*) and 'civilization' (*wén*) in pre-Qín texts, we are in a better position to make sense of these Old Chinese concepts while trying to respect their language-specific nature and meanings.

In the Warring States period, the word *wén* in the new sense of the acquired 'moral refinement/civility' of an individual was used in ways similar to the sixteenth- to eighteenth-century English (and French) words *civility*, *civilize*, and *civilized*. Early Modern English *civility* was obtained by a slow process of 'polishing' manners. Being *civil/civilized* or *polite* entailed being *polished* through *polite studies* and other edifying practices. Similarly, the fact that the basic meaning of the term *wén* was 'pattern' meant that it was well suited to the crafts metaphors of pattern-carving for self-cultivation used to articulate the virtue ethics of the *Analects* and the *Xúnzǐ*. Being *wén* entailed having had the 'pattern' of 'ritualized civility' (*wén*) carved onto one's 'human nature' (*xìng* 性) by engaging in 'polite studies'/'pattern imitation' (*wénxué* 文學) and other edifying practices.

The semantic shift in the meaning of the word *wén* occurred in tandem with semantic changes in a number of other terms, such as *jūnzǐ* 'nobleman' → 'noble

76 *From 'awe-inspiringly beautiful' to 'morally refined'*

man' and *dé* 'power' → *dé* 'virtue.' The aesthetically grounded and interpreted 'awe-inspiring beauty' (*wén*) of the 'nobleman' was the manifestation of his religio-political power in the Shāng and Western Zhōu periods. In contrast, in the Warring States period the ethically interpreted 'moral refinement/civility' (*wén*) of the 'noble man' was the manifestation of his 'moral virtue' (*dé*). While the kings of the various states were still at the top of the *sociopolitical* pyramid, the philosophers, such as Confucius and Xúnzǐ, placed themselves at the top of the *moral* hierarchy and were therefore in a position to lecture the rulers on how to rule by 'decorating/polishing' their 'morally refined' (*wén*) 'virtue' (*dé*).

As in Western Europe, the epistemic changes that led to the crystallization of a pre-Qín concept of acquired 'civility' took place in tandem with significant sociopolitical changes. Such changes included (i) the erosion of the ritualized lineage-based system of government of the Western Zhōu; (ii) a slow shift from charismatic modes of authority to more bureaucratic modes of authority manifested itself in a redefinition of aesthetically expressed 'awe-inspiring beauty' (*wén*) as 'moral refinement/civility' (*wén*); (iii) increasing professionalization of the officials in charge of government administration and military management; and (iv) the emergence of a market of cultural capital in which theories of 'civilization' could be formulated and exchanged. These changes helped create a sociopolitical infrastructure that enabled an emergent group of specialists of statecraft and moral philosophy to formulate and exchange their ideas. It was in this group of specialists vying for official positions that the concepts and terms through which civilizational consciousness could be articulated were first coined in pre-Qín China. Again, the first step in this process was the change from aesthetic understanding of *wén* as 'awe-inspiringly beautiful' to an ethical understanding of the term as 'morally refined,' and also the emergence of a concept of 'ritualized/patterned civility.' As indicated in row (V) in Figure 2.3, the next step in the evolution of the term *wén* was the extension of the word *wén* in the meaning 'ritualized civility' to an indigenous universal concept of 'civilization.' This is the topic of Chapter 3.

Notes

1 *Analects* 1.15, Chéng Shùdé (1997: 54–6), tr. adapted from Legge (1861: 8).
2 Furetière (1727: italics and bold fonts added). French: "civilizer: polir les mœurs."
3 Based on a passage in "Basic Annals of the Zhōu" in the *Historical Records* (*Shǐjì* 史記), Shaughnessy (1999a: 302) concludes that in 1058 BCE the Shāng king Dì Xīn (aka Emperor Zhòu) granted King Wén the "exclusive privilege to conduct military campaigns in the areas to the West of Shāng." According to the same passage, "the next year [i.e., 1057 BCE based on Shaughnessy's chronology] the Lord of the West [= King Wén] chastised the Quǎn-Róng [people]" (Nienhauser 1994: 58, tr. Wade-Giles changed to Pinyin).
4 Whether King Wén assumed the name during his lifetime or whether it was a posthumous title is debated. According to Shaughnessy (1999a: 302), Chāng "assumed the title Wen Wang 文王 (the Cultured King)" shortly after 1058 BCE. While solid evidence is sparse, I agree with Shaughnessy's assumption that it is possible Chāng may have "assumed the title Wen Wang" during his lifetime. For criticism of the translation

From 'awe-inspiringly beautiful' to 'morally refined' 77

of King Wén as the "Cultured King," see the subsection titled "Translating *Wén* in pre-Warring States texts" below.

5 The analyses of civilizational vocabulary in chapters 2–5 are based on a comprehensive corpus of received texts and recently discovered manuscripts from before the Qín unification in 221 BCE. Aiming to include most of the extant pre-Qín textual material, I have used a range of concordances, databases, and individual texts. Databases consulted include the Chinese Ancient Texts database (CHANT) at www.chant.org/, Chinese Text Project database at http://ctext.org, the Gugong Hanquan database at http://210.69.170.100/s25, the Wuhan University Ancient Chinese Excavated Manuscripts at www.bsm-whu.org/zxcl/, among others. More information on sources used will be provided when discussing specific words.

6 Part of the analysis *wén* presented here is based on Bergeton (2013). A shorter version of the analysis of *wén* presented in this chapter will appear in the *Journal of the American Oriental Society*; see Bergeton (forthcoming). Previous studies of *wén* focus on various aspects of the term. Chow (1979) focuses on expressions referring to 'writing' and 'literature.' Kern (2001) explores the use of the term *wénzhāng* to refer to "written textual compositions." Schaberg (2001a) focuses on its uses in the *Zuǒzhuàn* to refer to rhetorically patterned speech (*wén cí*). Gawlikowski (1988, 1987) contains a study of the *wén-wǔ* 'civil–martial' dichotomy and its role in political theory. Falkenhausen (1996) studies *wén* in Western Zhōu Bronze inscriptions. Shirakawa Shizuka (1983) briefly discusses different pre-Qín takes on the concept '*wén*.' Péng Yàfēi (1996, 2005) also discusses different views of *wén* in the pre-Qín period. Powers (2006) highlights the role of pattern decorations (*wén*) in the construction of personhood. More recently, Liú Shàojǐn (2010) analyzes the role of *wén* in pre-Qín theories of aesthetics. The term *wén* 文 never stopped developing new uses and meanings. For the period from the seventh to the twelfth centuries, see Bol (1992). For an excellent study of *wén* in medieval to modern China, see Blitstein (2016).

7 Underhill and Fang (2004: 135), Chang (1980: 235), and Keightley (2012: 33–62).

8 As observed by Powers (2006), the shapes of the 'patterns' (*wén* 文) decorating status objects, such as jades and bronze vessels, played a role in the construction of social hierarchies. During the Shāng and early Zhōu, patterns were rigid and highly stylized. Powers sees this as a reflection of fixed social hierarchies. In contrast, the more fluid patterns on Warring States decorations indicate dynamic social hierarchies and higher levels of social mobility.

9 Weber (1957: 358–9).

10 Weber (1968: 20) discusses charismatic authority in China. See also his essay on the "Chinese literati" in Weber (1991: 416–44). Although I adopt parts of Weber's concepts of "charismatic authority," "routinization," and "bureaucratization," I do not adopt all aspects of his analysis of the "Chinese literati" and bureaucratization in pre-Qín China. The term *wén rén* 文人, often translated as *literati* in English, did not exist in this sense in the Warring States period. At that time, many serving in official positions were 'retainer–officials'/'men of service' (*shì* 士).

11 Donlan (1973) and Adkins (1960).

12 Donlan (1973: 370).

13 As observed by Donlan (1973: 370, fn. 14), in the *Iliad* "Thersites' social inferiority and lack of *arête* are shown by his physical ugliness, and in general what a man looked like was a reliable index of his total worth."

14 *Odyssey* 9.513–16, tr. from Verity (2016: 122). Verity translates *kalós* as "handsome" in this passage. Bryant (2015: 179) translates *kalós* as "of noble presence" which indicates a meaning very close 'awe-inspiringly beautiful.'

15 Weber (1957: 359).

16 Morton (1971) analyzes the shift in the meaning of *jūnzǐ* from aristocratic 'nobleman' to morally refined 'noble man.' See also Rubin (1968) and Rubin (1976: 20) for studies

78 *From 'awe-inspiringly beautiful' to 'morally refined'*

of this shift in the meaning of the term *jūnzǐ*. More recently, Meyer (forth.: 103–05) has revisited the reconceptualization of the term *jūnzǐ* from " 'person of high social standing' to denoting a person of moral integrity." For the meanings of the *jūnzǐ* in *Zuǒzhuàn* and *Analects*, see also the excellent study by Gassmann (2007: 411–36).

I am grateful to Maria Khayutina for pointing out that while texts such as the *Book of Songs* provide evidence that the term *jūnzǐ* was used to refer to aristocratic 'noblemen' in the Spring and Autumn period, there is no solid evidence that it was used in this meaning in Shāng and Western Zhōu times. Shāng oracle bone inscriptions feature the expression *duō jūn* 多君 'the many lords,' or 'the many rulers.' The expression *jūnzǐ* 君子 appears only once in an obscure context in one Shāng inscription (*H*03272), where it is not clear exactly what it means. As observed by Khayutina (p.c.), in "Western Zhou bronze inscriptions, the word *jūn* means 'ruler,' 'lord,' or 'lineage's head' and it is applicable both to males and females. It is unlikely that it was a general designation for nobility vs. commoners; rather it is related to the relationships of subordination on various levels. *Jūn* are opposed to *chén* 'servitors' or simply subordinates, who are also members of the nobility." That is, the "*jūn* did not refer to any member of nobility, but only to an overlord. Not every member of the group that shares descent with the ruling lineage in a polity is a *jūn* . . . We can observe on the archaeological materials that within such kinship groups, only a very small number of people accumulated a great wealth and many symbols of power in their hands. Other members of the group had the same origin, but they were not nobles. It is very difficult to determine who belonged to the 'elite' during the Western Zhou period" (Khayutina, p.c.). According to Khayutina, this situation changed during the Spring and Autumn period, when the term of *jūnzǐ* came to be used to refer to aristocratic 'noblemen' in a broader sense. These *jūnzǐ* were not necessarily 'sons of a polity's ruler,' but they were also members of various aristocratic lineages of different origins within the polity. For an analysis of the social composition of polities during the Spring and Autumn period related to this shift, see Blakeley (1977–1979).

17 In addition to the pre-Warring States parts of the *Book of Songs*, the *Book of Changes*, the *Shàngshū*, and the *Annals*, the pre-Warring States corpus used here also includes the oracle bone and bronze inscriptions in the CHANT database (www.chant.org/) and print concordances such as Zhāng Yàchū's (2012) *Concordance Shāng and Zhōu Bronze Inscriptions*; and collections of inscriptions including: *Yīn Zhōu jīnwén jíchéng* (1984–1994) and Liu Yu and Lu Yan (2002).

18 Máo 128, *SSJZS* (1980: 370). The *Book of Songs* is referred to as the *Shījīng* (lit. 'song/poem' (*shī*) 'classic' (*jīng*)) in modern Chinese. In pre-Qín texts, before it began to be referred to as a 'classic' (*jīng*), it was simply referred to as the *Poems* or *Songs* (*shī*). This collection of songs/poems is also often referred to in English as the *Book of Poems/Odes/Songs*. Here I use *Book of Songs* when translating the Chinese phrase to *Shījīng* (lit. 'song/poem' (*shī*) 'classic' (*jīng*)) and *Songs* when translating reference to this work as the *Shī* (lit. 'the *Songs/Poems/Odes*'). Individuals *Songs* are referred using the Máo edition numbering. I adopt the consensus view that the *Shījīng* was composed in the period from the end of the second millennium BCE to the late Spring and Autumn period (770–481 BCE); see Loewe (1993b: 415–23) and Qū Wànlǐ 屈萬 里 (1983: 327–36). For hypotheses on relatively more precise dates of composition of different parts of the *Shījīng*, I will cite specific studies as needed.

19 Wáng Xiānqiān (2008: 254).

20 Máo 177, *SSJZS* (1980: 425). According to Zhèng Xuán (127–200), "*zhī* 織 refers to a woven emblem [in this passage] (織徽織也) (*SSJZS* 1980: 425).

21 The term *zhāng* 章 here refers to 'rank-indicating insignia.' In Warring States texts, *zhāng* and *wén* often occur together in the expression *wénzhāng* 文章, which can refer to: (i) 'emblems and insignia,' or (ii) more broadly to colorful and ornamented chariots, clothes, banners, and flags, and other status-indicating objects.

22 Máo 299, *SSJZS* (1980: 611).

From 'awe-inspiringly beautiful' to 'morally refined' 79

23 Máo 55, *SSJZS* (1980: 321), tr. adapted fr. Karlgren (1950: 37). Reading *fěi* 匪 as *fěi* 斐 'elegant,' see Schuessler (1987: 160).

24 The origin of the system of posthumous names (*shì fǎ* 謚法) is controversial; see Wāng Shòukuān (1995). Wáng Guówéi (1987: 895–96), places it in the middle of the Western Zhōu period, while Guō Mòruò (1954: 89a–101b) dates it to the Warring States period. I follow Falkenhausen's (1996) theory that an early form of posthumous naming existed in the late Shāng and was further developed in the Western Zhōu period.

25 This list of terms which can be modified by *wén* is based on Falkenhausen (1996).

26 Falkenhausen (1996: 3).

27 This does not diminish the value of Falkenhausen's (1996) excellent study of posthumous titles in bronze inscriptions.

28 Overall, I agree with Pines' (2002b) assessment, based on careful study of lexical usage patterns, "that insofar as the *Lunyu* reflects sayings by Confucius (trad. 551–479 B.C.) and the first two generations of his disciples, the vocabulary of this text should belong to the fifth century B.C. or slightly later, but is still akin to that of the bulk of the *Zuo*." However, it is also clear that the *Analects* is a stratified text consisting of material composed in different periods. According to Brooks and Brooks (1998), the *Analects* was composed over the span of several centuries: (i) *Analects* 4, 5, 6, 7, 8, 9 composed in the fifth century BCE; (ii) *Analects* 1, 2, 3, 10, 11, 12, 13, 14, 15 composed in the fourth century; and (iii) *Analects* 16, 17, 18, 19, 20 composed in the third century BCE. For criticism of Brooks and Brooks (1998), see Schaberg (2001b: 31–9). I agree with Schaberg that Brooks and Brooks attempt to date subparts of the *Analects* with greater precision than warranted by the available evidence. It nevertheless seems likely that much of the *Analects* was composed in the late fifth or fourth century BCE and other parts may have been composed even later. However, for the purposes of this study all that matters is that the bulk of the *Analects* was composed in the Warring States period and therefore reflects Warring States lexical usage patterns. For other discussions of the composition and compilation of the *Analects*, see also Cheng (1993b: 313–23); Makeham (1996); Qū Wànlǐ (1983: 382–9); and Hunter (2017).

29 Máo 262, *SSJZS* (1980: 574).

30 Karlgren (1950: 234).

31 Legge (1876: 344). Qū Wànlǐ (1983: 334) dates Máo 262 to the reign of King Xuān of Zhōu (r. 827/25–782).

32 Xiàng Xī 向熹 (1986: 485).

33 A Warring States period example of *wéndé* meaning 'morally refined virtue' can be found in *Analects* 16.1 where the ruler is advised to make people submit to him by 'cultivating his moral virtue' (*xiū wéndé* 修文德), see Chéng Shùdé (1997: 1137).

34 Puett (2001: 29). Since Puett (2001) is not a study of *wén*, the translation *cultured* does not diminish its value. Máo 275 may have been composed as early as under Duke of Zhōu (r. 1042–1036) or King Chéng (r. 1042/35–1006), see Qū Wànlǐ (1983: 334).

35 See, for example, the translations of *JC* 6011–12 and 6013 in Cook and Goldin (2016: 81–2).

36 Waley (1996: 295) renders this line "Mighty are you, Hou Ji." Karlgren (1950: 243) has "Fine are you, Hou Tsi."

37 See the conveniently collected paleographic studies of <文> in the *Gǔwénzì gǔlín* 古文字詁林.

38 Jì Xùshēng (2010: 731). See also Lǐ Zōngkūn (2012: 1292).

39 Jì Xùshēng (2010: 732).

40 As mentioned in the subsection titled "What's in a word" in chapter 1, it is important not to confuse the ways words are written with the words themselves. The vast majority of graphs are not pictographic depictions of things in the world but rather graphs that contain components indicating the sounds of the word the graphs are intended to

80   *From 'awe-inspiringly beautiful' to 'morally refined'*

write; see Baxter and Sagart (2014). The graph <來> was used in early inscriptions to write the word 'wheat plant.' Since the pronunciation of the Old Chinese word 'wheat' was similar to the word for the verb 'to come,' the graph <來> was also used to write 'to come' (*lái*). The graph <來> eventually evolved into the modern graph <來> now used to write the word 'to come.' In this case, knowing that the graph <來> for the word 'to come' evolved from <來> depicting a sprouting plant tells us nothing about the meaning of the word 'to come' (*lái*). We therefore need to be careful when using the shape of graphs to infer anything about word meanings.

41 I am grateful to Maria Khayutina (p.c.) for pointing out the potential issues with the hypothesis that *wén* originally meant 'tattoo.' It should be noted that both hypotheses ([i] that *wén* originally meant 'tattoo,' and [ii] that *wén* originally meant 'pattern decoration') are compatible with the analysis of 'awe-inspiringly beautiful' from an earlier meaning, be it 'tattoo' or 'pattern decoration.' Existing data on the meaning of *wén* does not allow us to definitively rule out either hypothesis.

42 For the purposes of the analysis of *wén*, it does not matter whether the original basic meaning of the word as 'tattoo' and 'pattern.' Both hypotheses are compatible with the semantic history of the term proposed here.

43 See Xú Zhōngshū (2006: 996).

44 As in the expression *wén mǔ* 'awe-inspiringly beautiful [deceased] mother,' attested in bronze inscriptions and the *Book of Songs*.

45 For archaeological evidence for the sociopolitical changes that took place between the Western Zhōu and the Warring States period, see Falkenhausen (2006).

46 For and overview of Western Zhōu history, see Shaughnessy (1999a: 292–351). The dates for the Western Zhōu and the conquest of the Shāng are from Shaughnessy (1999b: 25).

47 The term 'lord–protector' (*bà* 霸) is often used to refer to the 'hegemon' or 'lord–protector' of the Spring and Autumn period, beginning with Lord Huán of Qí (685–643). See, for example, Hsu's (1999: 551–62) discussion of the "*ba*-system" in the Spring and Autumn period. However, as observed by Eric Henry (p.c.), there is little evidence that the *bà*-institution existed in the Spring and Autumn period. It does not appear in any excavated texts from the pre-Warring States period. It also does not appear in the *Chūnqiū*, the *Songs* (*Shī*), or the pre-Warring States parts of the *Shàngshū* and the *Changes*. It may therefore be a fifth century BCE invention. For a discussion of the absence of the term *bà* from pre-Warring States texts, see note 85.

48 This comparison was made for the first time by Franke (1930: 162).

49 Lewis (1999), Lewis (2007), Hui (2005), Yáng Kuān (2003), and Yáng Kuān (1999).

50 See Yáng Kuān (2003). I am grateful to Maria Khayutina (p.c.) for pointing out that the "Jìsūn line descended from Duke Huán of Lǔ, which means that this was the younger branch of the ruling lineage of Lǔ. The Jì usurpation is therefore an internal power struggle within a hereditary ruling structure. That the direct line retained its nominal position up to 220s BCE [indicates that, although weakened,] the ritualized hierarchy was still in place and collateral lineages did not dare to replace the ruler."

51 As observed by Li (2008b), it is important not to conflate the idealized ritual system of offices and ranks described in the *Rituals of the Zhōu* (*Zhōulǐ*), which was likely composed during the Warring States period or later, with the system actually in place during the Western Zhōu. For a list of official titles in Western Zhōu bronze inscriptions, see Li (2008a: 305–14).

52 *Zuǒzhuàn* Yǐn 5.7, tr. adapted from Durrant, Li, and Schaberg (2016: 38–9).

53 *Analects* 3.1, Chéng Shùdé (1997: 136).

54 See the commentaries to *Analects* 3.1 in Chéng Shùdé (1997: 136–40). In Confucius' time institutionalized ritual prerogatives were highly conspicuous manifestations of political power. Usurping ritual prerogatives of one's superiors was thus tantamount to subverting the political order and destroying the fabric of society.

From 'awe-inspiringly beautiful' to 'morally refined'   81

55 For a recent re-evaluation of the issue of hereditary office-holding and promotion based on merit in the early Zhōu, see Li Feng (2008a: 190–234). As Li Feng correctly observes, it is possible to argue that Western Zhōu government possessed some elements of bureaucratization. While this is certainly true, it is also true that Western Zhōu society did not support the same kind of market of cultural capital that developed in the Warring States period. The difference is a matter of degree, not a dichotomy between a fully fledged bureaucracy and total absence of all elements of bureaucracy.

56 Advances in metallurgy during this period include the ability to produce iron vessels and implements; see Hsu (1999: 578–80).

57 Yáng Kuān (2003), Hsu (1965), Hsu (1999: 545), Gernet (1982), Gernet (1999), Lewis (1999).

58 For a study of the development of currency economies in the pre-Qín period, see Kakinuma (2015).

59 As observed by Pines (2002a:107), "the growing commercialization of the Warring States economy galvanized inter-regional connections and increased regional interdependence, with economic ties transcending boundaries of individual states, contributing thereby to a sense of economic unity of All under Heaven." See also Yáng Kuān (2003) and Hsu (1965: 116–26).

60 As observed by Pines (2002a: 107), "Almost all of the known Warring States thinkers routinely crossed boundaries in search of better appointment and many served more than one state." See also Lewis (1999: 632–34), and Meyer (2012: 233–34).

61 Lewis (2007: 32). For a succinct historical overview of the history of warfare in early China, see Yates (1999). For the period down to the end of the Spring and Autumn period, see also Kolb (1991).

62 These include the *Sūnzǐ* 孫子, the *Sūn Bìn* 孫臏, the *Wúzǐ* 吳子, and the *Wèi Liáozǐ* 尉繚子, among others; see Yates (1988), Lewis (1999), Gawlikowski (1985), and Sawyer (1993).

63 Lewis (2007).

64 For the "militarization of society" proposed in the *Book of Lord Shang*, see Pines (2016: 97–134).

65 Lewis (2007: 32). See also Lewis (1990: 54–60). For changes in state bureaucracy and military organization, see also Yates (1987), Yates (1988), Yates (1994), and Yates (1995). Before Lewis and Yates, Dù Zhèngshèng 杜正勝 (1979) suggested applying the city-state model to the Spring and Autumn period. The city-state model is controversial and is not accepted by all scholars. See for example, Li Feng's (2008a: 23; 294–98) alternative "kin-ordered settlement-state" model.

66 These changes are described in Yáng Kuān (2003), Hsu (1965), and Hsu (1999). The term 'man of service'/'retainer–official' (*shì* 士) is difficult to define and different translations abound. For discussion of this term, see Yú Yīngshí (1987), Liú Zéhuá (2004) and Pines (2009: 115–86).

67 Wang (2000: 125). See also Lewis (1990: 12) and Yates (1994: 57).

68 Allan (1991), Keightley (1999), Keightley (2000), Wheatley (1971).

69 Wang (2000: 27).

70 Wang (2000: 34ff).

71 Wang (2000: 125). For the concept of the 'Five Phases' and a critique of the term "correlative cosmology," see Nylan (2010).

72 Wang (2000: 77).

73 Wang (2000: 77; 126).

74 As observed by Dirk Meyer, the Warring States period constitutes a "threshold period" (German *Sattelzeit*) in Reinhart Koselleck's theory of conceptual history. A threshold period refers to "an epoch where key concepts and guiding terms undergo principal conceptual transformation. Prime denotations become reformulated and change their meaning. Koselleck devised the threshold period to describe the fundamental

82 *From 'awe-inspiringly beautiful' to 'morally refined'*

transformations in the conceptual range of the sociopolitical terminology between the years 1750 and 1850. . . See Brunner, Conze, and Koselleck (1972–1979: vol. 1: xiv ff. (1972); vol. 2: 363 ff; 625 ff. (75); 107; 349 f. (79))" (Meyer forth.: 102).

75 Confucius himself traveled between states in search of employment; see Nylan and Wilson (2010: 1–2). The *Analects* mention him being on the road, e.g., *Analects* 9.5 in (2) in chapter 3. Other traveling thinkers include Mencius, Xúnzǐ, and Hán Fēi.

76 *Hánfēizǐ* 35, Wáng Xiānshèn (2006: 337). Generally assumed to be a Warring States text, parts of the *Hánfēizǐ* may have been composed in early Hàn. However, this passage still captures the market of ideas in place in the late Warring States period.

77 In the *Hánfēizǐ*, serving in office is a transactional exchange of services for wealth and rank. For Confucius and other coiners of *wén*, serving in office was a vocation in the Weberian sense of the word. However, since they also peddled their cultural capital to gain employment, they still were part of a 'market of cultural capital.'

78 However, this does not mean that I endorse causal explanations in which changes in sociopolitical and institutional structures directly cause intellectual changes. Intellectual and sociopolitical changes occur in tandem in a complex process of mutual influence that cannot be reduced to simple causality.

79 While Warring States period mention sayings attributed to earlier kings, sages, and statesmen, they do not contain quotations from argument-based texts from pre-Warring States times. For the absence of argument-based philosophical texts from the pre-Warring States period, see also Meyer (2012).

80 Incidentally, the Greek word *kalós* which, as discussed above, referred to physical 'beauty' in pre-Classical times, also came to be interpreted in ethical terms to mean 'morally good' in the Classical period. It is a central concept in Plato's theories of aesthetics and ethics. As observed, by Taylor (1957: 231), in Plato's dialogues the terms 'beautiful' (*kalós*) and 'good' (*agathós*) are often convertible. That is, similarly to *wén*, *kalós* started out as a predominantly aesthetic descriptor meaning 'beautiful' which was then later reinterpreted ethically to mean 'morally good.'

81 Morton (1971).

82 Chéng Shùdé (1997: 267–69), tr. adapted from Watson (2007: 34).

83 The term *virtue ethics* is used by philosophers to refer to theories of ethics that emphasize cultivating virtuous impulses and behaviors until they become part of one's moral character. After an individual has internalized moral values through self-cultivation and education, she will be spontaneously reacting appropriately in any given situation. Virtue ethics is also sometimes referred to as *aretaic* ethics after the classical Greek word for 'virtue,' *areté*. See Carr and Steutel (1999: 22).

84 The translating *jūnzǐ* as *noble man* has the advantage of being phonologically similar to the word *nobleman*. However, other translations (e.g., 'morally superior person,' 'ideal gentleman,' 'man of quality') are also possible, and in many cases capture the meaning of the word *jūnzǐ* (in the sense 'morally refined person') better.

85 The dating of the composition of the *Zuǒzhuàn* is controversial. Pines' (2002b: 691–705) study of lexical usage patterns demonstrates that the vocabulary of the *Zuǒzhuàn* is very similar to that of the *Analects*. Unlike Karlgren (1929) and Dobson's (1967) studies of grammatical particles, Pines (2002b) focuses on content words, more specifically the seven expressions 'crossbow' (*nǔ* 弩), 'benevolence and propriety' (*rényì* 仁義), 'ten thousand things' (*wànwù* 萬物), 'ten thousand chariots' (*wànshèng* 萬乘), 'inner structure, principle' (*lǐ* 理), *yīn yáng* 陰陽 as 'cosmic forces,' and 'plain-clothed' (*bù yī* 布衣). These expressions appear frequently in mid- to late Warring States texts such as the *Mencius*, the *Xúnzǐ*, the *Hánfēizǐ*, and the *Lǚshì Chūnqiū*. Pines provides a compelling argument that the absence of all these expressions from the *Analects* and the *Zuǒzhuàn* indicates that the bulk of these two texts were composed in the fifth century BCE or earlier. In chapter 5, I argue that the absence of the word *sú* 俗 in the meaning 'customs' from the *Analects* and the *Zuǒzhuàn* can be added to the list of mid- to late Warring States expressions that

From 'awe-inspiringly beautiful' to 'morally refined'   83

indicate that the *Analects* and the *Zuǒzhuàn* have similar lexical usage patterns. That is, I agree with Pines' conclusion that the fact that none of these terms appear in "the *Zuo* and the *Lunyu* . . . support[s] the assertion that these two texts indeed reflect earlier linguistic layers than other Zhanguo writings" (Pines 2002b: 702). However, I do not believe that the absence of the seven expressions from the *Zuǒzhuàn* by itself provides compelling evidence for Pines' assumption that the *Zuǒzhuàn*'s "vocabulary, except for the narrator's remarks, should reflect that of the Chunqiu period" (Pines 2002b: 694). That is, the absence of the seven expressions from both the *Analects* and the *Zuǒzhuàn* does not by itself prove that the *Zuǒzhuàn* reflects linguistic usage patterns of the Spring and Autumn period while the *Analects* reflects the vocabulary of the early Warring States period. Of course, Pines (2002b) also does not explicitly make this claim. However, Pines (2002c: 37–8) does argue that the frequency of the terms 'benevolence' (*rén* 仁) and 'the Way' (*dào* 道) increases in speeches from the period 722–613 BCE to the period 541–468 BCE and that this indicates that the *Zuǒzhuàn* reflects linguistic usage patterns of the Spring and Autumn period. Pines (2002c: 217–20) also discusses pairs of grammatical particles, such as (i) *yú* 于 / *yú* 於 and (ii) *qí* 其 / *qǐ* 豈 and argues that changes in their chronological distribution in the *Zuǒzhuàn* follow general developments in the distribution of these terms from the Western Zhōu to the Warring States period. However, he also admits that the picture is complicated by the fact that the distribution of these particles is subject to stylistic factors such as the difference between direct speech and narrative. In sum, Pines' hypothesis that the *Zuǒzhuàn* reflect the vocabulary of the Spring and Autumn period seems to find some support in changes in the distribution of content words and grammatical particles and is certainly in the realm of the possible. However, the existing evidence does not seem sufficient to conclusively prove this hypothesis beyond any doubt. It is thus still possible to entertain alternative hypotheses about the date of composition and vocabulary of the *Zuǒzhuàn* which can also be supported by chronological changes in word distributions.

I adopt the hypothesis that the language of the *Zuǒzhuàn* is similar to the (older layers of the) *Analects* (which Pines also argues) and that this indicates that it largely reflects the vocabulary of the late fifth or early fourth century BCE. This hypothesis finds substantial support in the similarities between the terse language of the *Chūnqiū Annals* (without the *Zuǒzhuàn* parts), which almost all scholars agree were composed in the Spring and Autumn period, and bronze inscriptions from the pre-Warring States period. As I will argue in chapter 4, the compound ethnonyms *mán-yí* 蠻夷 and *sì yí* 四夷 are found neither in the *Chūnqiū* nor in bronze inscriptions from before the Warring States period, but they occur frequently in Warring States texts and the *Zuǒzhuàn*. Of course, this is not conclusive evidence that the *Zuǒzhuàn* reflects Warring States-era vocabulary. To be sure, one must be careful when using absence of evidence as evidence (in this case of absence of *mán-yí* 蠻夷 and *sì yí* 四夷 from bronze inscriptions). But it does provide an example where the language of extant bronze inscriptions (and the *Chūnqiū*) differ from the *Zuǒzhuàn*. Other examples of words that occur in Warring States texts and the *Zuǒzhuàn* but not in any pre-Warring States texts include the expression 'war chariot' (*bīngchē* 兵車) and 'military affairs' (*wǔshì* 武事). *Bīngchē* 兵車 is attested in the *Analects* and the *Zuǒzhuàn*. But it does not occur in bronze inscriptions or received pre-Warring States texts such as the *Chūnqiū*, the *Songs* (*Shī*), and the pre-Warring States parts of the *Shàngshū*. Similarly, *wǔshì* 武事 occurs in the *Zuǒzhuàn* and in later texts such as in the *Shāngjūnshū*, the *Guǎnzǐ*, and the *Gǔliángzhuàn*. But it also does not occur in bronze inscriptions, the *Chūnqiū*, the *Songs* (*Shī*), or the pre-Warring States parts of the *Shàngshū*. Another example is the word 'overlord/hegemon' (*bà* 霸, Middle Chinese: paeH). The character <霸> does occur in bronze inscriptions, where it only seems to be used (in expressions such as *shēng pò* 生霸, *sǐ pò* 死霸, Middle Chinese: phaek) as a calendrical term referring to the monthly recurring emergence of the moon. According to Chén Chūshēng 陳初

84 *From 'awe-inspiringly beautiful' to 'morally refined'*

生 (2004: 689–90), <霸> is not used in the meaning 'overlord/hegemon' in bronze inscriptions. The word 'overlord/hegemon' (*bà* 霸) is also not found in received pre-Warring States texts such as the *Chūnqiū*, the *Songs* (*Shī*), and the pre-Warring States parts of the *Shàngshū*. It is, however, found in both the *Zuǒzhuàn* and the *Analects*, as well as many Warring States texts (*Mencius, Xúnzǐ*, and so forth):

i 齊始霸也。
  Qí began acting as 'overlord' (*bà*). (*Zuǒ*, Zhuāng 15.1, tr. adapted from Durrant, Li, and Schaberg [2016: 117])
ii 子曰：「管仲相桓公，霸諸侯。
  When Guǎn zhòng served as prime minister to Duke Huán, he made him 'overlord' (*bà*) of the other feudal lords. (*Analects* 14.17, tr. adapted from Slingerland 2003a: 161).

The compound expression 'overlord king/hegemon king' (*bà wáng* 霸王), which is very frequent in numerous Warring States texts, also occurs in the *Zuǒzhuàn* (*Zuǒ*, Mǐn 1.2) but is not attested in any pre-Warring States text. If the term *bà* 霸 and *bà wáng* 霸王 were frequently used in meaning 'overlord' in the language of the reigns of Duke Zhuāng (r. 693–662 BCE) and Duke Mǐn (r. 661–660 BCE), then one would expect it to also be attested in other pre-Warring States texts, many of which focus on the doings of rulers. While all these examples may not constitute conclusive evidence that the *Zuǒzhuàn* reflects the Warring States vocabulary of its Warring States authors/compilers, they do at least bolster this hypothesis.

This, however, does not invalidate Pines' assumption that the *Zuǒzhuàn* "is largely based on the scribal records from various Chunqiu states" (2002c: 16). That is, I agree with Pines that the authors/compilers of the *Zuǒzhuàn* likely had access to earlier records, as well as to orally transmitted material. However, I suggest that authors of the *Zuǒzhuàn* mostly used fifth-century BCE vocabulary when they recounted the events mentioned in the records from the Spring and Autumn period that were available to them. This does not mean that I reject Pines' general assumption that the *Zuǒzhuàn* is a valuable source for the study of the history of the Spring and Autumn period. Sīmǎ Qiān recounted many earlier events based on records from those earlier periods. The fact that the *Shǐjì* 史記 largely reflects Hàn dynasty linguistic usage obviously does not completely invalidate its use as a source for the study of the pre-Hàn period.

Other scholars also place the composition of the *Zuǒzhuàn* in the Warring States period. See, for example, Brooks and Brooks (2015), who date the composition of the bulk of the content of the *Zuǒzhuàn* the mid-fourth century BCE. For discussion of other theories of the date and authenticity of the *Zuǒzhuàn*, see also Cheng (1993a: 67–76), Yáng Bójùn (1979: 65–75), Karlgren (1926: 1–65), Durrant, Li, and Schaberg (2016: xxxviii–lix), and Schaberg (2001a), among others.

86 *Zuǒ*, Xiāng 31.10, Yáng Bójùn (1990: 1191), tr. adapted from Durrant, Li, and Schaberg (2016: 1284–85).
87 This does not preclude later interpolations, or even the possibility of parts dating from the Qín or early Hàn periods. See John Knoblock (1988–1994: vol. 1: 105–28), Loewe (1993a: 178–88), and Hutton (2014).
88 Powers (1995: 223) translates *fǔfú* 黼黻 as "noble designs" and suggests that "by mid-Warring States times, the term often served simply as metonymy for any sumptuous counterchange pattern, i.e., a pattern in which figure and ground are reversible."
89 *Xúnzǐ* 10.9, Wáng Xiānqiān (1988: 185).
90 *Mán-yí* refers to the '(civilizationally inferior) non-Zhōu peoples (to the south-east)'; see the subsection titled "Ethnonym compounds" in chapter 4.
91 *Zuǒ*, Xiāng 31.13, Yáng Bójùn (1990: 1193–5), tr. adapted from Durrant, Li, and Schaberg (2016: 1292–93).
92 Baxter and Sagart (2014: 101) reconstruct the Old Chinese word which is later written <威> in received versions of pre-Qín texts as *ʔuj (> *wēi*) and the word written <畏>

as *ʔuj-s (> *wèi*). Both derive from the root *ʔuj. The *-s* suffix indicates a transitive verbal meaning. The word *ʔuj-s (> *wèi*) thus probably meant 'to fear; to frighten; threaten.' The word *ʔuj (> *wēi*) was a noun 'fright; fear' or adjective 'frightening; awe-inspiring.' Some excavated documents use the graph <畏> to write both the word *ʔuj and the word *ʔuj-s; see Gǔwénzì gǔlín (1999: vol. 9; 784).

93 Here both meanings ('nobleman' and 'noble man') appear to be evoked.

94 *Zuǒ*, Huán 2.2, Yáng Bójùn (1990: 86–9), tr. adapted from Durrant, Li, and Schaberg (2016: 76–7).

95 The word *dé* 德 is one of the words which becomes reanalyzed at the same time as the words *jūnzǐ* and *wén*. In the pre-Warring States period, *dé* referred to externally observable 'charismatic power.' It started to be reinterpreted in moral terms as 'moral virtue' at around the beginning of the Warring States period. Here I translate it as 'power' since it predominantly refers to the charismatic power of the ruler, be it defined aesthetically or ethically.

96 *Zuǒ*, Xī 24.1, Yáng Bójùn (1990: 418–9), tr. adapted from Durrant, Li, and Schaberg (2016: 378–79).

97 See Schaberg (2001a: 64).

98 For the dates of composition of the *Analects*, see note 28.

99 "The Explanation of the System of Posthumous Names" chapter in the *Yì Zhōu shū* 逸周書 describes the circumstances under which a person may be given various posthumous names. Though traditionally attributed to the Duke of Zhōu, it probably dates to Warring States or early Hàn times; see Shaughnessy (1993: 229–33). That it defines *wén* in moral terms also indicates that it is a Warring States text: "Someone whose Way and virtue is broad and thick may be called *wén*; someone who has studied assiduously and been fond of asking questions may be called **wén**; someone who has been kind and gracious in caring for the people may be called *wén*; someone who has had sympathy with the people and graciously performed the rites may be called **wén**" 道德博厚曰文，學勤好問曰文，慈惠愛民曰文，愍民惠禮曰文 (Huáng Huáixìn 黃懷信, Zhāng Màoróng 張懋鎔, and Tián Xùdōng 田旭東 2007: 635–7).

100 *Analects* 5.15, Chéng Shùdé (1997: 325).

101 Being part of the eulogizing lore following the death of high-status individuals, most (but not all) of posthumous titles are based on positive terms such as *wén* 'awe-inspiringly beautiful,' *líng* 靈 'potent'/'numinously efficacious,' and *huì* 惠 'wise.' Such positive posthumous titles were often less reflective of the carriers' true mettle than of the power and influence which their family and supporters kept exerting after their deaths.

102 It is important to distinguish between the historical Confucius and the persona(s) of Confucius portrayed in the *Analects*. A similar distinction must be made between the historical Xúnzǐ and the persona of Xúnzǐ created by the author(s) of the *Xúnzǐ*, the historical Mencius and the persona of Mencius presented in the *Mencius*, as well as for many other pre-Qin thinkers and their various persona(s). When I state that "Confucius justified Kǒng Yǔ's posthumous title by citing positive traits" this should be read as "the author(s) of *Analects* 5.15 portray Confucius as justifying Kǒng Yǔ's posthumous title by citing positive traits."

103 See also *Analects* 14.18, Chéng Shùdé (1997: 996–7), for a similar discussion of *wén* in posthumous titles.

104 *Xúnzǐ* 3.4, Wáng Xiānqiān (1988: 40–1).

105 Cf. Kryukov (1995: 314–33). For a somewhat different analysis of 'power/virtue' (*dé*) in pre-Qín texts, see Nivison (1996: 17–48) and Nivison (1978–79).

106 See the discussion of *dé* in Schwartz (1985: 76).

107 *Analects* 3.24 and 9.5 portrays Confucius as believing that 'Heaven' (*Tiān* 天) had destined him to spend his life teaching and promoting the 'Way' (*dào* 道) and

86 *From 'awe-inspiringly beautiful' to 'morally refined'*

'civility/civilization' (*wén*) of the founding Kings of the Zhōu dynasty; see Slingerland (2003a: 27; 71). In contrast, the "Discourse on Heaven" chapter in the *Xúnzǐ* clearly espoused a non-religious, proto-naturalistic view of 'heaven' (*tiān* 天) as the 'sky/atmosphere,' see Hutton (2014: 175–82) and Wáng Xiānqiān (1988: 306–20).

108 See the passage from Máo 262 discussed above in the subsection titled "From 'beautiful' (*wén*) 'nobleman' (*jūnzǐ*) to 'morally refined' (*wén*) 'noble man' (*jūnzǐ*): ethical re-interpretation of aesthetic *wén*" above.

109 *Analects* 16.1, Chéng Shùdé (1997: 1137). See also note 33 above.

110 *Analects* 1.15, Chéng Shùdé (1997: 136), tr. adapted from Slingerland (2003a: 6–7).

111 Slingerland (2003b: 53).

112 Since the concept of *wén* retains the connotation 'externally applied decorative pattern,' it fits well into the craft metaphors in the *Analects* and the *Xúnzǐ*. Slingerland's (2003b) metaphor analysis thus helps us understand why *wén* plays a central role in these works. According to Slingerland (2003b: 50), "[t]he primary metaphor for self-cultivation in the *Analects* is that of adornment. The SELF-CULTIVATION AS ADORNMENT schema informs the metaphor pair of 'native stuff' (*zhì* 質) and 'cultural refinement' (*wén* 文; lit. lines, strokes), as well as the most common term for self-cultivation itself, *xiu* 修 – literally, decorating or adorning a surface. This primary metaphor is often supplemented by and mixed with a related metaphor, SELF-CULTIVATION AS CRAFT, where the process of education is understood as an actual reshaping of the 'stuff' of the Self rather than the adornment of its surface." For *wén* and *zhì* contrast, see also Chong (1998) and Chong (2007: 1–19).

113 *Analects* 14.12, Chéng Shùdé (1997: 969), tr. adapted from Slingerland (2003a: 158).

114 *Analects* 6.18, Chéng Shùdé (1997: 400): "The Master said, 'When native substance dominates *wén*, then one is crude. When *wén* dominates native substance, one is a stickler. Only when *wén* and native substance are balanced, then you are a noble man'" 質勝文則野，文勝質則史，文質彬彬，然後君子.

115 See *Analects* 7.25, Chéng Shùdé (1997: 486): "The Master used four things to teach: *wén*, behavior, loyalty, and trust" 子以四教：文、行、忠、信.

116 See *Analects* 9.11, Chéng Shùdé (1997: 593–5): "Yán Huí, sighing, said . . . The Master . . . has broadened me with *wén* and restrained me with the rites (*lǐ*)" 顏淵喟然歎曰 . . . 夫子 . . . 博我以文，約我以禮.

117 In contrast, in the *Book of Songs*, and in the rest of the pre-Warring States corpus, *jūnzǐ* refers to 'rulers/lords' or 'noblemen.' Pre-Warring States texts contains no examples of the term *jūnzǐ* used exclusively in the sense 'morally refined gentleman (regardless of birth).' That is, in pre-Warring States texts *jūnzǐ* never refers to men of non-noble birth.

118 Technically the explicit comparison of 'pattern imitation' (*wénxué*) with cutting and carving to make jade discs is a simile rather than a metaphor. However, in Lakoff and Johnson's (1999) definition of conceptual metaphor, it still counts as a metaphor. That is, it uses a source domain of embodied experience (i.e., carving and polishing jade) to structure the abstract meanings in the target domain (i.e., the virtue–ethical notion of education and moral edification as a slow, gradual process).

119 The term *shì* 士 is notoriously difficult to translate. For lack of a better word, I use 'retainer–officials' as a stopgap translation.

120 *Xúnzǐ* 27.84, Wáng Xiānqiān (1988: 508), with <天子> emended as <天下> and <贛> changed to <貢>.

121 Although *wénxué* 文學 can mean 'literature' or 'literary studies' in later periods, I agree with Kern (2001) that such readings are anachronistic in pre-Qín texts. It is therefore unlikely that this is what it means in *Xúnzǐ* 27.84. Rather than referring narrowly to 'texts' or 'writing,' pre-Qín uses of *wén* in the expression *wénxué* refer to 'patterned civility/civilization' understood as social and moral 'patterns' (be they in sacrifice, rites, music, etc.). A better translation of *wénxué* would be 'polite studies' in the eighteenth-century sense referring to the study of the 'polite arts,' i.e., poetry, music, eloquence, and so forth. Legge (1861: 340) lists 'polite studies' as one of the

From 'awe-inspiringly beautiful' to 'morally refined'   87

possible translations of *wén* in his character index. As discussed below, the English word *polite* in the expression *polite studies* derives from the word *polished* through metaphorical extension. *Polite* and *wén* thus share the same connotations of being 'externally applied' to human behavior through education in the same way that a decorative pattern is applied to the surface of a physical object. For a different analysis of *wénxué*, see Chow (1979).

122 This image can be found online: www.harvardartmuseums.org/collections/object/ 204830. I am grateful the Harvard Art Museums/Arthur M. Sackler Museum for granting permission to reprint it here.

123 Lakoff and Johnson (1999).

124 This analysis of crafts metaphors in the *Xúnzǐ* is based in large part on Slingerland (2003b: 237).

125 *The Songs* did not have to have been written down to form the basis of an exegetical tradition. The *Songs* originated as a collection of popular songs and court liturgy and continued to be transmitted and expounded on as an oral tradition down into the Warring States period, in addition to being transmitted in writing. In India, the *Vedas* were passed down faithfully for centuries before they were written down and oral transmission continues to highly valued even today, more than two millennia after the emergence of writing in India; see Salomon (1998) and Daniels and Bright (1996).

126 According to *Analects* 7.1, Confucius himself said that he "trusted and loved the old ways" and that he "transmitted but did not innovate." As discussed above, ideally he would have liked the world to return to the golden age of the early Zhōu dynasty. In that sense, he is clearly conservative. Especially from the point of view of thinkers, such as Hán Fēi, who believe that contemporary problems need contemporary solutions and who on multiple occasions ridicule the *rú* for their desire to return to old ways. However, it should not be forgotten that Confucius' reinterpretation of the 'awe-inspiringly beauty' (*wén*) of 'noblemen' as the 'moral refinement' (*wén*) of 'noble men' (*jūnzǐ*) is in itself a major innovation. If Confucius' non-aristocratic students traveled back in time, they would likely be surprised to see that their revered King Wén would not recognize them as the 'morally refined' (*wén*) 'noble men' (*jūnzǐ*) that Confucius judged them to be, but rather as the commoners that they were, socially speaking. At the time of King Wén, *wén* did not mean 'morally refined' but rather 'awe-inspiringly beautiful.'

127 See Schaberg (1999) for analysis of rhetorical use of intertextual references to the *Songs* in early Chinese historiographical writing.

128 For a detailed account of the emergence of a body of canonical texts in early China, see Nylan (2001).

129 Original French: "Les peuples qui ont *poli* tous les autres ont été commerçants" (Raynal 1794 [1770]: vol. 1; 5).

130 Original Fr.: "Qui est-ce qui a rassemblé, vêtu, *civilisé* ces peuples? . . . C'est le commerce." (Raynal 1794 [1770]: vol. 1; 5).

131 The English word *polite* is now a dead metaphor. For most people being *polite* no longer evokes the idea of being *polished*. In contrast, in French the homonymy of *poli* 'polite' and *poli* 'polished' has kept the metaphorical association alive.

132 Shapin (2003: 171).

133 The word *wén* is attested in the meaning 'awe-inspiringly beautiful' in the earliest written records from the late Shāng, ca. 1300–1100 BCE. Although we have no attestations of the *wén* in the meaning 'pattern' from this period, it is still likely that this was the original meaning of the word. It is easy to explain how a word that means 'pattern' can be extended to mean 'patterned' > 'pattern-decorated' > 'decorated' > 'beautifully decorated' > 'beautiful.' It is less obvious how a word that means 'beautiful' should come to mean 'pattern.' Based on the relative plausibility of a path of lexicalization from going from 'pattern' to 'beautiful,' it seems reasonable to assume that the basic meaning of *wén* was 'pattern.' Note that this also explains why the word

88 *From 'awe-inspiringly beautiful' to 'morally refined'*

> *wén* continues to be used to refer to various kinds of 'patterns,' and why the extended meanings such as 'civility' has connotations related to 'patterns,' e.g., the jade carving metaphors for self-cultivation that imply that 'ritualized civility' (*wén*) is a 'pattern' (*wén*) carved unto 'human nature' (*xìng* 性) or 'native substance' (*zhì* 質).

134 Given the absence of attested writing before this period, we naturally have no way of determining when these semantic changes happened. Hence, in Figure 2.3, I write "????" instead of a specific time period.

135 The diachronic lexical semantic mapping of the polysemy of word *wén* in Figure 2.3 is inspired by Geeraerts (1997: 47–62). Other meanings of the *wén*, e.g., 'rhetoric' (i.e., 'decorated/patterned speech'), 'graphical sign/writing,' and so forth, are not directly relevant to tracing the metaphorical extension from 'pattern' to 'civility/civilization' and have not been included here.

References

Adkins, Arthur W. H. 1960. *Merit and Responsibility: A Study in Greek Values* (Clarendon Press: Oxford).

Allan, Sarah. 1991. *The Shape of the Turtle: Myth, Art, and Cosmos in Early China* (SUNY Press: Albany).

Baxter, William Hubbard, and Laurent Sagart. 2014. *Old Chinese: A New Reconstruction* (Oxford University Press: Oxford).

Bergeton, Uffe. 2013. 'From Pattern to "Culture"? Emergence and Transformations of Metacultural *Wén*', Dissertation, The University of Michigan.

———. forthcoming. 'From "Awe-Inspiringly Beautiful" to "Patterns in Conventionalized Behavior": Historical Development of the Metacultural Concept of *Wén* in Pre-Qín China', *Journal of the American Oriental Society*.

Blakeley, Barry B. 1977–1979. 'Functional Disparities in the Socio-Political Traditions of Spring and Autumn China, Pts. I-III', *Journal of the Economic and Social History of the Orient*, 20 & 22: pt.1 (Jan 1979): 81–118; pt.2 (May 77): 208–43; pt.3 (Oct 77): 307–43.

Blitstein, Pablo Ariel. 2016. 'From "Ornament" to "Literature": An Uncertain Substitution in Nineteenth-Twentieth Century China', *Modern Chinese Literature and Culture*, 28.

Bol, Peter Kees. 1992. *"This Culture of Ours": Intellectual Transitions in T'ang and Sung China* (Stanford University Press: Stanford, CA).

Brooks, Bruce, and Taeko Brooks. 1998. *The Original Analects: Sayings of Confucius and His Successors* (Columbia University Press: New York).

———. 2015. *The Emergence of China: From Confucius to the Empire* (Warring States Project: University of Massachusetts at Amherst).

Brunner, Otto, Werner Conze, and Reinhart Koselleck (eds.). 1972–1979. *Geschichtliche Grundbegriffe: historisches Lexikon zur politisch-sozialen Sprache in Deutschland* (E. Klett: Stuttgart).

Bryant, William Cullen. 2015. *The Odyssey*. Translated into blank verse by William Cullen Bryant (Calla Editions: New York).

Carr, David, and Jan W. Steutel. 1999. *Virtue Ethics and Moral Education* (Routledge: London).

Chang, Kwang-chih. 1980. *Shang Civilization* (Yale University Press: New Haven).

Chén Chūshēng 陳初生. 2004. *Jīnwén chángyòng zìdiǎn* 金文常用字典 (Shanxi ren min chu ban she: Xi'an).

From 'awe-inspiringly beautiful' to 'morally refined' 89

Cheng, Anne. 1993a. 'Ch'un ch'iu 春秋, Kung yang 公羊, Ku liang 穀梁 and Tso chuan 左傳', in Michael Loewe (ed.), *Early Chinese Texts: A Bibliographical Guide* (Society for the Study of Early China: Berkeley, CA).

———. 1993b. 'Lun yü 論語', in Michael Loewe (ed.), *Early Chinese Texts: A Bibliographical Guide* (Society for the Study of Early China: Institute of East Asian Studies & University of California Press: Berkeley, CA).

Chéng, Shùdé 程樹德. 1997. *Lúnyǔ jíshì* 論語集釋 (Zhōnghuá shūjú: Běijīng).

Chong, Kim-Chong. 1998. 'The Aesthetic Moral Personality: *Li, Yi, Wen*, and *Chih* in the *Analects*', *Monumenta Serica*, 46: 69–90.

———. 2007. *Early Confucian Ethics: Concepts and Arguments* (Open Court: Chicago & La Salle, IL).

Chow, Tse-tsung. 1979. 'Ancient Chinese Views on Literature, the *Tao* and Their Relationship', *Chinese Literature: Essays, Articles, Reviews (CLEAR)*, 1: 1–29.

Collins, Randall. 1998. *The Sociology of Philosophies: A Global Theory of Intellectual Change* (Belknap Press of Harvard University Press: Cambridge).

Cook, Constance A., and Paul R. Goldin (eds.). 2016. *A Source Book of Ancient Chinese Bronze Inscriptions* (Society for the Study of Early China: Berkeley, CA).

Daniels, Peter T., and William Bright. 1996. *The World's Writing Systems* (Oxford University Press: New York).

Dobson, W. A. C. H. 1967. 'Authenticating and Dating Archaic Chinese Texts', *T'oung Pao*, 53: 233–42.

Donlan, Walter. 1973. 'The Origin of Kalos Kagathos', *The American Journal of Philology*, 94: 365–74.

Dù Zhèngshèng 杜正勝. 1979. *Zhōu dài chéng bāng* 周代城邦 (Lianjing: Taipei).

Durrant, Stephen W., Wai-yee Li, and David Schaberg. 2016. *Zuo Tradition: Zuozhuan* (University of Washington Press: Seattle).

Falkenhausen, Lothar von. 1996. 'The Concept of Wen in the Ancient Chinese Ancestral Cult', *Chinese Literature: Essays, Articles, Reviews (CLEAR)*, 18: 1–22.

———. 2006. *Chinese Society in the Age of Confucius (1000–250 BC). The Archaeological Evidence* (Cotsen Institute of Archaeology University of California Press: Los Angeles, CA).

Febvre, Lucien. 1973. *A New Kind of History: From the Writings of Febvre* (Harper & Row: New York).

Franke, Otto. 1930. *Geschichte des Chinesischen Reiches: eine Darstellung seiner Entstehung, seines Wesens und seiner Entwicklung bis zur neuesten Zeit* (Walter de Gruyter: Berlin).

Furetière, Antoine. 1727. *Dictionnaire universel* (P. Husson: Paris).

Gassmann, Robert H. 2007. 'Die Bezeichnung jun-zi: Ansätze zur Chun-qiu-zeitlichen Kontextualisierung und zur Bedeutungsbestimmung im Lun Yu', in Hermann Marc and Christian Schwermann (eds.), *In Zurück zur Freude: Studien zur chinesischen Literatur und Lebenswelt und ihrer Rezeption in Ost und West: Festschrift für Wolfgang Kubin* (Institut Monumenta Serica: Sankt Augustin), pp. 411–36.

Gawlikowski, Krzysztof. 1985. 'The School of Strategy (*bing jia*) in the Context of Chinese Civilization', *East and West*, 35: 167–210.

———. 1987. 'The Concept of Two Fundamental Social Principles: *Wen* and *Wu* in Chinese Classical Thought (Part I)', *Annali*, 47: 397–433.

——. 1988. 'The Concept of Two Fundamental Social Principles: *Wen* and *Wu* in Chinese Classical Thought. (Part II)', *Annali*, 48: 35–62.

90 *From 'awe-inspiringly beautiful' to 'morally refined'*

Geeraerts, Dirk. 1997. *Diachronic Prototype Semantics: A Contribution to Historical Lexicology* (Clarendon Press: Oxford).

Gernet, Jacques. 1982. *A History of Chinese Civilization* (Cambridge University Press: Cambridge).

———. 1999. *Le monde chinois* (A. Colin: Paris).

Guō Mòruò 郭沫若. 1954. *Jīnwén cóngkǎo* 金文叢考, 3 vols (Kexue: Beijing).

Gǔwénzì gǔlín. 1999. *Gǔwénzì gǔlín* 古文字詁林 (Shànghǎi jiàoyù chūbǎnshè: Shànghǎi).

Hsu, Cho-yun. 1965. *Ancient China in Transition: An Analysis of Social Mobility, 722–222 B.C.* (Stanford University Press: Stanford, CA).

———. 1999. 'The Spring and Autumn Period', in Michael Loewe and L. Edward Shaughnessy (eds.), *Cambridge History of Ancient China: From the Origins of Civilization to 221 B.C.* (Cambridge University Press: Cambridge).

Huáng Huáixin 黃懷信, Zhāng Màoróng 張懋鎔, and Tián Xùdōng 田旭東. 2007. *Yìzhōushū huìjiào jízhù* 逸周書彙校集注 (Shànghǎi gǔjí chūbǎnshè: Shànghǎi).

Hui, Victoria Tin-bor. 2005. *War and State Formation in Ancient China and Early Modern Europe* (Cambridge University Press: Cambridge).

Hunter, Michael. 2017. *Confucius Beyond the Analects* (Brill: Leiden).

Hutton, Eric L. 2014. *Xunzi* (Princeton University Press: Princeton).

Jì Xùshēng 季旭昇. 2010. *Shuōwén xīn zhèng* 說文新證 (Fújiàn rénmín chūbǎnshè: Fúzhōu).

Kakinuma, Yohei. 2015. *Chūgoku kodai no kahei: okane o meguru hitobito to kurashi* (Yoshikawa Kōbunkan: Tokyo).

Karlgren, Bernhard. 1926. 'On the Authenticity and Nature of the *Tso Chuan*', *Göteborgs Högscholas Årsskrift*, 32: 1–65.

———. 1929. 'The Authenticity of Ancient Chinese Texts', *Bulletin of the Museum of Far Eastern Antiquities*, 29: 165–83.

———. 1950. *The Book of Odes* (Museum of Far Eastern Antiquities: Stockholm).

Keightley, David N. 1999. 'The Shang: China's First Historical Dynasty', in Michael Loewe and L. Edward Shaughnessy (eds.), *Cambridge History of Ancient China: From the Origins of Civilization to 221 B.C.* (Cambridge University Press: Cambridge), pp. 232–91.

———. 2000. *The Ancestral Landscape: Time, Space, and Community in late Shang China, ca. 1200–1045 B.C.* (University of California Center for Chinese Studies: Berkeley, CA).

———. 2012. *Working for His Majesty: Research Notes on Labor Mobilization in Late Shang China (ca. 1200–1045 B.C.)* (Institute of East Asian Studies & University of California Press: Berkeley, CA).

Kern, Martin. 2001. 'Ritual, Text, and the Formation of the Canon: Historical Transitions of "Wen" in Early China', *T'oung Pao*, 87: 43–91.

Knoblock, John. 1988–1994. *Xunzi: A Translation and Study of the Complete Works* (Stanford University Press: Stanford, CA).

Kolb, Raimund Theodor. 1991. *Die Infantrie im alten China: ein Beitrag zur Militärgeschichte der Vor-Zhan-Guo-Zeit* (P. von Zabern: Mainz am Rhein).

Kryukov, Vassili. 1995. 'Symbols of Power and Communication in Pre-Confucian China (On the Anthropology of "de"): Preliminary Assumptions', *Bulletin of the School of Oriental and African Studies*, 58: 314–33.

Lakoff, George, and Mark Johnson. 1999. *Philosophy in the Flesh: The Embodied Mind and Its Challenge to Western Thought* (Basic Books: New York).

Legge, James. 1861. *The Chinese Classics* (Trübner & Co.: London).

———. 1876. *The She King, or: The Book of Ancient Poetry* (Trubner: London).

From 'awe-inspiringly beautiful' to 'morally refined'   91

Lewis, Mark Edward. 1990. *Sanctioned Violence in Early China* (SUNY Press: Albany).

———. 1999. 'Warring States Political History', in Michael Loewe and L. Edward Shaughnessy (eds.), *Cambridge History of Ancient China: From the Origins of Civilization to 221 B.C.* (Cambridge University Press: Cambridge), pp. 587–650.

———. 2007. *The Early Chinese Empires: Qin and Han* (Belknap Press of Harvard University Press: Cambridge, MA).

Li, Feng. 2008a. *Bureaucracy and the State in Early China: Governing the Western Zhou* (Cambridge University Press: Cambridge).

———. 2008b. 'Transmitting Antiquity: The Origin and Paradigmization of the "Five Ranks"', in Dieter Kuhn and Helga Stahl (eds.), *Perceptions of Antiquity in Chinese Civilization* (Edition Forum: Heidelberg).

Lǐ Zōngkūn 李宗焜. 2012. *Jiǎ gǔ wén zì biān* 甲骨文字編 (Zhonghua shuju: Beijing).

Liú Shàojǐn 刘绍瑾. 2010. 'Zhōu dài lǐ zhì de "wén" huà yǔ Rú jiā měi xué de wén zhì guān 周代礼制的"文"化与儒家美学的文质观', *Wén yì yán jiū* 文艺研究: 40–8.

Liu Yu 劉雨, and Lu Yan 盧岩 (eds.). 2002. *Jìnchū Yīn-Zhōu jīnwén jílù* 近出殷周金文集錄 (Zhonghua shuju: Beijing).

Liú Zéhuá 刘泽华. 2004. *Xiān Qín shìrén shèhuì* 先秦士人与社会 (Tiānjīn rénmín chūbǎnshè: Tiānjīn).

Loewe, Michael. 1993a. 'Hsün tzu 荀子', in Michael Loewe (ed.), *Early Chinese Texts: A Bibliographical Guide* (Society for the Study of Early China: Institute of East Asian Studies & University of California Press: Berkeley, CA), pp. 178–88.

———. 1993b. 'Shih ching 詩經', in Michael Loewe (ed.), *Early Chinese Texts: A Bibliographical Guide* (Society for the Study of Early China: Institute of East Asian Studies & University of California Press: Berkeley, CA), pp. 415–23.

Makeham, John. 1996. 'The Formation of Lunyu as a Book', *Monumenta Serica*, 44: 1–24.

Meyer, Dirk. 2012. *Philosophy on Bamboo: Text and the Production of Meaning in Early China* (Brill: Leiden).

———. forthcoming. *Traditions of Documents* 書 *and Political Argument in Early China.* (Walter de Gruyter: Berlin).

Morton, W. Scott. 1971. 'The Confucian Concept of Man: The Original Formulation', *Philosophy East and West*, 21: 69–77.

Nienhauser, William H., Jr. 1994. *The Grand Scribe's Records, Volume I. The Basic Annals of Pre-Han China by Ssu-ma Ch'ien* (Indiana University Press: Bloomington & Indianapolis).

Nivison, David S. 1978–1979. 'Royal "Virtue" in Shang Oracle Inscriptions', *Early China*, 4: 52–5.

———. 1996. *The Ways of Confucianism: Investigations in Chinese Philosophy* (Open Court: Chicago).

Nylan, Michael. 2001. *The Five "Confucian" Classics* (Yale University Press: New Haven).

———. 2010. '*Yin-yang*, Five Phases, and *Qi*', in Michael Nylan and Michael Loewe (eds.), *China's Early Empires: A Re-Appraisal* (Cambridge University Press: Cambridge), pp. 398–414.

Nylan, Michael, and Thomas A. Wilson. 2010. *Lives of Confucius: Civilization's Greatest Sage Through the Ages* (Doubleday: New York).

Péng Yàfēi 彭亚非. 1996. 'Xiān Qín lùn "wén" sānchóng yàoyì 先秦论"文"三重要义', *Wén shǐ zhé* 文史哲: 41–5.

———. 2005. 'yuán "wén" – lùn "wén" zhī chū shǐ yì jí yuán hán yì 原"文" – 論"文"之初始義及元涵義', *Wén xué píng lùn* 文学评论: 75–82.

92   *From 'awe-inspiringly beautiful' to 'morally refined'*

Pines, Yuri. 2002a. 'Changing Views of *Tianxia* in Pre-Imperial Discourse', *Oriens Extremus*, 43: 101–16.

———. 2002b. 'Lexical Changes in Zhanguo Texts', *Journal of the American Oriental Society*, 122: 691–705.

———. 2002c. *Foundations of Confucian Thought: Intellectual Life in the Chunqiu Period (722–453 B.C.E.)* (University of Hawaii Press: Honolulu).

———. 2009. *Envisioning Eternal Empire: Chinese Political Thought of the Warring States Era* (University of Hawaii Press: Honolulu).

———. 2016. 'A "Total War"? Rethinking Military Ideology in the Book of Lord Shang', *Journal of Chinese Military History*, 5: 97–134.

Powers, Martin Joseph. 1995. 'The Figure in the Carpet: Reflections on the Discourse of Ornament in Zhou China', *Monumenta Serica*, 43: 211–33.

———. 2006. *Pattern and Person: Ornament, Society, and Self in Classical China* (Harvard University Asia Center: Cambridge, MA).

Puett, Michael. 2001. *The Ambivalence of Creation: Debates Concerning Innovation and Artifice in Early China* (Stanford University Press: Stanford, CA).

Qū Wànlǐ 屈萬里. 1983. *Xiān-Qín wénshǐ zīliào kǎobiàn* 先秦文史資料考辨 (Lianjing chuban shiye gongsi: Taibei).

Raynal, G. T. 1794 [1770]. *Histoire philosophique et politique des établissemens et du commerce des Européens dans les deux Indes* (chez Berry: Paris).

Rubin, Vitaliĭ. 1968. 'Chelovek v drevnekitaiskoi mysli [Man in the Ancient Chinese Thought]', *Narody Asii i Afriki*, 6: 73–8.

———. 1976. *Individual and State in Ancient China: Essays on Four Chinese Philosophers* (Columbia University Press: New York).

Salomon, Richard. 1998. *Indian Epigraphy: A Guide to the Study of Inscriptions in Sanskrit, Prakrit, and the Other Indo-Aryan Languages* (Oxford University Press: Oxford).

Sawyer, Ralph D. 1993. *The Seven Military Classics of Ancient China* (Westview Press: Boulder, San Francisco & Oxford).

Schaberg, David. 1999. 'Song and the Historical Imagination in Early China', *Harvard Journal of Asiatic Studies*, 59: 305–61.

———. 2001a. *A Patterned Past: Form and Thought in Early Chinese Historiography* (Harvard University Asia Center: Distributed by Harvard University Press: Cambridge, MA).

———. 2001b. 'Review: "Sell It! Sell It!": Recent Translations of Lunyu', *Chinese Literature: Essays, Articles, Reviews (CLEAR)*, 23: 115–39.

Schuessler, Axel. 1987. *A Dictionary of Early Zhou Chinese* (University of Hawaii Press: Honolulu).

Schwartz, Benjamin I. 1985. *The World of Thought in Ancient China* (Belknap Press of Harvard University Press: Cambridge, MA).

Shapin, Steven. 2003. 'The Image of the Man of Science', in David C. Lindberg and Ronald L. Numbers (eds.), *The Cambridge History of Science*. Vol. 4. Eighteenth-Century Science (Cambridge University Press: Cambridge), pp. 159–79.

Shaughnessy, Edward J. 1993. 'I Chou shu 逸周書', in Michael Loewe (ed.), *Early Chinese Texts: A Bibliographical Guide* (Society for the Study of Early China: Institute of East Asian Studies & University of California Press: Berkeley, CA), pp. 229–33.

———. 1999a. 'Western Zhou History', in Michael Loewe and L. Edward Shaughnessy (eds.), *Cambridge History of Ancient China: From the Origins of Civilization to 221 B.C.* (Cambridge University Press: Cambridge), pp. 292–351.

From 'awe-inspiringly beautiful' to 'morally refined' 93

——. 1999b. 'Calendar and Chronology', in Michael Loewe and L. Edward Shaughnessy (eds.), *Cambridge History of Ancient China: From the Origins of Civilization to 221 B.C.* (Cambridge University Press: Cambridge), pp. 19–29.

Shirakawa Shizuka 白川靜. 1983. *Zhōngguó gǔdài wénhuà* 中國古代文化 (Wenjin chubanshe: Taibei).

Slingerland, Edward G. 2003a. *Analects: With Selections from Traditional Commentaries* (Hackett: Indianapolis).

——. 2003b. *Effortless Action: Wu-wei as Conceptual Metaphor and Spiritual Ideal in Early China* (Oxford University Press: Oxford).

SSJZS. 1980. *Shísān jīng zhù shū* 十三經注疏 (Zhōnghuá shūjú: Běijīng).

Taylor, A. E. 1957. *Plato: The Man and His Work* (Meridian Books: New York).

Underhill, Anne P., and Hui Fang. 2004. 'Early State Economic Systems in China', in Gary M. Feinman and Linda M. Nicholas (eds.), *The Economics of Ancient Chiefdoms and States* (University of Utah Press: Salt Lake City).

Verity, Anthony. 2016. *The Odyssey.* Translated by Anthony Verity (Oxford University Press: Oxford).

Waley, Arthur. 1996. *The Books of Songs* (Grove Press: New York).

Wang, Aihe. 2000. *Cosmology and Political Culture in Early China* (Cambridge University Press: Cambridge).

Wáng Guówéi 王國維. 1987. *Guāntáng jílin* 觀堂集林, 4 vols (Zhonghua: Beijing).

Wāng Shòukuān 汪受寬. 1995. *Shì fǎ yán jiū* 谥法研究 (Shanghai guji chubanshe: Shanghai).

Wáng Xiānqiān 王先謙. 1988. *Xúnzǐ jíjiě* 荀子集解 (Běijīng Zhōnghuá shūjú: Běijīng).

——. (eds.). 2008. *Shìmíng shūzhèng bǔ* 釋名疏證補 (Zhonghua shuju: Beijing).

Wáng Xiānshèn 王先慎. 2006. *Hánfēizǐ jíjiě* 韓非子集解 (Běijīng Zhōnghuá shūjú: Běijīng).

Watson, Burton. 2007. *The Analects of Confucius* (Columbia University Press: New York).

Weber, Max. 1957. *The Theory of Social and Economic Organization.* Translated by A. M. Henderson and Talcott Parsons (Free Press: Glencoe).

——. 1968. *Max Weber on Charisma and Institution Building: Selected Papers* (Chicago University Press: Chicago).

——. 1991. *From Max Weber: Essays in Sociology* (Routledge: London & New York).

Wheatley, Paul. 1971. *The Pivot of the Four Quarters: A Preliminary Enquiry into the Origins and Character of the Ancient Chinese City* (University of Chicago Press: Chicago).

Xiàng Xī 向熹. 1986. *Shījīng cídiǎn* 詩經詞典 (Sìchuān rénmín chūbǎnshè: Chéngdū).

Xú Zhōngshū 徐中舒. 2006. *Jiǎgǔwén zìdiǎn* 甲骨文字典 (Sichun cishu chubanshe: Chengdu).

Yáng Bójùn 楊伯峻. 1979. '*Zuǒzhuàn* chéngshū niándài lùnshù 《左傳》成書年代論述 (Discussion and Exposition of the Compilation of the *Zuǒzhuàn*)', *Wenshi*, 6: 65–75.

——. 1990. *Chūnqiū Zuǒzhuàn zhù* 春秋左傳注 (Zhonghu shuju: Beijing).

Yáng Kuān 楊寬. 1999. *Xī Zhōu shǐ* 西周史 (Shànghǎi rénmín chūbǎnshè: Shànghǎi).

——. 2003. *Zhànguó shǐ* 戰國史 (Shànghǎi rénmín chūbǎnshè: Shànghǎi).

Yates, Robin D. S. 1987. 'Social Status in the Ch'in: Evidence from the Yun-meng Legal Documents. Part One: Commoners', *Harvard Journal of Asiatic Studies*, 47: 197–231.

——. 1988. 'New Light on Ancient Chinese Military Texts: The Development of Military Specialization', *T'oung Pao*, 74: 212–48.

——. 1994. 'Body, Space, Time, Bureaucracy: Boundary Creation and Control Mechanisms in Early China', in John Hay (ed.), *Boundaries in China* (Reaktion Books: London), pp. 56–80.

94 *From 'awe-inspiringly beautiful' to 'morally refined'*

———. 1995. 'State Control of Bureaucrats Under the Qin: Techniques and Procedures', *Early China*, 20: 331–66.

———. 1999. 'Early China', in Kurt A. Raaflaub and Nathan Stewart Rosenstein (eds.), *War and Society in the Ancient and Medieval worlds: Asia, the Mediterranean, Europe, and Mesoamerica* (Harvard University Press: Cambridge, MA), pp. 9–46.

Yīn Zhōu jīnwén jíchéng 殷周金文集成引得. 1984–1994. (Zhonghua shuju: Beijing).

Yú Yīngshí 余英時. 1987. *Shi yu Zhongguo wenhua* (Shanghai ren min chu ban she: Shanghai).

Zhāng Yàchū 張亞初. 2012. *Yīn Zhōu jīnwén jíchéng yǐndé* 殷周金文集成引得 (Zhonghua shuju: Beijing).

3 Coiners and critics of 'civility/civilization' (*wén*)

The Master [that is, Confucius] said, "As for the Zhōu, it could inspect the two [preceding] dynasties [that is, the Xià and the Shāng]. How splendid! How 'civilized' (wén) indeed! I follow the [the ways of the] Zhōu."

—*Analects*, 3.14[1]

'Civility/Civilization' (wén) destroyed their inner substance and broad learning drowned people's heart-minds. They began to be confused and disordered . . . From this we can see that the age had lost the Way and the Way had lost the age.

—*Zhuāngzǐ*, "Mending Nature"[2]

By the Warring States period (481–221 BCE), the term *wén* had begun to refer to an early Chinese concept of 'civility' understood as 'moral refinement' or the 'refinement of manners and conduct' of a 'noble man' (*jūnzǐ*). The question follows whether it could also be used in extended meanings to refer to an indigenous concept of 'civilization' similar to the early modern European universal concept of 'civilization.' Determining the extent to which a language-specific pre-Qín concept refers to a combination of semantic molecules akin to those of the language-specific eighteenth-century European universal concept of 'civilization' will shed light on the question of when a particular form of civilizational consciousness was coined in pre-Qín China. In addition to the 'civility' of *individuals*, discussed in Chapter 2, we shall examine if it is possible to identify the semantic component of 'police' (institutions and government regulations, laws, etc.) of *social formations* such as a states or empires, and if the meaning components of 'progress,' 'distinction(s),' and 'universality' are present in one form or another.

The concept of *wén* was a contentious topic in Warring States philosophical debates. In the virtue ethics of *Analects* and the *Xúnzǐ*, the idea of 'civility/civilization' (*wén*) was one of the key theoretical concepts of moral philosophy and statecraft. In contrast, other pre-Qín works, such as the *Mòzǐ*, the *Hánfēizǐ*, and the "Mending Nature" chapter of the *Zhuāngzǐ*, either explicitly rejected or simply had no use for the concept of 'civility/civilization' (*wén*). Examining these varying appraisals of the concept of 'civility/civilization' (*wén*) helps us understand the complex fragmentation of pre-Qín civilizational consciousness. We can

96 *Coiners and critics of 'civility/civilization' (wén)*

also solve a hitherto overlooked mystery: why did Mencius, who like Xúnzĭ was a self-proclaimed follower of Confucius and who also proposed a moral philosophy based on virtue ethics, avoid using the term *wén* as a philosophical concept? Since 'civility/civilization' (*wén*) is a key concept in the philosophies of the *Analects* and the *Xúnzĭ*, the *Mencius*' silence regarding this concept is striking.

Coiners of civilizational consciousness: from 'civility' to 'civility/civilization'

Like the early modern European universal concept of 'civilization,' the pre-Qín notion of 'civility/civilization' (*wén*) was a moralizing, prescriptive concept that referred to ideal traits of people and social formations. Not surprisingly, pre-Qín coiners and promoters of the concept of 'civility/civilization' (*wén*), such as the authors of the *Analects* and the *Xúnzĭ*, tended to be moral philosophers who embraced a form of virtue ethics based on the belief that innate human nature needs improvement through moral education and self-cultivation. They saw social institutions and regulations ('police') as the product of a long process of discovery of the ideal patterns of human behavior initiated by the ancient sage–kings.[3] For the coiners of *wén* in the meaning 'civility/civilization' civilizing the world by spreading knowledge of the ideal conventions of 'civility' and 'police' established by the founders of the Zhōu dynasty was part of a vocation to promote the ideal 'Way' (*dào*) of living a human life and ruling a state.

'Moral refinement' (wén) of 'dynasties' and 'states': an element of 'police'

Uses of *wén* to describe social formations such as states or dynasties as 'morally refined' indicate that *wén* contains a semantic molecule similar to the semantic molecule of 'police' of the early European concept of 'civilization.' As discussed in Chapter 2, the reinterpretation of adjectival uses of *wén* from 'awe-inspiringly beautiful' to 'morally refined' in descriptions of individuals was one of the early steps in the development of abstract uses of *wén* as a noun referring to a language-specific concept of 'civility/civilization' in pre-Qín texts. After this semantic shift had taken place, the new meaning of *wén* as 'moral refinement' or 'civility' could then be used to describe entire dynasties as 'morally refined'/'civilized,' as Confucius is reported to have done in the *Analects*:

(1) The Master [Confucius] said, "As for the Zhōu, when viewed on the background of the two [preceding] dynasties [i.e., the Xià and the Shāng], how splendid! How **'civilized'/'morally refined'** (*wén*) indeed! I follow the [the ways of the] Zhōu." (子曰周監於二代，郁郁乎文哉！吾從周)[4]

Confucius sets apart the Zhōu as the most 'morally refined' or 'civilized' (*wén*) of the three 'dynasties' (*dài* 代).[5] But what does it mean to say that a dynasty is 'morally refined'? An individual's moral refinement is observable in her behavior and

*Coiners and critics of 'civility/civilization' (*wén*)* 97

demeanor, that is, her 'civility.' In contrast, the 'moral refinement' of social formations, such as 'states' (*guó* 國) or 'dynasties' (*dài* 代), is manifested in the sophis-
tication and appropriateness of their institutions, values, and regulations, that is,
their 'police.' For Confucius, the ritualized government of the Western Zhōu—or
at least his view of what it was like—was the best possible system of government.
It is therefore not surprising that he would call the Zhōu dynasty 'morally refined'
or 'civilized' (*wén*). As illustrated by the analysis of the early modern European
concept of 'civilization' in Chapter 1, while individuals improve along the dimension of 'civility,' larger social formations (states, dynasties, etc.) improve along
the dimension of 'police' by developing better government institutions. The use
of adjectival *wén* in (1) thus includes an element of 'police.'

A passage in the *Zuǒzhuàn* describes 'morally refined power/virtue' (*wén dé*
文德) as something that a 'state' (*guó* 國) can either have or lack: "There is no
greater disaster than if a small state is without 'morally refined virtue' (*wén dé*) but
still [wants to] have military achievements."[6] This implies that 'states' (*guó*) can
be 'morally refined' (*wén*). As in (1), this 'moral refinement' or 'civility' of a state
refers to the refinement of its institutionalized regulations and values, that is, its
'police.' In other words, 'civilized' (*wén*) states are well-governed and 'policed.'

The *Analects* 9.5 contains one of the earliest attested uses of *wén* as a noun
referring to a concept of a 'morally refined tradition of values and institutions' or
'civilization' comprising the semantic molecules of 'civility' and 'police':

(2) When the Master was threatened in Kuāng, he said: After King **Wén** had
died, did **'civility/civilization' (*wén*)** not remain here? If Heaven was going
to destroy this **'civility/civilization' (*wén*)**, those of us dying after [King
Wén] would never have been able to participate in this **'civility/civilization'
(*wén*)**. And since Heaven has not yet destroyed this **'civility/civilization'
(*wén*)**, what can the people of Kuāng do to me? (子畏於匡，曰：文王既
沒，文不在茲乎？天之將喪斯文也，後死者不得與於斯文也；天之未
喪斯文也，匡人其如予乎)[7]

When Confucius allegedly uttered this statement, King Wén had been dead for
half a millennium. It is therefore unlikely that *wén* referred to King Wén's personal 'moral refinement.' King Wén's more enduring legacy, which had been
passed down and could still be observed, was the refined elite tradition of manners
('civility') and government institutions ('police') established under his virtuous
rule, that is, the 'civility/civilization'(*wén*) of the early Western Zhōu. The passage in (2) implies that 'Heaven' (*tiān* 天), the highest deity in the Zhōu pantheon,
had destined Confucius to carry on the civilizing project of King Wén.

Professionalization of the arts of peace and war and the emergence of a 'civil' versus 'military' contrast of principles of government

Indications that the concept of 'civility/civilization' (*wén*) could comprise an element of 'police' can also be found in the emergent contrast between 'civil' (*wén*)

98   Coiners and critics of 'civility/civilization' (wén)

and 'military' (*wǔ* 武) 'officials' (*guān* 官).[8] While the earliest attested explicit formulations of this contrast may date to the Qín or early Hàn, it has roots in the frequent uses in Warring States texts of the terms *wén* and *wǔ* to refer to contrasting methods of dealing with the affairs of a state in times of peace and war, respectively.[9] As illustrated by the following passage from the *Lǐjì* 禮記, from the Warring States period onward, the two revered founding kings of the Zhōu dynasty (1045–256 BCE), King Wén (r. 1099/56–1050 BCE) and King Wǔ (r. 1049/45–1043 BCE), became eponymously associated with these contrasting *wén* and *wǔ* principles of governance:

(3)   King Wén used 'civility/civilization' (*wén*) to govern, King Wǔ used 'war/ military force' (*wǔ*) achievements to rid the people of disasters. (文王以文治 武王以武功去民之菑)[10]

In this passage, 'civility/civilization' (*wén*) is explicitly described as a tool used by King Wén (文) in the process of 'governing' (*zhì* 治).[11] A passage from the *Lǔshì Chūnqiū* stating that "King Wǔ (武) won all under Heaven through 'warfare' (*wǔ* 武), but held on to it through 'civilization/civility' (*wén*)" (武王以武得之，以文 持之) similarly uses *wén* to refer to the peaceful methods of governing through which a ruler may consolidate 'military' (*wǔ*) conquests.[12] For many of the thinkers embracing the concept of 'civility/civilization' (*wén*), employing 'civility/ civilization' (*wén*) to govern a state means using the institutionalized 'rites' (*lǐ*) of the early Zhōu to elevate the level of 'moral refinement' or 'civility' of the people and to improve government policies, institutions, and regulations (i.e., the 'police' of the state). These uses of *wén* thus contain elements of both 'civility' and 'police.'

The concept of the 'rites' (lǐ) embodies both 'civility' and 'police'

That the Warring States concept of 'civility/civilization' (*wén*) comprises an element of 'police' is further indicated by the fact that it is often mentioned in conjunction with the 'rites' (*lǐ* 禮) in discussions of how to run a state.[13] In the Warring States period, the concept of the 'rites' (*lǐ*) encompassed elements of both 'civility' and 'police.' Although the word was occasionally used in pre-Qín texts to refer to 'conventionalized liturgy'—such as the appropriate behavior when sacrificing to gods or ancestors—it was also used in numerous ways that go far beyond the common meanings associated with the English words *rites* or *rituals*.[14] In the ritualized government system of the pre-Warring States period, the 'rites' (*lǐ*) referred to codified sumptuary regulations and inherited prerogatives of the nobility that both legitimized and perpetuated social hierarchies. Manifested as institutionalized sociopolitical performance, the 'rites' were a highly conspicuous part of everyday life which governed how people of different social rank should behave toward each other.[15]

In the pre-Warring States period, the term 'rites' (*lǐ*) still referred narrowly to this institutionalized social decorum of the aristocratic elite of Zhōu 'noblemen' (*jūnzǐ*). Adherence to the 'rites' (*lǐ*) was what distinguished members of the Zhōu

Coiners and critics of 'civility/civilization' (wén)   99

aristocracy from non-aristocratic members of Zhōu society.[16] While the term 'rites' (lǐ) acquired many new meanings and uses in the Warring States period, it still retained older meanings. In one passage in the *Xúnzǐ*, the role of 'civility/civilization' (*wén*) in the system of ritualized distinctions between people of high and low rank is explicitly linked to the 'rites' (lǐ). According to the *Xúnzǐ*, the " 'rites' (lǐ) . . . use [markers of distinctions between] noble and base to create 'patterns' (*wén*) [of social distinction]."[17] The 'rites' were part of an institutionalized social hierarchy that was a key element of the government system and thereby included elements akin to the sixteenth- to eighteenth-century English concept of 'police' discussed in Chapter 1.

As with the evolving meanings of the terms 'power' → 'virtue' (dé), 'nobleman' → 'noble man' (jūnzǐ), and 'awe-inspiringly beautiful' → 'morally refined' (*wén*), discussed in Chapter 2, evidence of a reinterpretation of the term 'rites' (lǐ) by emphasizing the moral (virtue ethical) aspect of behavior is also present in the *Analects*. In order to become a truly 'morally refined' (*wén*) 'noble man' (jūnzǐ), it was not enough to simply go through the actions prescribed by the 'rites'; one also had to feel that these actions were the right thing to do. For example, the 'rites' (lǐ) prescribed that a truly 'filial' (xiào) son should take good care of his parents. But for Confucius as he is portrayed in *Analects*, it was not enough to simply feed, clothe, and shelter one's parents; one should also sincerely feel that this is the right thing to do.[18] That is, the term 'rites' (lǐ) was given a new moral interpretation in the virtue ethics of *Analects*, *Mencius*, and *Xúnzǐ*. By the Warring States period, the expression 'the rites' (lǐ) thus no longer referred narrowly to the ritualized decorum of aristocratic 'noblemen' (jūnzǐ); it had also begun to be used to refer to the ideal 'moral decorum' of morally refined 'noble men' (jūnzǐ), regardless of social rank.[19] This shift in the meaning of the term 'rites' (lǐ) thereby coincided with and mutually reinforced the coining of the word 'civility/civilization' (*wén*).

In addition to nominal uses of *wén* denoting a pre-Qín concept of 'civility/civilization' directly, as in (2), *wén* was also used nominally in related meanings referring to various institutionalized ritual practices used to rule people and run a state—that is, elements of 'police.' The *Xúnzǐ* contains nominal uses of *wén* referring to prescriptive 'institutionalized patterns' in funeral sacrifices and music, which both played an important role in pre-Qín state governance. Understanding ancestral sacrifice and implementing it in the most appropriate way was an integral part of the art of kingship. As shown in (4), the *Xúnzǐ* explicitly describes how the former kings established the ideal 'institutionalized patterns' (*wén*) for sacrificial rites in order to help the mourners control and channel their emotions in socially appropriate ways:

(4) The former kings consequently established the 'patterns of moral refinement/civility' (*wén*) for these situations. . . . Therefore, I say: As for sacrifice . . . it is the [manifestation] of utmost loyalty, trust, caring and respect; [it is] the perfection of the rites and restraint and of 'morally refined/civilized' (*wén*) appearance. (故先王案為之立文 . . . 故曰祭者 . . . 忠信愛敬之至矣禮節文貌之盛矣)[20]

100 *Coiners and critics of 'civility/civilization' (wén)*

The 'institutionalized patterns' (*wén*) for sacrifice regulate behavior in an appropriate manner and give the mourner a dignified 'civil/morally refined' (*wén*) 'appearance' (*maò* 貌).[21]

In the theories of statecraft presented in the *Analects* and the *Xúnzǐ*, 'music' (*yuè* 樂) also played an important role in harmoniously ruling the people and bringing order to the state.[22] In this sense, institutionalized use of 'music' (*yuè*) was part of 'police' as well. A passage in the *Xúnzǐ* describes how "the former kings diligently 'made' (*wéi* 為) 'institutionalized patterns' (*wén*)" for music because they knew that "sounds and music penetrate deep into people, and their transformation of people is swift."[23] The implication, spelled out in the continuation of this passage, is that the ideal 'institutionalized patterns' (*wén*) established by the former kings ensured harmonious and balanced music that made the people behave correctly and thereby prevented disorder.[24] Without the 'institutionalized patterns' (*wén*) established by the sages, music as a tool for governing the people would be much less efficacious. Indeed, subversive music that was not *wén* could endanger the state.[25] The 'morally refined patterns' (*wén*) that the sages established for music slowly become carved into one's 'inborn nature' (*xìng*) by listening to and performing the right kind of music. 'Music' (*yuè*) was an important part of the curriculum an aspiring 'noble man' had to study to become 'morally refined/civilized' (*wén*). It connected the 'civility' of the individual to the 'police' of the larger social formation in which she lived. The 'rites' (*lǐ*) and 'institutionalized patterns' (*wén*) were important tools used by the sage–kings to rule their domains and, according to the *Analects* and the *Xúnzǐ*, should be used by any ruler hoping to become a true king of the entire civilized realm 'under Heaven' (*tiānxià*).

'Universality': 'civility/civilization' (wén) and 'all under Heaven' (tiānxià)

The expression 'all under Heaven' (*tiānxià*) began to refer to the 'civilized realm' in the Warring States period in ways that reveal the assumed 'universality' of the pre-Qín concept of 'civility/civilization' (*wén*). Seeing the former kings as responsible for establishing prescriptive 'institutionalized patterns' (*wén*) for sacrificial practice and music, the *Xúnzǐ* develops a theory of kingship that includes perfecting the 'civility/civilization' (*wén*) of the ruler's own person ('civility') and of his state ('police') in order to display it to 'all under Heaven' (*tiānxià*):

(5) The king . . . is the most worthy and is thereby able to save the unworthy. He is the strongest and is thereby able to be broadminded toward the weak. If he engages in warfare then he will necessarily defeat [his enemy] but he still considers it shameful to fight with anyone. Indeed, he perfects 'civility/civilization' (**wén**) [in his own person and in the institutions of his state] in order to display it to 'all under Heaven' (*tiānxià*) so that aggressive states will be at peace and transform themselves. (王者 . . . 致賢而能以救不肖，致彊而能以寬弱，戰必能殆之而羞與之鬥，委然成文，以示之天下，而暴國安自化矣)[26]

Coiners and critics of 'civility/civilization' (wén)   101

Observing the 'civility' (wén) of the true king and the 'civilization' (wén) embodied in the perfect government institutions ('police') established under his rule, 'aggressive states' will 'transform themselves' and be at peace. Elsewhere in the *Xúnzǐ* the transformative power of the display of 'civility/civilization' (wén) is captured in the saying: "if those above embody 'civility/civilization' (wén), then those below will be peaceful" (shàng wén xià ān 上文下安).[27] The ideal ruler of the realm 'under Heaven' (tiānxià) pacifies potential enemies by perfecting 'civility/civilization' (wén), understood as his own personal 'civility'/'moral refinement' and the 'police'/'ideal patterns of government institutions,' such as the 'institutionalized patterns' (wén) for social distinctions, music, and sacrifice described above.[28]

The pre-Qín promoters of the concept of 'civility/civilization' (wén) often equated 'all under Heaven' (tiānxià) with the 'civilized' realm as a "regime of value" defined by the shared practices of the Zhōu elite.[29] This is illustrated by Confucius' evaluation of the legacy of Guǎn Zhòng (d. 645 BCE), the famous prime minister of the state of Qí. Before serving Duke Huán of Qí (r. 685–643 BCE), Guǎn Zhòng had served Duke Huán's brother and had even tried to kill Duke Huán during the fratricidal struggle for the throne of Qí.[30] Guǎn Zhòng had a tarnished reputation because of this. According to the samurai-like code of honor adhered to by retainers and men of service, it was shameful to survive the slaying of one's lord, and, if one did, the honorable thing to do was to commit suicide. One of Confucius' disciples therefore asked Confucius, "Guǎn Zhòng was not a Good (rén)[31] person, was he?" In response, Confucius allegedly said:

(6)   When Guǎn Zhòng served as Duke Huán's Prime Minster, he allowed him to become lord-protector over the lords of the states, uniting and ordering **'all under Heaven' (tiānxià)**. To this day, the people continue to enjoy the benefits of his achievements—if it were not for Guǎn Zhòng, we would all be wearing our hair loose and fastening our garments on the left. How could he be expected to emulate the petty fidelity of a common husband or wife, going off to hang himself and die anonymously in some gully or ditch? (管仲相 桓公，霸諸侯，一匡天下，民到於今受其賜。微管仲，吾其被髮左衽 矣！豈若匹夫匹婦之為諒也，自經於溝瀆而莫之知也)[32]

Although in this passage Confucius gives credit to Guǎn Zhòng for bringing peace and order to 'all under Heaven' (tiānxià), he is aware that Guǎn Zhòng had stabilized only parts of the known world; but, as observed by Yuri Pines, "this did not matter: the Central States were coterminous with All under Heaven. For Confucius the limits of the civilized world were evidently the limits of the universe."[33] According to the 'rites,' adult male members of the Zhōu elite should always tie up their hair in a bun and wear a hat corresponding to their rank and position.[34] "Wearing one's hair loose" and "fastening one's garments on the left," as discussed by Confucius in (6), were considered uncouth conventional practices of the 'uncivilized,' lower levels of society, and non-Zhōu others.[35] Since the limits of 'all under Heaven' (tiānxià), understood as the "regime of value" informed by

102 *Coiners and critics of 'civility/civilization' (wén)*

the concept of 'civility/civilization' (*wén*), were defined in terms of adherence to pan-Zhōu elite decorum and institutions, non-Zhōu groups following their own 'local customs' (*sú* 俗) were not included.[36] The pre-Qín coiners and promoters of the concept of 'civility/civilization' (*wén*) assumed that the 'rites' of the Zhōu elites were universally applicable. By contrast, 'local customs' (*sú* 俗) were limited to a specific localities and time periods. The numerous different 'states' (*guó* 國) and different 'ages' (*shì* 世) had different 'local customs' (*sú* 俗), but there was only one 'all under Heaven' (*tiānxià*), understood as a 'realm of value' defined by a set of allegedly eternally valid civilizational *wén*-patterns and 'rites' (*lǐ*).[37] For Confucius, Guǎn Zhòng was therefore a hero who had saved the civilized realm of 'all under Heaven' (*tiānxià*) from being polluted by uncivilized 'vulgar customs' (*sú*).[38]

Changes in the meanings and uses of the expression *tiānxià* over time can help us date the emergence of civilizational consciousness. The expression *tiānxià* only occurs a few times in received texts from the first half of the first millennium BCE and is not attested in pre-Warring States bronze inscriptions.[39] In pre-Warring States texts, the expression *tiānxià* appears to refer mainly to 'the limited domain under royal jurisdiction' rather than to a 'regime of value.'[40] It occurs only once in the pre-Warring States parts of the *Book of Documents (Shū)*: "He who is in the position of king should be first in 'charismatic power' (*dé*); then the people will emulate him in the domain 'under Heaven' (*tiānxià*), and the king will be [even] more illustrious."[41] As argued by Pines (2002a: 102), here *tiānxià* evidently refer narrowly to the "area under the jurisdiction of the Zhōu Kings" rather than a "regime of value."[42] Uses of the term 'all under Heaven' (*tiānxià*) to refer to the 'civilized world' as a "regime of value" informed by 'civility/civilization' (*wén*) and 'rites' (*lǐ*), as in (5) and (6), emerge around the middle of the first millennium BCE in tandem with the coining of civilizational consciousness.[43] Not surprisingly, the texts in which the term *tiānxià* is first (and/or most frequently) used in this meaning (e.g., the *Zuǒzhuàn* and the *Analects*) are the same texts in which *wén* meaning 'moral refinement' and 'civility/civilization' occurs first and/or most frequently. It therefore seems plausible that the coining of the concept of 'civility/civilization' (*wén*) and the use of the expression *tiānxià* to refer to a 'regime of value'/'civilized world' arose together in a relation of interdependence. In sum, the Old Chinese concept of 'civility/civilization' (*wén*) embodied an element of 'universality.'

Pre-Qín concept of 'progress'

The early European universal concept of 'civilization' is intimately linked to the idea of 'progress.' As discussed in Chapter 1, the modern European idea of 'progress' emerged in the sixteenth to the eighteenth century, when people began to see themselves as morally, institutionally, and technologically more 'advanced' than the ancient Greek and Roman societies. Similarly, as detailed below, Warring States thinkers also observed that their contemporary society was more advanced than societies of people living in the remote, more 'primitive' past, not just in

Coiners and critics of 'civility/civilization' (wén) 103

terms of technology but also with respect to 'civility' and 'police.'[44] As illustrated by the following *Lǚshì Chūnqiū* passage, a notion of 'progress,' understood as 'change for the better,' was also a constituent component of the pre-Qín concept of 'civility/civilization':

(7) Long ago, in great antiquity, there were no rulers. People lived together in flocks. They knew their mothers but not their fathers. There were no distinctions between close and distant relatives, older and younger brothers, husbands and wives, and male and female; no 'Way' (*dào*) for dealing with superiors and inferiors or older and younger; no 'rites' (*lǐ*) governing advancing and withdrawing in court or bowing and yielding; nor such conveniences as clothing, shoes, belts, houses, and storehouses; nor any such facilities as tools and utensils, boats and carts, inner and outer city walls, or border fortifications. These hardships existed because there were no rulers. (昔太古嘗無君矣，其民聚生群處，知母不知父，無親戚兄弟夫妻男女之別，無上下長幼之道，無進退揖讓之禮，無衣服履帶宮室畜積之便，無器械舟車城郭險阻之備，此無君之患)[45]

Having no government or rulers, people in the remote past lived in a state of nature without any 'police.' Lacking social conventions, living without distinctions between different ranks or between male and female duties, and without 'rites' to guide their actions, they also lacked 'civility.' Furthermore, they had none of the technological inventions (houses, clothing, tools, boats, carts, etc.) that made life comfortable and convenient in the Warring States period. People ate uncooked food and took shelter in caves or in nests in the trees. They did not have 'cities' and, according to another Warring States account, 'lived in the wild' (*yě chǔ* 野處).[46]

Many of the phrases used to describe the primitive practices of the pre-sage–king ancestors of the Zhōu are also used in Warring States texts to describe contemporary non-Zhōu peoples as primitive and uncivilized. Since 'living in the field/wild' (*yě chǔ*) was a feature of their own primitive ancestors, the Zhōu regarded as primitive many of the non-Zhōu groups who were perceived as lacking the complex state infrastructures characteristic of the Central States, whose governments were seated in 'walled cities' (*guó* 國).[47] Similar to descriptions of the Zhōu ancestors in the remote past, contemporary non-Zhōu groups are described as dwelling in caves and nests, eating raw food, and not having boats or carts.[48] Being socially unsophisticated, they lacked appropriate government institutions and 'rites' (*lǐ*). In sum, both the 'primitive' ancestors of the Zhōu and the contemporary non-Zhōu 'barbarians' (*yí*) lacked 'civility/civilization' (*wén*).

According to Warring States narratives, humankind had been liberated from the brutish conditions of 'living in the wild' by sages and sage–kings who taught people the use of various technologies such as using fire, building houses, making clothes, agriculture, transportation, and writing. The *Xúnzǐ* also contains several passages describing how the intervention of the former kings saved humanity from an original Hobbesian-like state of chaos in which people's uncontrolled

104 *Coiners and critics of 'civility/civilization' (*wén*)*

desires caused endless fighting for resources (food, mates, etc.).[49] By ruling over the people and actively managing the affairs of the state (such as irrigation projects and turning wild marshes and forests into fertile farmland), it was thought, the sage–kings improved the standard of living; and by introducing government institutions, social hierarchies, and conventions for interpersonal behavior, they taught people how to live together in harmony.[50] Although Warring States thinkers disagreed on the value of technological and social developments and, in some cases, attributed them to different individuals and different times in history, none denied such changes had taken place.

In contrast to the linear, modern European concept of 'progress,' which is often projected endlessly into the future, the Warring States thinkers such as the composers of the *Analects* and the *Xúnzǐ* had a more cyclical concept of 'change for the better' based on the assumption that that the pinnacle of moral and institutional development had been reached during the golden age of the Western Zhōu, as illustrated by the *Analects* passages in (1) and (2). The *Mencius* describes this process of alternating progress and decline as follows:

(8) By the time of the tyrant Zhòu (the last ruler of the Shāng dynasty), all under Heaven was again in a state of great confusion. Zhōu Gōng assisted King Wǔ, and destroyed Zhòu. . . . He chased off the tigers, leopards, rhinoceroses, and elephants to remote places. And all [the people] under Heaven was greatly delighted. The *Book of Documents* says, "Great and splendid were the plans of King Wén! Greatly were they carried out by the energy of King Wǔ! They assist and instruct us descendants. They all apply the upright and are without deficiencies." Again, the age fell into decay, and the Way faded. Aberrant teachings and violent actions arose. There were cases of ministers murdering their rulers and of sons murdering their fathers. Confucius was afraid, and composed the *Annals*. What the *Annals* contain are affairs of the Son of Heaven [the Emperor] . . . Sage–kings ceased to arise, and the princes of the States gave the reins to their lusts. Idle retainer-officials indulged in unreasonable debates. (及紂之身天下又大亂。周公相武王誅紂 . . . 驅虎豹犀象而遠之。天下大悅。《書》曰『丕顯哉文王謨！丕承哉武王烈！佑啟我後人，咸以正無缺。』世衰道微邪說暴行有作，臣弒其君者有之，子弒其父者有之。孔子懼作《春秋》。《春秋》天子之事也 . . . 聖王不作，諸侯放恣，處士橫議)[51]

After the technological and sociopolitical advances allegedly made during the reigns of the sage–kings Yáo, Shùn, and Yǔ, 'all under Heaven' (*tiānxià*) fell into a period of decline that culminated under the corrupt last ruler of the Shāng dynasty. Then the founding rulers of the Western Zhōu—King Wén, King Wǔ, and the Duke of Zhōu—overthrew the Shāng and developed conventionalized behavior and government institutions to their peak. Subsequently, another period of decline began. Confucius, Mencius, and Xúnzǐ thus believed they lived in a period of moral decline and considered it their duty to return 'all under Heaven' (*tiānxià*) to the ideal Golden Age of King Wén, as seen in (1) and (2) above.

Coiners and critics of 'civility/civilization' (wén)   105

The 'progress' that took place in their version of history had occurred during the period from the first sages and rulers, such as Huáng Dì, Yáo, Shun, and Yǔ in the third millennium BCE (and earlier), to the peak of 'civility/civilization' (*wén*) during the early Western Zhōu.

Like the modern European universal concept of 'civilization,' the pre-Qín concept of 'civility/civilization' (*wén*) of thinkers such Confucius and Xúnzǐ was also intimately linked to an idea of 'progress' or 'change for the better.' Although the Old Chinese language of the pre-Qín period did not have a single word with a meaning similar to Modern English *progress*, a notion of 'progress' could still be articulated through combinations of words for its semantic molecules, i.e., as 'change (*biàn* 變), or transformation (*huà* 化), in things or states of affairs resulting in better things or states of affairs.'[52] By introducing technological inventions and establishing appropriate government institutions and traditions of conventionalized behavior, the sage–kings and their ministers had saved humanity from a brutish existence in nature. This clearly represented a 'change in for the better' or, in other words, 'progress.'

The optimistic idea of (or belief in) improvement in the future is at the core of the early modern European concept of 'progress.' 'Progress' is what defines the modern Franglophone concept of 'civilization.' In the words of J. B. Bury, progress is "the animating and controlling idea of western civilization. . . . The phrase *civilisation and progress* has become stereotyped, and illustrates how we have come to judge a *civilisation* good or bad according as it is or is not progressive."[53] In contrast, Confucius and Xúnzǐ did not envision progress as a linear and potentially endless process extending into the future.[54] For both, the ideal was to return to the 'civility/civilization' (*wén*) of the Western Zhōu, and remain there, as illustrated by (1) and (2) above. When asked what he observed during his visit to the state of Qín, Xúnzǐ reportedly praised the people, functionaries, retainer–officials, and grand ministers as resembling those in 'ancient times' (*gǔ* 古), meaning in the time of the early Western Zhōu.[55] With respect to 'police,' that is, government institutions and social regulations, no progress beyond the early Zhōu Golden Age was needed or even possible. The more static pre-Qín notion of 'progress' or 'change for the better' (as having peaked at some point in the past) therefore informed a quite different language-specific conceptualization of 'civility/civilization' than the more dynamic concept of 'civilization' informed by the modern European notion of 'progress' (assumed to continue endlessly into the future).

Around the middle of the first millennium BCE the early Zhōu system of hereditary office-holding was eroding. In the midst of what they perceived as a crisis of tradition, conservative, moralistic thinkers such as Confucius and his followers began to create a proto-anthropological terminology with which they could criticize the subversive effects of contemporary 'local customs' (*sú*) and extol the importance of returning what they saw as the universally valid, ideal 'civility/civilization' (*wén*) of the early Zhōu.[56] In the *Analects*, Confucius himself expressed the ideal of conservative preservation, or revival, of the idealized institutions of the early Zhōu by describing himself as a faithful custodian of

106 *Coiners and critics of 'civility/civilization' (wén)*

tradition who "transmits [the past] without 'creating' (*zuò* 作) anything himself and is trustworthy and loves 'ancient ways' (*gŭ* 古)."[57] Similarly, in the *Xúnzĭ* the highest kind of *rú* 儒 are those who "model themselves on the former kings" and "use ancient ways to manage contemporary affairs."[58]

While Confucius and Xúnzĭ thought the social development of the 'police' aspect of human 'civility/civilization' (*wén*) had peaked in the institutions and values of the early Zhōu, as discussed in Chapter 2, they still believed each individual needed to go through an arduous process of self-cultivation to carve a pattern of 'civility' (*wén*) onto innate 'human nature' (*xìng*). The notion of continual 'progress' on this path of character building was therefore very much alive ontogenetically. *Analects* 2.4 describes Confucius' own life-long process of education and edification, which ended with him being able to follow his heart's desire without ever transgressing (or even wanting to transgress) the 'rites.' Similarly, passage (11) in Chapter 2 illustrates how even 'commoners' (*pǐfū* 匹夫) can aspire to become 'sages' (*shèng rén* 聖人) if they make enough progress in moral cultivation. While the development of 'police' (i.e., government institutions and normative values) of *social formations* (e.g., states and empires) had reached perfection during the Western Zhōu, Confucius and Xúnzĭ did not see an end point for each *individual*'s development of 'civility' (*wén*).

Contrasting the Xià elites of the Zhōu realm and 'non-Zhōu others'

Civilizational consciousness is by nature comparative. One of its main functions is to construct and contrast identities of a 'civilized self' versus 'uncivilized others.' It therefore tends to flourish in historical contexts where different traditions of social mores are confronted.[59] As described in Chapter 1, in early modern Europe the encounter with 'exotic' overseas populations whose lives differed dramatically from those of the European explorers and colonizers triggered an interest in ways of describing the perceived contrast between the so-called "civilized" and the "barbarians." A similar situation occurred in China around 600–400 BCE, when a proto-anthropological interest emerged in cross-cultural comparison between the 'elegant, proper' (*yǎ* 雅) 'civility/civilization' (*wén*) and 'rites' (*lĭ*) of the elite of the 'Great ones' (*Xià*) inhabiting the 'Central States' (*Zhōng guó* 中國) on the one hand and the practices of the various non-Zhōu peoples on the other.

The practices of the non-Zhōu others were often referred to as 'local/vulgar customs' (*sú* 俗) but never as 'civilization/civility' (*wén*) or 'rites' (*lĭ*). Territorial and military expansion brought the Zhōu elite in contact with an increasingly wide range of non-Zhōu peoples who adhered to alien practices and in some cases spoke languages incomprehensible to the Zhōu.[60] To be sure, there had certainly also been extensive contact with non-Zhōu peoples in pre-Warring States times.[61] However, as discussed in Chapters 4–5, it was not until 600–400 BCE that moral philosophers began to explicitly formulate a perceived contrast between the superior Zhōu 'civility/civilization' (*wén*) and the 'vulgar customs' (*sú*) of the 'civilizationally inferior non-Zhōu others' or 'barbarians' (*yí* 夷). They sometimes

*Coiners and critics of 'civility/civilization' (*wén*)* 107

condescendingly compared the 'civilizationally inferior non-Zhōu other' (*yí*) to 'birds and beasts.'[62] In other contexts, they described them as potentially capable of becoming 'morally refined' or 'civilized' (*wén*) if they adopted the 'superior mores' or 'rites' (*lǐ*) and values of the Zhōu elite tradition.[63]

In the *Zuǒzhuàn*, which was composed mainly in the fifth to fourth centuries BCE (with later additions), 'civility/civilization' (*wén*) is described as an ideal to which the rulers of less 'civilized' states of the pan-Zhōu realm aspired. These states include Chǔ 楚, Wú 吳, and Yuè 越, all located on the southern fringe of the ancestral Zhōu heartland. One passage describes a battle in which the state of Chǔ thoroughly defeated the Jìn 晉 army. Although representing the victor, a Chǔ officer initiated post-battle negotiations with Jìn by apologizing for the Chǔ ruler's lack of mastery of 'civility' (*wén*). "In his youth, our ruler met with sorrowful bereavement, and as a consequence he is not able to 'act with civility' (*wén*)" (寡君少遭閔凶不能文).[64] This passage suggests that being able 'to *wén*' (i.e., 'to comport oneself according to the ideal patterns of civility (*wén*)') was a skill that was taken for granted by people from states from the Zhōu heartland but had not yet been fully acquired by the ruling elites of the south.

In another *Zuǒzhuàn* passage, the ruler of Wú, another southern state with a peripheral status in the Zhōu realm, is described in the following terms by one of his ministers:

(9) Wú is a distant descendant of Zhōu who has been abandoned on the coast of the sea and is no longer in communication with the Jī clan of the Zhōu. However, now [the state of] Wú has begun to be great again, and can begin to be compared to the 'Flowery' (*Huá*) states. Prince Guāng [of Wú] is extremely **'civil/morally refined' (*wén*)**, and will surely by himself become like the former kings. (吳，周之冑裔也，而棄在海濱，不與姬通，今而始大，比于諸華。光又甚文，將自同於先王)[65]

Like 'the Great ones' (*Xià*), the term 'the Flowery' (*Huá*) is used by the pan-Zhōu elites to distinguish themselves from non-Zhōu groups.[66] The role that 'civility' or 'moral refinement' (*wén*) plays in the argument in (9) is revealing. Having the same family name as Western Zhōu rulers, Jī 姬, Prince Guāng claimed descent from Zhōu royalty. Since 'civility/civilization' (*wén*) is conceived of as the embodiment of the ideal Zhōu traditions, mores, and institutions, it is not surprising that the state of Wú's anticipated return to the center of the Zhōu community should be foreshadowed by Prince Guāng's perfection of correct 'moral refinement/civility' (*wén*). Through schemes and political maneuvering, he eventually became king and ruled the state of Wú as King Hé Lǘ 闔廬 from 514 BCE to 496 BCE.

Taken together, these two *Zuǒzhuàn* passages indicate that at the time when they were composed (probably in the fifth or fourth century BCE) the rulers of Zhōu states considered to be on the margins of the 'civilized' Zhōu realm were assumed to be deficient in 'moral refinement/civility' (*wén*); in contrast, the rulers of the core Zhōu states were expected to rule their people through display of their

108 Coiners and critics of 'civility/civilization' (wén)

mastery of 'civility/civilization' (*wén*). The coining of the term *wén* in the new meaning 'civility/civilization' therefore seems likely to have occurred around the middle of the first millennium BCE in the context of a heightened interest in comparing the conventionalized behavior and traditions of the Zhōu elite with those of their non- or semi-Zhōu neighbors.

*Summary: the coining of 'civility/civilization' (*wén*)*

Around the middle of the first millennium BCE, a subset of the emerging community of masters of statecraft and moral philosophers began to coin the terms necessary to formulate and thus be conscious of the idea of a belonging to a 'civilization.' This indigenous pre-Qín concept of 'civilization' had similar, albeit language-specific, semantic molecules to the eighteenth-century European concept of 'civilization.' At a certain level of abstraction, the shared conceptual core of both the language-specific pre-Qín concept of 'civility/civilization' and the language-specific European concept of 'civilization' can be paraphrased as follows: 'a social formation (state, empire, realm) that has undergone a "universal" process of "progress" (/"change for the better") operating on individuals and social formations along the dimensions of "civility" (refinement of manners, behavior, etc.) and "police" (laws, government institutions), which resulted in the establishment of value-laden distinctions between self (the civilized) and others (the barbarians) and between a primitive past and an advanced era (understood as either a Golden Age or the present/future).' As shown in row (V) in Figure 3.1 (same as Figure 2.3 in Chapter 2), *wén* is coined in this meaning around the eve of the Warring States period, thereby completing a long process of semantic extension: 'pattern' → 'decoration' → 'awe-inspiringly beautiful' → 'morally refined'/'civility' → 'civility/civilization.'

As argued in Chapter 2, *wén* first acquired the meaning 'morally refined' from the earlier meaning 'awe-inspiringly beautiful,' which itself had been derived by metaphorical extension from the meanings 'pattern' and 'decoration.' In the

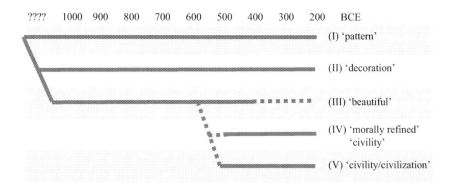

Figure 3.1 Tracing the history of the meaning changes of the word *wén* (same as Figure 2.3).

*Coiners and critics of 'civility/civilization' (*wén*)* 109

Warring States period, it began to be used in extended meanings to refer to an emergent language-specific universal concept of 'civility/civilization,' as in (2). The word *wén* thus followed a path of lexicalization similar to the English word *civility*. The Franglophone term *civility* and the pre-Qín term *wén* both originally referred to a form of 'refinement of manners and demeanor' of the hereditary nobility. Eventually, as described in the subsection titled "Historical context of the emergence of the universal concept of 'civilization'" in Chapter 1 and the subsection titled "From 'beautiful' (*wén*) 'nobleman' (*jūnzǐ*) to 'morally refined' (*wén*) 'noble man' (*jūnzǐ*): ethical re-interpretation of aesthetic *wén*" in Chapter 3, they were interpreted ethically as 'morally refined' comportment and behavior of a morally 'noble man,' regardless of birth. 'Morally refined' (*wén*) *individuals* were characterized by 'civility' or 'refinement of manners' (*wén*). By extension, 'morally refined' *social formations* (states, dynasties, tribes, etc.) were said to have 'civility/civilization' (*wén*). As discussed in the subsection titled "1500–1760s: multiple ways of expressing the universal concept of 'civilization'" in Chapter 1, *civility* was also occasionally used to refer to the concept of 'civilization' before it was eclipsed in this use by the word *civilization* in the 1770s. In these ways, the coining of 'civility/civilization' (*wén*) resembles the coining of the pre-1770s English term *civility* to mean 'civilization.'

The coining of *wén* in this new meaning of 'civility/civilization' in the Warring States period indicates that a small community of the Zhōu elite whose shared lexicon included this word had attained a particular language-specific form of collective civilizational consciousness at that time.[67] Although there are significant differences between the pre-Qín concept of 'civility/civilization' (*wén*) and the early Franglophone concept of 'civilization,' at a certain level of abstraction it is still possible to identify similar semantic components and internal structure. Breaking these two complex language-specific concepts down into combinations of semantic molecules facilitates cross-linguistic comparison. As argued above, both can be broken down into five key semantic components: 'progress,' 'civility' (of an individual), 'police' (of institutions and government regulations, laws, etc.), 'distinction(s),' and 'universality.'

As shown in Chapter 2, the word *wén* was used to refer to the 'moral refinement,' 'civility,' or 'polished manners and demeanor' of an individual, which is depicted in row 2 of Figure 3.2. As indicated in row 3, the element of 'police' or 'refinement of laws and government institutions' was also implicitly present in the occurrences of *wén* used to describe social formations such as 'states' (*guó* 國) or 'dynasties' (*dài* 代). The semantic component of 'universality' was lexicalized in the compound term *tiānxià* 'all under Heaven,' which by the Warring States period had begun to be used to refer to the 'civilized world' as a 'realm of value' informed by 'civility/civilization' (*wén*), indicated in row 5. Though not lexicalized as a single word, a notion of 'progress' can be expressed through paraphrases that describe 'changes' (*biàn* 變) for the 'better' (row 1). Finally, as indicated in row 4 and as will be discussed in Chapter 4, a 'distinction' was made between the Zhōu elite, who referred to themselves with the autonym 'Great ones' (*Xià*), and the 'civilizationally inferior non-Zhōu others' or 'barbarians' (*yí* 夷).

110 *Coiners and critics of 'civility/civilization' (wén)*

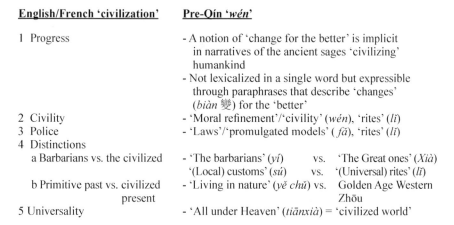

Figure 3.2 Comparing the modern European and pre-Qín universal concepts of 'civilization.'

While sharing kindred semantic molecules and semantic structure, the modern European word *civilization* and the pre-Qín word 'civility/civilization' (*wén*) still have widely different language-specific connotations. Many of these differences stem from the fact that their semantic molecules are coined in words that have different language-specific meanings and connotations. As discussed in the subsection titled "Semantic molecules of the universal concept of 'civilization'" in Chapter 1 and the subsection titled "Pre-Qín concept of 'progress'" in this chapter, the European and pre-Qín concepts of 'progress' and the related distinction between a 'barbaric' past and a later 'civilized' state differ considerably. Both are based on the basic idea of 'change for the better.' The original state of 'living in nature' in the remote past is deemed to be inferior to later stages characterized by technological inventions, improvement of mores and institutions, and so forth. However, while the linear European concept of 'progress' tends to look optimistically to the future for potentially unlimited civilizational development, the cyclical pre-Qín concept of 'progress' adopted by the coiners of the word 'civility/civilization' (*wén*) looks back to the assumed pinnacle of human 'civility/civilization' (*wén*) achieved in the Golden Age of King Wén.

The shared element of 'civility' is also fleshed out quite differently in pre-Qín China and sixteenth- to eighteenth-century Europe. The three years of mourning prescribed by the 'rites' (*lǐ*) after the passing of a parent, for example, which involved refraining from working or actively engaging in social life, wearing coarse garments, and so forth, would (and did) appear exotic and even 'barbaric' to European thinkers of this time. Conversely, European funerary practices and the conspicuous absence of institutionalized ancestor worship would have been considered 'barbaric' by Confucius. Many other such differences could be highlighted.

Similarly, the element of 'police' is manifested quite differently in the two traditions. For many of the coiners of 'civilization' in early modern Europe, such as

Adam Smith, legal protection of private property and free commerce was a central component of the concept of 'police' (government institutions, laws). For pre-Qín thinkers such as the authors of the *Analects* and the *Xúnzǐ*, this emphasis on commerce would seem not only crass and vulgar but also disastrously misguided. Instead, they would propose the establishment of a government based on an institutionalized form of the 'rites' (*lǐ*). And they would emphasize the use of ritualized musical performances of the *Songs* to ensure stable government through moral education of the people. Again, although both the modern European and the pre-Qín concepts of 'civilization' encompassed an element of 'police' (government institutions), the specific manifestations of this element of 'police' were informed by two very different traditions of normative values and conventionalized practices.

One may wonder whether *wén* could be translated into English as *culture* in Warring States texts. In fact, *wén* is frequently translated as *culture* in passages such as (2). Indeed, if understood in the nineteenth-century sense 'high culture,' then it is a reasonably good translation. Like the word *civilization* in the universal sense, the now somewhat quaint—or for some even obsolete—phrase *high culture* refers to a tradition of values and practices assumed to be universally valid. However, unlike *civilization*, the meaning of word *culture* (even as it is/was used in the phrase *high culture*) refers mainly to customs (different traditions of food, architecture, arts, manners, etc.) and tends not include a component of 'police' (government institutions). Furthermore, in contemporary usage, the word *culture* is no longer readily interpreted as referring to a prescriptive, ethnocentrically grounded concept of 'high culture' assumed to be universal. Today it is most often used to denote a descriptive ethnographic concept of 'culture' defined as a set of values and conventionalized practices *sui generis* characterizing a specific group. All peoples, in any location and time period, are assumed to have their particular "culture" understood as a distinct set of values and traditions. Since this is not what *wén* meant in pre-Qín texts, translating *wén* as *culture* is problematic.[68]

Critics of the concept of '*wén*'

The word *wén* in the sense 'civility/civilization' was part of the shared vocabulary of the literate elite during the Warring States period. However, opinions on the value and relevance of this concept differed greatly. The term 'civility/civilization' (*wén*) first emerged in texts such as the *Zuǒzhuàn* and the *Analects* in the fifth and fourth centuries BCE and was further developed in the *Xúnzǐ* in the third century BCE. These texts discuss the concept of *wén* in highly positive terms, both as the ideal, institutionalized 'patterns of conventionalized behavior' or 'civilization' of the early Zhōu and as the externally visible 'moral refinement' of 'noble men' (*jūnzǐ*) acquired through imitation of those ideal patterns. However, the pre-Qín corpus also contains voices that are fiercely critical of this concept of *wén*. While other works could have been included, I will limit myself here to the *Mòzǐ*, the *Hánfēizǐ*, and the "Mending Nature" chapter of the *Zhuāngzǐ*, which illustrate three different criticisms of 'civility/civilization' (*wén*) from the fourth and third centuries BCE. Analyzing these radically different takes on 'civility/civilization' (*wén*) provides insight

112   *Coiners and critics of 'civility/civilization' (wén)*

into the complex fragmentation of the Zhōu elite's self-reflective understanding and evaluation of their own traditions and mores. Although a collective civilizational consciousness had been coined, there was no consensus as to how to relate to it.

The *Hánfēizǐ*: 'civility/civilization' *(wén) versus 'laws'* (fǎ)

The concept of 'civility/civilization' (*wén*) has no place in the theory of statecraft of the *Hánfēizǐ*, a third-century work eponymously attributed to Hán Fēi 韓非 (c. 280–233 BCE).[69] Hán Fēi dismissed the virtue ethics of thinkers such as Confucius, Mencius, and Xúnzǐ as outdated and impractical and developed a theory of state governance that was in many ways the antithesis of those found in the *Analects* and the *Xúnzǐ*. As a manual of statecraft intended for a paranoid ruler, the *Hánfēizǐ* paints a dark picture of humankind as essentially driven by greed and fear. It outlines a Machiavellian system of governance that aims to regulate the behavior of the masses by strictly enforcing the distribution of punishments and rewards. Trusting no one and keeping his motives hidden, the ruler maintains power by retaining the ultimate authority to reward and punish. The development of 'moral virtue' (*dé*) as the basis for interpersonal trust plays no role in the *Hánfēizǐ*'s system of governance. The *Hánfēizǐ* therefore has no use for the edification processes proposed in the *Analects* and the *Xúnzǐ*, which transform men into 'morally refined' (*wén*) 'noble men' (*jūnzǐ*) through emulation of the 'civility/ civilization' (*wén*) established by the ancient sage–kings. Indeed, the *Hánfēizǐ* explicitly criticizes the concept of 'civility/civilization' (*wén*) and argues that it should be replaced by a rigid system of 'laws' or 'promulgated models' (*fǎ* 法) designed to control behavior through punishments and rewards.[70]

According to the *Hánfēizǐ*, Confucius' and Xúnzǐ's concept of 'civility/civilization' (*wén*) allows people to subvert the government system of promotion by seeking to bypass government-regulated routes to wealth and rank.[71] Several passages discuss the pernicious influence of 'civility/civilization' (*wén*) and of people 'pursuing polite studies' (*wénxué zhě* 文學者), whom he identified as the group of 'ritual specialists' called the *rú*, to which Confucius, Xúnzǐ, and Mencius belonged.

(10) The *rú* disorder the 'laws' (*fǎ*) through their 'civility/civilization' (*wén*). The 'independent warriors' (*xiá* 俠) violate prohibitions through their 'martial prowess' (*wǔ*). However, the ruler of men still honors both. This is why there is disorder. Those who stray from the 'laws' (*fǎ*) are guilty. However, all the masters of learning are selected for office based on their 'polite studies' (lit. '*wén* studies'). . . . Therefore, those who practice 'Goodness and duty' (*rén yì* 仁義), are not to be praised. If one praises them, then one would hamper [concrete] accomplishments. Those who [engage in] 'polite studies' (lit. '*wén* studies') should not be employed; if one employed them, one would disorder the laws. (儒以文亂法，俠以武犯禁，而人主兼禮之，此所以亂也。夫離法者罪，而諸先生以文學取 . . . 故行仁義者非所譽，譽之則害功；文學者非所用，用之則亂法)[72]

Coiners and critics of 'civility/civilization' (wén) 113

According to the *Hánfēizǐ*, the 'masters of ritual' (*rú*) and the 'independent warriors' (*xiá*) both constitute a threat to the order of the state. Although they bypass or deviate from the 'laws' (*fǎ*), rulers often promote them for their erudition and skill in martial arts. The state machinery proposed in the *Hánfēizǐ* relies on strict adherence to government regulations and laws. Having entire groups of the population operating outside the laws would undermine the authority of the government's system of laws and imperil its very existence. By emphasizing the development of the virtues of 'Goodness and duty' (*rén yì*), which are central concepts in the *Analects*, *Mencius*, and *Xúnzǐ*, the *rú* set up an alternative system of normative values that competes with, and therefore threatens, the system of 'laws' (*fǎ*). Beyond leveling a broadside against the concept of 'civility/civilization' (*wén*), this passage also indicates that Warring States thinkers associated the idea of 'civility/civilization' (*wén*) with the 'masters of ritual' (*rú*).

The *Hánfēizǐ* outlines a state in which rewards in the shape of either material emoluments or rank are based solely on one's achievements in productive labor (agriculture, weaving, etc.) or military service. The *Hánfēizǐ* therefore criticizes those who engage in 'polite studies' (*wénxué* 文學), obtain employment, and receive emoluments without having accumulated any merits in either labor or the military:

(11) At present, if by refining 'polite studies' (lit. '*wén* studies') and rehearsing sayings and speeches one can be without the hard work of plowing and yet have the fruits of wealth; and if one can be without the dangers of war and yet have the honor of noble rank, then who among people will not do so? Hence, a hundred men will engage in knowledge and [only] one will use his physical force. When those engaging in knowledge are many, then the 'laws' (*fǎ*) will fail. If those who use physical force are few, then the state will be poor. That is why this age is disordered. (今修文學、習言談，則無耕之勞、而有富之實，無戰之危、而有貴之尊，則人孰不為也？ 是以百人事智而一人用力，事智者眾則法敗，用力者寡則國貧，此世之所以亂也)[73]

'Polite studies' (*wénxué*) is used here in the eighteenth-century sense to refer to the study of the 'polite arts,' i.e., poetry, music, eloquence, history, and so forth. Here the *Hánfēizǐ* uses it to refer to the typical *rú* curriculum of the *Book of Songs* (*Shī*), the *Book of Documents* (*Shū*) and the 'rites' (*lǐ*).[74] Since the pursuit of 'polite studies' (*wénxué*) could be used as a shortcut to rank and material wealth (bypassing the toils of productive labor and the mortal danger of the battlefield), it could eventually come to be viewed as a possible career path, even for the average person without noble birth (*pǐfū*).[75] Hence, people would stop tilling in order to study. As a result, the fields would lay in waste and the state would be impoverished. Indeed, according to two anecdotal accounts from the district of Zhōngmóu, the ruler's unjustified promotion of people of learning inspired as many as half of the population to stop tilling their fields and to sell their farms and houses in order to pursue 'polite studies' (*wénxué*) as a shortcut to wealth and rank.[76] Though

114　*Coiners and critics of 'civility/civilization' (wén)*

this is probably a gross exaggeration, the *Hánfēizǐ* points out the contradiction between wanting to "enrich the state through agriculture and fend off foes with recruited soldiers while at the same time honoring the 'retainer–officials pursuing polite studies' (*wénxué zhī shì* 文學之士)."[77] The only way to do away with these problems would be to "abolish polite studies and make visible the laws and regulations."[78]

In sum, there are two main reasons why the *Hánfēizǐ* is critical of Confucius' concept of 'civility/civilization' (*wén*). First, *wén* subverts the strict implementation of the system of 'laws' (*fǎ*) by introducing an alternative set of normative values such as 'Goodness and duty/rightness' (*rén yì*). The *wén*-edified 'noble man' (*jūnzǐ*) behaves and is promoted according to a set of norms that do not necessarily conform to 'laws' (*fǎ*).[79] Second, by rewarding people for their achievement in 'polite studies' (*wénxué*) rather than for their material contribution (as farmers) or for their military service, the pursuit of *wén-practices* lures the 'common man' (*pǐfū*) away from the toils of farming and the perils of warfare, which in turn impoverishes the state, leaving it vulnerable to enemy attack.

The Mòzǐ: utilitarian rejection of the wasteful practices of 'civility/civilization' (wén)

The *Mòzǐ* is an eponymous work attributed to Mòzǐ (fl. fifth to early fourth centuries BCE), one of the earliest critics of Confucius. The bulk of it appears to have been composed in the fourth century BCE by followers of Mòzǐ and his teachings.[80] It proposes an anti-elitist, utilitarian philosophy based on consequentialist maximization of 'benefit' (*lì* 利) defined as (i) increasing the population of the state, (ii) increasing order, and (iii) increasing wealth to secure the material well-being of the people.[81] The *Mòzǐ* rejects the notion of *wén*, both in the Warring States senses of 'civility/moral refinement' of the 'noble man' (*jūnzǐ*) and in its older use to refer to the 'awe-inspiringly beautiful' appearance of the 'nobleman' (*jūnzǐ*) manifested in lavishly decorated ritual objects and markers of institutionalized social status, such as emblems (*wén*) and insignia. While the term *wén* occurs multiple times in the *Mòzǐ*, it is never used as a noun meaning 'civility/civilization.' Instead, the *Mòzǐ* criticizes rúist *wén*-practices (e.g., elaborate funeral practices, musical performances) and the 'decorated' (*wén*) artifacts (e.g., ornamented chariots, embroidered garments) that were part of the material manifestation of the institutionalized social hierarchy of early Zhōu elite society.

Like the *Analects* and the *Xúnzǐ*, the *Mòzǐ* supports promoting people to official positions based on competence and moral integrity.[82] But in contrast to the *Analects* and the *Xúnzǐ*, where moral worth and character are the result of a long and slow edification process emphasizing imitation of 'the ideal prescriptive patterns of conventionalized behavior and government institutions' (*wén*) instituted by the former kings, in the consequentialist philosophy of the *Mòzǐ* there is a more direct line from knowing what is right to acting on it. To use a contemporary example, for Mòzǐ, you have succeeded in getting a person to quit smoking as soon as you have persuaded her that quitting is in her best interest. Action automatically

*Coiners and critics of 'civility/civilization' (*wén) 115

follows logical persuasion. In contrast, in the virtue ethics of the *Analects*, changing behavior (such as making a person quit smoking) is a gradual process of character building that requires slowly instilling a set of new habits until they become second nature. Hence, according to the *Mòzǐ*, engaging in rúist 'polite studies' (*wénxué*) to acquire 'civility/moral refinement' (*wén*) is a wasteful practice of elite snobbery.[83] Rather than measuring a man's worth by his mastery of the *Book of Songs* and the elite decorum of the 'rites' (*lǐ*) manifested in the externally observable 'civility/moral refinement' (*wén*) of his appearance and demeanor, the *Mòzǐ* examines the extent to which his actions contribute to the maximization of 'benefit' (*lì*) for the state and its people. According to the *Mòzǐ*, serving as an official is a utilitarian imperative to maximize 'benefit' (*lì*), not a mission to spread knowledge of 'civility/civilization' (*wén*) in 'all under Heaven' (*tiānxià*). In the *Mòzǐ* 'all under Heaven' (*tiānxià*) is not coterminous with the civilized realm of the 'Central States' (*Zhōng guó* 中國) but extended to the "entire known world," including non-Zhōu areas inhabited by non-Zhōu peoples adhering to their own local 'customs' (*sú*). For the *Mòzǐ*, people everywhere, regardless of their local customs and values, can potentially be persuaded to emphasize 'utility' when maximizing 'benefit.'[84]

The *Mòzǐ* depicts the wasteful practices of rulers attempting to demonstrate their own personal 'civility' and the degree of 'civilization' of their states as a source of social disorder. In its version of history, the ancient sage–kings did not engage in lavish practices such as the procurement of costly garments embroidered with 'emblems' (*wén*), elaborately 'decorated chariots' (*wénxuān* 文軒), and other accouterments that served to display status and authority. Instead they are said to have valued 'practical utility' (*yòng* 用):

(12) Therefore, when the sages made clothes and garments, they [were made to] fit their bodies and harmonize with the skin and that was sufficient. [Clothes were] not [made] to dazzle the ears and the eyes in order to impress ignorant people. . . [As for] carvings and engravings, 'pattern-(decorations) and [variegated] colors' (*wéncǎi* 文采), [people] did not know that they were delightful . . . Therefore the people . . . were not led astray by external things. Thus, the people were frugal and easy to govern and the ruler was restrained in his use of resources and easily supported. (故聖人之為衣服適身體和肌膚而足矣。非榮耳目而觀愚民也 . . . 刻鏤文采不知喜也 . . . 故民 . . . 不感於外也。是以其民儉而易治，其君用財節而易贍也)[85]

Unlike the theories of 'civility/civilization' (*wén*) in the *Zuǒzhuàn*, the *Analects*, and the *Xúnzǐ*, which are based on a social hierarchy manifested in outer appearance and regulated by sumptuary 'rites' (*lǐ*), the *Mòzǐ* finds the maintenance of such a system to be a waste of precious resources and labor. The context preceding passage (12) contains a description of how the moral decline of the rulers of the Xià and Shāng dynasties stemmed from their increasingly opulent displays of material wealth and status. The *Mòzǐ* thus views 'pattern(-decorations) and variegated colors' (*wéncǎi*) as signs of moral depravity and decline; garments should

116 *Coiners and critics of 'civility/civilization' (wén)*

be designed simply to fit and to keep the body comfortable, not to "impress igno-rant people" (觀愚民). In such a world, no resources are wasted and the people will be "frugal" and "easy to govern."

In Warring States texts, *wén* in the concrete sense of 'pattern decoration' on clothing and accouterments is closely linked to *wén* in the more abstract/metaphorical senses of 'decoration' as a marker of social distinction and the con-cept of 'civility/civilization' (*wén*). In the *Zuǒzhuàn*, the *Analects*, and the *Xúnzǐ*, the ruler's engagement in *wén-practices* and his *wén-appearance* and demeanor are considered central to successful government. 'Civility/civilization' is physi-cally manifested in concrete 'decorative patterns' (*wén* 文) on 'emblems and insignia' (*wénzhāng* 文章) in order to maintain a harmoniously stratified society. Conversely, the *Mòzǐ*, which rejects 'moral refinement,' also finds the production and display of decorated, rank-indicating luxury items unnecessary for, or even detrimental to, the functioning of government.

Although the *Mòzǐ* is fiercely critical of the concepts of 'civility/civilization' (*wén*) developed by Confucius and his followers, it never—unlike the explicit criticism of *wén* in the *Hánfēizǐ*—directly discusses abstract concepts of 'civility/civilization' (*wén*). The *Xúnzǐ* is the first pre-Qín work to explicitly formulate the *Mòzǐ*'s rejection of 'civility/civilization' (*wén*):

(13) Mòzǐ was blinded by 'utility' (*yòng*) and did not understand **'civility/civilization' (*wén*)**. (墨子蔽於用而不知文)[86]

While the utilitarian philosophy of the *Mòzǐ* emphasizes 'utility' (*yòng*) and the maximization of 'benefit' (*lì* 利), the virtue ethics of the *Analects* and the *Xúnzǐ* stress the moral dimensions of human actions. In the *Xúnzǐ*, the 'noble man' has been 'morally refined' (*wén*) by a lifetime of embodying the ideal 'social mores' (*lì*) established by the sage–kings. That the *Xúnzǐ* found it necessary to criticize Mòzǐ for his lack of understanding of *wén* illustrates that *wén* was a topic of dis-pute in the late Warring States period. The *Xúnzǐ* passage quoted in (5) in Chapter 2 explicitly emphasizes the need for rulers to 'beautify' (*měi*) and 'decorate' (*shì*) themselves with 'emblems' (*wén*) and status symbols in order to "fill the eyes of the people" (以塞其目) and thereby awe them into submission.[87] However, as if anticipating the criticism of the followers of the teachings of the *Mòzǐ*, *Xúnzǐ* 10.1 states that emblems (*wén*) and insignia (*zhāng*) only serve to maintain the social hierarchy and were "not intended for ostentatious display" (不求其觀).[88]

The contrasting takes on *wén* found in the *Mòzǐ* and the *Xúnzǐ* are illustrated most clearly by their views on music and funeral practices. The *Xúnzǐ*, as discussed above, firmly states that one of the greatest contributions of the former kings was 'to establish' (*lì* 立) the 'institutionalized patterns' (*wén*) that regulate and structure institutionalized practices of music and mourning. Such 'institutionalized patterns' (*wén*) were the very foundation of peaceful rule, without which humankind would be unable to maintain social hierarchies and, as a consequence, would return to the state of bird and beasts.[89] In contrast, the *Mòzǐ* contains two chapters entitled "Against Music"[90] and "Moderation in Funerals"[91] in which the *rúist* emphasis on lavish musical performances and funeral rites, advocated by Confucius, Mencius,

Coiners and critics of 'civility/civilization' (wén)   117

and Xúnzǐ, is fiercely criticized. According to the *Mòzǐ*, such *wén*-practices were a frivolous waste of resources. Hence, as observed in the *Xúnzǐ*, the *Mòzǐ* rejects 'civility/civilization' (*wén*) and emphasizes 'utility' (*yòng*) and 'benefit' (*lì*).

*Disfiguring 'human nature' (*xìng*) by trying to mend it with 'civilization' (*wén*)*

The "Mending Nature (Shàn xìng 繕性)" chapter in the heterogeneous compilation of texts known as the *Zhuāngzǐ* contains a scathing criticism of 'civility/civilization' (*wén*). As observed by A. C. Graham, with respect to style and philosophical content it is quite unlike the rest of the *Zhuāngzǐ*. Likely composed toward the end of the Warring States period,[92] it conceives of "the ideal community as living in a spontaneous oneness without a ruler at all"[93] and assumes that the sage–kings who founded human 'civility/civilization' (*wén*) by inventing technologies and creating government institutions did positive harm to humankind by making it impossible for them to live in the original, ideal state of undifferentiated oneness:

(14)   The people of old lived in the midst of primordial undifferentiatedness. They were one with their time and obtained tranquility and unperturpedness in it. . . . The myriad creatures were unharmed. None of the host of living beings came to a premature end. Although people had knowledge, they had no place to use it. This is called ultimate 'oneness' (*yī* 一). At that time, no one 'consciously managed [anything]' (*wéi* 為) and all things were constantly 'so of themselves' (*zì rán* 自然).
   A time came when 'power/virtue' (*dé* 德) declined, until Suì Rén [the inventor of fire] and Fú Xī [the inventor of writing, fishing, and trapping] began to 'consciously manage' 'all under Heaven' (*tiānxià*). Because of this, there was compliance but not oneness. 'Power/virtue' declined further, until Shén Nong [who invented agriculture] and the Yellow Emperor began to 'consciously manage' (*wéi*) 'all under Heaven' (*tiānxià*). Because of this, there was peaceful control but not compliance. 'Power/virtue' declined further, until Yáo and Yǔ began to 'consciously manage' (*wéi*) all under Heaven. By initiating the fashion of transforming people through governing, they diluted what was concentrated and broke up the 'unhewn [block of wood]' (*pǔ* 樸), parted from the 'Way' (*dào* 道) in order to become good, endangered 'power/virtue' (*dé*) in order to act, so that people deserted their 'nature' (*xìng* 性) to follow their 'heart-mind' (*xīn* 心).[94] One heart-mind recognized the knowledge of another heart-mind, but it was not enough to stabilize all under Heaven. They then appended 'civility/civilization' (*wén*) to people's heart-minds and augmented them with 'broad learning' (*bó* 博). But 'civility/civilization' (*wén*) destroyed their 'inner substance' (*zhì* 質) and 'broad learning' (*bó* 博) drowned their 'heart-minds' (*xīn*). Then the people began to be confused and disordered. From this we can see that the age had lost the 'Way' (*dào*) and the 'Way' (*dào*) had lost the age. (古之人在混芒之中，與

118 *Coiners and critics of 'civility/civilization' (*wén*)*

一世而得澹漠焉。當是時也 . . . 萬物不傷群生不夭，人雖有知，無所
用之，此之謂至一。當是時也莫之為而常自然。逮德下衰及燧人伏
羲始為天下，是故順而不一。德又下衰及神農黃帝始為天下，是故安
而不順。德又下衰及唐虞始為天下，興治化之流，澆淳散樸，離道以
善，險德以行，然後去性而從於心。心與心識知而不足以定天下，然
後附之以文，益之以博。文滅質，博溺心，然後民始惑亂，無以反其
性情而復其初。由是觀之，世喪道矣，道喪世矣)[95]

The ideal primordial state of 'oneness' (*yī*) celebrated in this passage is closely
related to the concept of 'being so by itself' (*zì rán*). In the original state of undifferentiated oneness, all people (as well as all other creatures) simply are 'the way
they are/thus' (*rán*) 'by themselves' (*zì*) without any external interference. No ruler
is needed to 'consciously manage' (*wéi*) anything. The inventions of the sage–kings
are not a positive development, but a sign that 'power/virtue' (*dé*) is in decline.[96] In
the words of A. C. Graham (1986: 319), "Mending Nature" treats "all government
as a deviation from the original tribal Utopia." Being against any form of government and explicitly rejecting 'civility/civilization' (*wén*), the authors of the "Mending Nature" chapter are against serving as government officials. The best option is
to 'hide' (*yǐn* 隱) and live as a recluse to avoid becoming even more alienated from
original 'oneness' by serving. Should the world return to its original undifferentiated
oneness, then there would still be no need for administrators 'actively managing
affairs' (*wéi*), because everything would be as it should by itself.

"Mending Nature" presents an internalist view of human nature (*xìng*).[97] That
is, knowledge of normative values is assumed to be innate in human nature. In
the original natural state before the intervention of 'civility/civilization' (*wén*),
humans spontaneously knew what to do. There was no external tradition of learning. Knowledge of how to behave must therefore be internal, that is, innately
present in human nature (*xìng*). It is part of the original 'substance' (*zhì*) from
which humans are made. The 'unhewn block of wood' (*pǔ*) metaphorically captures this initial complete and intact state of human 'substance' (*zhì*). Once the
sage–kings emerged and began creating or discovering distinctions, this 'original
block' (*pǔ*) of 'oneness' (*yī*) was carved up. As an artificial pattern of 'civility/
civilization' (*wén*) was carved onto humans, their 'substance' (*zhì*) was destroyed.[98]
Like Rousseau and the satirical article "Civilisation" in *Punch*, in Figure 1.5 in
Chapter 1, "Mending Nature" would agree that people are "disfigured by civilization." Rather than benefitting humankind, the 'civilizing' efforts of the sage–kings
and their ministers alienated people from their own 'human nature' (*xìng*) and the
true 'Way' (*dào*) of living in the world.

The overlooked neglect of 'civility/civilization' (*wén*) in the *Mencius*

Unlike the *Analects* and the *Xúnzǐ*, in which the concept of 'civility/civilization'
(*wén*) plays a central role, the word *wén* is never used in this sense in the *Mencius*.[99] Surprisingly, this conspicuous absence appears to have eluded scholarly

*Coiners and critics of 'civility/civilization' (*wén*)* 119

attention—especially since both Mencius and Xúnzǐ were self-proclaimed followers of Confucius, who, according to the *Analects*, viewed *wén* as a key element of his teachings. The neglect of *wén* in the *Mencius* is not likely to be arbitrary and needs to be explained.

Traditionally, the *Mencius* has been considered to be closer to the *Analects* than the *Xúnzǐ*. The *Analects* and the *Xúnzǐ* mainly use craft metaphors in discussions of the role of human nature (*xìng* 性) and education. This contrasts sharply with the predominant use of agriculture metaphors in the *Mencius*. This indicates that the *Analects* and the *Xúnzǐ* share an externalist philosophy that views the source of normative values as external to 'human nature' (*xìng*). In contrast, the internalist philosophy of the *Mencius* takes normative values to be innately present in embryonic form in 'human nature' (*xìng*) akin to the potential existing in a seed. To the best of my knowledge, scholars have not yet observed that this contrast is supported by the fact that uses of *wén* to refer to concepts of 'civility,' 'institutionalized patterns,' and 'civilization' play a central role in the moral philosophies of *Analects* and the *Xúnzǐ*, while they are absent from the *Mencius*.

In the *Mencius*, the word *wén* is predominantly used in names, such as King Wén. The term *wén* only occurs four times in other passages, none of which explicitly discusses the concept of 'civility/civilization.'[100] First, in *Mencius* 6A17, *wén* is used in the concrete sense of 'ornamental decoration' or 'pattern embroidery' on a garment.[101] Second, in *Mencius* 5A4, *wén* refers to 'rhetoric' or the 'ornamental structuring' of a linguistic utterance.[102] Third, in *Mencius* 4B21, *wén* appears to be used in the meaning '(rhetorical) style' to describe the particular manner in which a certain type of historical annals were written.[103]

Finally, the fourth occurrence of *wén* in *Mencius* 4A27 appears to be a verb in the general sense of 'refining' or 'patterning/structuring':

(15) The content of 'Goodness' (*rén* 仁) is the serving of one's parents. The content of 'dutifulness' (*yì* 義) is obedience to one's elder brothers. The content of wisdom is to understand these two and to hold fast to them. The content of the rites is to regulate and to 'pattern/refine' (***wén***) these two. (仁之實事親是也。義之實從兄是也。智之實知斯二者弗去是也。禮之實節文斯二者是也)[104]

Here, as in the *Analects*, 'serving one's parents' (*shì qīn* 事親) or 'filial piety' (*xiào* 孝), as well as 'serving elder brothers' (*cóng xiōng* 從兄) or 'respecting/deferring to elder brothers' (*tì* 悌), are the purpose or meaning of 'Goodness' (*rén* 仁) and 'rightness/duty' (*yì* 義), respectively.[105] The purpose or meaning of the 'rites' (*lǐ*) is to 'restrain' (*jié* 節) and 'pattern' (*wén*) these two virtues of 'Goodness' and 'rightness/duty.' The *Mencius*' use of *wén* as a transitive verb in this passage is perhaps best compared to a similar use of the term in *Analects* 14.12, which describes the 'complete person' (*chéng rén* 成人) as someone who has been 'refined/decorated/patterned' (*wén*) through 'rites and music' (*lǐ yuè* 禮樂).[106] But while the verbal use of *wén* in *Analects* 14.12 refers to the process of 'morally refining' or 'civilizing' an individual through the 'rites,' in (15) it describes one

120   *Coiners and critics of 'civility/civilization' (wén)*

of the functions of the 'rites' as the process of 'polishing'[107] or 'refining' the two virtues of 'filial piety' and 'respect for elder brothers.'

Thus, in the *Mencius* the term *wén* is never used as a noun referring to the concept of 'civility/civilization.' In this respect, it differs sharply from the *Analects* and the *Xúnzǐ*, which both frequently discuss the concept of 'civility/civilization' (*wén*) explicitly as a key term in their theories of moral education. How can we explain this difference? The *Analects* and the *Xúnzǐ* both emphasize the role of the teachers (and sages) in fashioning or molding people into decent human beings by teaching them to behave according to the ideal norms of behavior established by the sage–kings. Human beings are believed to be born without innate knowledge of proper social norms—hence their need to emulate the external models of behavior embodied in the Zhōu tradition. If not, they will end up as 'birds and beasts' (*qín shòu*).[108] This shared assumption of the *Analects* and the *Xúnzǐ* (that human nature is a moral 'blank slate') is reflected in the fact that both tend to use craft metaphors to describe the process of edification. As discussed in Chapter 2, the jade-carving metaphors for moral edification found in the *Analects* and the *Xúnzǐ* imply that the raw material or input, or 'human nature' (*xìng*), is devoid of an innate potential to develop moral values and correct behavior on its own. In the same way that a raw piece of jade needs to be worked on by an expert jade carver in order to transform it into a beautifully decorated vessel, so also human nature needs to receive knowledge of normative values from the outside (teachers, writings, etc.).[109]

In contrast to the *Analects* and the *Xúnzǐ*, the dominant metaphor for moral edification in the *Mencius* is taken from agriculture. Unlike the *Analects* and the *Xúnzǐ*, the *Mencius* assumes that human beings are born with the innate potential to develop knowledge of normative values on their own. Just as humans are born with four limbs, the *Mencius* assumes that they are also born with four 'sprouts' (*duān* 端) of virtue that have the innate potential to grow and flourish if they are tended to in the appropriate way.[110] In other words, human beings are more like domesticated plants than raw jade, clay, or dead wood. A passage in the *Mencius* compares young men to a crop of barley. "In good years the young men are mostly lazy, while in bad years they are mostly violent." This difference is not due to "Heaven-bestowed endowment" but rather to "what ensnares their hearts." This is similar to growing barley: "Sow the seeds and cover them with soil. The place is the same and the time of sowing is also the same. The plants shoot up and by the summer solstice they all ripen. If there is any unevenness, it is because the soil varies in richness and there is no uniformity in the fall of rain and dew and the amount of human effort devoted to tending it."[111]

Although the teacher is still necessary, his role is not as important as in the *Analects* and the *Xúnzǐ*. In contrast to stones and clay, which are completely reliant on external effort, barley seeds will still sprout and grow (albeit without flourishing) without a caring farmer weeding, fertilizing, and watering his fields. But just as a farmer is needed to achieve a bountiful crop, so too is the teacher important in ensuring the best outcome of the edification process. Like a diligent farmer,

*Coiners and critics of 'civility/civilization' (*wén*)* 121

he provides the proper environment in which the student can develop his innate moral potential. In sum, as Slingerland (2003b) notes, "domesticated plants thus represent for Mencius the perfect marriage of human effort with natural tendencies, and thereby serve as the ideal metaphor for the 'cultivation'" needed to bring to maturation innate but latent moral tendencies.[112]

The incompatibility of *wén* and Mencian theories of moral edification is revealed by the following passage from Mencius' dialogue with Gàozǐ, who endorsed a more externalist approach to moral education:

(17) Gàozǐ said, "Human nature is like the [wood of the] *qǐ* willow. Duty is like cups and bowls. To make Goodness and duty (*rényì* 仁義) out of human nature is like making cups and bowls out of the [wood of the] *qǐ* willow." Mencius replied, "Can you follow the nature of the *qǐ* willow when making your cups and bowls? Or is it in fact the case that you will have to mutilate the *qǐ* willow when making it into cups and bowls? If you have to mutilate the *qǐ* willow when making it into cups and bowls, must you then also mutilate people when making them Good and dutiful?" (告子曰性猶杞柳也；義猶桮棬也。以人性為仁義猶以杞柳為桮棬。孟子曰子能順杞柳之性而以為桮棬乎? 將戕賊杞柳而後以為桮棬也? 如將戕賊杞柳而以為桮棬，則亦將戕賊人以為仁義與?)[113]

Gàozǐ's woodcarving metaphor indicates that he assumes normative values must have a source external to human nature. Devoid of normative values, un-edified individuals must rely on a teacher to 'carve them into shape.'[114] In contrast, for Mencius, woodcarving results in the destruction of the wood's originally innate potential. Mencius is not against the 'rites' or the refined tradition of the Zhōu elite, but he avoids the term 'civility/civilization' (*wén*) because it has connotations of an 'externally applied pattern' that clashes with his internalist assumption about human nature.

Conclusion

A particular language-specific form of civilizational consciousness emerged in small coteries around thinkers such as Confucius around 600–400 BCE. In the framework developed in Chapter 1, this collective consciousness can be called "civilizational" because it is articulated through combinations of meaning components akin to the five semantic molecules of the early European concept of 'civilization,' that is, 'progress,' 'civility,' 'police,' 'distinctions,' and 'universality.' The civilizational consciousness that emerged among a segment of the Zhōu elite on the eve of the Warring States period is much later than the "origin of Chinese civilization" proposed by most archaeologists, which tend to range from 4000 BCE to 1000 BCE. As mentioned in the introduction, asking when "Chinese civilization" emerged is very different from asking when civilizational consciousness emerged. The first question uses the word *civilization* in the archaeological sense to refer

122   *Coiners and critics of 'civility/civilization' (*wén*)*

to a set of criteria for "civilization" (monumental architecture, writing, and so forth; see Figures 1.7 and 1.8 in Chapter 1). The second asks when an indigenous, language-specific universal concept of 'civilization' (as mapped in Figure 1.4 in Chapter 1, and Figure 2.3 in Chapter 2) was first explicitly articulated, either in phrasal combinations of words for its semantic molecules, or in a single word, such as 'civility/civilization' (*wén*).

Dating pre-Qín civilizational consciousness to the middle of the first millennium BCE allows us to avoid anachronistic translations of the name King Wén in pre-Warring States texts as the 'civil/cultured/accomplished King.' As discussed in Chapter 2, before the Warring States period King Wén meant '(awe-inspiringly) beautiful King.' Although Warring States texts state that King Wén used 'civility/civilization' (*wén*) to rule (see [3] above), we now know that King Wén and his contemporaries did not use the word *wén* in this meaning. The chronology of the coining of the word 'civility/civilization' (*wén*) proposed here enables us to avoid being influenced by the problematic tendency in the commentarial tradition to project Warring States meanings onto words in pre-Warring States texts.

While the word 'civility/civilization' (*wén*) entered the shared vocabulary of the literate community of moral philosophers and masters of statecraft in the Warring States period, attitudes toward it differed greatly. As I have argued, it was embraced in externalist virtue–ethical philosophical frameworks such as the *Analects* and the *Xúnzǐ*, but proponents of other philosophies either rejected or ignored it. According to the *Mencius*, anti-*wén* utilitarian philosophy of the *Mòzǐ* as well as anti-*wén* primitivist ideas akin to those promoted by "Mending Nature" chapter were popular during the Warring States period. Anti-*rú* theories of statecraft based on the concept of 'laws' or 'promulgated models' (*fǎ*), such as the *Hánfēizǐ*, also flourished in the late Warring States period. As discussed above, these philosophies were all critical of the rúist concept of 'civility/civilization.' Even a virtue-ethical thinker and self-proclaimed *rú* and follower of Confucius such as Mencius shied away from using the term 'civility/civilization' (*wén*) because it was informed by an externalist 'pattern' metaphor that clashed with his own internalist assumptions about human nature. Thinkers embracing the concept 'civility/civilization' were not in the majority, and critical voices abounded. It would therefore be wrong to assume that a single monolithic civilizational consciousness was widely shared in the Warring States period.

Unlike the English word *civilization*, which has enjoyed immense popularity since its introduction in the eighteenth century, the word 'civility/civilization' (*wén*) never caught on in a comparable way in the Warring States period. Part of the explanation for this may be found in the cutthroat internecine wars that characterized the period leading up to the Qín unification of the Zhōu realm in 221 BCE. Incessant warfare forced the rulers of the mutually competing states to develop the most efficient ways to mobilize their populations and extract wealth from their domains to fund their armies. In this context, the virtue–ethical theories of statecraft in the *Analects* and the *Xúnzǐ* were less appealing than the more practical theories of the *Hánfēizǐ*.[115] The *Analects* and the *Xúnzǐ* told the rulers of

Coiners and critics of 'civility/civilization' (wén) 123

the various states that they could only become the ruler of 'all under Heaven' by engaging in moral self-cultivation and returning the system of government institution to that of the early Western Zhōu. By displaying the 'civility/civilization' (*wén*) of their own persons and of the institutions of their states, enemy states would submit peacefully (see [5]). Most rulers found such doctrines too idealistic and impractical.

By contrast, the *Hánfēizǐ* provided detailed blueprints for 'law'-based state machineries designed to extract resources and to produce conscript soldiers for the army. The fact that ideas akin to those proposed in the *Hánfēizǐ* began to be implemented in the state of Qín in the mid-fourth century BCE—and arguably contributed to making Qín the strongest of the Central States[116]—undoubtedly further contributed to the lack of interest in Confucius' concept of 'civility/civilization' (*wén*). To the rulers of the various states of the late Warring States period, ruling through strict application of 'laws' (*fǎ*) evidently seemed more successful than the virtue–ethical model of rule through a slow and painstaking process of refinement of 'civility/civilization' (*wén*). State-sponsored interest in the models of statecraft based on moral self-cultivation and a return to the 'civility/civilization' (*wén*) of the early Zhōu proposed in the *Analects* and the *Xúnzǐ* were only rekindled later with the emergence of state supported studies of pre-Qín 'Classics' in the Hàn dynasty. In the imperial ideology of the Hàn dynasty, a rhetoric of protecting the 'civilized realm' against the 'barbarians' served to justify military action.

Notes

1 *Analects* 3.14, Chéng Shùdé (1997: 182), tr. adapted from Legge (1861: 203). 子曰：「周監於二代，郁郁乎文哉！吾從周。」
2 *Zhuāngzǐ*, "Shàn xìng," Guō Qìngfán (2008: 552). Chinese: 文滅質，博溺心，然後民始惑亂 . . . 由是觀之，世喪道矣，道喪世矣。
3 For an excellent study of difference between "discovery" and "creation" of "culture" in early Chinese texts, see Puett (2001).
4 *Analects* 3.14, Chéng Shùdé (1997: 182), tr. adapted from Slingerland (2003a: 23, bold and italics added). *Wén* can also be translated as a noun here, i.e., "How splendid [its] 'civility/civilization' (*wén*) indeed!"
5 As mentioned in note 102 in the Chapter 2, it is important to distinguish between the historical Confucius and the persona(s) of Confucius presented in the *Analects* and other early Chinese texts. The words reportedly uttered by Confucius according to the *Analects* may or may not in fact have been his actual words. Due to the scarcity of sources, it is impossible to know. Hence, when I refer to the ideas of "Confucius," again it should be understood as a shorthand for "the ideas attributed to Confucius by the Warring States composers of the texts later put together as the *Analects*."
6 *Zuǒ*, Xiāng 8.3, Yáng Bójùn (1979: 956), tr. adapted from Durrant, Li, and Schaberg (2016: 942–43). Chinese: 小國無文德而有武功，禍莫大焉。
7 *Analects* 9.5, Chéng Shùdé (1997: 576–79). Some commentaries suggest that 畏 should be emended to 圍 *wéi* '(to be) surround(ed).' However, according to the reconstruction of Baxter and Sagart (2014), 畏 *ʔuj-s (> *wèi*) and 圍 *ɢʷəj (> *wéi*) were too different phonologically to be interchangeable. Hence, in *Analects* 9.5 the graph 畏 refers to *ʔuj-s (> *wèi*) 'to fear; to frighten; threaten, to be threatened'; see also Chéng Shùdé (1997: 576).

124 *Coiners and critics of 'civility/civilization' (*wén*)*

8 For studies of the *wén-wǔ* contrast, see Gawlikowski (1987/1988) and chapter 2 in Rand (2017).

9 The *Wèi Liáozǐ* contains one of the earliest explicit formulations of the distinction between *wén* and *wǔ* officials (*guān*): "Officers are divided into 'civil' (*wén*) and 'military' (*wǔ*)" 官分文武 (*Wèi Liáozǐ*, chapter 10.5 "Yuán Guān," Zhōng Zhàohuá 钟兆华 (1982: 47), tr. adapted from Sawyer (1993: 259)). Though a manuscript version of the *Wèi Liáozǐ* has been excavated from a Western Hàn tomb, parts of the *Wèi Liáozǐ* may date to the Warring States period. The "*Yòu guān* 幼官" chapter of the *Guǎnzǐ* 管子 may also be interpreted as contrasting *wén guān* and *wǔ guān*: "There should be virtuous civil and awe-inspiring military officials" 必得(德)文威武官, tr. adapted from Rickett (1985: 168–69). However, rejecting the emendation of 得 to 德, this sentence can also be translated "it is necessary to obtain officials who are 'morally refined' (*wén*), 'awe-inspiring' (*wēi*), and 'martial' (*wǔ*).'" "*Yòu guān*" dates from the late Warring States or early Hàn; see Rickett (1985: 168–69). The *Hánfēizǐ* passage in (10) also bears witness to a professionalization of 'war.'

10 *Lǐjì*, "Jì Fǎ 祭法," *SSJZS* (1980: 1590), tr. adapted from McNeal (2012: 13). An alternative translation based on the punctuation in the *SSJZS* would be "King Wén used *wén* to govern; King Wǔ used *wǔ* to gain merit; thereby they rid the people of disaster(s)."

11 The *wén-wǔ* contrast is also found in the Shanghai Museum bamboo manuscripts, and thus likely dates to the fourth century BCE: "If one is trusted in *wén*, then one will obtain officials, if one is trusted in *wǔ*, then one will obtain fields. 'Morally refined' (*wén*) charismatic power [serves to] govern, 'martial' (*wǔ*) charismatic power [serves to] attack. *Wén* brings to life and *wǔ* kills" 信文得吏信武得田文德治武德伐文生武殺 ("Tiān zǐ jiàn zhōu 天子建州," strip 5, Mǎ Chéngyuán 馬承源 (2007: 316–18)).

12 *Lǚshì Chūnqiū*, 23/6.1, tr. adapted from Knoblock and Riegel (2000: 602). Elsewhere the *Lǚshì Chūnqiū* describes an official called Níng Yuè who excelled at both 'civility/civilization' (*wén*) and 'war/military force' (*wǔ*): "When he used 'warfare' (*wǔ*), he won through force. When he used **'civility/civilization' (*wén*)**, he won through moral virtue/power" 用武則以力勝，用文則以德勝 (*Lǚshì Chūnqiū*, 15/6.4, tr. adapted from Knoblock and Riegel (2000: 361–2)).

13 As observed by Masayuki Sato 佐藤將之 (2013: 227–33), several passages in the *Xúnzǐ* reveal close connections between 'civility/civilization' (*wén*) and the 'rites' (*lǐ*).

14 'Ritualized liturgy' appears to be an early meaning of the word *lǐ*, from which later meanings derived.

15 Pines (2000: 1–41). For analysis of the 'rites' (*lǐ*) as social performance, see Fingarette (1972).

16 Pines (2000: 1–41).

17 *Xúnzǐ* 19.3, Wáng Xiānqiān (1988: 357). Original Chinese: 禮者 . . . 以貴賤為文. See also *Xúnzǐ* 27.45, Wáng Xiānqiān (1988: 497).

18 See, for example, *Analects* 2.7, Chéng Shùdé (1997: 85–8), tr. Slingerland (2003a: 10).

19 Pines (2000: 1–41).

20 *Xúnzǐ* 19.11, Wáng Xiānqiān (1988: 375), for alternative translation; see also Hutton (2014: 216).

21 As discussed in chapter 2, 'awe-inspiringly beautiful' (*wén*) was reinterpreted to mean 'morally refined' by the time of Confucius. However, here the expression *wén maò* 'morally refined appearance' indicates that morally reinterpreted *wén* could also refer to the external 'appearance and charisma of moral perfection' manifested in a person's physical appearance, actions, and demeanor. For physical correlates of 'virtue' in early China, see Csikszentmihalyi (2004).

22 For analysis of the concept of 'music' (*yuè*) in early Chinese theories of governance, see Brindley (2012: 25–85). As observed by Brindley (2012: 44), the authors of the *Zuǒzhuàn* "link music to the ideal, single, civilized culture" of the Zhōu elite traditions.

23 *Xúnzǐ* 20.2, Wáng Xiānqiān (1988: 380). Chinese: 夫聲樂之入人也深，其化人也速，故先王謹為之文.

Coiners and critics of 'civility/civilization' (wén) 125

24 The close interconnections between 'music' and the 'rites' in good governance are also illustrated in the following *Xúnzǐ* passage: "When music is played, intentions gain purity. When rites are cultivated, conduct comes to fruition. They (music and the rites) make the ears keen hearing and the eyes bright. They harmonize and balance blood and 'material energy' (*qì*). They modify mores and changes 'customs' (*sú*), [so that] all under heaven is tranquil and those who are beautiful and good delight in each other" 樂行而志清，禮脩而行成，耳目聰明，血氣和平，移風易俗，天下皆寧，美善相樂 (*Xúnzǐ* 20, Wáng Xiānqiān (1988: 382), tr. Hutton (2014: 221)). For discussion of this passage, see Brindley (2012: 33ff).

25 See the *Xúnzǐ* passage in (2) in chapter 5.

26 *Xúnzǐ* 7.1, Wáng Xiānqiān (1988: 108). For an alternative translation, see Hutton (2014: 48).

27 *Xúnzǐ* 14.6, Wáng Xiānqiān (1988: 263). The idea that 'those above' (*shàng*), who have *wén*, rule 'those below' (*xià*) is also present in the passage from *Zuǒzhuàn* Xiāng 31.13 discussed as (6) in chapter 2 where those governed 'fear'/'are in awe' (*wèi*) over the 'dignified' (*wēi*) *wén*-appearance and demeanor of their superiors.

28 These passages thus indicate that 'civility/civilization' (*wén*) was mainly conceived of as a property of the ruler and ruling elite, that is 'those above' (*shàng* 上). Like the modern Franglophone concepts of 'civility' and 'civilization' which could be referred to by the term *civility* in sixteenth- to eighteenth-century English and French, pre-Qín 'civility/civilization' (*wén*) was also an elitist concept designed by the Zhōu elite to justify and maintain their place at the top of the social hierarchy.

29 See Pines (2002a: 101),"Joseph Levenson defined the traditional concept of *tiānxià* 天下 ('world,' 'All under Heaven') as referring primarily to a cultural realm, being 'a regime of value,' as opposed to a political unit, *guó* 國, 'a state.'" See Levenson (1952). See also Pines (2000), Pines (2008), Pines (2009).

30 Though ostensibly set in the seventh century BCE, this story was likely written two centuries later in the early Warring States period.

31 'Goodness' (*rén*) is the highest stage of moral perfection in the *Analects*. Someone who is Good (*rén*) fully embodies Confucius' ideal of spontaneously following the 'Way' (*dào*). Other translations of *rén* include 'benevolent' and 'humane.'

32 *Analects* 14.17, Chéng Shùdé (1997: 989–96), tr. adapted from Slingerland (2003a: 161).

33 Pines (2002a: 104).

34 That members of the Zhōu elite considered it uncouth to step outside without first tying up one's hair is also indicated by the following passage from *Mencius*: "Now if a fellow-lodger is involved in a fight, it is right for you to rush to his aid with your hair hanging down and your cap untied. But it would be misguided to do so if it were only a fellow villager. There is nothing wrong with bolting your door" 今有同室之人鬥者救之雖被髮纓冠而救之可也。鄉鄰有鬥者被髮纓冠而往救之則惑也雖閉戶可也 (*Mencius* 4B29, tr. Lau (2004: 95)). For the *rú*, who were specialists of the Zhōu 'rites' (*lǐ*), wearing one's hair loose was considered an uncivilized, inferior 'local custom' (*sú*). For "unbound hair" as marker of non-Zhōu identity, see also Brindley (2015: 143–44). The "civilized" Zhōu realm is referred to in the *Lǚshì Chūnqiū* as the "states where people wear caps and belts" 凡冠帶之國 (*Lǚshì Chūnqiū* 17/6.2, tr. adapted from Knoblock and Riegel (2000: 328)).

35 As observed by Pines (2002a: 103), several *Zuǒzhuàn* passages support interpreting *tiānxià* as a "regime of value" based on the shared values and traditions of the Zhōu elite. Pines (2002a: 102, n. 11) analyzes *tiānxià* in *Zuǒ*, Zhuāng 12: 192; Cheng 2: 804; Xiāng 26: 1112; Xiāng 31: 1195; Zhāo 8: 1302; Dìng 10: 1583 as referring to the "public opinion" of the pan-Zhōu elite.

36 According to Pines (2002a), in the *Zuǒzhuàn* the limits of *tiānxià* "never surpassed that of the Zhōu world: alien tribes were apparently beyond the fringes of All under Heaven" (see, for example, *Zuǒ*, Xi 24). "Tiānxià is . . . coterminous with Zhōngguó,

126 *Coiners and critics of 'civility/civilization' (*wén*)*

and the Róng are evidently excluded from it, just as barbarians were often excluded from the Greek oikoumenē" (Pines 2002a: 103).

37 "*Tiānxià* was a supra-political unit, larger than the manageable *Zhōngguó*, 'the Central States'" (Pines 2002a: 101).

38 'Barbarians' and non-elite members of Zhōu society could become part of the civilized realm of 'all under Heaven' (*tiānxià*) by abandoning their misguided local customs and adopting the universally applicable 'rites' of the Zhōu elite. For criticism of this view, see Yang Shao-yun (2014: xii–xxviii).

39 Pines (2002a: 102). As observed by Pines (2002a: 102, n. 6), *tiānxià* does occur in one bronze inscription from the late fourth century BCE; see also Mattos (1997: 104–11). The expression *tiānxià* 天下 is frequently found in Warring States period texts. It was "introduced into political discourse relatively late, and is largely a creation of the middle to late Spring and Autumn period (722–453)" (Pines 2002a: 101). For the origin of the concept of *tiānxià*, see also Gān Huáizhēn (2010).

40 Pre-Warring States *tiānxià* may also mean '[everything] under [the supreme deity] Heaven'; see Pines (2002a: 102).

41 "Shao Gao," tr. adapted from Legge (1960: 432). Original Chinese: 其惟王位在德元，小民乃惟刑；用于天下，越王顯。 According to Nylan (2001: 135), the "Shao Gao" was likely composed in pre-Warring States times.

42 Support for this reading of *tiānxià* can be found the phrase *tiān zhī xià* 天之下 in Máo 205: "Everywhere 'under Heaven' is the King's land, each of those who live on the land is the King's servant" 溥天之下，莫非王土，率土之濱，莫非王臣 (SSJZS (1980: 463), tr. Pines (2002a: 102). For discussion of other occurrences of *tiānxià* in the *Book of Poetry*, see Pines (2000).

43 Pines (2002a: 102).

44 In Koselleck's terminology, both the period from the sixteenth to the eighteenth century in Europe and the Warring States period in China can be characterized as "threshold periods" (or "saddle period" after Koselleck's German term *Sattelzeit*).

45 *Lǚshì Chūnqiū*, 20/1.2, tr. adapted from Knoblock and Riegel (2000: 511).

46 The "Xì Cí," a Warring States addition to the *Changes*, states "[i]n the remote past [people] lived in 'caves and dwelt in the wild' [*yě chǔ*]; in later times the sages replaced [these] with palaces and halls" 上古穴居而野處後世聖人易之以宮室 (*SSJZS* 1980: 87). As observed by Shaughnessy (1993: 216; 21), commentaries of the *Changes* included in the received *Book of Changes* [including the "Xì Cí"] "reflect the worldview of the Late Warring States or Han periods" and probably "attained their present form in the mid-third to the early second century B.C."

47 See Cho-Yun Hsu (1999: 548): "Intermingled among the Zhōu states were numerous non-Zhōu peoples who appear not to have formed complicated statehood structures. When the Zhōu conquered the eastern territory, their vassal states were mainly garrison stations at strategic spots, many of them already inhabited . . . texts refer to these natives as 'people of the field' (*yě rén* 野人) . . . They were regarded as aliens probably because they held distinctive cultural identities." As observed by Li (2008: 286), the distinction between 'people inside the city' (*guó rén* 國人) and "people of the field" (*yě rén* 野人), probably did not emerge "until the Eastern Zhou period." Western Zhōu bronze inscriptions do not refer to cities as *guó* 國 and their inhabitants as *guó rén* 國人; "instead *yi* 邑 and *yiren* 邑人 are terms to express such concepts" (Li 2008: 286).

48 See, for example, (6) in chapter 4 and examples (1–4) in chapter 5.

49 See, for example, *Xúnzǐ* 10.105–138, Wáng Xiānqiān (1988: 179–80), tr. Hutton (2014: 85–6), which describes how early rulers ended primordial strife by creating communities based on social hierarchies. Several Warring States "narratives presented the origins of civilization as a process in which humans separated themselves from animals" (Sterckx 2002: 93). *Mencius* 3A4, tr. Lau (2004: 59–60), describes humankind originally living in a bestial state of nature before sage–kings and their ministers created a civilized realm through technological advances (agriculture, flood-control, etc.)

Coiners and critics of 'civility/civilization' (wén)   127

and the establishment of social conventions (proper relations between husband and wife, etc.) and government institutions (rulers, ministers, etc.). See also *Mòzǐ* 6.1–6, Johnston (2010: 39–45).

50 For an overview of mythological figures credited with 'civilizing' humankind, see Lewis (2009). Chang (1999: 68–70) lists "heroes" and their "inventions" (*zuò* 作). As observed by Lewis (1990: 170), "the idea that humanity was created through the work of sages was common to all the philosophical schools of the period, but each school defined its own ideal of society through naming different innovations as the crucial ones that set men apart from beasts." See also Puett (2001).

51 *Mencius* 3B9, tr. adapted from Lau (1970: 113–114). Although, as discussed in subsection titled "The overlooked neglect of 'civility/civilization' (*wén*) in the Mencius" below, the *Mencius* avoids the term 'civility/civilization' (*wén*), its history of progress and decline is similar to that found in the *Analects* and the *Xúnzǐ*.

52 While the coiners of the early modern European concept of 'civilization' could refer to the conceptual component of 'progress' explicitly with the term *progress*, pre-Qín notions of 'progress' understood as 'changes for the better' were not independently lexicalized as a single word. However, such a notion of 'change for the better' was clearly present in the 'distinction' between a primitive past and a more advanced golden age. This notion of 'changes for the better' could be expressed through paraphrases involving the word 'change' (*biàn* 變). According to the *Mencius*, "[i]f [a ruler] follows the Way of the present day without changing current customs (*sú*), then even if 'All under Heaven' were given to him, he would not be able to hold onto it for a single morning 由今之道，無變今之俗，雖與之天下，不能一朝居也 (*Mencius*, tr. Lau (2004: 141)). 'Change' (*biàn*) clearly implies 'change for the better.'

53 Bury (1921: vii).

54 The pre-Qín notion of 'progress' resembles Ancient Greek notions of 'progress.' As observed by Bury (1921: 16), the Epicureans had a notion of 'progress.' "For them, the earliest condition of men resembled that of the beasts, and from this primitive and miserable condition they laboriously reached the existing state of civilization [sic.], . . . by the exercise of human intelligence throughout a long period. The gradual amelioration of their existence was marked by the discovery of fire and the use of metals, the invention of language, the invention of weaving, the growth of arts and industries, navigation, the development of family life, the establishment of social order by means of kings, magistrates, laws, the foundation of cities." As observed by Robert Nisbet and Ludwig Edelstein, notions of progress understood as 'change for the better brought about by technological and sociopolitical developments' can be found in the works of Xenophanes (c. 570–475 BCE) and Plato (c. 428/427 or 424/423–348/347 BCE). According to Xenophanes, "the gods did not reveal to men all things in the beginning, but men through their own search find in the course of time that which is better" (as quoted in Edelstein (1967: 3) and Nisbet (1980: 11)). As described in Nisbet (1980: 24–31), Plato's works contain descriptions of the progress of humankind from an original state of nature to advanced stages of sociopolitical development. Notions of 'progress' understood broadly as 'change for the better' clearly exist beyond European modernity.

55 *Xúnzǐ* 16, Wáng Xiānqiān (1988: 302–4), tr. adapted from Hutton (2014: 171–2). In spite of his positive comparison of Qín to the state of affairs in the Golden Age of the 'ancient period' (*gǔ* 古) [=the early Western Zhōu]), Xúnzǐ criticizes Qín for its absence of *rú* scholars. Without the 'civilizing' presence of the *rú* scholars, the state of Qín lacks the moral compass of the 'civility/civilization' (*wén*) of the early Zhōu.

56 Ethnographic and sociological terminology are clearly not exclusively modern European inventions. As also pointed out by Baali (1988: 107), since the fourteenth-century Arab thinker Ibn Khaldun's work contains sophisticated sociological theories, Western sociologists are wrong to "believe that sociology began with Comte who coined the term sociology."

128 *Coiners and critics of 'civility/civilization' (wén)*

57 *Analects* 7.1, Chéng Shùdé (1997: 431). Chinese: 述而不作信而好古.
58 *Xúnzĭ* 8, Wáng Xiānqiān (1988: 140–41), tr. Hutton (2014: 64). Chinese: 法先王 . . . 以 古持今 . . . 是大儒者也.
59 Patterson (1997: 87–116).
60 For the role of language in the construction of Zhōu identity, see Behr (2010).
61 For interaction between the Shāng and surrounding peoples, see Liu and Chen (2003), Thorp (2006), among others.
62 For discussion of reference to the non-Zhōu as 'birds and beasts' (*qínshòu* 禽獸), see Di Cosmo (2002), Pines (2005), Schaberg (2001), Sterckx (2002), and Fiskesjö (2012).
63 See chapter 4 below. See also Lewis (2003) and Pines (2005).
64 *Zuŏ*, Xuān 12.2, Yáng Bójùn (1990: 733). Here *wén* is used as a verb. For discussion of this passage, see also Schaberg (2001: 252). Other translations of *wén* in Xuān 12.2 may include 'to decorate his speech with rhetorical flourishes' or 'express himself with rhetorical flourishes.' For the use of *wén* to describe 'patterned' speech, see Schaberg (2001). Durrant, Li, and Schaberg (2016: 650–51) translate 不能文 in *Zuŏ*, Xuān 12.2 as "not capable of fine expression." They explain that "although the word *wen* 文 has a broad range of meanings, here it refers primarily to the rhetoric of diplomatic speeches. See also Xi 26.3f, when Zhao Cui is recommended to represent Jin in a diplomatic meeting because he is more 'cultured' (*wen*)" (Durrant, Li, and Schaberg 2016: 650, fn. 217).
65 *Zuŏ*, Zhāo 30.3, Yáng Bójùn (1990: 1508), tr. adapted from Legge (1960: 734; ii) and Durrant, Li, and Schaberg (2016: 1708–09), who here translate *wén* as "cultured."
66 See the subsection titled "The rise of the 'Great ones' (*Xià*): Zhōu elite self-identity" in chapter 5 for discussion of the terms *Xià* and *Huá*.
67 See the discussion of consciousness and collective consciousness in the subsection titled "The lexicon as historical source" in chapter 1.
68 For the history of the tendency to render *wén* as *culture* in English translations of the *Analects*, see Bergeton (forthcoming a).
69 While the *Hánfēizĭ* may contain Qín or Hàn interpolations, the bulk was likely composed during the pre-Qín period, if not by Hán Fēi himself then by followers (Levi 1993: 116–7); see also Lundahl (1992) and Pines (2002b: 695).
70 The term *fă* is often translated as 'laws.' However, this translation obscures the important differences between the modern Western concept of 'law' and the pre-Qín concept of 'promulgated models/regulations' (*fă*). Laws, in the modern Western sense, not only limit the actions of citizens but also protect the rights of the individual vis-à-vis the authorities. In contrast, people living in the Warring States period were not citizens with rights protected by laws; they were subjects of autocrats controlling the populace to serve their own interests. These rulers were assisted by masters of statecraft, such as *Hán Fēi*, who designed systems of 'promulgated models' (*fă*). The *fă* were not "laws" protecting citizens in a system characterized by the *rule of law* but rather regulations and restrictions imposed on the population to control the population and ensure peaceful extraction of resources through taxation and conscription. The *fă* were 'promulgated models' of behavior which the people had to follow under threat of punishment. This was *rule by law* rather than *rule of law*. For the concept of *fă*, see also Brown and Sanft (2011).
71 For the critique of the *rú* notion of *wén* in the *Hánfēizĭ*, see also Péng Yàfēi (1996: 42) among others.
72 *Hánfēizĭ* 49, Wáng Xiānshèn (2006: 449).
73 *Hánfēizĭ* 49, Wáng Xiānshèn (2006: 452).
74 For the translation of *wénxué* as 'polite studies,' see note 121 in chapter 2.
75 See also *Hánfēizĭ* 49: "Thus, in the calculations of the 'common man' (*pĭfū*), nothing compares . . . to practicing 'polite studies' (*wénxué*) . . . Having practiced **polite studies' (*wénxué*)** he will become a renowned master. . . . Thus, if one has no merit but obtains office, and if one has no rank but is illustrious, and if government is practiced

Coiners and critics of 'civility/civilization' (wén)   129

in this way, then the state will by necessity be disordered and the ruler will by necessity be endangered" 然則為匹夫計者，莫如... 習文學。... 文學習則為明師... 然則無功而受事，無爵而顯榮。為有政如此，則國必亂，主必危矣 (Wáng Xiānshèn (2006: 450, boldface added)). Elsewhere the *Hánfēizǐ* explicitly identifies 'retainer–officials pursuing **polite studies' (*wénxué*)** 文學之士 as "people who depart from the 'laws' (*fǎ*)" 離法之民 (*Hánfēizǐ* 46, Wáng Xiānshèn (2006: 415)).

76 See *Hánfēizǐ* 32.1, Wáng Xiānshèn (2006: 263) and *Hánfēizǐ* 32.4, Wáng Xiānshèn (2006: 270).

77 See *Hánfēizǐ* 49, Wáng Xiānshèn (2006: 450). Chinese: 富國以農，距敵恃卒，而貴文學之士.

78 *Hánfēizǐ* 47, Wáng Xiānshèn 王先慎 (2006: 425). Chinese: 息文學而明法度. This passage explicitly criticizes Confucius and Mòzǐ as parasites pursuing futile knowledge while neglecting to "plough and weed."

79 See *Analects* 13.18 (Chéng Shùdé (1997: 922–26), tr. Slingerland (2003a: 147)) where Confucius explicitly states that filial piety overrides the legal system.

80 The *Mòzǐ* was composed over an extended period of time; see Graham (1993: 336–41). Based on the criticism of Mòzǐ in the *Mencius*, we know that that ideas attributed to Mòzǐ circulated in the fourth century BCE. I assume that the *Mòzǐ* passages discussed here reflect the intellectual milieu of the early fourth century BCE. According to Pines (2002b: 695), the core chapters of the *Mòzǐ* "originated within Mozi's lifetime (ca. 460–390 B.C.) or shortly thereafter." See also Maeder (1992).

81 I am using the term *consequentialist* as defined in Van Norden (2007).

82 See, for example, the "Promoting the Worthy" chapters in the *Mòzǐ* (Johnston 2010: 54–89).

83 For the *Mòzǐ*'s critique of the *rú* notion of *wén*, see also Péng Yàfēi (1996: 42).

84 See Pines (2002a: 108ff): "Mozi saw the Central States as part of All under Heaven rather than its totality."

85 *Mòzǐ* 6.3, Johnston (2010: 40–1).

86 *Xúnzǐ* 21.4, Wáng Xiānqiān (1988: 392), tr. adapted from Knoblock (1988–1994: III; 102).

87 *Xúnzǐ* 10.9, Wáng Xiānqiān (1988: 185).

88 See *Xúnzǐ* 10.1, Wáng Xiānqiān (1988: 180). This passage appears to respond to Mòzǐ's criticism of displays of *wén*-accouterments in (12) above which Xúnzǐ considered important to the establishment of social hierarchies.

89 For an alternative analysis of the concept of *wén* in the *Xúnzǐ*, see Chén Yǒngchāo (1997).

90 *Mòzǐ* 32, Johnston (2010: 306–17).

91 *Mòzǐ* 25, Johnston (2010: 210–31).

92 It may also be a Qín or Western Hàn text. For the composition of the *Zhuāngzǐ*, see Roth (1993) and Klein (2010).

93 Graham (1981: 170).

94 This is in direct opposition to Xúnzǐ's emphasis on using conscious deliberations of the 'heart-mind' (*xīn*) to guide actions.

95 *Zhuāngzǐ*, "Shàn xìng," Guō Qìngfán (2008: 552), tr. adapted from Graham (1981: 171–2) and Mair (1994: 149–50). See also Skaja (1998).

96 As similar negative appraisal of the civilizing efforts of ancient sage–rulers is expressed in *Lǎozǐ* 17, 18, and 38.

97 I am using the terms *internalist* and *externalist* as defined in Slingerland (2003b). Externalist works (such as the *Analects* and the *Xúnzǐ*) assume that normative values are not innately present in human nature; they must be acquired from external sources (e.g., transmitted traditions of the sages). In contrast, for internalist thinkers, "we already are good, and we merely need to allow this virtuous potential to realize itself. *Zhuangzi*, *Laozi* and the *Mencius* fall into this camp" (Slingerland 2003b: 12).

130 *Coiners and critics of 'civility/civilization' (*wén*)*

98 As discussed in the subsection "'As if carved, as if polished': '*wén*' as acquired cultural capital" in chapter 2, 'substance' (*zhì*) is also contrasted with 'civility/civilization' (*wén*) in *Analects* 6.18. However, the *Analects* advocates pursuing a balance between 'civility/civilization' (*wén*) and 'substance' (*zhì*).

99 The *Mencius* was likely composed in the late fourth or early third century BCE; see Lau (1993) and Pines (2002b: 695). The analysis of *wén* presented in this subsection is based in part on Bergeton (2017). I am grateful to the editors of the *Southeast Review of Asian Studies* (*SERAS*) for granting me permission to reprint passages from this article.

100 In 47 of the 51 occurrences of <文> in the *Mencius* it is part of a name; King Wén alone is mentioned 36 times.

101 "Pattern-embroidered [garments]" 文繡, M6A17, tr. adapted from Lau (1970: 169).

102 According to Mencius, "when explaining the *Songs*, one should not allow 'rhetoric/eloquence' (*wén*) to obscure the statements, nor the statements to obscure the intended meaning" 說詩者，不以文害辭，不以辭害志 (M5A4, tr. adapted from Lau (1970: 142)). As argued in Bergeton (2013) and Bergeton (2017), here *wén* most likely refers to the 'rhetorical patterning/decoration' (*wén*) of an 'utterance/statement' (*cí* 辭). For other readings, see Dīng Xiùjú (2011), Hú Wèi (2006) and Zhōu Yùkǎi (2002).

103 "The *Shèng* of the Jìn, the *Táo Wù* of Chǔ and the *Chūnqiū* of Lǔ are [all] one [kind of historical records]. The events recorded [in them] concern Duke Huán of Qí and Duke Wén of Jìn, and the 'style/form' (*wén*) is that of the official historian" 晉之《乘》楚之《檮杌》魯之《春秋》一也。其事則齊桓晉文，其文則史 (M4B21, tr. adapted from Lau (2004: 92)). In spite of the diversity of opinions on the meaning of *wén* in *Mencius* 4B21, there is no evidence that it means 'civility' or 'civilization.' Lau's (2004: 92) reading of *wén* in this passage as 'rhetoric' or '(rhetorical) style,' which is also followed by Van Norden (2008: 108), seems most plausible. M4B21 describes which aspects of the study of historical records Confucius considered most important. The study of history was one of the topics that Confucius viewed as contributing to the 'civility/moral refinement' (*wén*) of the 'noble man' (*jūnzǐ* 君子). The *Mencius* implies that one should extract the moral instruction (*yì* 義) of historical works from both the examples of good and bad behavior in the events *wén* recorded therein as well as from the style (*wén*) in which they are composed, that is, the style of a 'historical scribe' (*shǐ* 史).

104 M4A27, tr. adapted from Lau (1970: 127).

105 See *Analects* 1.2, 1.6.

106 See *Analects* 14.12, Chéng Shùdé (1997: 969), also discussed in the subsection "'As if carved, as if polished': '*wén*' as acquired cultural capital" in chapter 2.

107 Pre-eighteenth-century French dictionaries define *civilizer* as 'to polish manners' (*polir les mœurs*). It may be possible to translate *wén* in (15) as 'polish' in this sense.

108 A *Xúnzǐ* passage describes the 'rites' (*lǐ*) as something 'patterned/decorated/refined' (*wén*) which must be applied to native 'human nature' (*xìng* 性) to make people 'elegant/proper' (*yǎ* 雅) 'noble men' (*jūnzǐ*) and save them from becoming like birds and beasts (*Xúnzǐ* 26.1, Wáng Xiānqiān 王先謙 (1988: 472–3)). For discussion of pre-Qín ideas of how a lack of adherence to the rites (*lǐ*) makes people become like 'birds and beasts,' see also Lewis (1990), Sterckx (2002), Pines (2005) and Fiskesjö (2012).

109 Slingerland (2003b).

110 *Mencius* 2A:6. The basic meaning of *duān* 端 is 'tip.' The word *duān* can refer to the 'tips' or 'sprouts' of plants as they emerge from the ground. In *Mencius* 2A:6 the word is used metaphorically to refer to the innate 'sprouts' of human virtues.

111 *Mencius* 6A:7; tr. adapted from Lau (1970: 164). Chinese: 富歲子弟多賴；凶歲子弟多暴。非天之降才爾殊也，其所以陷溺其心者然也。今夫麰麥，播種而耰之，其地同，樹之時又同，浡然而生，至於日至之時，皆熟矣。雖有不同，則地有肥磽，雨露之養、人事之不齊也。

112 Slingerland (2003b: 15). For an explicit self-cultivation as agriculture metaphor, see the anecdote about a farmer from Song in *M*2A:2.

113 *Mencius* 6A:1; tr. adapted from Slingerland (2003b:150).
114 Slingerland (2003b: 234).
115 The *Book of Lord Shang* proposed reforms similar to those outlined in the *Hánfēizǐ*. For the militarization of society proposed in the *Book of Lord Shang*, see Pines (2016: 97–134). For a translation of the *Book of Lord Shang*, see Pines (2017).
116 See Lewis (2007: 30–50).

References

Baali, Fuad. 1988. *Society, State, and Urbanism: Ibn Khaldun's Sociological Thought* (SUNY Press: Albany).
Baxter, William Hubbard, and Laurent Sagart. 2014. *Old Chinese: A New Reconstruction* (Oxford University Press: Oxford).
Behr, Wolfgang. 2010. 'Role of Language in Early Chinese Constructions of Ethnic Identity', *Journal of Chinese Philosophy*, 37: 567–87.
Bergeton, Uffe. 2013. 'From Pattern to "Culture"? Emergence and Transformations of Metacultural Wén', Dissertation, The University of Michigan.
———. 2017. 'The Overlooked Neglect of "Civility/Civilization" (*Wén*) in Mencius', *Southeast Review of Asian Studies (SERAS)*, 39: 1–13. www.asia-studies.com/asia/SERAS/2017/1.pdf.
———. forthcoming a. 'Found (and Lost) in Translation: The Emergence of "Culture" in the Analects', *Harvard Journal of Asiatic Studies*.
———. forthcoming b. 'From "Awe-Inspiringly Beautiful" to "Patterns in Conventionalized Behavior": Historical Development of the Metacultural Concept of Wén in Pre-Qín China', *Journal of the American Oriental Society*.
Brindley, Erica. 2012. *Music, Cosmology, and the Politics of Harmony in Early China* (SUNY Press: New York).
———. 2015. *Ancient China and the Yue: Perceptions and Identities on the Southern Frontier, c.400 BCE–50 CE* (Cambridge University Press: Cambridge).
Brown, Miranda, and Charles Sanft. 2011. 'Categories and Legal Reasoning in Early Imperial China: The Meaning of Fa in Recovered Texts', *Oriens Extremus*, 50: 283–306.
Bury, J. B. 1921. *The Idea of Progress: An Inquiry into Its Origin and Growth* (Macmillan and Company: London).
Chang, Kwang-Chih. 1999. 'China on the Eve of the Historical Period', in Michael Loewe and L. Edward Shaughnessy (eds.), *Cambridge History of Ancient China: From the Origins of Civilization to 221 B.C.* (Cambridge University Press: Cambridge), pp. 37–73.
Chén Yǒngchāo 陈泳超. 1997. 'Xúnzi "guì wén" sīxiǎng jí qí měixué yìyì 荀子"贵文"思想及其美学意义', *Jianghai Academic Journal* 江海学刊: 169–73.
Chéng Shùdé 程樹德. 1997. *Lúnyǔ jíshì* 論語集釋 (Zhōnghuá shūjú: Běijīng).
Csikszentmihalyi, Mark. 2004. *Material Virtue: Ethics and the Body in Early China* (Brill: Leiden).
Di Cosmo, Nicola. 2002. *Ancient China and Its Enemies: The Rise of Nomadic Power in East Asian History* (Cambridge University Press: Cambridge).
Dīng Xiùjú 丁秀菊. 2011. 'Mèngzi "yǐ yì nì zhì" de yǔyìxué quánshì——jī yú xiūcí lǐjiě jiǎodù 孟子"以意逆志"的语义学诠释——基于修辞理解角度', *Shāndōng dàxué xuébào* 山东大学学报: 141–46.
Durrant, Stephen W., Wai-yee Li, and David Schaberg. 2016. *Zuo Tradition: Zuozhuan* (University of Washington Press: Seattle).
Edelstein, Ludwig. 1967. *The Idea of Progress in Classical Antiquity* (Johns Hopkins Press: Baltimore).

132 *Coiners and critics of 'civility/civilization' (wén)*

Fingarette, Herbert. 1972. *Confucius: The Secular as Sacred* (Harper & Row: New York).

Fiskesjö, Magnus. 2012. 'The Animal Other: China's Barbarians and Their Renaming in the Twentieth Century', *Social Text*, 109, 29: 57–79.

Gān, Huáizhēn 甘怀真. 2010. 'Analysis and Discussion of the Establishment of the Concept of All Under Heaven (Tiānxià gàiniàn chénglì de zài tàntǎo 天下概念成立的再探讨)', *Běijīng dàxué zhōngguó gǔwénxiàn yánjiū zhōngxīn jíkān* 北京大学中国古文献研究中心集刊: 1–24.

Gawlikowski, Krzysztof. 1987/1988. 'The Concept of Two Fundamental Social Principles: *Wen* and *Wu* in Chinese Classical Thought. (Parts I & II)', *Annali*, 47/48: 397–433, 35–62.

Graham, Angus C. 1981. *Chuang-tzǔ: The Seven Inner Chapters and Other Writings from the Book Chuang-tzǔ* (Allen & Unwin: London).

———. 1986. *Studies in Chinese Philosophy and Philosophical Literature* (SUNY Press: New York).

———. 1993. 'Mo tzu 墨子', in Michael Loewe (ed.), *Early Chinese Texts: A Bibliographical Guide* (Society for the Study of Early China: Berkeley, CA), pp. 336–41.

Guō Qìngfán 郭慶藩. 2008. *Zhuāngzǐ jí jiě* 莊子集解 (Zhonghua shu ju: Beijing).

Hsu, Cho-yun. 1999. 'The Spring and Autumn Period', in Michael Loewe and L. Edward Shaughnessy (eds.), *Cambridge History of Ancient China: From the Origins of Civilization to 221 B.C.* (Cambridge University Press: Cambridge), pp. 545–86.

Hú Wèi 胡蔚. 2006. ' "yǐ wén hài cí" xīn shì – guān yú wén xué chǎn shì xué zhōng yī gè gǔ lǎo mìng tí de shāng què "以文害辞" 新释 – 关于文学阐释学中一个古老命题的商榷', *Theoretical Studies in Literature and Art* (*Wenyi lilun yanjiu* 文艺理论研究), 2006: 79–83.

Hutton, Eric L. 2014. *Xunzi* (Princeton University Press: Princeton).

Johnston, Ian. 2010. *The Mozi. A Complete Translation* (Columbia University Press: New York).

Klein, Esther. 2010. 'Were There "Inner Chapters" in the Warring States? A New Examination of Evidence About the Zhuangzi', *T'oung Pao*, 96: 299–369.

Knoblock, John. 1988–1994. *Xunzi: A Translation and Study of the Complete Works* (Stanford University Press: Stanford, CA).

Knoblock, John, and Jeffrey Riegel. 2000. *The Annals of Lü Buwei* (Stanford University Press: Stanford, CA).

Lau, D. C. 1970. *Mencius* (Penguin: Harmondsworth).

———. 1993. 'Meng tzu 孟子', in Michael Loewe (ed.), *Early Chinese Texts: A Bibliographical Guide* (Society for the Study of Early China: Berkeley, CA), pp. 331–35.

———. 2004. *Mencius* (Penguin: London).

Legge, James. 1861. *The Chinese Classics* (Trübner & Co.: London).

———. 1960. *The Chinese Classics. Vol. 5: The Ch'un Ts'ew with the Tso Chuen. London, Trübner, 1862; rpt.* (Hong Kong University Press: Hong Kong).

Levenson, Joseph Richmond. 1952. 'T'ien-hsia and Kuo, and the "Transvaluation of Values"', *The Far Eastern Quarterly*, 11: 447–51.

Levi, Jean. 1993. 'Han fei tzu 韓非子', in Michael Loewe (ed.), *Early Chinese Texts: A Bibliographical Guide* (Society for the Study of Early China: Berkeley, CA), pp. 115–24.

Lewis, Mark Edward. 1990. *Sanctioned Violence in Early China* (SUNY Press: Albany).

———. 2003. 'Custom and Human Nature in Early China', *Philosophy East and West*, 53: 308–22.

Coiners and critics of 'civility/civilization' (wén)   133

————. 2007. *The Early Chinese Empires: Qin and Han* (Belknap Press of Harvard University Press: Cambridge, MA).

————. 2009. 'The Mythology of Ancient China', in John Lagerwey and Marc Kalinowski (eds.), *Early Chinese Religion, Part One: Shang Through Han (1250 BC–220 AD)* (Brill: Leiden), pp. 543–94.

Li, Feng. 2008. *Bureaucracy and the State in Early China: Governing the Western Zhou* (Cambridge University Press: Cambridge).

Liu, Li, and Xingcan Chen. 2003. *State Formation in Early China* (Duckworth: London).

Lundahl, Bertil. 1992. *Han Fei Zi: The Man and the Word* (Institute of Oriental Languages: Stockholm).

Mǎ Chéngyuán 馬承源. 2007. *Shànghǎi bówùguǎn cáng zhànguó Chǔ zhúshū* 上海博物館藏戰國楚竹書, Vol. 6 (Shànghǎi gǔjí chūbǎnshè: Shànghǎi).

Maeder, Erik W. 1992. 'Some Observations on the Composition of the "Core Chapters" of the Mozi', *Early China*, 17.

Mair, Victor H. 1994. *Wandering on the Way: Early Taoist Tales and Parables of Chuang Tzu* (University of Hawaii Press: Honolulu).

Masayuki Sato 佐藤將之. 2013. *Xúnzǐ lǐzhì sīxiǎng de yuānyuán yǔ zhànguó zhūzi zhī yánjiū* 荀子禮治思想的淵源與戰國諸子之研究 (Guólì Táiwān dàxué chūbǎn zhōngxīn: Táiběi).

Mattos, Gilbert Louis. 1997. 'Eastern Zhou Bronze Inscriptions', in Edward J. Shaughnessy (ed.), *New Sources of Early Chinese History: An Introduction to Reading Inscriptions and Manuscripts* (Society for Study of Early China: Berkeley, CA), pp. 85–124.

McNeal, Robin. 2012. *Conquer and Govern: Early Chinese Military Texts from the Yi Zhou Shu* (University of Hawaii Press: Honolulu).

Nisbet, Robert A. 1980. *History of the Idea of Progress* (Basic Books: New York).

Nylan, Michael. 2001. *The Five "Confucian" Classics* (Yale University Press: New Haven).

Patterson, Thomas C. 1997. *Inventing Western Civilization* (Monthly Review Press: New York).

Péng Yàfēi 彭亚非. 1996. 'Xiān Qín lùn "wén" sān zhòng yàoyì 先秦论 "文" 三重要义', *Wén shǐ zhé* 文史哲: 41–5.

Pines, Yuri. 2000. 'Disputers of the Li: Breakthroughs in the Concept of Ritual in Preimperial China', *Asia Major*, 13: 1–41.

————. 2002a. 'Changing Views of *tianxia* in Pre-Imperial Discourse', *Oriens Extremus*, 43: 101–16.

————. 2002b. 'Lexical Changes in Zhanguo Texts', *Journal of the American Oriental Society*, 122: 691–705.

————. 2005. 'Beasts or Humans: Pre-Imperial Origins of Sino-Barbarian Dichotomy', in Reuven Amitai and Michal Biran (eds.), *Mongols, Turks, and Others: Eurasian Nomads and the Sedentary World* (Brill: Leiden), pp. 59–102.

————. 2008. 'Imagining the Empire? Concepts of "Primeval Unity" in Pre-imperial Historiographic Tradition', in Fritz-Heiner Mutschler and Achim Mittag (eds.), *Conceiving the Empire: China and Rome Compared* (Oxford University Press: Oxford), pp. 67–90.

————. 2009. *Envisioning Eternal Empire: Chinese Political Thought of the Warring States Era* (University of Hawaii Press: Honolulu).

————. 2016. 'A "Total War"? Rethinking Military Ideology in the *Book of Lord Shang*', *Journal of Chinese Military History*, 5: 97–134.

————. 2017. *The Book of Lord Shang* (Columbia University Press: New York).

134   Coiners and critics of 'civility/civilization' (wén)

Puett, Michael. 2001. *The Ambivalence of Creation: Debates Concerning Innovation and Artifice in Early China* (Stanford University Press: Stanford, CA).

Rand, Christopher C. 2017. *Military Thought in Early China* (SUNY Press: New York).

Rickett, W. Allyn. 1985. *Guanzi: Political, Economic, and Philosophical Essays from Early China* (Princeton University Press: Princeton).

Roth, H. D. 1993. 'Chuang tzu 莊子', in Michael Loewe (ed.), *Early Chinese Texts: A Bibliographical Guide* (Society for the Study of Early China: Berkeley, CA), pp. 56–66.

Sawyer, Ralph D. 1993. *The Seven Military Classics of Ancient China* (Westview Press: Boulder, San Francisco & Oxford).

Schaberg, David. 2001. *A Patterned Past: Form and Thought in Early Chinese Historiography* (Harvard University Asia Center: Distributed by Harvard University Press: Cambridge, MA).

Shaughnessy, Edward J. 1993. '*I ching* 易經', in Michael Loewe (ed.), *Early Chinese Texts: A Bibliographical Guide* (Society for the Study of Early China: Berkeley, CA), pp. 216–28.

Skaja, Henry G. 1998. 'How to Interpret Chapter 16 of the *Zhuangzi*: "Repairers of Nature (Shan Xing)"', in Roger T. Ames (ed.), *Wandering at Ease in the* Zhuangzi (SUNY Press: Albany), pp. 102–24.

Slingerland, Edward G. 2003a. *Analects: With Selections from Traditional Commentaries* (Hackett: Indianapolis).

———. 2003b. *Effortless Action: Wu-wei as Conceptual Metaphor and Spiritual Ideal in Early China* (Oxford University Press: Oxford).

SSJZS. 1980. *Shísān jīng zhù shū* 十三經注疏 (Zhōnghuá shūjú: Běijīng).

Sterckx, Roel. 2002. *The Animal and the Daemon in Early China* (SUNY Press: Albany).

Thorp, Robert L. 2006. *China in the Early Bronze Age: Shang Civilization* (University of Pennsylvania Press: Philadelphia).

Van Norden, Bryan W. 2007. *Virtue Ethics and Consequentialism in Early Chinese Philosophy* (Cambridge University Press: New York).

———. 2008. *Mencius* (Hackett: Indianapolis).

Wáng Xiānqiān 王先謙. 1988. *Xúnzǐ jíjiě* 荀子集解 (Běijīng Zhōnghuá shūjú: Běijīng).

Wáng Xiānshèn 王先慎. 2006. *Hánfēizǐ jíjiě* 韓非子集解 (Běijīng Zhōnghuá shūjú: Běijīng).

Yáng Bójùn 楊伯峻. 1979. '*Zuǒzhuàn* chéngshū niándài lùnshù 《左傳》成書年代論述 (Discussion and Exposition of the Compilation of the *Zuǒzhuàn*)', *Wenshi*, 6: 65–75.

———. 1990. *Chūnqiū Zuǒzhuàn zhù* 春秋左傳注 (Zhonghu shuju: Beijing).

Yang, Shao-yun. 2014. 'Rhetorical and Philosophical Uses of the Yi-Di in Mid-Imperial China, 600–1300', Dissertation, University of California Press, Berkeley, CA.

Zhōng Zhàohuá 钟兆华. 1982. *Wèiliáozi xiàozhù* 尉缭子校注 (Zhōngzhōu shūhuàshè: Zhèngzhōu shì).

Zhōu Yùkǎi 周裕锴. 2002. '"yǐ yì nì zhì" xīn shì 以意逆志" 新释', *Theoretical Studies in Literature and Art* (*Wén yì lǐ lùn yánjiū* 文艺理论研究): 71–8.

4   Inventing the 'barbarian'

From 'belligerent others' to 'civilizationally inferior others'

King Wén was born in Qí Zhōu and died in Bì Yǐng. He was a Western barbarian.

—*Mencius* 4B:1[1]

The description of King Wén (r. 1099/56–1050 BCE) as a 'Western barbarian' (*xī-yí* 西夷) in the epigraph above may seem surprising or even contradictory. King Wén was revered by many as one of the founding fathers of the Zhōu dynasty (1045–256 BCE). Confucius as well as many Warring States thinkers considered him one of the sage–rulers who brought 'civility/civilization' (*wén*) to its highest level of perfection (see the passages from *Analects* 3.14 and 9.5 in (1) and (2) in Chapter 3). In the Warring States period, King Wén's name even came to be eponymously associated with the concept of 'civility/civilization' (*wén*) itself. Why then would Mencius, who explicitly stated that he followed the teachings of Confucius, describe King Wén as a 'barbarian' (*yí* 夷)? And why did he not use one of the quasi-synonymous expressions *xī-róng* 西戎 or *róng* 戎 '(member of the) *róng* (group) who live in the west' instead of the term 'Western *yí*' (*xī-yí*)? To answer these questions, we need to explore the extent to which the word *yí* can be said to mean 'barbarian,' and how the coining of the word in this sense is related to the emergence of the concept of 'civility/civilization' (*wén*).

In this chapter, I trace the coining of the term *yí* in the meaning of '(civilizationally inferior) others' or 'barbarians' and its use as a default term for non-Zhōu groups. The construction of a dichotomy between a "civilized" self and "uncivilized" others is a central component of civilizational consciousness as defined in Chapter 1. In early modern Western Europe, the Classical term *barbarian* was well known to people reading Latin, which was standard fare for anyone acquiring an education. During the period when the early modern European universal concept of 'civilization' began to emerge in the sixteenth to the eighteenth century, Anglophone Europeans were applying the English word *barbarian* to groups they considered 'civilizationally inferior.'[2] A similar process occurred on the other side of the world some two thousand years earlier: around the beginning of the Warring States period (481–221 BCE) moral philosophers coined the term 'civility/civilization' (*wén*) and began distinguishing between the 'Great ones' (*Xià*) and

136 *Inventing the 'barbarian'*

the 'civilizationally inferior others' (*yí*). Since the dating of the emergence of a *Xià–yí* contrast is controversial, I analyze the evolution of the systems of terms for 'others' from the pre-Warring States to the Warring States period. Looking not just at semantic changes in *individual terms*, I show how *structural changes in paradigms of ethnonyms* can be used to trace the coining of words for the emerging concept of 'civilizationally inferior others' or 'barbarians.'[3]

A consensus is emerging in the growing body of work on pre-Qín identities that the Zhōu versus non-Zhōu dichotomy was defined largely in terms of differences in conventionalized behavior, such as, for example, differences in clothing, food, dwellings, burial customs, language, moral decorum, normative values, and so forth.[4] However, the question of when this dichotomy arose is still debated. I argue that the narrative that informed the conceptualization of non-Zhōu groups changed from 'warfare' in pre-Warring States times to proto-anthropological concepts (e.g., 'civility/civilization' [*wén*], 'rites' [*lǐ*] and 'customs' [*sú*]) around 600–400 BCE. In pre-Warring States times, non-Zhōu groups were typically referred to with expressions denoting specific peoples with whom the Zhōu were engaged in warfare, or with the word 'belligerent others' (*róng* 戎). In the Warring States period, the emphasis turned to differences in conventionalized values and practices both in individual behavior and government institutions. Consequently, new words for the concepts of 'civilizationally different' or 'civilizationally inferior' non-Zhōu groups developed. Within the emerging new systems of compound ethnonyms, the word *yí* 夷 had the greatest combinatorial potential and emerged as the default expression for the new concept of 'civilizationally inferior others.' The resulting *Xià–yí* dichotomy thereby became a key element of the Zhōu elite's civilizational consciousness.

Pre-Warring States vocabulary of identity: non-Zhōu as 'belligerent others'

In the Western Zhōu (1045–771 BCE) and early Spring and Autumn period (770–481 BCE), the Zhōu elite had not yet explicitly articulated a collective civilizational consciousness. That is, although they shared a ritual decorum (i.e., a set of values and practices regulating social behavior) and, to a large extent, a material culture (bronze vessels, jades, etc.), they had not yet explicitly formulated the idea of belonging to a 'civilization.'[5] At end of the Western Zhōu, the political power and influence of the Zhōu court was disintegrating. According to traditional accounts, in 771 BCE allied forces of the Western Róng and the states of Western Shen and Zheng attacked the Zhōu capital, thereby marking the end of the Western Zhōu.[6] Around the beginning of the Spring and Autumn period, a small number of large states began to emerge as powerful players in inter-state affairs, each fending for itself through diplomacy and alliance formation. Under such circumstances, *Realpolitik* overrode common heritage and often led Central States to ally with non-Zhōu groups or statelets in order to engage fellow Central States militarily. In pre-Warring States times, a 'civilizationally' defined distinction between Zhōu and non-Zhōu was therefore less important than practical security concerns and pragmatic inter-state diplomacy.[7]

Inventing the 'barbarian' 137

Before the Warring States period non-Zhōu groups were frequently conceptualized as 'belligerent others.'[8] Texts from this period often mention non-Zhōu
groups as military opponents.[9] This state of affairs is reflected in the terms for
non-Zhōu others. Pre-Warring States inscriptions on bronze vessels and received
texts such as the *Book of Songs* and the *Annals* abound in ethnonyms referring to
specific non-Zhōu groups with whom the Central States were interacting, either
through hostile warfare or peaceful alliances. Received texts and inscriptions
also contain numerous battle descriptions in which non-Zhōu groups are usually
referred to using ethnonyms referring to specific non-Zhōu enemies such as the
Huáiyí and *Mán-Jīng* in (1). Bold fonts are used to highlight the expressions:

(1) (a) Here the **Yí of Huái** come to submit . . . We have quieted the **Yí of
Huái** . . . the **Yí of Huái** have all been dealt with. . . . From afar the **Yí of
Huái** come. (淮夷攸服 . . . 既克淮夷 . . . 淮夷卒獲 . . . 憬彼淮夷)[10]
(b) Foolish were you, **Mán of Jīng**, who made a great nation into your
foe. [Fang-shu] . . . made the **Mán of Jīng** afraid. (蠢爾蠻荊，大邦
為讎！ . . . 蠻荊來威)[11]

The *Huáiyí* 淮夷 in (1a), one of the non-Zhōu groups most often mentioned in the
Book of Songs and the *Annals*, inhabited the Huái River area. The *Mán-Jīng* 蠻荊
in (1b) were a people settled in Jīng 荊, somewhere between the Han River and
the Yangzi, in what is now northern Húběi.[12] *Huái* and *Jīng* are names of places,
or toponyms, which, combined with the ethnonyms *yí* and *mán*, form what I call
'toponym compounds.'[13]

Pre-Warring States bronze inscriptions and received texts (that is, the *Annals*, the
Book of Songs, and the pre-Warring States parts of the *Changes* and the *Shàngshū*)
lack explicit anthropological descriptions of the values and conventional practices of non-Zhōu groups and indicate a greater concern with practical interaction with specific groups on a case-by-case basis, than with an across-the-board
delineation of a "civilized" world versus an "uncivilized" periphery grounded in
ethnographic differences. A strongly delineated, civilizationally defined Zhōu–
barbarian dichotomy is thus unlikely to have existed before 600–400 BCE.

Róng as general term for 'armed opponents' or 'belligerent others'

While there was no word for 'civilizationally inferior others' or 'barbarians' in the
pre-Warring States period, the word *róng* 戎 was often used to refer to non-Zhōu
groups as 'armed opponents' or 'belligerent others.' Occurrences of the word
róng in both inscriptional material and received texts from the Western Zhōu and
Spring and Autumn periods can be divided into two main uses. First, it was used
as a specific ethnonym (or part of ethnonyms) for the *Róng* peoples.[14] Second, it
was used to refer to various aspects of 'warfare,' such as 'weapons,' 'war chariots,' and 'military accomplishments.'[15] Due to its widespread use to refer to warfare and military accouterments, the term *róng* also came to be used in extended
meanings to express the dominant pre-Warring States concept of 'otherness,' that

138 *Inventing the 'barbarian'*

is, 'belligerent others.'[16] In this meaning *róng* is frequently used in pre-Warring States texts to refer to peoples and groups that could also be referred to more specifically by other ethnonyms, such as the *Xiǎnyǔn* 獫狁 in (2).[17]

(2) You used our chariots sweepingly attacking the *Xiǎnyǔn* at Gaoyin; you cut off many heads and took many prisoners. The *Róng* (戎) greatly gathered and followed chasing you, and you and the *Róng* (戎) greatly slaughtered and fought 汝以我車宕伐獫狁于高隆，汝多折首、執訊。戎大同從追汝，汝及戎大敦搏.[18]

Such uses of *róng* to refer to peoples who already had other specific names indicate that it served as a blanket term for 'belligerent others' in the pre-Warring States period.[19] Poo (2005: 46) suggests that in (2) *róng* may be "a general term referring to the foreign barbarians." The English word *barbarians* (like its Classical Greek predecessor *bárbaroi*) tends to mean 'civilizationally inferior others.'[20] However, if, as argued here, a concept of 'civilizationally inferior others' or 'barbarians' did not emerge before the middle of the first millennium BCE, then using the term *barbarian* to translate the pre-Warring States term *róng* in (2) is anachronistic. In this period, *róng* could mean 'armed enemies' or 'belligerent other(s)' but not 'barbarians,' understood as 'civilizationally inferior others.' As observed by Li (2006: 286), "it is likely that when a people was called 'Rong' the Zhōu considered them as political and military adversaries, rather than as cultural and ethnic 'others.'"

Diminishing relevance of toponym compounds

Throughout the pre-Warring States period non-Zhōu groups were found, not just outside the realm of the Central States, but also inside. At that time the area that is now China was much less densely populated than today. The elite of the Zhōu states lived inside walled cities. Between these cities lay farmland and (in many cases) uncultivated wilderness. This led to a distinction between 'people inside the city' (*guó rén* 國人), referring to the Zhōu elite, and 'people of the field' (*yě rén* 野人), which referred to non-Zhōu peoples as well as to the non-elite Zhōu population living outside the city walls.[21] In other words, in the pre-Warring States period the Zhōu often lived in relatively close proximity to non-Zhōu groups and tended to perceive these non-Zhōu groups not in terms of a civilizationally informed Zhōu versus non-Zhōu dichotomy, but rather in terms of concrete forms of interaction, whether hostile or peaceful. Hence, when the Zhōu referred to non-Zhōu groups they mostly used specific ethnonyms referring to particular peoples in particular geographical areas, as in (1), rather than blanket terms for 'barbarians.'

When the politically and militarily dominant Zhōu group expanded through military conquests and population growth, they slowly pressed non-Zhōu groups further and further away from fertile lands until some of the non-Zhōu ended up living in mountainous regions or inhospitable swamps before (in some cases) eventually disappearing completely through intermarriage and acculturation.[22] In

Inventing the 'barbarian' 139

the Warring States period, references to specific Róng, Dí, and Yí groups became scarce.[23] This indicates that the Zhōu states had begun to absorb smaller non-Zhōu peoples in their areas of influence. By the Qín unification in 221 BCE, all but pockets of non-Zhōu groups seem to have disappeared from certain areas of the Central Plain.[24]

The idea of an increasing homogenization of the Zhōu heartland vis-à-vis a non-Zhōu periphery is reflected in Warring States texts. As argued by Pines (2005: 84–5), the mythological geography found in the *Lǐjì* of a 'civilized' center of the 'Central States' (*zhōng guó*) surrounded by increasingly 'uncivilized' concentric circles of uncivilized peoples is in large part a Warring States invention.[25] To be sure, even during the Warring States period this idealized mythological worldview of a 'civilized' center surrounded by an 'uncivilized' periphery was far removed from the complex situation on the ground. Although some ethnic homogenization had taken place, it seems likely that the emergent civilizational consciousness and the accompanying, idealized dichotomy between the 'elegant' or 'civilized' (*yǎ*) 'Great ones' (*Xià*) and the 'vulgar' (*sú*) 'civilizationally inferior others' (*yí*) played the most important role in the formulation of the mythological geographies of a 'civilized' center surrounded by a periphery of increasingly 'uncivilized others.' Together these sociopolitical and epistemic changes help explain why ethnonyms referring to specific non-Zhōu groups are less frequent in Warring States texts than blanket terms for 'civilizationally different/inferior non-Zhōu others.'

The relative frequencies of three types of compound ethnonyms based on the four single-syllable ethnonyms *mán* 蠻, *yí* 夷, *róng* 戎, and *dí* 狄—that is, (i) top-onym compounds, (ii) directional compounds, and (iii) ethnonym compounds— changed significantly from the pre-Warring States to the Warring States period. These changes in relative frequencies support the hypothesis that Zhōu construc-tions of non-Zhōu groups shifted from being grounded in 'warfare' in the pre-Warring States period to being informed by a concept of 'civility/civilization' (*wén*) in the Warring States period, and that these changes took place in tandem with the emergence of a specific form of civilizational consciousness.

Toponym compounds consist of one of the four ethnonyms *mán*, *yí*, *róng*, and *dí*, combined with descriptive terms indicating a specific geographical location or group affiliation, as illustrated in (3).

(3) Toponym compounds:

a.	*Huái-yí*	淮夷	'the *Yí* of Huái'
b.	*Mán-Jīng*	蠻荊	'the *Mán* of Jīng'
c.	*Jiāng-róng*	姜戎	'the Jiāng *Róng*,' etc.

Huái and Jīng are both specific geographical names referring to the Huái River and the Jīng area, respectively. Jiāng is a term referring to people of the Jiāng clans. The term 'toponym compound' is not restricted to compounds that include place names (toponyms) but is used as a general term for ethnonyms referring to specific non-Zhōu groups that contain a word marking some type of geographical location or name of a particular group.

140   *Inventing the 'barbarian'*

Directional compounds are composed of one of the four terms *mán, yí, róng*, and *dí*, preceded by a word referring to one of the cardinal directions, as listed in (4).[26] Finally, ethnonym compounds are combinations of *mán, yí, róng*, and *dí*; see (5).

(4)   Directional compounds:

    a.   *dōng-yí*   東夷   'the *Yí*, who live in the east'
    b.   *xī-róng*   西戎   'the *Róng*, who live in the west'
    c.   *běi-dí*   北狄   'the *Di*, who live in the north'
    d.   *nán-mán*   南蠻   'the *Mán*, who live in the south'

(5)   Ethnonym compounds:

    a.   *mán-yí*   蠻夷   'The *Mán-yí*'
    b.   *róng-dí*   戎狄   'The *Róng-dí*'
    c.   *yí-dí*   夷狄   'The *Yí-dí*,' etc.

The changes in the relative frequency of the toponym compounds versus directional and ethnonym compounds in pre-Warring States versus Warring States texts indicate a shift from a system of ethnonyms based predominantly on toponyms to a system based more on directional and ethnonym compounds.[27] A comparison of selected samples of received texts from the two periods indicates that the frequency of toponym compounds (relative to directional and ethnonym compounds) fell from 84% in pre-Warring States texts (such as the *Annals*, the *Book of Songs*, and the pre-Warring States parts of the *Changes* and the *Shàngshū*) to 18% in texts from the Warring States period (such as the *Mencius*, the *Xúnzǐ*, the *Lǚshì Chūnqiū*, and the *Zuǒzhuàn*). The relative frequency of toponym compounds similarly declines in archaeological texts from 74% in Western Zhōu bronze inscriptions (BI) to 0% in recently discovered Warring States bamboo manuscripts (such as the Guōdiàn, Shàngbó, and Qīnghuá manuscripts).[28] This decline in the use of toponym compounds is likely a reflection of the sociopolitical changes that occurred in the transition from the Western Zhōu to the Warring States period, such as, for example, the reduction in the number of non-Zhōu groups and statelets in close proximity to the Central States in the center of the Zhōu realm due to acculturation and military expansion.

While these demographic and sociopolitical factors may partially account for the decrease in the number of the toponym ethnonyms, they do not account for the simultaneous rise in the frequency of directional compounds (e.g., *dōng-yí*, *xī-róng*) and ethnonym compounds (e.g., *mán-yí, róng-dí*). In pre-Warring States texts (received texts and BI combined), directional and ethnonym compounds make up 18% of the total number of compound ethnonyms of the types in (3–5); in Warring States texts (received and archaeological combined), they make up 82%. I argue that the emergence of these two paradigms of compound ethnonyms was closely linked to the inter-state Zhōu elite's emerging view of themselves as belonging to a shared 'civility/civilization' and to the Warring States invention of the concept of 'civilizationally inferior others' or 'barbarians.'

Yí as default term for 'civilizationally inferior non-Zhōu others' or 'barbarians'

It has been claimed that pre-Qín Chinese lacked a single term corresponding to the Greek word *bárbaroi* 'barbarians' (*βάρβαροι*) and instead relied on a number of different compound ethnonyms, such as *yí-dí*, *mán-yí*, *róng-dí*, *mányí-róngdí*, and so forth, to refer to 'civilizationally inferior others' in general.[29] The shared written lingua franca of the Zhōu elite during the Warring States period did indeed sometimes use these as general terms for 'non-Zhōu others' or 'civilizationally inferior others.' But, as argued here, careful analysis of the three types of compound ethnonyms based on the four mono-morphemic ethnonyms—*mán*, *yí*, *róng*, and *dí*—in (3–5) shows that the single morpheme ethnonym *yí* 夷 eventually became the default expression for 'non-Zhōu others,' both in compounds and when used on its own. Thus, while there were several expressions referring to non-Zhōu others in general, only one non-compound word, *yí*, could be used in this way.[30] Around the middle of the first millennium BCE the word *yí* became the default word for the emerging concept of 'civilizationally inferior others.'[31]

The periphery–center worldview that emerged in the Shāng dynasty was a precursor to the Warring States period view of the central states as a 'civilization' surrounded by an uncivilized periphery. In Shāng mythological geography, the Shāng realm was conceived of as a large square within the 'Shāng center' (*Zhōng Shāng* 中商) surrounded by a peripheral domain divided into 'four regions' (*sì fāng* 四方), or 'four lands' (*sì tǔ* 四土), corresponding to the four cardinal directions.[32] This worldview continued into later periods, with the 'Central States' (*Zhōng guó*) replacing the 'Shāng center' (*Zhōng Shāng*) at the center. However, it was not before the coining of civilizational consciousness around the eve of the Warring States period that this view of the world as a square became part of the Zhōu elite's self-understanding as a 'civilization.' This happened when the terms *mán*, *yí*, *róng*, and *dí* became systematically associated with the four cardinal directions, as shown in Figure 4.1.

Figure 4.1 Directional associations of *mán*, *yí*, *róng*, and *dí*.

142 *Inventing the 'barbarian'*

The association of ethnonyms with cardinal directions is explicitly stated in the *Lǐjì*:

(6) The **people to the east were called Yí**. They had their hair unbound, and tattooed their bodies. Some of them ate their food without its being cooked. **Those to the south were called Mán**. They tattooed their foreheads, and had their feet turned in toward each other. Some of them (also) ate their food without its being cooked. **Those to the west were called Róng**. They had their hair unbound, and wore skins. Some of them did not eat grain-food. **Those to the north were called Dí**. They wore skins of animals and birds, and dwelt in caves. Some of them also did not eat grain-food. The people of the **Central States (*zhōng guó*)**, and those of **Yí, Mán, Róng, and Dí**, all had their dwellings, where they lived at ease; their flavors which they preferred; the clothes suitable for them; their proper implements for use; and their vessels which they prepared in abundance. (東方曰夷，被髮文身，有不火食者矣。南方曰蠻，雕題交趾，有不火食者矣。西方曰戎，被髮衣皮，有不粒食者矣。北方曰狄，衣羽毛穴居，有不粒食者矣。中國、夷、蠻、戎、狄，皆有安居和味宜服利用備器)[33]

This passage establishes a geographical association of the *yí* with the 'east' (*dōng* 東), the *mán* with the 'south' (*nán* 南), the *róng* with the 'west' (*xī* 西) and the *dí* with the 'north' (*běi* 北). The 'customs' (*sú*) attributed to the non-Zhōu in the four directions in (6)—such as eating uncooked food, living in caves, and wearing animal skins—marked them as civilizationally inferior to the Zhōu inhabitants of the Central States who had mastered the technologically advanced practices of cooking, building houses, and weaving garments of silk and hemp. As discussed previously (Chapter 3, subsection titled "Pre-Qín concept of 'progress'"), Zhōu descriptions of the 'primitive' conventionalized behaviors of non-Zhōu others often resembled descriptions of the Zhōu ancestors before the sage–kings and their ministers initiated the 'civilizing process.' The authors of the schematic descriptions of non-Zhōu groups in the four cardinal directions in (6) are not engaging in ethnographic description; they are using non-Zhōu groups as a foil for the 'civility/civilization' of the Zhōu elite.[34] The passage from the *Guǎnzǐ* in (7) illustrates how the four terms eventually fused with their matching directional terms to form the directional compounds *dōng-yí*, *xī-róng*, *nán-mán*, and *běi-dí*. Together with the Central States, these four directional compounds referred to all the subjects of the Zhōu realm.

(7) Therefore, of the 'Yí, who live in the east' (*dōng-yí*), the 'Róng, who live in the west' (*xī-róng*), the 'Mán, who live in the south' (*nán-mán*), and the 'Dí, who live in the north' (*běi-dí*), as well as of all the Lords of the 'Central States' (*Zhōng guó*), there were none who did not submit. (故東夷西戎南蠻北狄中國諸侯莫不賓服)[35]

After the terms *mán, yí, róng*, and *dí* became associated with the cardinal directions in the Warring States period, as shown in (6–7), the single morpheme ethnonyms

Inventing the 'barbarian' 143

(*mán, yí, róng, dí*) and the more redundant corresponding directional compounds (*nán-mán, dōng-yí, xī-róng, běi-dí*) could be used more or less synonymously.[36] This change spans the first two stages in the development of the paradigm of directional compound ethnonyms, as shown in (8).

(8)　　(i) Stage 1　　　　　　　　(ii) Stage 2

　　a.　*róng* 戎　　　=>　　　*róng* 戎 ≈ *xī-róng* 西戎
　　b.　*dí* 狄　　　　=>　　　*dí* 狄 ≈ *běi-dí* 北狄
　　c.　*mán* 蠻　　　=>　　　*mán* 蠻 ≈ *nán-mán* 南蠻

The 'four (civilizationally inferior) non-Zhōu others' (sì yí)

The expression 'four (civilizationally inferior) non-Zhōu others' (*sì yí* 四夷) can also be used to date the emergence of the systems of directional compounds. The terms 'four lands' (*sì tǔ*) and 'four sides/regions' (*sì fāng*) were used in Shāng and Western Zhōu times to refer to the four lands or regions surrounding the center, be it the 'Central *Shāng*' (*Zhōng Shāng*) or the 'Central States' (*Zhōng guó*). However, these early center–periphery terms were not yet informed by a collective civilizational consciousness as defined in Chapter 1 and Chapter 3.[37] The expression 'four non-Zhōu others' (*sì yí*) therefore did not emerge until around the middle of the first millennium BCE, when it was used as a blanket term referring to all the '(civilizationally inferior) non-Zhōu others of the four directions.' The earliest attested occurrences of the expression 'four non-Zhōu others' (*sì yí*) are from texts from the late fifth or fourth century BCE, such as the *Zuǒzhuàn* and the *Mòzǐ*; see (9).

(9) a.　In general when the lords of the states gain victory over any of the **'four civilizationally inferior non-Zhōu others' (sì yí)**, then they present the spoils to the [Zhōu] king, who uses them to serve as warning to the **'civilizationally inferior non-Zhōu others' (yí)**. This is not the case of [spoils of war taken by one of] the **Central States** [from another]. **The lords of the states** also do not present prisoners of war to one another (凡諸侯有四夷之功則獻于王，王以警于夷。中國則否。諸侯不相遺俘)[38]

　　b.　After King Wǔ had conquered the Shāng dynasty . . . he opened up communications with the **'four non-Zhōu others' (sì yí** 四夷) so that there was no one in **'the realm under Heaven' (tiānxià)** who did not pay him allegiance. (王既已克殷 . . . 通維四夷而天下莫不賓)[39]

From the contexts of the passages in (6–7) and (9), it is clear that the expression 'four non-Zhōu others' (*sì yí*) refers to the sum of the 'non-Zhōu others' of the four cardinal directions, i.e., the *mán* ≈ *nán-mán*, *yí* ≈ *dōng-yí*, *róng* ≈ *xī-róng*, and *dí* ≈ *běi-dí*.

Although it is a commentary on events that took place during the reign of Duke Zhuāng of the state of Lǔ (r. 693–662 BCE), the *Zuǒzhuàn* passage in (9a) was

144 *Inventing the 'barbarian'*

likely composed during Warring States period. The ruler of the state of Qí had come to present the Duke of Lǔ with *Róng* prisoners and spoils of war. This was against ritual decorum, since he should have presented the spoils of war to King Huì of Zhōu (r. 676–652) and not to the ruler of Lǔ. Furthermore, the passage also distinguishes between the Central States and the '(civilizationally inferior) four non-Zhōu others' (*sì yí* 四夷) who did not belong to the Zhōu "realm of value"; spoils from the latter could be presented to the Zhōu king, but not spoils from the former, who, by definition, were already subjects of the Zhōu ruler and therefore part of the Zhōu "realm of value."

The *Mòzǐ* passage in (9b) relates King Wǔ's (r. ca. 1049/45–1043 BCE) conquest of the Shāng dynasty in 1045 BCE. However, it does so from the perspective of promoters of Mòzǐ's ideas who likely composed it in the fourth century BCE. Here the expression 'four non-Zhōu others' (*sì yí*) refers to all the non-Zhōu peoples 'under Heaven' (*tiānxià*) who lived to the four sides of the central realm of newly established Zhōu dynasty.[40]

In traditional Chinese historiography, passages such as those in (9) have often been used to push the *Xià–yí* dichotomy back to the Spring and Autumn and early Western Zhōu periods, since the events related in them purportedly took place during those periods. This is highly problematic. The expression 'four non-Zhōu others' (*sì yí*) is not attested in pre-Warring States texts. Since the passages in (9) were composed in the Warring States period, their use of the expression 'four non-Zhōu others' (*sì yí*) reflects Warring States (rather than pre-Warring States) linguistic usage patterns and thought. The expression 'four non-Zhōu others' (*sì yí*) is attested in a broad range of Warring States texts.[41] In contrast, the logically possible numeral compounds *sì-róng* 四戎 'four róng,' *sì-dí* 四狄 'four dí,' and *sì-mán* 四蠻 'four mán' are not found in pre-Qín texts.[42] Not only can this distribution of the expression 'four non-Zhōu others' (*sì yí*) be used to date the establishment of the paradigm of cardinal direction ethnonyms to the middle of the first millennium BCE, it also indicates that *yí* was the only non-compound term used as a default term for the concept of '(civilizationally inferior) non-Zhōu others' or 'barbarians.'

Greater combinatorial potential of yí 夷 *as default term for 'barbarians'*

In addition to the expression 'non-Zhōu others to the four directions' (*sì yí*), the fact that *yí* has the greatest combinatorial potential of the four terms *mán*, *yí*, *róng*, and *dí* in directional compounds strongly supports the hypothesis that it had come to be the default for non-Zhōu others in the Warring States period. In a morphological paradigm of directional ethnonyms composed of one of the four directional prefixes *dōng-*, *xī-*, *nán-*, *běi-* followed by one of the four single morpheme ethnonyms terms *mán*, *yí*, *róng*, and *dí*, there are 16 possible combinations. However, only eight are attested in the corpus studied here.

In pre-Warring States texts, the only directional compounds attested are *dōng-yí*, *nán-yí*, *xī-róng*, and *běi-róng*.[43] Rather than forming part of a system of

Inventing the 'barbarian' 145

directional compounds (referring to various geographically defined sets of 'barbarians'), they are either ethnonyms referring to specific groups, as in the case of 'the Eastern Yí' (*Dōng-Yí*) and 'the Southern Yí' (*Nán-Yí*), or expressions that refer to the 'belligerents' (*róng*) from various directions, such as 'the belligerents from the west' (*xī-róng*) and 'belligerents from the north' (*běi-róng*).[44]

The non-matching directional compound *nán-yí* 南夷 is found in both pre-Warring States bronze inscriptions and received texts, such as the passage from the *Book of Songs* in (10).

(10) The **Yí of the Huái River** came to terms, there were none that did not obey. . . . The **Yí of Huái**, the *Mán*, and the *Mò*, and the **southern Yí** (*nán-yí*), there were none that did not obey. (淮夷來同，莫不率從 . . . 淮夷蠻貊，及彼南夷，莫不率從)[45]

The expression *nán-yí* in (10) is listed along with other ethnonyms referring to specific non-Zhōu groups in the south and the east—the *Yí* of Huái, the *Mán*, and the *Mò*. The fact that *nán-yí* and *Huáiyí* are mentioned in the same line as two different peoples clearly shows that, at the time of the *Book of Songs*, *Nán-yí* did not refer to all the non-Zhōu 'barbarians' in the south, but rather to a particular group, the southern *Yí*.[46] The expression *Dōng-yí* also occurs in Western Zhōu bronze inscriptions. But rather than referring to the 'all the barbarians to the east,' it refers to particular groups, for example, "indigenous societies in the hinterland of the Jiaodong peninsula," as the 'eastern *Yí*.'[47] In sum, the fact that *expressions* such as *dōng-yí* and *nán-yí* occur in bronze inscriptions cannot automatically be taken as evidence that a system of directional ethnonyms used to refer to a *concept* of 'civilizationally inferior barbarians in the four directions' had already been established in the pre-Warring States period.

The expression *xī-róng* was used to refer *Xiǎnyǔn* groups in pre-Warring States texts[48]:

(11) Awe-inspiring is Nán-zhòng, he attacks **the Western Róng (or, 'the western belligerents')**. . . . Awe-inspiring is Nán-zhong, the **Xiǎnyǔn** are pacified. (赫赫南仲，薄伐西戎。 . . . 赫赫南仲，獫狁于夷)[49]

In this passage from the *Book of Songs*, the great military leader Nán-zhòng is praised for having defeated the *Xiǎnyǔn* who are also referred to as the 'Western belligerents' (*xī-róng*). This occurrence of *xī-róng* thus reflects the old, pre-Warring States system of ethnonyms grounded in a narrative of 'warfare.' It can therefore not be used to show that the system of directional ethnonyms, in which *róng* and *xī-róng* came to be used interchangeably to refer to the '(civilizationally inferior) non-Zhōu others to the west' (see [8] above), had already been established in the pre-Warring States period.

Finally, let us take a closer look at the expression *běi-róng*. We find it in the same laconic pre-Warring States passage from the *Annals* quoted in the *Zuǒ*, *Gǔliáng*, and *Gōngyáng* commentaries: "In summer, the Prince of Qí and the

146 *Inventing the 'barbarian'*

Head of Xǔ attacked the Northern Róng (*běi-róng*)."[50] In this context it evidently refers either to a particular ethnic group, the Northern Róng, or to the 'belligerents from the north.' There is no evidence to support translating it as the 'barbarians to the north.'

The fact that the four expressions *dōng-yí*, *nán-yí*, *xī-róng*, and *běi-róng* are attested in pre-Warring States texts thus cannot be taken as evidence that a system of directional ethnonyms had already been established in the pre-Warring States period. That the expressions *běi-róng* (north-west), and *nán-yí* (south-east) are directional 'mismatches' further indicates that the terms *mán*, *yí*, *róng*, and *dí* had not yet become systematically associated with the four cardinal directions, and that, as a consequence, the cardinal direction paradigm of compound ethnonyms composed of matching directional prefixes and single morpheme ethnonyms had not yet been established. This conclusion is also supported by the absence of the compound '(civilizationally inferior) non-Zhōu others of the four regions' (*sì yí*) from pre-Warring States texts.

In contrast, the meanings and uses of directional compounds in Warring States texts clearly point to the existence of a fully fledged morphological paradigm of directional compounds. In the Warring States period, directional compounds referring to different sub-segments of the non-Zhōu others began to become more frequent than the toponym compounds (referring to specific ethnic groups) which dominate pre-Warring States texts. The overall percentage of directional compounds increased from 22.5% in pre-Warring States texts to 50% in Warring States texts.[51] Frequently attested in Warring States texts are the four matching directional compounds where the prefix and single morpheme ethnonym both indicate the same cardinal direction, as illustrated in (4), (7), and (8) above: 'the *yí* who live to the east' (*dōng-yí*), 'the *róng* who live to the west' (*xī-róng*), 'the *mán* who live to the south' (*nán-mán*), and 'the *dí* who live to the east' (*běi-dí*). Rather than adding a distinguishing feature, the directional prefix simply reinforces the cardinal direction already associated with the following mono-morphemic ethnonym.

In addition to the matching expression 'non-Zhōu others who live to the east (*dōng*)' (*dōng-yí*), the term *yí* can also be found with the three other non-matching directional prefixes: 'non-Zhōu others who live to the west (*xī*)' (*xī-yí*), 'non-Zhōu others who live to the east' (*dōng-yí*), 'non-Zhōu others who live to the south (*nán*)' (*nán-yí*), and 'non-Zhōu others who live to the north (*běi*)' (*běi-yí*). In contrast, the *dí* can only be found with the matching *běi*- 'north' prefix. Likewise, *mán* can only be found with the matching *nán*- 'south' prefix. Similarly, *róng* is often found with the matching *xī*- 'west' prefix and occasionally with the non-matching *běi*- 'north' prefix.[52] Only the term *yí* can be found with all four directional prefixes. That only *yí* has realized its full combinatorial potential strongly suggests that it had become the default term for 'civilizationally inferior other' or 'uncivilized barbarian' in the Warring States period. This development is illustrated by the third stage in the evolution of the vocabulary of identity, illustrated in (12). Here, the main changes are indicated by the forms outside the parentheses; those inside parentheses are 'relics' from earlier layers of the language that continued to function as quasi-synonyms in later stages.

Inventing the 'barbarian' 147

(12)	(i) **Stage 1**		(ii) **Stage 2**		(iii) **Stage 3**
	Single word		**Matching directional**		*Yí* **Combined with**
	ethnonyms		**ethnonyms**		**all directions**
a.	*róng*	=>	*xī-róng* (≈ *róng*)	=>	*xī-yí* (≈ *xī-róng* ≈ *róng*)
b.	*mán*	=>	*nán-mán* (≈ *mán*)	=>	*nán-yí* (≈ *nán-mán* ≈ *mán*)
c.	*dí*	=>	*běi-dí* (≈ *dí*)	=>	*běi-yí* (≈ *běi-dí* ≈ *dí*)
d.	*yí*	=>	*dōng-yí* (≈ yí)	=>	*dōng-yí* (≈ *yí*)

In the first stage, the terms *mán*, *yí*, *róng*, and *dí* became firmly associated with the four cardinal directions (as shown in Figure 4.1 and illustrated in [6]). The addition of a 'matching' directional prefix at the second stage led to the formation of semantically redundant forms in which the cardinal direction is marked twice (e.g., *xī-róng* [west–west], *nán-mán* [south–south], etc.; see [12ii]). Since *běi-dí*, *xī-róng*, and so forth, are redundant expressions, they could be replaced by the *yí*-based directional compounds in (12iii) without becoming ambiguous. The directional prefix now retained the distinctive semantic feature needed to tell the 'non-Zhōu others' of the four cardinal directions apart, and we end up with stage 3 in (12), where *xī-yí* is quasi-synonymous with both *xī-róng* and *róng*, and so on. The emergence of this new type of purely *yí*-based directional compounds (*xī-yí*, *nán-yí*, *běi-yí*, *dōng-yí*) and the numeral compound 'four *yí*' (*sì yí*) clearly demonstrates the expression *yí*'s role as a default term for '(civilizationally inferior) other' and contributed to its being used with this meaning on its own.

Terms for 'civilizationally inferior non-Zhōu others' in the Mencius

A central assumption in the *Mencius* is the superiority of the Zhōu elite's rites and social mores vis-à-vis the customs of the non-Zhōu others. Since there is wide agreement that the *Mencius* can be reliably dated to the late fourth or third century BCE, and since its vocabulary of identity is representative of the mid-Warring States period, it is a good choice for a case study of ethnonyms. The *Mencius* illustrates that the increasing replacement of specific ethnonyms (e.g., *xī-róng* and *běi-dí*) with the semantically more neutral *yí*-based ethnonyms (e.g., *xī-yí* and *běi-yí*)—i.e., the shift from stage 2 to stage 3 in (12) above—reflects changes in intellectual history: the culturally defined Zhōu–barbarian dichotomy was hardening, and the Zhōu elite were seeing themselves more as belonging to a 'civilization.' The *Mencius* contains 14 compound ethnonyms of the three types illustrated in (3–5) above.[53] Only one (1/14 = 7%), i.e., *kūn-yí* 昆夷, is a toponym ethnonym. The remaining 13 compounds (13/14 = 93%) are of the new types that only emerged in the Warring States period, i.e., directional (71.5%) or ethnonym compounds (21.5%). Furthermore, most of the directional compounds are *yí*-based (e.g., *dōng-yí* [1 attestation], *xī-yí* [4], *běi-yí* [1], *sì yí* [1]). This is the direct opposite of the distributional patterns of the pre-Warring States vocabulary of identity.

Why did an *yí*-based system of directional ethnonyms appeal to the authors of the *Mencius*? More specifically, why are specific mono-morphemic ethnonyms,

148 *Inventing the 'barbarian'*

such as *róng*, replaced by the more general term *yí* 夷 in directional compounds, as illustrated in expressions in stage 3 in column (iii) in (12)? Mencius' provocative claim that Shùn and King Wén—two of the most respected sage–kings in Chinese history—were of 'barbarian' stock may help us answer this question.

(13) Shùn was born in Zhū Féng, moved to Fù Xià, and died in Míng Tiáo. He was an **Eastern Yí (*dōng-yí*)**. King Wén was born in Qí Zhōu and died in Bì Yǐng. He was a **Western Yí (*xī-yí*)**. Their native places were over a thousand *li* apart, and there were a thousand years between them. Yet when they had their way in the **Central Kingdoms (*Zhōng guó*)**, their actions matched like the two halves of a tally. The standards of the two sages, one earlier and one later, were identical. (舜生於諸馮遷於負夏卒於鳴條東夷之人也。文王生於岐周卒於畢郢西夷之人也。地之相去也，千有餘里；世之相後也，千有餘歲。得志行乎中國，若合符節。先聖後聖其揆一也)[54]

Many late Warring States readers of the *Mencius* would undoubtedly have been shocked by the statement that Shùn was an 'eastern barbarian' (*dōng-yí*) and that King Wén was a 'western barbarian' (*xī-yí*). As argued by Pines (2005: 73–4), there is reason to believe that the author(s) of this passage intended to shock his audience in order to persuade them to adopt his belief in an innate potential for 'Goodness' (*rén* 仁) shared by all humans, regardless of their geographic or class origins. In other words, by stating that the famous sage–kings started out as 'uncivilized barbarians' (*yí*) but eventually, through self-cultivation, transformed themselves into paragons of virtue and founding fathers of the much revered Zhōu dynasty, Mencius implied that everyone is born with the potential to become 'civilized' through the practice of Zhōu rites (*lǐ*).

However, one question remains. Why did Mencius choose the expression *xī-yí* to refer to King Wén as a 'western barbarian' rather than the quasi-synonymous expressions *xī-róng* or *róng*, which were also available to him? Based on the above analysis of the emergence and evolution of the paradigm of directional compounds, we are now in a position to answer that question. Due to the specific ethnic associations attached to some uses of the term *róng* in Warring States usage, the author(s) of the *Mencius* preferred to use *yí* as a more neutral term for 'non-Zhōu others,' one that was devoid of specific ethnic connotations. As shown by the *Zuǒ* passage in (14), reportedly uttered by a Róng leader, Róng ethnic identity was defined by particular conventionalized behaviors—specific non-Zhōu food, drink, clothing, and language.

(14) The food, drink, and clothing used by **our various Róng groups** are not the same as those of **the Huá**; gifts do not pass back and forth; and language is not understood. (我諸戎飲食衣服不與華同，贄幣不通，言語不達)[55]

Going back to (13), the main point of this passage in the *Mencius* is to emphasize the common human potential for change through self-cultivation. Using a blanket term like *yí* to refer to peoples who are 'non-Zhōu' and do not adhere to Zhōu

Inventing the 'barbarian' 149

practices is therefore more appropriate than using either *róng* or *xī-róng*, both of which would have invoked a number of distinctive ethnic traits that would be both unnecessary and distracting in this context. Furthermore, by choosing a neutral term devoid of reference to a specific existing non-Zhōu group, Mencius also avoids undesirable political implications. In Mencius' lifetime, Róng groups still existed. A claim that King Wén derived from the Róng might give this group prestige that could be used politically. By choosing *xī-yí* rather than *xī-róng* (or *róng*), the *Mencius* elegantly avoids these complications and leads the reader to the main point of the passage: the inclusive claim that anyone, regardless of origin, has the potential to transcend the Zhōu–barbarian dichotomy by adopting the ways of the Zhōu elite.[56]

The *Mencius* contains explicit references to a 'civilizationally' defined dichotomy between the 'Great ones' (*Xià*) of the Central States (*zhōng guó*) and the 'civilizationally inferior non-Zhōu others' or 'barbarians,' referred to with the single morpheme ethnonym *yí*.[57] The idea of non-Zhōu 'barbarians' (*yí*) converting to the ways of the 'Great ones' (*Xià*) is discussed in the *Mencius* passage in (15).

(15) I have heard of the 'Great ones' (*Xià*) converting **'barbarians' (*yí*)** to their ways, but not of the 'Great ones' (*Xià*) being converted to **'barbarian' (*yí*)** ways. . . . A *Lǔ Song* says, "It was the ***Róng*** and ***Dí*** that he attacked; It was ***Jīng*** and ***Shū*** that he punished." It is these people that the Duke of Zhōu was going to punish and you want to learn from. That is not a change for the better, is it? (吾聞用夏變夷者，未聞變於夷者也。 . . . 魯頌曰： 「戎狄是 膺，荊舒是懲。」周公方且膺之，子是之學，亦為不善變矣)[58]

This passage is part of a lecture given by Mencius to Chén Xiāng, who had "converted" to the agriculturalist teachings of the philosopher Xǔ Xíng (fourth century BCE) after the death of his former master, Chén Liáng.[59] Although a native of the 'barbarian' state of Chǔ,[60] Chén Liáng, in the words of Mencius "had been delighted with the way of Duke of Zhōu and Confucius" and had become an "outstanding scholar" by studying in the northern (more civilized) Central States. In that sense, he was an example of an *Yí* converting to *Xià* ways. In contrast, Chén Xiāng's switching his loyalties to Xǔ Xíng is an example of a *Xià* converting to *Yí* ways. To emphasize the enormity of Chén Xiāng's error, Mencius refers to Xǔ Xíng as a "southern barbarian (*nán-mán*) with a twittering tongue, who condemns the way of the Former Kings."[61] Mencius even quotes a song from the *Book of Songs*, also quoted in (17) below, that indicates (or so he anachronistically implies) that the Duke of Zhōu punished the 'barbarians' of *Jīng* because of their uncivilized ways. Since the state of Chǔ was sometimes referred to as *Jīng*, he is able to criticize Chén Xiāng for wanting to learn from the very 'barbarians' that the Duke of Zhōu, one of the founding fathers of Zhōu 'civilization' (according to Mencius), wanted to punish. Although the phrases "*Róng* and *Dí*" and "*Jīng* and *Shū*" referred to specific sets of peoples in the pre-Warring States *Song* from which he is quoting, Mencius lumps them together using the Warring States term 'barbarians' (*yí*).

150　*Inventing the 'barbarian'*

The use of the expression 'barbarians' (*yí*) in (15) provides evidence of a fourth stage in the evolution of the vocabulary of identity—that is, the emergence of the use of *yí* on its own to refer to 'civilizationally inferior others' or 'uncivilized barbarians,' illustrated in (16).

(16) **(i) Stage 2**　　　　　　**(ii) Stage 3**　　　　　　　**(iii) Stage 4**
　　　Matching directional　　*Yí* **combined with**　　　*yí* **as default term**
　　　ethnonyms　　　　　　**all directions**　　　　　　*for* **all directions**

a.	*xī-róng* (≈ *róng*)	=>	*xī-yí* (≈ *xī-róng* [≈ *róng*])	=>	*yí*
b.	*běi-dí* (≈ *dí*)	=>	*běi-yí* (≈ *běi-dí* [≈ *dí*])	=>	*yí*
c.	*nán-mán* (≈ *mán*)	=>	*nán-yí* (≈ *nán-mán* ≈ [*mán*])	=>	*yí*
d.	*dōng-yí* (≈ *yí*)	=>	*dōng-yí* (≈ *yí*)	=>	*yí*

Although Mencius still uses directional compounds of the more specific 'matching' types (e.g., *běi-dí* and *nán-mán*, see [16i]),[62] he clearly prefers the neutral *yí*-based type directional compounds (e.g., *xī-yí*, *běi-yí*, see [13] and [16ii]). From the point of view of his moral philosophy, there is no need to subdivide the different non-Zhōu groups by adding specific geographic modifiers such as 'west' (*xī*), 'north' (*běi*). What is important to him is that they are all defined negatively as 'civilizationally inferior others' (*yí*) by their failure to adhere to elite Zhōu practices and mores, as shown in (15) and (16iii). Independent evidence for this comes from the fact that the author(s) of the *Mencius* also used the compound 'four non-Zhōu others' (*sì yí*) to refer to all 'barbarians.'[63] In the Warring States period, *yí* had thus become the default single-morpheme word for 'barbarian' as illustrated in (15).

Ethnonym compounds

The system of ethnonym compounds—i.e., compounds made up exclusively of combinations of the ethnonym terms *mán*, *yí*, *róng*, and *dí*; see (5)—that became established in the Warring States period provides another window into how terms for '(civilizationally inferior) non-Zhōu others' were coined. As shown above, the term *yí* was the only single-morpheme ethnonym that could be used alone in the meanings 'non-Zhōu others' and 'civilizationally inferior others' or 'barbarians' in the Warring States period. However, the ethnonym compounds *mányí-róngdí* and *yídí* were also used in similar meanings. In a morphological paradigm of bi-morphemic ethnonym compounds composed of the four single morpheme ethnonym terms *mán*, *yí*, *róng*, and *dí*, there are 12 possible two-word combinations (leaving out the unattested reduplicative forms *mán-mán*, etc.). However, only three, that is, *yí-dí*,[64] *mán-yí*,[65] and *róng-dí*,[66] are attested with any significant frequency in Warring States texts as general terms for 'civilizationally inferior others' or 'barbarians.' How can this be explained?

A few other sequences of the terms *mán*, *yí*, *róng*, and *dí* are attested (i.e., *róng-yí*, *dí-róng*, *róng-mán*, *yí-mán*). However, rather than true compound

Inventing the 'barbarian' 151

ethnonyms stored in the shared lexicon, these are either proper names or syntactically conjoint noun phrases and not lexicalized compound words. Thus, for example, the sequence *yí mán* only occurs once in the pre-Qín corpus in the following *Lǐjì* passage: "As for the *Mèi* [tune], it is the music of the *dōng-yí*; as for the *Rèn* [tune], it is the music of the *nán-mán*. The music of the *yí* [and the] *mán* was introduced into grand temple to express the greatness of Lǔ in the realm under Heaven."[67] Here *yí mán* is clearly a phrasal unit of conjoined nouns meaning 'the *yí* and the *mán*,' where *yí* refers back to the *dōng-yí* and *mán* refers back to the *nán-mán*. Even the word order is determined by the fact that *dōng-yí* is mentioned earlier than *nán-mán* in the preceding context. Thus, *yí mán* is clearly not a lexicalized compound ethnonym, but rather a sequence of conjoint noun phrases.[68] The attested sequences *róng-yí*, *dí-róng*, *róng-mán* are also either phrasal constructions or part of proper names rather than lexicalized compounds.[69] As we shall see, the association of the terms *mán*, *yí*, *róng*, and *dí* with the cardinal directions that emerged in the Warring States period plays a crucial role in structuring the paradigm of ethnonym compounds and sheds light on why the only lexicalized ethnonym compounds are *mányíróngdí*, *yídí*, *mányí* and *róngdí*.

The system of ethnonym compounds emerged around 600–400 BCE.[70] Ethnonym compounds of the type illustrated in (5) are not attested in inscriptions on oracle bones or bronze vessels. In the body of pre-Warring States received texts, only one potential ethnonym compound is found—*róngdí*; see (17).

(17) The **Róng** and the **Dí** he withstood. The Jīng and the Shu he repressed. (戎狄是膺荊舒是懲)[71]

While at first glance the sequence *róng dí* (戎狄) in (17) may look like it would be a compound ethnonym, the parallelism with the conjoined ethnonyms 'the Jīng and the Shu' in the following line indicates that *róng dí* is instead a phrasal unit of conjoined mono-morphemic ethnonyms referring to two separate non-Zhōu peoples, the Róng and the Dí.[72] In other words, there is no direct evidence that a formal system of ethnonym compounds existed in pre-Warring States times. Such a system evidently emerged around 600–400 BCE at about the same time as the association with the terms *mán*, *yí*, *róng*, and *dí* with the four cardinal directions and the expression 'four *yí*' (*sì-yí*).

The *Zuǒzhuàn* passages in (18) and (19) illustrate some of the earliest attested uses of *mányí* and *róngdí* as general terms for subsets of 'barbarians,' which are contrasted either with the Central States (*zhōng guó*), as in (18), or with 'all the Xià (states)' (*zhū-Xià* 諸夏), as in (19).

(18) Wú attacked Tán. Tán reached an accord with Wú. Jì Wénzǐ said, "The **'Central States'** (*zhōng guó*) are not putting their forces in order. The **Mán-yí** enter and attack, and none has any concern for the domain in its plight." (吳伐郯，郯成。季文子曰：中國不振旅，蠻夷入伐，而莫之或恤)[73]

152   *Inventing the 'barbarian'*

(19) **The Dí** invaded Xíng. Guǎn Jìngzhòng spoke to the Prince of Qí, "**The Róng-Dí** are jackals and wolves and cannot be satisfied. The various [**states of**] **the Great ones (*zhū-Xià*)** are close intimates and cannot be abandoned." (狄人伐邢。管敬仲言於齊侯曰：戎狄豺狼，不可厭也；諸夏親暱，不可棄也)[74]

While the contrasts with the 'Central States' (*zhōng guó*) and 'all the Xià' (*zhū-Xià*) in (18–19) indicate that *mányí* and *róngdí* were general terms for 'non-Zhōu others,' these passages also contain specific geographical information that shows a semantic difference between *mányí* and *róngdí*. In (18), the term *mányí* refers to the state of Wú, located southeast of the Central Plain area. As explained by Durrant, Li, and Schaberg (2016: 763), "the concept of barbarian is fluid and relational. As a victim of Wú, sometimes decried for its barbarian mores, Tán is considered one of the [Central States]."[75] In (19), the term *róngdí* refers to the '*Dí* people' (*Dí rén* 狄人), who attacked Xíng in the state of Qí, which was located in the northeastern corner of the Zhōu realm.[76] In other words, these passages indicate that *mányí* was the general term for 'barbarians from the south or east,' while *róngdí* was the general term for 'barbarians from the north or west.'[77]

In this respect, *mányí* and *róngdí* are similar to the Modern Chinese terms *xiōngdì* 'brothers' and *jiěmèi* 'sisters.' *Xiōngdì* and *jiěmèi* can be considered general terms for 'siblings' in that they refer to male and female subsets of 'siblings' respectively; see (20).

(20) Words for 'siblings' in Modern Chinese:

a.	*xiōng*	兄	'older brother'
b.	*dì*	弟	'younger brother'
c.	*jiě*	姐	'older sister'
d.	*mèi*	妹	'younger sister'
e.	*xiōng-dì*	兄弟	'brothers'
f.	*jiě-mèi*	姐妹	'sisters'
g.	*xiōngdì-jiěmèi*	兄弟姐妹	'brothers and sisters, siblings'

Similarly, as shown in (21), *mányí* and *róngdí* are general terms that refer to different subsets of '(civilizationally inferior) non-Zhōu others.'

(21) Words for 'non-Zhōu others' in Warring States Old Chinese:

a.	*yí*	夷	'the non-Zhōu others to the east'
b.	*róng*	戎	'the non-Zhōu others to the west'[78]
c.	*dí*	狄	'the non-Zhōu others to the north'
d.	*mán*	蠻	'the non-Zhōu others to the south'
e.	*mán-yí*	蠻夷	'the non-Zhōu others to the south and the east'

f.	*róng-dí*	戎狄	'the non-Zhōu others to the west and the north'
g.	*mányí-róngdí*	蠻夷戎狄	'the non-Zhōu others to the south, east, west, and north'

As indicated in (20g) and (21g), the structural parallels between the pre-Qín system of ethnonym compounds and the modern Chinese paradigm of terms for 'siblings' are due to the fact that both are based on four words denoting subsets of total set of 'others' and 'siblings' respectively. The parallels can be pushed even further. Modern Chinese lacks semantically general mono-morphemic words for 'brother(s)' and 'sister(s),' and uses the compounds *xiōng-dì* '(lit.) older brother–younger brother' and *jiě-mèi* '(lit.) older sister–younger sister' instead. Modern Chinese also lacks a mono-morphemic word for 'sibling(s),' and instead uses a combination of the compounds for 'brothers' and 'sisters' (i.e., *xiōngdì-jiěmèi* '[lit.] older brother–younger brother–older sister–younger sister,' which is semantically equivalent to the English word 'siblings'). That is, the Modern Chinese word for 'siblings' (*xiōngdì-jiěmèi*) has the internal structure in (22).

(22)

xiōng-dì jiě-mèi 兄弟姐妹 'siblings'

As the *Xúnzǐ* passage in (23) shows, Warring States Chinese used a similar four-morpheme compound, composed of the ethnonym compounds *mán-yí* and *róng-dí*, as a general term for 'barbarians,' that is, *mányí-róngdí*.

(23) And so, the states of the **Xià** are the same in serving the king and have the same standards of conduct. In contrast, the states of the **Mányí-róngdí** (蠻夷戎狄) are the same in serving the king, but do not have the same regulations. The area within the King's borders constitutes the "tillage" zone. Beyond that, the area just outside the King's borders constitutes the "lords" zone. Beyond that, the next region constitutes the "retainers" zone. Beyond that, the **Mányí** constitute the "controlled" zone. Beyond that, the **Róngdí** constitute the "wilderness" zone. (故諸夏之國同服同儀，蠻夷戎狄之國同服不同制。封內甸服，封外侯服，侯衛賓服，蠻夷要服，戎狄荒服)[79]

In (23), the 'total set of the [four kinds of] (civilizationally inferior) non-Zhōu others' (*mányí-róngdí*) are contrasted with the 'all the Xià' (*zhūxià*).[80] Furthermore, in the immediately following context, the *mányí* are distinguished from the *róngdí* with respect to their service to the Zhōu court. This indicates that the internal structure of *mányí-róngdí* as a general term for 'non-Zhōu others' or 'barbarians'

154 *Inventing the 'barbarian'*

is similar to that of *xiōngdí-jiěmèi* as a general term for 'siblings' in modern Chinese. Compare (22) and (24a).

(24)

a. *mán -yí róng -dí*   蠻夷戎狄   'barbarians'
b. *. . . -yí . . . -dí*   夷狄   'barbarians'

As mentioned above, the expressions *mányí* and *róngdí* refer to two different subsets of the total set of non-Zhōu others that are defined in a spatially defined semantic field: *róngdí* 'non-Zhōu others to the west and north,' and *mányí* 'non-others to the south and east.' The passage from the *Xúnzǐ* in (23) indicates that they had different meanings that went beyond their spatially defined meanings. The *mányí* were closer to the civilizational center and therefore more domesticated and controllable than the *róngdí*, who were further out on the 'wild' fringes of the civilized realm. Hence, translating both as 'barbarians' is inadequate.[81]

The stark topographic and climatic differences between the northwest of the area now known as China and the southeast contributed to reinforcing perceived differences between non-Zhōu groups in these areas. Since the high plateaus of the northwest are dominated by arid and cold climate, many peoples there lived by herding livestock on the large plains. In contrast, the warmer and wetter lowlands of the southeast encouraged other means of sustenance, including agriculture. Living mainly as sedentary farmers in the temperate middle, the Zhōu tended to perceive the peoples in the southeast, some of whom also lived as farmers, as less threatening than the groups of herders to the northwest.

Early modern English distinguished between two kinds of 'civilizationally inferior others': (i) the *barbarians* and the (ii) *savages*. The term *savages* was often used to refer to groups whom the Europeans deemed devoid of any elements of 'civilization.' These were the peoples living in nature with only the barest rudiments of 'police' and 'civility.' In contrast, *barbarians* referred to peoples such as the Indians and the Chinese who had ancient traditions and written records bearing witness to well-established elements of 'police' and 'civility' as well as a high degree of technological advancement.[82] While not unproblematic, translating the terms *róngdí* and *mányí* as 'savages' and 'barbarians,' respectively, in contexts such as (23) may be more suggestive of their mutual differences than translating both as 'barbarians.'

As shown in (24b), I analyze the compound 'barbarians' (*yídí*) as an abbreviated form of *mányí-róngdí*.[83] Since it is a synecdochic reduction of a combination of the ethnonym compounds *mányí* and *róngdí*, it could not have come into existence before the expressions *mányí* and *róngdí* had been coined as terms for subsets of non-Zhōu others. Interestingly, the bulk of the attestations of the expression *yídí* are found in late Warring States or early Hàn texts such as the *Gǔliáng* (17 instances) and *Gōngyáng* (20 instances) commentaries, where it is used as a general term for 'civilizationally inferior others,' which is often contrasted with the

Inventing the 'barbarian' 155

Central States (*zhōng guó*).[84] In contrast, in the *Zuǒzhuàn*, which has the highest number of the compounds *mányí* (9 occurrences) and *róngdí* (12 occurrences), not a single instance of *yídí* is found. This complementarity in the distribution of *yídí*, *mányí*, and *róngdí* in the *Zuǒ* versus the *Gōngyáng* and *Gǔliáng* is all the more striking since these three works are commentaries on the *Annals*; it may thus be an indication that they were composed at different times. While *mányí* and *róngdí* are both attested in a wide variety of Warring States texts,[85] besides the *Gōngyáng* and *Gǔliáng* commentaries, only four occurrences of *yídí* are found elsewhere— two in the *Analects*[86] and one each in the *Mencius*[87] and the *Lǐjì*.[88] Assuming the *Gōngyáng* and *Gǔliáng* were written later than the *Zuǒzhuàn*,[89] this seems to indicate that *yídí* became widely used as a general term for '(civilizationally inferior) non-Zhōu others' or 'barbarians' at a slightly later time than *yí*, *mányí*, and *róngdí*. Indeed, *yídí* becomes one of the most frequently used expressions to refer to 'others' in Hàn and post-Hàn times.[90]

Conclusion: coining of terms for the new concept of 'civilizationally inferior others'

Using the history-word-by-word approach to study lexical changes in ethnonymies (i.e., paradigms of ethnonyms) offers insight into the epistemic changes the Zhōu elite's conceptualization of non-Zhōu others. In pre-Warring States times, the Zhōu elite had not yet developed a strong collective civilizational consciousness as defined in Chapter 1. The Zhōu frequently interacted with a number of non-Zhōu peoples who often lived inside, or in close geographical proximity to, the Central States. The main narrative of otherness was 'warfare,' and non-Zhōu peoples were often conceptualized as 'belligerent others.' They were most often referred to by specific toponym compounds denoting specific groups living in specific geographic locations such as *Quǎn-róng* 'the Dog Róng,' *Huái-yí* 'the Yí of the Huái region,' etc. The term *róng* was also used as a general word for 'belligerent other' or 'armed enemies.'

With the coining of civilizational consciousness, as described in Chapter 3, this old paradigm of ethnonyms was replaced by a new set of terms grounded in the theories of 'civility/civilization' (*wén*) that emerged around the beginning of the Warring States period. With the advent of the idea of a politically unified 'realm of value' or 'empire'[91] and the idea of a distinction between the 'civilized' 'Great ones' (*Xià*) and various 'uncivilized' non-Zhōu groups, the Zhōu elite felt a need for a word to refer to a complementary set of 'civilizationally inferior others.' Rather than creating a new word from scratch, various strategies were adopted to coin terms for 'civilizationally inferior others' using existing words, as summarized in Figure 4.2.

Figure 4.2 illustrates the central role the association of the four terms *mán*, *yí*, *róng*, and *dí* with the cardinal directions (in the box to the left of the arrow) played in the emergence of the five words *mányí*, *róngdí*, *mányíróngdí*, *yídí*, and *yí* used for 'non-Zhōu others' in Warring States texts (as illustrated by the four boxes to the right of the arrow). The boxes in Figure 4.2 are visual representations

156 *Inventing the 'barbarian'*

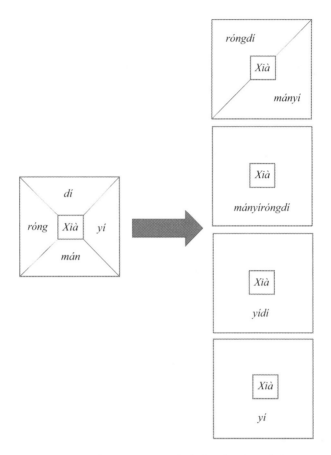

Figure 4.2 Coining of words for the concept of 'civilizationally inferior others.'

of the spatially organized semantic field of concepts of identity dividing humanity (as understood by the pre-Qín Zhōu elite) into five sets. The smaller box in the center of the larger boxes represent the set of the 'Great ones' (*Xià*). Around 600–400 BCE, this set began to be conceived of as being surrounded by four sets of 'non-Zhōu others,' referred to by the terms *mán* ('non-Zhōu others to the south'), *yí* ('non-Zhōu others to the east'), *róng* ('non-Zhōu others to the west'), and *dí* ('non-Zhōu others to the north'). From this system emerged the ethnonym compounds *mányí* and *róngdí*, which refer to the larger sets of 'non-Zhōu others to the south and east' (who tended to be viewed as sedentary and assimilable) and 'non-Zhōu others to the west and north' (who were often seen as less assimilable and belligerent), respectively, as well as three different expressions, that is *mányíróngdí*, *yídí*, and *yí*, for the concept of '(civilizationally inferior) non-Zhōu other' as the complementary set to the 'Great ones' (*Xià*).

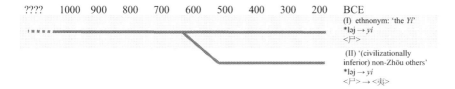

Figure 4.3 Tracing the history of the meaning changes of the word *yí*.[92]

The association of the terms *mán*, *yí*, *róng*, and *dí* with the four cardinal directions thus enabled the construction of the paradigms of ethnonyms from which the use of the term *yí* as the default term for non-Zhōu others emerged. As indicated in Figure 4.3, the coining of the word *yí* in the new meaning '(civilizationally inferior) non-Zhōu others' took place around 600–400 BCE in tandem with the coining of the term *wén* in the new meaning 'civility/civilization.'

As indicated in row (II) in Figure 4.3, at some point the graph used to write this word changed from <尸> to <夷>. Since this change in the writing system happened independently of the coining of the word *yí* in the new meaning 'civilizationally inferior other' that took place around 600–400 BCE, I will not explore it further here.[93] Instead, in the following chapter, I will return to the question of whether we are justified in translating *yí* as 'barbarian.' To do so, I examine the meaning changes in the other half of the *Xià–Yí* dichotomy—the Zhōu self-appellation the 'Great ones' (*Xià* 夏) and its relationship to the adjective 'elegant, proper' (*yǎ* 雅). Exploring the emergent contrast between 'rites' (*lǐ* 禮) of the 'Great ones' (*Xià* 夏) with the 'customs' (*sú* 俗) of the 'civilizationally inferior non-Zhōu others' (*yí*) will shed further light on these questions.

Notes

1 Tr. adapted from Legge (1861: 192); see also (13) below.
2 See Stocking (1987: 10–11) and Patterson (1997: 87–116).
3 Not narrowly restricted to ethnically defined groups, the term *ethnonym* here also refers to terms ranging from specific group names to general terms for 'barbarians' and 'non-Zhōu others.'
4 Earlier studies that discuss the Zhōu-barbarian distinction include Poo Mu-chou (1999, 2005, 1998, 1994), Schaberg (2001), Di Cosmo (2002), Pines (2005), Bergeton (2006), Kim (2009), Beecroft (2010), Fiskesjö (1999, 2012), Huang (2013), Yang Shao-yun (2014), and Brindley (2003, 2015), among others. This subsection is based in part on Bergeton (2006).
5 Allan (2007: 461–96) proposes that an elite material culture (jades, bronzes, etc.) constitutes a "cultural hegemony" in the early second millennium BCE that marks the beginning of "Chinese civilization." It is possible to define the origin of "Chinese civilization" in this way. However, a shared material culture does not amount to a fully articulated civilizational consciousness, as defined in chapter 1. That is, Allan's "cultural hegemony" and civilizational consciousness (as defined in chapter 1) are two different theoretical concepts. The Shāng dynasty and Early Zhōu elites certainly stood apart from other groups through their distinct material culture (jades, bronzes, etc.).

158 *Inventing the 'barbarian'*

They also most likely were keenly conscious of belonging to a coherent and well-defined group. However, this does not necessarily mean that they had terms such as *wén* in the sense of 'civility/civilization' that allowed them to articulate their difference from others as a civilizational divide between the 'civilized' versus the 'barbarians.' Allan's (2007) brilliant study also does not make this claim. Since her analysis pursues a different question from the one asked in this book, it is not invalidated by the dating of the emergence of civilizational consciousness to around 600–400 BCE proposed here.

6 For a thorough study of the end of the Western Zhōu, see Li (2006: 193–232).

7 As observed by Yuri Pines (2005), the lack of a clearly defined division between Zhōu and non-Zhōu is reflected by the fact that the Zhōu elite often intermarried with non-Zhōu and that people of non-Zhōu origin could rise to high positions in the Central States. See for example *Zuǒ*, Zhuāng 28.2, which shows that children of non-Zhōu wives could aspire to the throne. See also Pines (2005: 84, note 78) for similar examples, such as *Zuǒ*, Xiāng 29 and Zhāo 17.

8 For views of foreigners as "enemies" in Ancient Egypt, Mesopotamia, and China, see Poo (2005: 68–79).

9 Peaceful interaction with non-Shāng and non-Zhōu groups may have been more common than extant records lead us to believe. A large proportion of pre-Warring States bronze vessel inscriptions describe specific battles. Most pre-Warring States period writings on perishable media have not been preserved; we do not know if they described more peaceful interaction with others.

10 Máo 299, SSJZS (1980: 612), tr. adapted from Waley (1996: 301–12).

11 Máo 178, SSJZS (1980: 426), tr. adapted from Waley (1996: 153).

12 See Waley (1996: 154, fn. 1).

13 Another type of archaic location- or group-specific ethnonyms are formed with the suffix *-fāng* 方 'side, region,' e.g., *Guǐ-fāng* 鬼方 'the *Guǐ*.' *Fāng*-compounds are not general terms for 'barbarians' but specific names for particular enemy groups (Keightley 1999: 269). See also Chang (1980: 216–20; 48–59), Keightley (2000: 66–72), and Di Cosmo (1999: 907–9).

14 E.g.: Máo 168, and Máo 300 in (11) and (17). See also *Annals*, Yǐn 7.6 and Zhuāng 18.2.

15 The word *róng* was often used as a modifier meaning 'military/war' as in *róng-chē* 戎車 'war-chariots' (Máo 178, 299). It was also used to mean 'war chariot,' 'arms,' 'weapons,' 'attack,' 'war'; see Schuessler (1987: 511–12).

16 The term *róng* was more widely used to refer to 'warfare' and related concepts in the pre-Warring States period than in the Warring States period when it was often replaced by quasi-synonymous terms, such as 'weapon; soldier' (*bīng* 兵), 'battle, war' (*zhàn* 戰), and 'martial, courageous; warfare' (*wǔ* 武).

17 According to Poo (2005: 45), the "term [Xiǎnyǔn] appears to have remained a specific ethnic name." *Xiǎnyǔn* was likely a loan-word transcription of a foreign autonym. See also Wáng (1987: 583–605), Průšek (1971: 18–19), Pulleyblank (1983: 449), Di Cosmo (1999: 919), and Li (2006: 343–46).

18 Buqi *gui*, *JC*: 4329, transcription and translation from Li Feng 2006:155. Shirakawa Shizuka (1962-: fascicle no. 49, entry no. 12:303). For a different translation, see Průšek (1971: 127). According to Poo (2005: 167, n. 58), "the author of this inscription obviously equated Xiǎnyǔn with Róng."

19 See also Poo (2005: 45, note 57). Shaughnessy (1991: 177–80) discusses a bronze inscription (Shirakawa Shizuka 白川靜 1962-: fascicle no. 49, entry no. 12:303) from King Mù's reign (956–918 BCE) in which the term *róng*, which he translates as 'belligerents,' refers to the people from the state of Hu, which was a member of the Huáiyí confederation.

20 For the concept of 'barbarians' in Classical Greece, see notes 29 and 82; see also page 172 and notes 2–4 in chapter 5.

Inventing the 'barbarian' 159

21 As observed by Li (2008: 286), the distinction between 'people inside the city' (*guó rén* 國人) and 'people of the field' (*yě rén* 野人) probably did not emerge "until the Eastern Zhōu period." Western Zhōu bronze inscriptions do not refer to cities as *guó* 國 and their inhabitants as 'city-dwellers' (*guó rén* 國人); "instead *yi* 邑 and *yiren* 邑人 are terms to express such concepts" (Li 2008: 286).

22 Pines (2005: 85). The following *Zuǒ* passage indicates that its Warring States authors believed that *Róng* groups had been relegated to infertile lands in the Spring and Autumn period (the term *róng* is used here as an ethnonym for specific groups, rather than in the meaning 'belligerent others'): "The chief of the Jiāng Róng . . . replied, 'Formerly, the men of Qín, relying on their numbers, and covetous of territory, expelled us, the various **Róng** tribes. Then Lord Huì . . . gave us the lands of Jin's southern marches, where jackals and wolves howled. All of us **Róng** removed and cut down their brambles and drove away their foxes and wild cats, jackals and wolves, and became subjects of the former lord.'" (*Zuǒ*, Xiāng 14, tr. adapted from Durrant, Li, and Schaberg (2016: 1009)). For discussion of this passage, see also Pines (2005: 85, fn. 79).

23 Pines (2005: 85).

24 The Central Plain area was not homogeneous ethnically and with respect to moral values and conventional practices in the Warring States period. However, the Zhōu expansion did reduce diversity in certain areas compared to earlier periods.

25 See, for example, the "Yǔ gòng" chapter of the *Shàngshū* (Legge 1960: 92–127), which Nylan (2001: 134–35) and Shaughnessy (1993: 378) date to the Warring States period. See also Pines (2005) and Di Cosmo (2002: 94–6). For discussion of the term *Zhōng guó* and other Zhōu autonyms (*Huá, Xià*, and *Huáxià*), see also Chén Suìzhēng (1993) and the discussion of *Xià* in chapter 5.

26 Referring to the four cardinal directions, 'the four non-Zhōu others' (*sì yí* 四夷) is counted here as a directional compound.

27 Many other types of compound ethnonyms are found in pre-Qín texts, e.g., color compounds (e.g., *chì-dí* 赤狄 'the Red *Dí*,' *bái-dí* 白狄 'White *Dí*'). However, for simplicity, the present analysis is based on the three compound types illustrated in (3–5).

28 The data in Table 4.1, see page 160, (and Table 4.2 in note 70) is based on representative subsets of texts from the Warring States and pre-Warring States periods. For both periods, both received and archaeological texts have been included. The fact that the *Zuǒzhuàn* was composed mainly in the fifth to fourth century BCE (for this assumption, see note 85 in chapter 2) and that the *Lǚshì Chūnqiū* was composed in the mid-third century does not matter here. Both represent Warring States (or roughly post-500 BCE) vocabulary. To be sure, there are significant differences in the language of the two texts. However, doing a fine-grained century-by-century chronology of linguistic changes from the fifth to the third century BCE goes beyond the scope of this book, which is limited to the difference between pre-Warring States and Warring States meanings and uses of ethnonyms.

29 See Lattimore (1962: 455); Di Cosmo (2002: 95, fn. 7); Hall (1997: 4); Pines (2005: 61, n. 8); and Beckwith (2009).

30 As observed by Yang (2014: xvi), Bergeton (2006) "demonstrated systematically that the Chinese of the Warring States period . . . began to use compounds like *Man-Yi*, *Rong-Di* and *Yi-Di*, as well as *Yi* and the numerical expression 'four Yi' . . . as standard synecdochic labels for all foreign peoples . . . Bergeton's study thus refutes. . . Beckwith's [(2009)] contention. . . 'that Chinese has no generic word equivalent to barbarian, or indeed any one word that is even close to it.' . . . Beckwith overlooks the fact that words like Yi could acquire generic or synecdochic semantic functions in addition to their original specific meanings."

31 Whether or not the term *yí* should be translated as 'barbarian' has been the topic of a debate triggered by Liu's (2004) claim that it came to mean 'barbarian' after the Opium Wars in the 1830s and 1840s, and that before 1830 it was a neutral way to refer to foreigners during the Qīng dynasty (1636–1911). Whether *yí* was a neutral or

Table 4.1 Relative frequency of different types of ethnonyms.

Period	Pre-Warring States			Warring States		
Texts	Annals, Book of Songs, pre-WS Shàngshū, pre-WS parts of Changes*	BI*1	Total pre-Warring States texts	Mencius, Xúnzǐ, Lǚshì Chūnqiū, Zuǒzhuàn	Bamboo manuscripts Guōdiàn, Shàngbó (vols 1–9), Qīnghuá (vols 1–4)	Total Warring States texts
a. Toponym compounds	16/19 = 84%*2	46*3 (74%)	62 (62/80=77.5%)	16/87 = 18%	0	16/89 = 18%
b. Directional + ethnonym compounds (+sì yí)	3/19 = 16%	15 (24%)	18 (18/80 = 22.5%)	71/87 = 82%	2	73/89 = 82%
c. Directional compounds	3*4	15*5	18	40	1*6	41
d. Ethnonym compounds	(3)*7	0	0*8	31	1*9	32

Notes to table 4.1:
Here I follow Nylan's (2001) suggestions as to which parts of Changes and the Shàngshū date to pre-Warring States period.
* BI = bronze inscriptions
*1 Counts are based on Zhāng Yàchū's (2012) Concordance Shāng and Zhōu Bronze Inscriptions.
*2 Book of Songs: 10 (Huái-yí [8], Kūn-yí [1], Chuàn-yí [1]); Annals: 6 (Máo-róng, Shān-róng, Luò-róng, Jiāng-róng, Huái-yí [2]).
*3 Nineteen of these are instances of Huái-yí 淮尸(夷).
*4 Book of Songs: 2 (Xī-róng [1], Nán-yí [1]); Annals: 1 (Běi-róng).
*5 Nán-yí 南尸(夷)[6], Dōng-yí 東尸(夷)[9]. Although the expressions Nán-yí and Nōng-yí occur in BI, they do not have the same meaning as in Warring States texts. Pre-Warring States Dōng-yí and Nán-yí are not 'the barbarians to the south/east' but refer to specific sub-groups of the ethnic group called the Yí: the 'Yí to the east' (Dōng-yí) and the 'Yí to the south' (Nán-yí). In contrast, the expression xī-yí used in the Mencius passage in (13) to describe King Wén means 'civilizationally inferior other to the West' not a 'person from the sub-group of the ethnic group Yí in the West.'
*6 Qīnghuá, Vol. 2, p. 138: 1 (Xī-róng).
*7 Book of Songs: 1 (Róng-dí); Annals: 2 (róng-mán(zi) 戎蠻(子) [2]). Since these occurrences of róng-dí and róng-mán are not true ethnonym compounds, they are not included in the total counts here; see the discussion of (17) below.
*8 Mán-róng occurs in one Spring and Autumn period BI where it appears to refer to a specific group.
*9 Qīnghuá, Vol. 2, p. 153: 1 (Mán-yí). Here the word mán 蠻 is written without <虫> as <蠻>, as is also usually the case in BI. The word yí 夷 is written as <尸>/<夷>, that is, with <二> added under the graph <尸> that normally is used to write the word yí 夷 in BI.

Inventing the 'barbarian' 161

pejorative term during the Qīng dynasty does not bear directly on the questions studied here. I will therefore not discuss it here. That term *yí* can have negative connotations in pre-Qín texts, as claimed here, has been pointed out in numerous studies; see Poo (1999, 2005, 1998, 1994), Fang Weigui (2001), Di Cosmo (2002), Pines (2005), Bergeton (2006), Kim (2009), Beecroft (2010), Fiskesjö (1999, 2012), Huang (2013), Yang (2014), Brindley (2003), Brindley (2015), and Schaberg (2001).

32 Keightley (1999: 269).

33 *Lijì*, "Wáng Zhì" 3.13, *SSJZS* (1980: 1338), tr. adapted from Legge (1960: 229–30). The "Wáng Zhì" passage in (6) was likely composed in the late Warring States or early Hàn periods.

34 Schaberg (2001).

35 *Guǎnzǐ*, "Xiǎo Kuāng," tr. Rickett adapted from (1985: 339). Although this passage describes Duke Huán of Qí (r. 685–643 BCE) subjugating of non-Zhōu peoples militarily, the use of ethnonyms reflects Warring States (or early Hàn dynasty) usage patterns and reflects late Warring States ideas. It was probably composed in the late third or early second century BCE.

36 In texts from the Warring States period, the directional compounds *dōng-yí, nán-mán,* and so forth, should be translated as 'the Yí, who live in the east,' 'the Mán, who live in the south,' and so forth. Translating these terms as 'the southern Mán,' 'the eastern Yí,' and so forth, might lead to the mistaken assumption that there is a distinction between the southern Mán, the eastern Mán, the northern Mán, and so on. Both the single-word ethnonyms (*mán, yí, róng,* and *dí*) in (6) and the directional compounds (*nán-mán, dōng-yí, xī-róng, běi-dí*) in (7) are used as general terms referring to 'non-Zhōu others' in various directions (south, east, north, west) rather than to specific peoples.

37 As also observed by Poo (2005: 47), it is "doubtful . . . if the Shang people had already developed a strong Sino-centric perspective that considered the Shang state as the center of the world, the unquestionable leader of civilization."

38 *Zuǒ*, Zhuāng 31.1, tr. adapted from Durrant, Li, and Schaberg (2016: 221).

39 *Mòzǐ*, "Against War III," tr. adapted from Watson (1963: 58).

40 The term 'four non-Zhōu others' (*sì yí*) does not mean the same in (9a) and (9b). In the *Zuǒ* passage in (9a), the 'four civilizationally inferior non-Zhōu others' (*sì yí*) are contrasted with the Central States, which are all part of the "realm of value" defined by 'civility/civilization' (*wén*). As discussed in chapter 3, the *Zuǒzhuàn* distinguishes between the 'civilized world' (*tiānxià*) of the 'Central States' (*zhōng guó*) and the 'barbarians' or 'civilizationally inferior others' (*yí*). In contrast, in the *Mòzǐ* passage in (9b), 'four non-Zhōu others' (*sì yí*) is a neutral term for all non-Zhōu peoples. As observed in chapter 3, the *Mòzǐ* is hostile to the concept of 'civility/civilization' (*wén*). Hence, in the *Mòzǐ*, 'all under Heaven' (*tiānxià*) is not limited to a 'civilized world' defined by 'civility/civilization' (*wén*), but also includes the non-Zhōu others. Thus, in the *Mòzǐ*, 'four non-Zhōu others' (*sì yí*) is not a pejorative term but a neutral way to refer to the totality of non-Zhōu groups; see also Pines (2005).

41 *Sì-yí* occurs four times in the *Zuǒzhuàn*, thrice in the *Zhōulǐ*, twice in the *Zhuāngzǐ* and the *Lǔshì Chūnqiū*, and once in the *Lijì*, the *Mencius*, the *Xúnzǐ*, the *Mòzǐ*, and the *Guǎnzǐ*. *Sì-yí* also occurs in three chapters of the *Shàngshū*, but according to Nylan (2001) all three are post-Hàn chapters.

42 The expression 'four Mán' (*sì-mán*) occurs once in the *Hánshī wàizhuàn*, which was likely composed around 150 BCE; see Hightower (1993).

43 In addition to the *Annals* and the *Book of Songs* as well as the pre-Warring States parts of the *Shàngshū* and the *Changes*, the corpus studied here also includes bronze inscriptions.

44 The expressions *xī-róng* and *běi-róng* can also function as toponym ethnonyms referring to the "Western Rong" and "Northern Rong," respectively.

45 Máo 300, SSJZS (1980: 426), tr. adapted from Waley (1996: 315).

162 *Inventing the 'barbarian'*

46 In the bronze inscriptions discussed in Shaughnessy (1991: 178–9) the 'Southern *Yí* (*Nán-yí*) refers to a specific non-Zhōu people, i.e., the *Huái-yí* who were fighting wars with the Zhōu.

47 Li (2006: 95). That is, *dōng-yí* is often used as "a generic term referring to the various indigenous peoples in the east" (Li 2006: 307), e.g., *JC*: 2739. *JC* refers to the *Yīn Zhōu jīnwén jíchéng* (1984–1994).

48 Li (2006: 343–46).

49 Máo 168, *SSJZS* (1980: 416), tr. adapted from Karlgren (1950: 112).

50 *Zuǒ*, Xī 10.4, Yáng Bójùn (1990: 332). tr. from Durrant, Li, and Schaberg (2016: 299), who translate *běi-róng* as "Northern Rong."

51 See Table 4.1 in note 28.

52 *Běi-róng* occurs four times in the *Zuǒzhuàn* commentary to the *Annals*: *Zuǒ*, Xuān 6.4; *Zuǒ*, Xuān 9.6; *Zuǒ*, Xuān 10.5; and *Zuǒ*, Yǐn 9.6. *Běi-róng* also occurs once in the *Bamboo Annals* (*Zhúshū jìnián*). For the date and authenticity of the *Bamboo Annals*, see Nivison (1993, 2009). In these cases, *běi-róng* refers to a specific ethnic group, 'the northern *Róng*' (*běi-róng*), attacking or being attacked by the states of Zhèng and Qí. It is not a general term for 'barbarians.'

53 Attestations in the *Mencius* of the three types of *mán-, yí-, róng-, dí*-based compound ethnonyms in (3–5):

   i   Toponym compounds in the *Mencius* (total 1/14 = 7%):
     kūn-yí 昆夷   'the Kūn groups'   (M1B:3)*

   ii Directional compounds (+*sì yí*) in the *Mencius* (total 10/14 = 71.5%):

a. *dōng-yí zhi-ren* 東夷之人	'Eastern barbarian'	(M4B:1)
b. *xī-yí* 西夷	'Western barbarians'	(3M1B:11, 3 MB:5, M7B:4)
c. *xī-yí zhi-ren* 西夷之人	'Western barbarian'	(M4B:1)
d. *běi-yí* 北夷	'Northern barbarians'	(M7B:4)
e. *běi-dí* 北狄	'Northern barbarians'	(M1B:11, M3B:5)
f. *nán-mán* 南蠻	'Southern barbarian'	(M3A:4)
g. *sì yí* 四夷	'barbarian groups on the four borders'	(M1A:7)

   iii Ethnonym compounds in the *Mencius* (3/14 = 21.5%):

a. *róng-dí* 戎狄	'barbarians in the north west'	(M3A:4, M3B:9, both from Máo 300)**
b. *yí-dí* 夷狄	'barbarians'	(M3B:9)

    * The expression *kūn-yí* 昆夷 is used in the *Book of Songs* (written with <混>) to refer to a people which whom the founders of the Western Zhōu fought. In the *Mencius* it is used as a relic from pre-Warring States usage.

   ** In *M*3A:4 and *M*3B:9 *Róng-dí* 戎狄 occurs in a quotation from Máo 300. As discussed in (17) below, while at first glance *róngdí* in this passage looks like a compound, it is most likely a phrasal unit of conjoined mono-morphemic ethnonyms referring to two separate non-Zhōu peoples.

54 *Mencius* 4B:1, tr. adapted from Lau (2004: 88).

55 *Zuǒ*, Xiāng 14.1, Yáng Bójùn (1990: 1007). tr. adapted from Schaberg (2001: 133).

56 Pulleyblank (1983: 421, Wade-Giles changed to Pinyin) discusses the hypothesis that the Zhōu may have had Róng origins: "Mencius may have been accurate in referring to King Wén as a Western Barbarian (*Xī-yí* 西夷) . . . If the Zhōu were originally Róng people, they must have undergone a process of sinicization before the conquest [in 1045 BCE] . . . Due to this acculturation the Zhōu lost their identity with those Róng who retained their own customs and language and turned against them."

57 The term *yí* is also used as a blanket term for barbarians' in the *Zuǒzhuàn* passage in (9a) and in *Zuǒ*, Dìng 10.2: "Aliens should not plot against the 'Great ones' (*Xià*); the

Inventing the 'barbarian'   163

'civilizationally inferior others' (*Yí*) should not disrupt the 'Flowery' (*Huá*) States"
裔不謀夏，夷不亂華 (Yáng Bójùn (1990: 1578), tr. adapted from Durrant, Li, and
Schaberg (2016: 1797)). For discussion of the *Huá-Yí* dichotomy in the *Zuǒzhuàn*, see
also Ogura Yoshihiko (1967).

58 *Mencius* 3A:4, tr. adapted from Lau (2004: 61).
59 Gardner (2007: 71). For agriculturalist theories of statecraft and the philosophy of Xǔ
Xíng, see Graham (1989: 64–74).
60 Chǔ had strong local traditions and a distinct material culture; see Cook and Major
(1999). People from the northern states, such as Qí and Lǔ, sometimes scornfully
referred to Chǔ as a 'barbarian' (*yídí*) state. See also Di Cosmo (2002) for discussion of the real-political implications of one of the Central States calling another state
'barbarian.'
61 *Mencius* 3A:4, tr. Lau (2004: 61). Chinese: 南蠻鴃舌之人，非先王之道.
62 See the examples in note 53.
63 *Mencius* 1A:7, tr. adapted from Lau (2004: 12).
64 *Yídí* occurs frequently in the *Gǔliáng* (17 occurrences) and *Gōngyáng* (20 occurrences). It occurs once in the *Lǐjì* and the *Mencius* and twice in the *Analects*. Since
the *Gǔliáng* and *Gōngyáng* may have been written in the Western Hàn, the number of
attestations of *Yídí* in (received) pre-Qín text can be counted one hand. *Yídí* also occurs
in the *Guóyǔ* (1) and the *Shuō yuàn* (5). *Yídí* is not found in the *Guōdiàn*, *Shàngbó* (vol.
1–9), or *Qīnghuá* (vols 1–4) manuscripts.
65 *Mán-yí* is found in a range of received Warring States texts: *Zhōulǐ* (1), *Zuǒzhuàn*
(9), *Xúnzǐ* (1), *Mòzǐ* (2), *Yànzǐ Chūnqiū* (1), *Guǎnzǐ* (1), *Lǚshì Chūnqiū* (2). *Mán-yí*
also occurs twice in the "Canon of Yao" chapter in the *Shàngshū*, which according
to Nylan (2001) was composed in late Warring States or early Hàn times. It also
occurs in the *Guóyǔ* (12), the *Shuō yuàn* (5), and the *Zhànguócè* (5). *Mán-yí* is
found once in the *Qīnghuá* manuscripts; see Lǐ Xuéqín (2010–2014: vol. 2: 153).
The passage in which it occurs describes a war between Chǔ and Jìn. The armies
of 'the various *Mán-yí*' are on the side of the southern state of Chǔ. In contrast, the
allied armies of the northern state of Jìn include the 'armies of the various *Róng*.'
Hence, the expression *mán-yí* here refers to the 'non-Zhōu others/groups to the
southeast'; see (21e).
66 *Róng-dí* is found in a wide range of received Warring States texts: *Zhōulǐ* (1), *Lǐjì*
(1), *Zuǒzhuàn* (12), *Gōngyáng* (1), *Mencius* (2), *Xúnzǐ* (1), *Yànzǐ Chūnqiū* (1), *Guǎnzǐ*
(1). *Róng-dí* also occurs in the *Guóyǔ* (17), the *Shuō yuàn* (1), and the *Zhànguócè*
(3). *Róng-dí* is not found in the *Guōdiàn*, *Shàngbó* (vols 1–9), or *Qīnghuá* (vols 1–4)
manuscripts.
67 *Lǐjì*, "Míng tang wèi," SSJZS (1980: 1489). For alternative tr. see Legge (1967: 33).
Chinese: 昧東夷之樂也；任南蠻之樂也。納夷蠻之樂於大廟，言廣魯於天下也。
68 This sequence *yí mán* can be compared to Modern Chinese nonce words such as *jiě-dì*
'older sister(s) and younger brother(s)': "Our father and mother gave birth to us two,
'older sister' (*jiě*) [and] 'younger brother' (*dì*)" (父母生我姐弟二人). Unlike the
compounds, 'brothers' *xiōng-dì* and 'sisters' (*jiě-mèi*), which are listed in dictionaries,
nonce expressions such as 'older sister and younger brother' (*jiědì*) and 'younger sister
and older brother' *mèi-xiōng* are not. They are phrasal constructions made up to serve
particular communicative purposes in specific contexts.
69 The instance of *Róng-Yí* in the *Lǐjì* passage in (3) in chapter 5 is a phrasal unit rather
than a compound. *Róng-Yí* also occurs once in the *Lièzǐ*. However, as observed by
Barrett (1993: 300–01), the *Lièzǐ* "cannot be used as a source for pre-Ch'in Chinese
thought without proof that the specific passage involved was incorporated into it from
an earlier work of that period." *Róngyí* is also attested in the *Lǚshì Chūnqiū*: "Qín is
a backward and vulgar place inhabited by *Róngyí* 秦國僻陋戎夷" (*Lǚshì Chūnqiū*, tr.
adapted from Knoblock and Riegel (2000: 607)). However, here *róng-yí* is a nonce
word alternative to *róngdí*, which is frequently used pejoratively to refer to the people

164 *Inventing the 'barbarian'*

of Qín as 'civilizationally inferior others.' It could also be a scribal corruption of *róngdí*. Finally, three instances of *róng-yí* in the *Lǚshì Chūnqiū* are emended as 式夷 *Shi Yí* (proper name); see Knoblock and Riegel (2000: 517; see also pp. 14–5).

The expression *dí-róng* occurs once in the pre-Qín corpus, namely *in Zuǒ*, Duke Ai 4.2, where it appears to be a nonce alternative to the more frequently found *róngdí*.

Two occurrences of the expression 'the viscount of the *Róng-mán*' (戎蠻子) are from Zhāo 16.2 and Ai 4.6 in the versions of the *Annals* attached to the *Zuǒzhuàn* and the *Gǔliáng* commentaries. The version of the *Annals* attached to the *Gōngyáng* has 曼 instead of 蠻. In a passage in the *Zuǒzhuàn* commenting on *Annals*, Zhāo 16.2, *Róng-mán* is likewise the name of a particular 'viscount' (*zǐ* 子) of a particular non-Zhōu people. According to the *Hànyǔ Dà Cídiǎn*, *Róng-mán* is the name of a tribe. Finally, one occurrence is found in the *Lièzǐ*. However, since the authenticity of the *Lièzǐ* as a pre-Qín text is problematic, its reference to "the country of the *Róng-mán*" cannot be used as evidence of pre-Qín usage.

70 The data set in Table 4.2, with zero true ethnonym compounds in pre-Warring States texts versus 32 in Warring States texts, strongly indicates that ethnonym compounds first arose on the eve of the Warring States period.

Table 4.2 Ethnonym compounds.

Period	*Pre-Warring States*			*Warring States*					
Text	*(i)* Annals (C)	*(ii)* Book of Songs (S)	*(iii)* W. Zhōu BI*[1]	*(iv)* Mencius (M)	*(v)* Xúnzǐ (X)	*(vii)* Lǚshì Chūnqiū (L)	*(viii)* Zuǒzhuàn (Z)	*(ix)* M+X+ L+Z	*(x)* Arch. manus.*[3]
a *mán-yí*	0	0	0	0	2	2	9	13	1
b *róng-dí*	0	(1)/0*[2]	0	2	1	0	11(12)	16	0
c *mányí-róngdí*	0	0	0	0	1	0	1	2	0
d *yídí*	0	0	0	1	0	0	1	2	0
Sum	0	0	0	3	4	2	22	31	1
Total	0								32

Notes to table 4.2:
*[1] Counts are based on Zhāng Yàchū's (2012) *Concordance Shāng and Zhōu Bronze Inscriptions (BI)*.
*[2] *Róng-dí* occurs in Máo 300; see (17), where it is a phrasal unit of conjoined ethnonyms referring to two separate non-Zhōu peoples. Máo 300 was likely composed during the reign of Duke Xi of Lǔ (r. 659-627); see Qū Wànlǐ 屈萬里 (1983: 334–35).
*[3] Arch. manus. = Archaeological manuscripts

71 Máo 300, SSJZS (1980: 617), tr. adapted from Karlgren (1950: 260), also quoted in the *Mencius* 3A:4 in (15) above.

72 According to Waley (1996: 315, fn. 3–4), "Jīng are the southern people known later as Chǔ. The Xu [=Shu] (in south-west Shandōng and Anhui) were regarded as non-Chinese, but at this period often fought in alliance with the Chinese."

73 *Zuǒ*, Chéng 7.1, Yáng Bójùn (1990: 832), tr. adapted from Durrant, Li, and Schaberg (2016: 763). Tán is a state located on the Shandong peninsula (Li 2006: 317).

74 *Zuǒ*, Mǐn 1.2, Yáng Bójùn (1990: 256), tr. adapted from Durrant, Li, and Schaberg (2016: 229).

75 In contrast, compared to the state of Lǔ, Tán is sometimes cast as the 'barbarian.' As observed by Durrant, Li, and Schaberg (2016: 763), "when the Tan ruler comes to the Lu court and shows unexpected mastery of esoteric knowledge (Zhao 17.3), Confucius declares that learning is lost at the center but found among 'tribes of the four quarters'

Inventing the 'barbarian' 165

(*siyi* 四夷). Compared with Lu, Tan's non-Zhōu status becomes obvious." Early Chinese texts contain numerous similar examples of Zhōu states calling other Zhōu states 'barbarians.' As described by Di Cosmo (2002: 100), the "states of Chin, Ch'u, and Wu were all branded at one time or another as Yi-Ti because of their violation of accepted norms." Archaeological evidence shows that the material cultures of Wú and Yuè differed from other Zhōu states; see Falkenhausen (1999: 525–39). For studies of Yuè identity, see also Henry (2007) and Brindley (2003, 2015).

76 For discussion of another *Zuǒ* passage relating an attack by the Dí, see Zhāng Huáitōng (2001: 21–7). For the location of the *róng-dí*, see Zhào Tiěhán (1965). For Róng and Zhōu interaction, see also Kodō Kinpei (1962).

77 According to Li (2006: 286), "the rise of self-awareness of the people in North China had led to the construction of a cultural divide between the 'Huaxia' population and the totality of 'Rongdi' 戎狄, which by the middle Spring and Autumn period had clearly gained a meaning similar to 'barbarian' as the word is used in English." As mentioned above, the expression *róngdí* does not occur in the *Annals* and BI and only occurs once as a phrasal sequence in the *Book of Songs*; see (17). Li (2006) may be basing his claim on the occurrences of *róngdí* in the *Zuǒzhuàn*, where *róngdí* does indeed refer to a concept of 'civilizationally inferior others.' However, since it may have been composed (based on records from earlier records) in the Warring States period (as argued in note 85 in chapter 2), using the *Zuǒzhuàn* to study Spring and Autumn period word meanings may be problematic. However, Li's (2006) hypothesis that *róngdí* had come to mean 'barbarian' by the "middle of the Spring and Autumn period" is still compatible with the proposal put forth in this chapter that a concept of non-Zhōu others as 'civilizationally inferior others' emerged sometime between 600 and 400 BCE. It is certainly possible that *róngdí* could mean 'barbarian' by the early sixth century BCE. However, if we exclude the *Zuǒzhuàn* from the corpus of texts composed before the Warring States period, then there are not enough attestations of the expression *róngdí* to demonstrate beyond doubt that it could mean 'barbarian' in pre-Warring States times.

78 The term *róng* does not always mean 'the non-Zhōu others to the west' as in (6). In some contexts – see (14) – it denotes a specific ethnic group. However, in the systems of directional and ethnonym compounds that emerged in the Warring States period, it often means 'civilizationally inferior non-Zhōu others to the west.' The same applies to the other expressions in (21a–d).

79 *Xúnzǐ* 18, Wáng Xiānqiān (1988: 329–30), tr. adapted from Hutton (2014:189).

80 Evidence that *mányí-róngdí* was used a compound can also be found in *Zuǒ*, Chéng 2.9: "When the 'civilizationally inferior non-Zhōu others to the south, east, west, and north' (*mányí-róngdí*) do not obey the royal commands, indulge in sensual excesses and wine, and flout the constants of order, then the king gives the command to attack them" 蠻夷戎狄，不式王命，淫湎毀常，王命伐之 (Yáng Bójùn (1990: 809), tr. adapted from Durrant, Li, and Schaberg (2016: 735). The expression *mányí-róngdí* also occurs twice in the *Guóyǔ*.

Other sequences of the mono-morphemic ethnonyms *mán, yí, róng*, and *dí* are attested. See, for example, the sequence *Yí, Mán, Róng*, and *Dí* (夷蠻戎狄) in the passage from the *Lǐjì* quoted in (6) above. However, here the sequence **yí mán róng dí** is likely a phrasal unit rather than a lexicalized compound like *mányí-róngdí* 'barbarians' on a par with modern Chinese *xiōngdì-jiěmèi* 'siblings.' This interpretation is supported by the fact that the unexpected order (*Yí, Mán, Róng, Dí*) mirrors the order in which the four 'barbarians' are discussed in the preceding context: "The groups on the east were called **Yí** . . . Those on the south. . . **Mán** . . . Those on the west. . . **Róng** . . . Those on the north. . . **Di**."

81 According to Di Cosmo (2002: 95, fn. 7), "the distinction made in these early differentiations between *yao* peoples (allied, and possibly 'absorbed,' also indicated with the

166 Inventing the 'barbarian'

binome *Man-Yi*) and *fan* peoples (independent, and possibly hostile, also designated with the binome *Jung-Ti* [=*Róng-dí*]) introduces a notion of conscious differentiation between close foreigners and far foreigners . . . This distinction is hopelessly obscured when the blanket term 'barbarian' is used indiscriminately."

82 For an etymological overview of the terms *barbarians* and *savages*, see also Stocking (1987: 10): "'Barbarian' derives from the Greek contrast between those who spoke intelligibly and those beyond the pale of civil life whose language seemed simply reiterative mumbling – notably the Scythians, who for centuries were the archetype of the barbarian nomads of the Eastern steppes. A second contrastive term derives not from language but from habitat: 'savages' (from the Latin 'sylva') were those who lived in the woods, rather than in the city and who, with the era of discovery, were more apt to be encountered by seafaring Europeans venturing West."

83 See Di Cosmo (2002: 100) for discussion of the *yídí* as general term for 'barbarians.' See also Yang (2014).

84 See, for example, *Gōngyáng*, Xī 4.3: "When Chǔ has a [true] king then they will submit [to the Son of Heaven]; lacking a [true] king they will be the first to revolt. They are *Yí-dí*, they often violate the Central States. The **Southern Yí** and the **Northern Dí** join together [to attack the Central States]. And the **Central States** are imperiled like a string that is about to break. Duke Huan saved the **Central States**, and resisted the **Yí-dí**, and finally pacified the Jīng Chǔ. And thereby he completed the task of a [true] king" 楚有王者則後服，無王者則先叛。夷狄也，而亟病中國，南夷與北狄交。中國不絕若線，桓公救中國，而攘夷狄，卒怗荊，以此為王者之事也 (SSJZS 1980: 2249). Here the state of Chǔ is branded as a 'barbarian' (*yídí*) state. See Di Cosmo (2002: 100) for discussion of such use of terms for 'barbarians' in inter-state political discourse. For Zhōu perceptions of the State of Chǔ, see also Pines (2005: 88). *Yídí* also occurs once in the *Guóyǔ* and five times in the *Shuō yuàn*.

85 See notes 65 and 66.

86 *Yídí* occurs in *Analects* 3.5 (see [1] in chapter 5), and in *Analects* 13.19, Chéng Shùdé (1997: 926), Slingerland (2003: 18; 148). As argued by Brooks and Brooks (1998: 102; 127), *Analects* 3.5 and 13.19 were likely composed toward the end of the fourth century BCE.

87 *Mencius* 3B:9.

88 *Lǐjì*, "Zhōngyōng," Legge (1960: 306), SSJZS (1980: 1627).

89 See Cheng (1993) and Pines (2002).

90 *Yídí* is frequently used in Sīmǎ Qiān's *Historical Records*. For a study of *yídí* from post-Hàn to Sòng times, see Yang (2014). As observed by Yang (2014: xvi), it is possible that "*Yi-Di* gained greater currency in through the field of *Chunqiu* exegesis." This explains why it came to be a very frequent way to refer to various concepts of 'barbarians' in Hàn and post post-Hàn times.

91 For the emergence of a concept of 'empire' in the Warring States period, see Pines (2009).

92 The term *yí* also had other meanings, e.g., 'to level (both concrete and abstract senses)'; 'to harmonize'; 'equal'; 'common.' Since they do not bear on the issues discussed here, I will not discuss them here.

93 In bronze inscriptions, the graph <尸> was used to write the word *lǝj* → *shī* 'corpse.' The asterisk '*' indicates reconstructions of Old Chinese. The arrow → indicates sound change between Old Chinese and Modern Mandarin. Since the Old Chinese pronunciation of the word for 'corpse' differed from the ethnonym *lǝj* → *yí* 'the *yí*' only in the voicing of the initial consonant (the little circle under the 'l' indicates that it is voiceless), in pre-Warring States texts the graph <尸> was also the standard way to write the word *lǝj* → *yí* 'the *yí*' which was later written <夷>. The graph <尸> represents a "person, seen from the side, with knees bent" and is often "indistinguishable from that for 人 *rén* 'person'" (Baxter and Sagart 2014: 401, fn. 90); see also Jì Xùshēng (2010: 651; 95–96). In received texts from the Warring States period, *lǝj* → *yí* 'the *yí*'

is generally written with various forms of the graph <夷>, while *ləj → *shī* 'corpse' continues to be written with <尸>. However, in archaeological manuscripts from the Warring States period, the word *ləj → *yí* is written <尼>/<🏹>; see *Qīnghuá* Vol. 2, p. 153: 1 (*Mán-yí*); see also the cases discussed in Richter (2013: 104–08). Graphic differentiation of words that used to be written with one graph but later came to be written with two different graphs are common and reflect a general tendency in the evolution of the pre-Qín writing system. The graphic differentiation of the words 夷 *ləj → *yí* 'the *Yí*' and 尸 *ləj → *shī* 'corpse' probably happened for phonological and orthographic reasons, independently of the semantic developments in the word *ləj → *yí* from the 'the *Yí*,' referring to a specific ethnic group, to 'the civilizationally inferior other.' It was the similarity in pronunciation which originally allowed the two words to be written with the same graph <尸>. The shift to the use of <夷> to write *yí* may have been triggered by sound changes making the two words sound more different. As suggested by Baxter (p.c.), *ləj → *shī* 'corpse' may have changed to *xəj thereby rendering <尸> phonetically unfit to write the word *ləj → *yí* 'the *Yí*,' which then had to be written differently. Early forms of the graph <夷> do occur in pre-Warring States archaeological texts such as oracle bone inscriptions; see *HJ* 17027. However, in early pre-Warring States archaeological inscriptions, the graph <夷> seems to have been used mainly in non-ethnonym meanings. It also occurred in personal names. The use of the graph <夷> as a loan graph for the ethnonym *ləj → *yí* 'the *yí*' seems to have been introduced rather late. Since the question of when this happened does not bear directly on the analysis of the emergence of the use of the word *ləj → *yí* to refer to 'civilizationally inferior others' (regardless of how it was written), I will not discuss it in more detail here.

It has recently been proposed by Basu (2014), citing earlier work by Tan (1973: 47–8), that <夷> "is a combination of a big man with a bow – a term also employed to convey the concept of conquest" (Basu 2014: 930). The implication seems to be that the composition of the graph <夷> is somehow related to the meaning of the word 'non-Zhōu other' (*ləj → *yí*). There are several problems with this explanation. First, it does not take into account that the word 'non-Zhōu other' (*ləj → *yí*) was originally written with the graph <尸>, which had nothing to do with 'bows' or 'big man.' Second, there is evidence that the <弓> element in <夷> is not a 'bow' but rather a string wrapped around an arrow <矢>. The explanation of the graph <夷> as consisting of 'bow' <弓> and 'big (man)' <大>, found in the *Shuōwén* 說文 dictionary, is thus a later misunderstanding; see Jì Xùshēng (2010: 796). Indeed, as observed by Jì Xùshēng (2010: 796; 489–90), in pre-Qín orthography the characters <夷> and <弟> look very similar; both graphs share the string-like component, later (mis)interpreted as 'bow' <弓>. Furthermore, 夷 *ləj was also similar in pronunciation to 弟 *lˤəjʔ.

References

Allan, Sarah. 2007. 'Erlitou and the Formation of Chinese Civilization: Toward a New Paradigm', *The Journal of Asian Studies*, 66: 461–96.

Barrett, T. H. 1993. 'Lieh tzu 列子', in Michael Loewe (ed.), *Early Chinese Texts: A Bibliographical Guide* (Society for the Study of Early China: Berkeley, CA).

Basu, Dilip K. 2014. 'Chinese Xenology and the Opium War: Reflections on Sinocentrism', *The Journal of Asian Studies*, 73: 927–40.

Baxter, William Hubbard, and Laurent Sagart. 2014. *Old Chinese: A New Reconstruction* (Oxford University Press: Oxford).

Beckwith, Christopher I. 2009. *Empires of the Silk Road: A History of Central Eurasia from the Bronze Age to the Present* (Princeton University Press: Princeton).

168 *Inventing the 'barbarian'*

Beecroft, Alexander. 2010. *Authorship and Cultural Identity in Early Greece and China: Patterns of Literary Circulation* (Cambridge University Press: Cambridge).

Bergeton, Uffe. 2006. 'The Evolving Vocabulary of Otherness in Pre-imperial China: From "Belligerent Others" to Cultural Others', Master's Thesis, University of Southern California.

Brindley, Erica. 2003. 'Barbarians or Not? Ethnicity and Changing Conceptions of the Ancient Yue (Viet) Peoples, ca. 400–50 BC', *Asia Major*, 16: 1–32.

———. 2015. *Ancient China and the Yue: Perceptions and Identities on the Southern Frontier, c.400 BCE-50 CE* (Cambridge University Press: Cambridge).

Brooks, Bruce, and Taeko Brooks. 1998. *The Original Analects: Sayings of Confucius and His Successors* (Columbia University Press: New York).

Chang, Kwang-chih. 1980. *Shang Civilization* (Yale University Press: New Haven).

Chén Suìzhēng 陳穗錚. 1993. 'Zhongguo cicheng de qiyuan yu yuanyi 中國詞稱的起源與原義', *Shi Yuan* 史原, 19: 1–38.

Cheng, Anne. 1993. 'Ch'un ch'iu 春秋, Kung yang 公羊, Ku liang 穀梁 and Tso chuan 左傳', in Michael Loewe (ed.), *Early Chinese Texts: A Bibliographical Guide* (Society for the Study of Early China: Berkeley, CA), pp. 67–76.

Chéng Shùdé 程樹德. 1997. *Lúnyǔ jíshì* 論語集釋 (Zhōnghuá shūjú: Běijīng).

Cook, Constance A., and John S. Major. 1999. *Defining Chu: Image and Reality in Ancient China* (University of Hawaii Press: Honolulu).

Di Cosmo, Nicola. 1999. 'The Northern Frontier in Pre-Imperial China', in Michael Loewe and L. Edward Shaughnessy (eds.), *Cambridge History of Ancient China: From the Origins of Civilization to 221 B.C.* (Cambridge University Press: Cambridge), pp. 885–966.

———. 2002. *Ancient China and Its Enemies: The Rise of Nomadic Power in East Asian History* (Cambridge University Press: Cambridge).

Durrant, Stephen W., Wai-yee Li, and David Schaberg. 2016. *Zuo Tradition: Zuozhuan* (University of Washington Press: Seattle).

Falkenhausen, Lothar von. 1999. 'The Waning of the Bronze Age: Material Culture and Social Developments, 770–481 B.C', in Michael Loewe and L. Edward Shaughnessy (eds.), *Cambridge History of Ancient China: From the Origins of Civilization to 221 B.C.* (Cambridge University Press: Cambridge), pp. 450–544.

Fang Weigui. 2001. 'Yi, Yang, Xi, Wai and Other Terms: The Transition from "Barbarian" to "Foreigner" in Nineteenth-Century China', in Michael Lackner, Iwo Amelung, and Joachim Kurtz (eds.), *New Terms for New Ideas: Western Knowledge and Lexical Change in Late Imperial China* (Brill: Leiden), pp. 95–123.

Fiskesjö, Magnus. 1999. 'On the "Raw" and "Cooked" Barbarians of Imperial China', *Inner Asia*, 1: 139–68.

———. 2012. 'The Animal Other: China's Barbarians and Their Renaming in the Twentieth Century', *Social Text*, 109, 29: 57–79.

Gardner, D. K. 2007. *The Four Books: The Basic Teachings of the Later Confucian Tradition* (Hackett: Indianapolis).

Graham, Angus C. 1989. *Disputers of the Tao: Philosophical Argument in Ancient China* (Open Court: La Salle, IL).

Hall, Jonathan M. 1997. *Ethnic Identity in Greek Antiquity* (Cambridge University Press: Cambridge).

Henry, Eric. 2007. 'The Submerged History of Yue', *Sino-Platonic Papers*, 176.

Hightower, James R. 1993. 'Han shih wai chuan 韓詩外傳', in Michael Loewe (ed.), *Early Chinese Text: A Bibliographical Guide* (Society for the Study of Early China: Berkeley, CA), pp. 125–28.

Inventing the 'barbarian' 169

Hutton, Eric L. 2014. *Xunzi* (Princeton University Press: Princeton).

Jì Xùshēng 季旭昇. 2010. *Shuōwén xīn zhèng* 說文新證 (Fújiàn rénmín chūbǎnshè: Fúzhōu).

Karlgren, Bernhard. 1950. *The Book of Odes* (Museum of Far Eastern Antiquities: Stockholm).

Keightley, David N. 1999. 'The Shang: China's First Historical Dynasty', in Michael Loewe and L. Edward Shaughnessy (eds.), *Cambridge History of Ancient China: From the Origins of Civilization to 221 B.C.* (Cambridge University Press: Cambridge), pp. 232–91.

———. 2000. *The Ancestral Landscape: Time, Space, and Community in Late Shang China, ca. 1200–1045 B.C.* (University of California Center for Chinese Studies: Berkeley, CA).

Kim, Hyun Jin. 2009. *Ethnicity and Foreigners in Ancient Greece and China* (Duckworth: London).

Knoblock, John, and Jeffrey Riegel. 2000. *The Annals of Lü Buwei* (Stanford University Press: Stanford, CA).

Kodō Kinpei 後藤均平. 1962. 'Shujū jidai no Shū to Ron 春秋時代の周と戎', in Chūgoku kodai shi kenkyūkai 中國古代史研究會 (ed.), *Chūgoku kodai shi kenkyū* 中國古代史研究 (Yoshikawa: Tokyo).

Lattimore, Owen. 1962. *Inner Asian Frontiers of China* (Beacon Press: Boston).

Lau, D. C. 2004. *Mencius* (Penguin: London).

Legge, James. 1861. *The Chinese Classics* (Trübner & Co.: London).

———. 1960. *The Shoo King or the Book of Historical Documents* (Hong Kong University Press: Hong Kong).

———. 1967. *Li chi: Book of Rites. An Encyclopedia of Ancient Ceremonial Usages, Religious Creeds, and Social Institutions*. Translated by James Legge. Edited with an introduction and study guide by Ch'u Chai and Winberg Chai (University Books: New York).

Li, Feng. 2006. *Landscape and Power in Early China: The Crisis and Fall of the Western Zhou, 1045–771 BC* (Cambridge University Press: Cambridge).

———. 2008. *Bureaucracy and the State in Early China: Governing the Western Zhou* (Cambridge University Press: Cambridge).

Lǐ Xuéqín 李學勤. 2010–2014. *Qīnghuá dàxue cáng zhànguó zhújiǎn* 清華大學藏戰國竹簡 Vol. 1–4 (Zhong xi shu ju: Shanghai Shi).

Liu, Lydia He. 2004. *The Clash of Empires: The Invention of China in Modern World Making* (Harvard University Press: Cambridge, MA).

Nivison, David S. 1993. 'Chu shu chi nien 竹書紀年', in Michael Loewe (ed.), *Early Chinese Texts: A Bibliographical Guide* (Society for the Study of Early China: Berkeley, CA), pp. 39–47.

———. 2009. *The Riddle of the Bamboo Annals* (Airiti Press: Taipei).

Nylan, Michael. 2001. *The Five "Confucian" Classics* (Yale University Press: New Haven).

Ogura Yoshihiko 小倉芳彦. 1967. 'I i no toriko: Saden no Ka I kannen 裔夷の俘 – 左傳の華夷觀念', in Chūgoku kodai shi kenkyūkai 中國古代史研究會 (ed.), *Chūgoku kodai shi kenkyū* 中國古代史研究 (Yoshikawa: Tokyo).

Patterson, Thomas C. 1997. *Inventing Western Civilization* (Monthly Review Press: New York).

Pines, Yuri. 2002. *Foundations of Confucian Thought: Intellectual Life in the Chunqiu Period (722–453 B.C.E.)* (University of Hawaii Press: Honolulu).

———. 2005. 'Beasts or Humans: Pre-Imperial Origins of Sino-Barbarian Dichotomy', in Reuven Amitai and Michal Biran (eds.), *Mongols, Turks, and Others: Eurasian Nomads and the Sedentary World* (Brill: Leiden), pp. 59–102.

170 *Inventing the 'barbarian'*

———. 2009. *Envisioning Eternal Empire: Chinese Political Thought of the Warring States Era* (University of Hawaii Press: Honolulu).

Poo, Mu-chou. 1994. 'The Emergence of Cultural Consciousness in Ancient Egypt and China: A Comparative Perspective', in Betsy M. Bryan and David Lorton (eds.), *Essays in Egyptology in Honor of Hans Goedicke* (Van Siclen Books: San Antonio, TX), pp. 191–200.

———. 1998. 'Encountering the Strangers: A Comparative Study of Cultural Consciousness in Ancient Egypt, Mesopotamia, and China', in *Seventh International Congress of Egyptologists* (Louven: Peters), pp. 885–92.

———. 1999. 'Gudai Zhongguo, Aiji yu Lianghe liuyu dui yizu taidu zhi bijiao yanjiu 古代中國、埃及與兩河流域對異族態度之比較研究 (A Comparative Study of the Attitudes toward the Aliens in Ancient China, Egypt, and Mesopotamia)', *Hanxue yanjiu* 漢學研究, 17: 137–69.

———. 2005. *Enemies of Civilization: Attitudes Toward Foreigners in Ancient Mesopotamia, Egypt, and China* (SUNY Press: Albany).

Průšek, Jaroslav. 1971. *Chinese Statelets and the Northern Barbarians in the Period 1400–300 B.C.* (Riedel: Dordrecht & Holland).

Pulleyblank, Edwin G. 1983. 'The Chinese and Their Neighbours in Prehistoric and Early Historic Times', in David N. Keightley (ed.), *The Origins of Chinese Civilization* (University of California Press: Berkeley, Los Angeles, CA & London), pp. 411–66.

Qū Wànlǐ 屈萬里. 1983. *Xiān-Qín wénshǐ zīliào kǎobiàn* 先秦文史資料考辨 (Lianjing chuban shiye gongsi: Taibei).

Richter, Matthias. 2013. *The Embodied Text* (Brill: Leiden).

Rickett, W. Allyn. 1985. *Guanzi: Political, Economic, and Philosophical Essays from Early China* (Princeton University Press: Princeton).

Schaberg, David. 2001. *A Patterned Past: Form and Thought in Early Chinese Historiography* (Harvard University Asia Center: Distributed by Harvard University Press: Cambridge, MA).

Schuessler, Axel. 1987. *A Dictionary of Early Zhou Chinese* (University of Hawaii Press: Honolulu).

Shaughnessy, Edward L. 1991. *Sources of Western Zhou History* (University of California Press: Berkeley, CA).

———. 1993. 'Shang shu 尚書 (Shu ching 書經)', in Michael Loewe (ed.), *Early Chinese Texts: A Bibliographical Guide* (Society for the Study of Early China: Berkeley, CA), pp. 376–89.

Shirakawa Shizuka 白川靜. 1962-. *Kinbun tsūshaku* 金文通釋 (Hakutsuru bijutsukanshi: Kobe).

Slingerland, Edward G. 2003. *Analects: With Selections from Traditional Commentaries* (Hackett: Indianapolis).

SSJZS. 1980. *Shísān jīng zhù shū* 十三經注疏 (Zhōnghuá shūjú: Běijīng).

Stocking, George W. 1987. *Victorian Anthropology* (Free Press & Collier Macmillan: New York & London).

Tan, Chung. 1973. 'On Sinocentrism: A Critique', *China Report*, 9: 38–50.

Waley, Arthur. 1996. *The Books of Songs* (Grove Press: New York).

Wáng, Guówéi 王國維. 1987. 'Guifang Kunyi Xianyun Kao 鬼方昆夷獫狁考', in *Guāntáng jílin* 觀堂集林 (Yi wen yin shu guan: Taipei).

Wáng Xiānqiān 王先謙. 1988. *Xúnzǐ jíjiě* 荀子集解 (Zhōnghuá shūjú: Běijīng).

Watson, Burton. 1963. *Mo Tzu Basic Writings*. Translated by Burton Watson (Columbia University Press: New York).

Yáng Bójùn 楊伯峻. 1990. *Chūnqiū Zuǒzhuàn zhù* 春秋左傳注 (Zhonghu shuju: Beijing).

Yang Huang. 2013. 'Perceptions of the Barbarian in Early Greece and China', *Center for Hellenic Studies Research Bulletin*, 2, published online at. http://nrs.harvard.edu/urn-3:hlnc.jissue:CHS_Research_Bulletin.Vol_02.Issue_01.2013.

Yang, Shao-yun. 2014. 'Rhetorical and Philosophical Uses of the Yi-Di in Mid-Imperial China, 600–1300', Dissertation, University of California Press, Berkeley, CA.

Yīn Zhōu jīnwén jíchéng 1984–1994. *Yīn Zhōu jīnwén jíchéng* (Zhōnghuá shūjú: Běijīng).

Zhāng Huáitōng 張懷通. 2001. 'Chūnqiū Zhuanggong sanshier nian faxing zhi "di" kao 春秋莊公三十二年伐邢之'狄'考', *Zhongyuan wenwu* 中原文物: 21–7.

Zhāng Yàchū 張亞初. 2012. *Yīn Zhōu jīnwén jíchéng yǐndé* 殷周金文集成引得 (Zhonghua shuju: Beijing).

Zhào Tiěhán 趙鐵寒. 1965. 'Chūnqiū shiqi de Rong-Di dili fenbu jiqi yuanliu 春秋時期的戎狄地理分析及其源流', *Gushi kaoshu* 古史考述: 314–47.

5 Ethnographic vocabulary of civilizational otherness

The 'elegant' 'rites' of the 'Great ones' versus the 'vulgar' 'customs' of the 'barbarians'

> The responsibilities of the Grand [Music] Master consist in preventing 'barbarian' (*yí* 夷) 'customs' (*sú* 俗) and deviant tunes from daring to bring disorder to the 'elegant/proper' (*yǎ* 雅) [standard].[1]
>
> —*Xúnzǐ* 20.60–92

In many respects, the development of a Zhōu–barbarian distinction in pre-Qín China mirrors that found in Ancient Greece. Before the fifth century BCE, the Greeks had not yet explicitly articulated a strong sense of civilizational identity and superiority. Differences in values and conventional practices were not emphasized in narratives mentioning enemies of the Greeks. In the Homeric epics, noblemen, whether Greek or non-Greek, have more in common than Greek noblemen have with Greek commoners or slaves.[2] Although a bitter foe, Hector is not viewed as a barbarian. It was only after the Persian wars (499–449 BCE) that non-Greek groups began to be described as 'barbarians' (*bárbaroi*) who "behave in ways which fell short of the standards of Hellenic virtue: they are emotional, stupid, cruel, subservient, or cowardly. Culturally their ways are barbarian; ethnographic material is used to distinguish their customs from those of Greeks."[3] Only after the middle of the first millennium BCE did the term *bárbaros* begin to refer to "the universal anti-Greek against whom Hellenic—especially Athenian—culture was defined."[4]

Prior to the Warring States period, the language of the Zhōu elite did of course include both autonyms, or names for the Zhōu elite themselves, and numerous specific ethnonyms, or names for other non-Zhōu groups. However, as shown in the previous chapter, it was not until the crystallization of civilizational consciousness in the term 'civility/civilization' (*wén*) around 600–400 BCE that a dichotomy between the Zhōu—who referred to themselves as the 'Great ones' (*Xià*)—and the 'civilizationally inferior' groups came to be conceptualized mainly in terms of differences in values and practices. This development coincided with and/or triggered the coining of a number of key terms used by the Zhōu elite to articulate their emerging civilizational consciousness even more explicitly. Thus, a new vocabulary used to describe 'civilizationally inferior others' in ethnographic terms began to be coined.[5]

Ethnographic vocabulary of civilizational otherness 173

Tracing the emergence of the Zhōu self-appellation 'the Great ones' (*Xià* 夏) and its close relationship to the term 'elegant, proper' (*yǎ* 雅) will provide a fuller picture of the contrast between the 'civilizationally inferior others' (*yí*) and a 'civilized' self. Exploring the coining of the noun 'customs' (*sú* 俗) and the related adjective 'vulgar' (*sú* 俗) offers yet another window into the lexicalization of civilizational consciousness that took place around the middle of the first millennium BCE. The lexicalization of the terms 'elegant, proper' (*yǎ*), 'customs' (*sú* 俗), and 'vulgar' (*sú* 俗) helped the coiners of civilizational consciousness describe the ethnographic differences between the 'elegant, proper' (*yǎ*) 'rites' (*lǐ* 禮) of the Zhōu elite and the 'vulgar' (*sú* 俗) 'customs' (*sú* 俗) of the 'civilizationally inferior non-Zhōu others' (*yí*). While these terms have all been discussed in the literature, I will show how semantic changes in these words are related to the emergence of civilizational consciousness and propose new semantic analyses and chronologies for the coining of the words 'the Great ones' (*Xià*), 'elegant, proper' (*yǎ* 雅), 'customs' (*sú* 俗), and 'vulgar' (*sú* 俗).

The rise of the 'Great ones' (*Xià*): Zhōu elite self-identity

The term *xià* 夏 has played a pivotal role in the grounding of Chinese self-identities. From the pre-Qín period to the present day, this word has served as both an autonym and the name of the myth-like first dynasty of China, the *Xià* dynasty (2070–1600 BCE). Since the Warring States period, the dichotomy between the 'civilized' 'Great ones' (*Xià*) versus the 'barbarians' (*yí*) has continued to influence the way people have constructed their identities, not just in China but also in other East Asian countries, such as Korea and Japan, that have adopted these traditional Chinese terms and made them their own.

The word *xià* had several different meanings and uses in the pre-Qín period, including: 'large,' 'great,' 'magnificent,' 'name of the Xià dynasty,' and 'Zhōu autonym.'[6] If and how these meanings are connected historically is debated. Figure 5.1 proposes a chronology of the historical connections between some of the meanings of the word *xià* that played a role in the articulation of pre-Qín civilizational consciousness. The figure also indicates the relationship between the self-appellation 'the Great ones' (*Xià*) and the adjective 'elegant/proper, *Xià*-like' (*yǎ*). Since the pronunciation has changed considerably since the pre-Qín period, phonological reconstructions of Old Chinese words are important in order to determine morphological relationships between words. The asterisk '*' indicates reconstructions of Old Chinese. The arrow → indicates sound change between Old Chinese and Modern Mandarin.

There is a great deal of disagreement on when the *xià* is first attested in the meanings listed Figure 5.1. In many cases, existing evidence is too sparse to definitively determine which of the many analyses proposed in the literature is correct. I have therefore used dotted lines to propose a tentative chronology which can be revised if further evidence emerges. My main argument is that the meanings in Figure 5.1 are connected through semantic extensions as follows: (I) 'large; big; great' → (II) 'great; splendid' → (III) 'the Great/Grand,' 'name of the

174 *Ethnographic vocabulary of civilizational otherness*

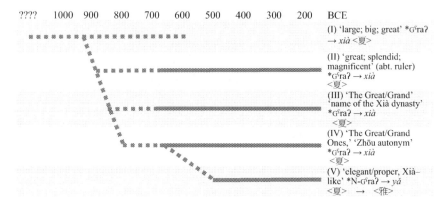

Figure 5.1 Tracing the history of the meaning changes of the words *xià* and *yǎ*.

Xià dynasty' → (IV) 'The Great/Grand Ones,' 'Zhōu autonym' → (V) 'elegant/ proper, *Xià*-like.' I assume that meanings (I–IV) must have emerged sometime during the period from the late Shāng to the Spring and Autumn period. Exactly when does not bear directly on the semantic derivations proposed here. Determining the date of the coining of the word 'elegant/proper, *Xià*-like' (*N-ɢˤraʔ → *yǎ*) in (V) in Figure 5.1, however, is relevant for my analysis of the expansion of the vocabulary used to articulate the Zhōu–barbarian distinction. I argue that it took place sometime around the eve of the Warring States period.

The etymology proposed in Figure 5.1 assumes that one of the earliest and most basic meanings of the word *xià* <夏> is 'large; big,' as indicated in row (I).[7] The Old Chinese pronunciation *ɢˤraʔ of the word eventually evolved into modern Mandarin *xià*.[8] There is evidence that Old Sinitic and Written Tibetan shared a word root with the basic meaning 'large, great.'[9] This etymology is supported by the fact that early Chinese dictionary-like word glosses also define the words 夏 (*ɢˤraʔ → *xià*) and 嘏 (*kˤraʔ → *jiǎ*) as sharing the meaning 'large; great' (*dà* 大).[10] It therefore seems plausible to assume that the (or an) early basic meaning of the word 夏 (*ɢˤraʔ → *xià*) was 'large, great.'[11]

As indicated in row (II), from the basic meaning (physically) 'large, great,' the more abstract meaning 'great' or 'magnificent,' used to describe rulers, was derived by semantic extension. The word 夏 (*ɢˤraʔ → *xià*) is used in the sense 'magnificent' sense to describe King Wén in *Ode* 241.7:[12] "[Lord on High (*dì*) said to King Wén:] 'in spite of your prominent **greatness** (夏 *ɢˤraʔ → *xià*) [your bright charismatic power] has not changed.'"[13]

As discussed in Chapter 2, the term *wén* was first used to describe individuals (usually rulers or members of the high aristocracy) as 'awe-inspiringly beautiful.' Then, after it was interpreted in ethical terms as 'morally refined,' it also came to be used to refer to 'states' (*guó*) and 'dynasties' (*dài*) as 'civilizationally refined' or 'civilized/policed.' The term 'great' (夏 *ɢˤraʔ → *xià*) may have undergone a

Ethnographic vocabulary of civilizational otherness   175

similar process. First it was used to describe individuals as 'great/magnificent,' as shown above. It then came to be used to modify collective groups and social formations, as in Máo 135: "The **great** household was very grand; but now, at every meal there is nothing left over." [14] Eventually, the term 'great' (夏 *ɢˤra? → *xià*) was used to describe and name the legendary first dynasty as the 'Great/Magnificent' (*Xià*) 'dynasty' (*dài*), as shown in row (III) in Figure 5.1.

The use of *Xià* as a dynastic title does not appear to be attested in pre-Warring States oracle bone or bronze inscriptions.[15] The word *Xià* used to refer to the dynasty preceding the Shāng does appear in the "Proclamation of Shao (召誥)" chapter of the *Shàngshū*: "We must survey the Xià dynasty . . . The Xià dynasty was to enjoy the favoring decree of Heaven just for (so many) years."[16] Nylan (2001: 133–5) tentatively places the composition of the "Proclamation of Shao" chapter in the earliest pre-Warring States strata of the *Shàngshū*, which she believes were composed ca. 1000–700 BCE.[17,18] The use of *Xià* to name a legendary dynasty that allegedly preceded the Shāng dynasty may therefore date back to the Western Zhōu.[19] The word *Xià* is also used in Máo 304 in the *Book of Songs*, which mentions the slaying of King Jié, the last king of the *Xià* dynasty. According to Qū Wànlǐ 屈萬里 (1984: 159), Máo 304 is likely to have been composed during the time of Duke Xiāng of Sòng (r. 650–637 BCE).

An early variant of the graph <夏> occurs in a Spring and Autumn bronze inscription in a context where it could be construed as referring to 'the Great ones,' meaning (IV) in Figure 5.1.[20] It is therefore likely that the term *Xià* was used by the Zhōu elite to refer to themselves by the Spring and Autumn period. It is also possible that *Xià* could have been used in this meaning even earlier.[21] However, the mere existence of the use of the term *Xià* as a Zhōu autonym meaning 'the Great/Grand ones' obviously does not by itself prove that a civilizational consciousness had been fully articulated during the first half of the first millennium BCE. Indeed, using words with positive meanings (such as 'great') as an autonym is attested in many other languages and traditions.[22] Autonyms deriving from positive words is a widespread linguistic phenomenon that does not correlate directly with the presence of fully articulated civilizational consciousness. If a civilizationally grounded *Xià–yí* distinction based on cultural differences between the 'civilized' *Xià* and the 'barbarians' (*yí*) had emerged before 600–400 BCE, then it difficult to explain when we do not find any more direct evidence of it in bronze inscriptions and received pre-Warring States texts.

The *Zuǒzhuàn* contains some of the earliest attestations of a civilizationally grounded *Xià–yí* contrast.[23] However, as mentioned above, the bulk of the *Zuǒzhuàn* was likely composed during (or after) the fifth century BCE. In contrast, the *Annals*, the *Book of Songs*, and the pre-Warring States parts of the *Documents* and the *Changes* contain no uses of the word *Xià* as an autonym meaning 'the Great ones.' Indeed, in the *Annals* the word *xià* is only used in the meaning 'summer' and in personal names.

The Spring and Autumn period can be compared to the period 1500–1750 in Europe. Both periods lead up to the explicit coining of civilizational consciousness

176 *Ethnographic vocabulary of civilizational otherness*

(around 600–400 BCE in China and around 1750–1800 in Europe). In both cases, the *concepts* that would eventually form the backbone of civilizational consciousness were slowly beginning to form, but the key *terms* which would eventually articulate civilizational consciousness had yet to be coined. Poo (2005: 48) is thus correct that "during the Eastern Zhōu period . . . a heightened consciousness of the conflict between the Chinese States and the foreign tribes was prevalent." The term *Xià* may have been used as an autonym to set the Zhōu apart from non-Zhōu enemies, but this contrast was still largely informed by the pre-Warring States perception of others as 'belligerent others.' As argued in Chapter 4, the view of non-Zhōu others as 'civilizationally inferior others' (*yí*) does not appear to have become prevalent before the coining of the word *wén* in the meaning 'civility/civilization' around 600–400 BCE.

The coining of the word 'elegant/proper, *Xià*-like' (**N-Gˤraʔ → yǎ*) indicated in row (V) in Figure 5.1 appears have taken place around the middle of the first millennium. I argue that it both informed and was triggered by the explicit coining of civilizational consciousness. As for the phonological and semantic relationship between the word 夏 'great' (**Gˤraʔ → Xià*) in the four meanings in rows (I–IV) and the word 雅 'elegant/proper, *Xià*-like' (**N-Gˤraʔ → yǎ*) in row (V), I follow Baxter and Sagart's (2014: 121) proposal that (V) **N-Gˤraʔ* 'elegant' is derived from (IV) **Gˤraʔ* 'Great ones' by adding the nasal prefix **N-*. Although the words 'Great ones' (*Xià* 夏) and 'elegant' (*yǎ* 雅) now have different pronunciations and are now written with different graphs, their Old Chinese pronunciations (**Gˤraʔ* and **N-Gˤraʔ*) differed only in the presence or absence of the *N*-prefix. There are other examples of the *N*-prefix being used to derive adjectives from nouns. According to Baxter and Sagart (2014: 7, 83), the adjective 'flowery' or 'flower-like' (華 **N-qʷʰˤra → huá*) was derived from the noun 'flower' (華 **qʷʰˤra → huā*) by adding the stative-intransitivizing prefix **N-*.[24] Furthermore, the fact that both words could be written with variants of the graph <夏> in pre-Qín documents also supports Baxter and Sagart's conclusion that they derived from the same root.[25]

Attestations of the word 'proper, elegant' **N-Gˤraʔ → yǎ* (whether written as <夏> or <雅>) do not predate middle of the first millennium by much. It is likely that it was coined sometime in the late Spring and Autumn or early Warring States period in order to satisfy a communicative need for a convenient way to refer to things and people that were *Xià*-like, that is, 'elegant/proper' as the 'civilized' 'Great/Grand ones' (*Xià*).[26] The word 'elegant/proper, *Xià*-like' **N-Gˤraʔ → yǎ* fulfilled this function and allowed the Zhōu elite to contrast their own 'elegant/proper, *Xià*-like' (**N-Gˤraʔ → yǎ*) 'rites' (*lǐ*) with the 'vulgar' 'customs' of the 'barbarians.'

The assumed civilizational superiority of the 'Great ones' (*Xià*) vis-à-vis the 'non-Zhōu others' (*yí*) has already been suggested by the passages in (6), (15), and (23) discussed in Chapter 4. The *Analects* passage in (1) below explicitly states that the 'non-Zhōu other' (*Yídí*) are 'inferior to' (lit. *bù rú* 不如 'not as good as') the *Xià*. The implication is that even when they have rulers (i.e., 'police'), they still lack the 'civility/civilization' (*wén*) embodied in the 'rites' (*lǐ*) of the Zhōu

Ethnographic vocabulary of civilizational otherness 177

tradition.[27] Hence, in passage (1), translating the term 'civilizationally inferior non-Zhōu others' (*Yídí*) as 'barbarians' appears fitting.

(1) The Master said, "The **'barbarians'** (*Yídí*), even with their rulers, are still inferior to the ***Xià* states** (***zhū-Xià***) without their rulers." (子曰：夷狄之有君，不如諸夏之亡也)[28]

(2) Sounds and music enter into people deeply and transform people quickly. Therefore, the former kings carefully made for these things a 'proper pattern' (*wén*). . . . Thus, the former kings valued the 'rites' (*lǐ*) and considered deviant tunes base. . . . The responsibilities of the Grand [Music] Master consist in preventing 'barbarian' (*yí* 夷) 'customs' (*sú* 俗) and deviant tunes from daring to bring disorder to the **'elegant/proper, *Xià*-like' (*yǎ*) [standard].** (夫聲樂之入人也深，其化人也速，故先王謹為之文 . . . 故先王貴禮樂而賤邪音 . . . 使夷俗邪音不敢亂雅，太師之事也)[29]

The *Xúnzǐ* passage in (2) illustrates how the word *N-Gˤraʔ → yǎ* (雅) was used to contrast the '*Xià*-like' or 'elegant, proper' (*yǎ*) standards of the 'civilizational patterns' (*wén*) of the musical tradition practiced by the 'Great ones' (*Xià*) with the 'deviant tunes' of the 'civilizationally inferior others' (*yí*).[30] It also illustrates how the Zhōu elite's civilizational consciousness informed the contrast between their own proper 'rites' (*lǐ*) and the 'local customs' (*sú*) of the '(civilizationally inferior) non-Zhōu others' (*yí*).

In sum, the uses of the word *Xià* as a Zhōu autonym and as a name for the dynasty preceding the Shāng may have preceded the explicit articulation of the civilizational consciousness of the Zhōu elite that emerged around 600–400 BCE, as shown in stages (I–IV) in Figure 5.1. In contrast, this civilizational consciousness is likely one of the factors that led to the coining of the word 'elegant/proper, *Xià*-like' (*N-Gˤraʔ → yǎ*) in stage (V). It is not a coincidence that the derivation of the word 'elegant/ proper, *Xià*-like' (*N-Gˤraʔ → yǎ*) by adding an *N*-prefix to the word 'Great ones' (*Gˤraʔ → xià*) took place around the same time as the coining of the word *wén* to mean 'morally refined' and 'civility/civilization,' as described in Chapters 2–3. The shift in the narratives informing the construction of 'non-Zhōu others' from 'belligerent others' to 'civilizationally inferior others' or 'barbarians,' described in Chapter 4, generated a need for a word like 'elegant, proper, *Xià*-like' (*yǎ*/*N-Gˤraʔ*) to refer to the Zhōu elite's own traditions and practices and contrast them with the 'vulgar' (*sú* 俗) 'customs' (*sú* 俗) of the 'civilizationally inferior others' (*yí*). The terms 'elegant, proper, *Xià*-like' (*yǎ*/*N-Gˤraʔ*), 'vulgar' (*sú* 俗), and 'customs' (*sú* 俗) are part of the emerging ethnographic vocabulary of civilizational otherness that allowed the Zhōu-barbarian dichotomy to be articulated with increasing clarity.

From 'desires' (*yù*) to 'vulgar' (*sú*) 'customs' (*sú*): practices bound in time and space[31]

The emergence of the *Xià-yí* contrast spurred interest in discussing the 'rites' (*lǐ*) of the Zhōu elite and the 'customs' (*sú* 俗) of both the Zhōu's own primordial primitive ancestors and their contemporary non-Zhōu 'barbarian' neighbors.

178 *Ethnographic vocabulary of civilizational otherness*

Tracing the chronology of the coining of the term *sú* in the meaning 'customs' therefore provides yet another window into the emergence of the civilizational self-consciousness of the Zhōu elite. While the concept of 'civility/civilization' (*wén*) incorporates the universal and timeless 'rites' (*lǐ*) of the Zhōu elite, the term *sú* is often used in pre-Qín texts to refer to the 'vulgar/common' (*sú*) non-Zhōu 'customs' (*sú*) anchored in time and place.[32] But when and how did *sú* begin to be used as a noun meaning 'customs' and as an adjective meaning 'common' or 'vulgar'? What do these developments tell us about the nature and chronological development of pre-Qín civilizational consciousness?

The word *sú* is not attested in the meaning 'customs' in received texts from the pre-Warring States period.[33] The graph <俗> does occur in pre-Warring States bronze inscriptions, but only as part of names or to write the word *yù* 'desire, want.'[34] An inscription on a bronze vessel from the ninth century BCE contains an instance of the graph <俗> that some scholars have interpreted to mean 'customs' (*sú*). However, there are compelling reasons to believe that <俗> is simply used in its most common way in pre-Warring States Old Chinese, that is, to write the word *yù* 'desire, want' (which is now written <欲>). First, several scholars take the graph <俗> in this inscription to write the word 'desire, want' (*yù*).[35] Second, the striking absence of discussion of *sú* 'customs' in texts from the early Warring States period—e.g., the early layers of the *Analects*, the *Zuǒzhuàn*—indicates that even by the fifth century BCE the term *sú* had not yet been coined to mean 'customs.' The absence of the word *sú* in the *Zuǒzhuàn* is remarkable given the numerous passages that compare conventionalized behaviors of the Zhōu elite with those of the non-Zhōu groups, as in the passage in (14) in Chapter 4. Had the word *sú* in the meaning 'customs' been available to the composers of the *Zuǒzhuàn*, then they surely would have used it in passages like these.

While the coining of the term *wén* in the meaning 'civility/civilization' signaled the crystallization of collective civilizational consciousness on the eve of the Warring States period, the term 'customs' (*sú*) emerged later as part of the technical vocabulary of fourth century BCE thinkers who were confronted with a politically fragmented realm and engaged in comparative discussions of local differences in conventional behavior and the different modes of governance embraced by the various Central States. The first attested instances of the term *sú* in the meaning 'customs' appear in fourth century BCE texts such as the *Mòzǐ*, the *Mencius*, and the "Kǒngzǐ shī lùn" from the Shàngbó manuscripts.[36] The term 'customs' (*sú*) often occurs in passages about thinkers who observe the conventionalized behaviors of people whenever entering an unfamiliar state. A passage in the *Lǐjì* states that "when entering a state, one should ask about its customs" (入國而問俗).[37] 'Customs' (*sú*) is one of the key terms in the proto-anthropological terminology that developed in the Warring States period to facilitate the formulation of theories about the role of local conventionalized behavior (or 'customs') in efforts to reform government institutions and the education aimed at the development of human nature (*xìng*).[38]

(3) In general, when it comes to the nature of the population [in various locations], it depends on [the differences in] land and sky, [and differences with respect to] heat and cold, dryness and humidity. The systems [for governing]

Ethnographic vocabulary of civilizational otherness 179

the broad valleys/plains and the mountain valleys are different and the **'customs' (sú)** of the people born in these places also differ. . . . The five flavors [of their cooking] are differently harmonized. Their systems of vessels and utensils are different. And clothes and garments are adapted to different needs. When adjusting the teaching of these peoples, one does not have to change their **'customs' (sú)** . . . The people of those five regions[39]—Central States, and the Róng, the Yí (and the other non-Zhōu groups)—had all their 'natures' (*xìng*), which they could not be made to alter. (凡居民材，必因天地寒煖燥溼，廣谷大川異制。民生其間者異俗 . . . 五味異和，器械異制，衣服異宜。修其教，不易其俗 . . . 中國戎夷，五方之民，皆有其性也，不可推移)[40]

As illustrated by the *Lǐjì* passage in (3), and the continuation of this passage in (6) in Chapter 4, as well as numerous late Warring States passages, the concept of 'customs' comprises various kinds of conventionalized behavior, including culinary practices, vessels and utensils, clothing, dwellings, body decorations (tattoos, hair style, etc.), music, and language.[41] Similar passages highlighting differences in material culture and conventionalized practices between the Zhōu elite and non-Zhōu others can be found in Warring States texts such as the *Lǚshì Chūnqiū*:

(4) The Mán-yí have backward tongues, exotic **'customs' (sú)**, and odd 'practices' (*xí* 習); furthermore, their clothes, caps and belts, houses and encampments, boats, carts, vessels, and tools; as well as their preferences of sound, sight, and flavor are all different from ours. (蠻夷反舌殊俗異習之國，其衣服冠帶，宮室居處，舟車器械，聲色滋味皆異)[42]

The 'customs' (*sú*) of the 'non-Zhōu others' were often (but, as we shall see, not always) viewed as just as backward and undeveloped as those of the Zhōu ancestors of remote antiquity.[43] They included eating uncooked food (due to ignorance of cooking), using animal skins as clothing (due to ignorance of hemp growing, sericulture, spinning, and weaving), living in caves (due to ignorance of how to build houses), and so forth. On a moral and institutional level, non-Zhōu others and the Zhōu ancestors of remote antiquity were portrayed in similar ways as having no rulers or government institutions and lacking a proper moral decorum regulating behavior (e.g., separation of genders, respect for elders).

For the authors of the *Analects* and the *Xúnzǐ*, the 'civilizationally inferior non-Zhōu others' (*yí*) lacked both the proper tradition of 'civility/civilization' (*wén*) and the 'rites' (*lǐ*) on which it was built. The words 'civility/civilization' (*wén*) and the 'rites' (*lǐ*) are never directly attributed to non-Zhōu others. As illustrated by the following passage from the *Xúnzǐ*, the Zhōu elite's self-identity as the 'elegant/proper, *Xià*-like' (*yǎ*) 'Great ones' (*Xià*) is based on strict adherence to the 'rites' (*lǐ*) in all aspects of everyday life, including food, clothing, and the movements of one's body:

(5) Food and drink, clothing and garments, houses and dwellings, motion and stillness [in behavior], should all be regulated and harmonized from 'rites'

(*lĭ*). If not, then one will encounter pitfalls, and develop ailments. If your countenance, bearing, movements, and stride accord with the 'rites' (*lĭ*), they will be 'elegant/proper' (or '*Xià*-like') (*yă*), if not, then they will be 'barbaric' (*yí*), obtuse, perverse, vulgar, and unruly. (食飲、衣服、居處、動靜，由禮則和節，不由禮則觸陷生疾；容貌、態度、進退、趨行，由禮則雅，不由禮則夷固、僻違、庸眾而野)[44]

Beyond material aspects of everyday life, the 'rites' are also the ultimate guide for moral behavior. In answer to his favorite disciple's question about how to realize the highest virtue of 'Goodness' (*rén*), Confucius is reported to have said, "Look not at what is contrary to the rites; listen not to what is contrary to the rites; speak not what is contrary to the rites; make no movement which is contrary to the rites."[45] Following '(local) customs' will not lead one to becoming 'Good' (*rén*); only living strictly according to the prescriptions of the assumed-to-be universally valid 'rites' (*lĭ*) will allow one to achieve this goal. According to the *Xúnzĭ*, since the 'vulgar customs' (*sú*) are by definition imperfect, and since the 'masters of the rites' (*rú*) embody the ideal tradition of the 'rites,' one of their roles when serving in office is to 'beautify' (*měi* 美) the 'vulgar customs' (*sú*) of the people:

(6) As for the 'masters of the rites' (*rú*), when they are serving in court then they beautify the government, when they are in lower positions then they 'beautify' (*měi* 美) 'customs' (*sú*). (儒者在本朝則美政，在下位則美俗)[46]

One reason the 'masters of the rites' (*rú*) look down on 'customs' (*sú*) is the perception that their purpose merely is to satisfy physical needs and 'desires' (*yù*) for food, shelter, clothing, and basic interpersonal interaction (marriage customs, etc.). Hence, they believed that 'customs' (*sú*) have to be 'beautified' (*měi* 美) to bring them in tune with the ideal practices of the 'rites' (*lĭ*) established by the sage–rulers of the Golden Age of the early Zhōu.[47]

Recent advances in phonological reconstruction provide evidence for a close connection between the words *yù* 'desire' and *sú* 'customs.' As shown in Figure 5.2, the reconstructions proposed by Baxter and Sagart (2014) enables us to hypothesize that the words **ɢ(r)ok → yù* 'desire' and **s-[ɢ]ok → sú* 'customs' derive from the same root **ɢok*.[48] The **s-* prefix added to form **s-[ɢ]ok → sú*

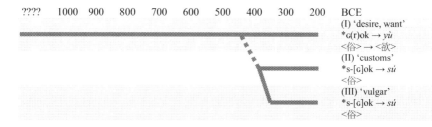

Figure 5.2 Tracing the history of the meaning changes of the words *yù* and *sú*.

Ethnographic vocabulary of civilizational otherness   181

'customs' indicates an oblique object 'that by which.' The derived word *s-[ɢ]ok → *sú* thus means 'that by which one obtains what one wants.'[49] That is, *sú* 'customs' are that by which one obtains shelter, food, spouses—in other words, the conventionalized behaviors that regulate the satisfaction of creature comforts.

As shown in (7), this analysis of the morphological relationship between the words *ɢ(r)ok → *yù* 'desire' and *s-[ɢ]ok → *sú* 'customs' is supported by the definition of the word *sú* 'customs' in the *Shìmíng*, a Hàn dictionary-like collection of word glosses:

(7) [The word] 'customs' (*sú*), is defined as 'to want/desire' (*yù*). It is that which '(vulgar) common' (*sú*) people 'want/desire' (*yù*). (俗，欲也，俗人 所欲也)[50]

The association of *sú* 'customs' with the crass satisfaction of base 'desires' (*yù*) eventually led to the lexicalization of *sú* in the adjectival meaning 'vulgar, civilizationally inferior.' The 'customs' (*sú*) of 'common people' (*sú rén*) are that by which they satisfy their basic needs and 'desires' (*yù*) for food, clothing, shelter, companionship, and so forth. For virtue ethical 'masters of the rites' (*rú*), such as Confucius and Xúnzǐ (as they are described in the *Analects* and the *Xúnzǐ*), merely satisfying basic material needs is not enough. What separates humans from animals and the 'elegant and proper' (or 'Xià-like') (*yǎ*), 'morally refined' (*wén*) 'noble man' (*jūnzǐ*) from 'common (vulgar) people' (*sú rén*) is the ability to constrain animalistic 'wants and desires' (*yù*) by always acting according to the ideal ritual decorum embodied in the 'rites' (*lǐ*).[51] While the 'rites' (*lǐ*) are assumed to be universally applicable and transcend physical 'needs/desires' (*yù*), 'customs' (*sú*) are viewed as 'vulgar' (*sú*) because they are associated with satisfaction of 'desires' (*yù*) and are bound to specific places and times.

By the third century BCE, as witnessed by texts such as the *Xúnzǐ*, adjectival *sú* in the meaning 'vulgar' began to be contrasted with the term *yǎ* 'elegant, proper, civilized, Xià-like,' which, as shown above, was a cognate of the autonym 'Great ones' (*Xià*) used by the Zhōu elite: "Thus there are 'vulgar' (*sú*) men, 'vulgar' (*sú*) *rú*, 'elegant' (*yǎ*) *rú*, and great *rú*."[52] If a ruler employs 'vulgar men' (*sú rén*), then his state will perish.[53] Though the states of rulers employing 'vulgar *rú*' (*sú rú*) may survive, only those employing 'elegant *rú*' (*yǎ rú*) can be made secure. In other words, the 'Great ones' (*Xià*) can emphasize the superiority of their own timeless 'civility/civilization' (*wén*) by explicitly describing its values and practices as 'elegant' (*yǎ*) and contrasting it with the 'vulgar' (*sú*) 'customs' (*sú*) of the 'civilizationally inferior non-Zhōu others' (*yí*) (see [2] and [5] above).[54]

Although the word 'customs' (*sú*) was part of the shared lexicon of the educated elite versant in the written lingua franca of the Zhōu realm, various thinkers displayed highly divergent attitudes toward the concept. Warring States *rú* texts, such as the *Xúnzǐ*, arguably reflect highly Zhōu-centric value systems founded on the assumption that the timeless, universal 'rites' (*lǐ*) of elite Zhōu tradition formed the social fabric of the civilized world, which was surrounded by 'civilizationally inferior peoples' (*yí*).[55] The tendency to blindly follow

182 *Ethnographic vocabulary of civilizational otherness*

'popular local customs' (*sú*) constituted a threat to the transmission and survival of the refined tradition of ritual decorum.[56] As shown in (2), Xúnzǐ was therefore very concerned about preventing the 'customs of the barbarians' (*yí sú*) from bringing disorder to the 'elegant/proper [standards]' (*yǎ*) of the 'Great ones' (*Xià*). In contrast, the authors of the *Mòzǐ* assumed a neutral understanding of 'customs' (*sú*) as a term that could be used to refer to the conventionalized behaviors of Zhōu and non-Zhōu alike.[57] One of the most direct attacks on *rú* conservatism and idealization of the ancient 'rites' (*lǐ*) of the Zhōu elite can be found in Mòzǐ's relativist pragmatism.

(8) Lord Wén of Lǔyáng, while talking to Master Mòzǐ, said, "To the south of Chǔ there is a state called Qiáo where cannibalism occurs. In this state, when the first-born son is born, then he is eaten alive; this is called satisfying the needs of the younger brothers. If he tastes good, then he is offered as a gift to the lord, and if the lord likes him, then he will reward the father. Is this not indeed a bad **'custom' (*sú*)**?" Mòzǐ said: "Even among the **'customs' (*sú*)** of the 'Central States' (*zhōng guó*), there are those [customs] which are similar to these. For how is killing the father and rewarding the son different from eating the son and rewarding the father? If one does not employ *rén* and *yì*, on what basis can one fault the **'non-Zhōu people' (*yí rén* 夷人)** for eating their sons?" (魯陽文君語子墨子曰：楚之南有啖人之國者橋，其國之長子生，則鮮而食之，謂之宜弟。美，則以遺其君，君喜則賞其父。豈不惡俗哉？ 子墨子曰：雖中國之俗，亦猶是也。殺其父而賞其子，何以異食其子而賞其父者哉?苟不用仁義，何以非夷人食其子也?)[58]

Mòzǐ appears to have aimed at shocking his audience by putting the cannibalistic 'customs' (*sú*) of a southern non-Zhōu people from the state of Chǔ on par with the 'customs' (*sú*) of the Central States. As shown in Chapter 3, Mòzǐ was portrayed by the authors of the *Xúnzǐ* as having been unable to understand the importance of the *wén*-paradigm of the 'masters of rites' (*rú*). The *Mòzǐ* also does not use the term 'all under Heaven' (*tiānxià*) to refer to a 'realm of value' or 'civilized world' defined by the adherence to the 'rites' (*lǐ*) but uses *tiānxià* instead to refer to the entire known world.[59] By his willingness to put the revered Zhōu traditions on the same level as the "barbaric" customs of the southern 'non-Zhōu others' (*yí*), Mòzǐ clearly positioned himself in opposition to the conservative ethnocentrism of contemporary *rú* thinkers. While *rú* texts condescendingly refer to local customs and foreign practices as *sú*, they reserve the term 'rites' (*lǐ*) for the revered ceremonies and rituals of early Zhōu times.[60] Hence, the same texts also tend to give the term *yí* the strongly pejorative meaning 'civilizationally inferior non-Zhōu others.' Translating *yí* as 'barbarian' (if by 'barbarian' we mean 'civilizationally inferior others') is clearly justified in texts such as the *Analects*, the *Mencius*, and the *Xúnzǐ*. In contrast, the fourth century BCE authors of the *Mòzǐ* leveled the playing field by using the term *sú* to refer to the 'customs' of both the Zhōu elite themselves and non-Zhōu groups referred to as 'non-Zhōu people(s)' (*yí rén* 夷人).

Ethnographic vocabulary of civilizational otherness 183

The *Mòzǐ* has little use for a civilizationally grounded *Xià–yí* distinction. Translating the expression *yí rén* 夷人 in a negative sense as 'barbarians' in (8) above is therefore somewhat problematic. In some respects, Mòzǐ resembles early European critics of the concept of 'civilization' such as Montaigne and Rousseau, discussed in Chapter 1. Like Montaigne, Mòzǐ also picked the practice of cannibalism, which he knew his target audience would find horrendously savage, and defended it as equal to the 'customs' of the 'Central States.' The fact that Mòzǐ referred to the 'customs' (*sú*) of the Central States rather than using the term 'rites' (*lǐ*) would also have been shocking to some.[61] As was discussed in Chapter 3, the *Mòzǐ* is not concerned with morality but with utilitarian strategies for maximizing 'benefit' (*lì* 利). If non-Zhōu groups can be persuaded to maximize 'benefit' (*lì*), then it does not matter what 'customs' (*sú*) they have as long as they do not obstruct the goal of maximizing 'benefit' (*lì*). While the terms *yí* and *sú* are used in the neutral senses 'non-Zhōu others' and 'customs' in texts such as the *Mòzǐ*, they are also used in the strongly pejorative senses 'civilizationally inferior others'/'barbarians' and 'vulgar customs' in others (e.g., the *rú* texts).[62]

Conclusion

An interest in labeling non-Zhōu groups as 'barbarians' (*yí*) and using ethnographic terms such as 'custom' (*sú*) to describe them as culturally different and inferior did not emerge before 600–400 BCE. This chapter has tied together in one narrative the chronologies of the coining of six key terms for key concepts in the Zhōu elite's understanding of themselves as a 'civilization.' As shown in Figure 5.3, these six terms form three pairs of opposites.

a. *xià* 夏 'the Great ones'   *yí* 夷 'civilizationally inferior others'
b. *lǐ* 禮 'rites/decorum' (of Zhōu elite)   *sú* 俗 'local customs'
c. *yǎ* 雅 'elegant/proper, *Xià*-like'   *sú* 俗 'vulgar; common'

Figure 5.3 Key terms articulating pre-Qín civilizational consciousness.

Chronologically, the dichotomy between 'the Great ones' (*Xià*) and the '(civilizationally inferior) others' (*Yí*) is the first pair of opposites. It emerged on the eve of the Warring States period, when the term *wén* also began to be used to refer to an emergent concept of 'civility/civilization.' About a century later, probably in the late fifth or fourth century BCE, the word *sú* in the meaning 'local customs' was coined by adding a prefix to the root *yù* 'desire, want.' Subsequently, the timeless and placeless 'rites/decorum' (*lǐ*) of the Zhōu elite could be contrasted with 'local customs' (*sú*) that varied from place to place and from generation to generation. Finally, sometime in the fourth or early third century BCE, *sú* was lexicalized as an adjective meaning 'vulgar.' Uses of the term *sú* to mean 'vulgar' are often contrasted with the adjective *yǎ* 'elegant/proper, *Xià*-like' that, in turn, derives from the same root as the autonym *Xià* 'the Great Xià.' With this last pair of opposites in place, the timeless tradition of the 'civility/civilization' (*wén*) of the 'Great ones' (*Xià*) could be explicitly articulated as 'elegant' (*yǎ*) and contrasted with

184 *Ethnographic vocabulary of civilizational otherness*

'vulgar' (*sú*) 'customs' (*sú*) of the non-Zhōu 'barbarians' (*yí*), customs that merely serve to satisfy basic 'desires' (*yù*) for food, clothing, dwellings, and so forth. It follows that from the fifth to the third century BCE the vocabulary used by the Zhōu elite to articulate their civilizational consciousness expands considerably.

The concept of 'civilization' articulated through the terms in Figure 5.3 (as well as in the terms in Figure 3.2 in Chapter 3) is found in a subset of pre-Qín texts represented by the *Analects* and the *Xúnzi*, among others. As also discussed in Chapter 3, not all pre-Qín texts shared this perspective, and it was not necessarily the most prominent view in the pre-Qín period. While it emerged in the pre-Qín period, this conceptualization of 'civilization' only became more prevalent than that of other groups of thinkers after the so-called Confucian classics became part of standard curriculum in the Hàn dynasty (206 BCE–220 CE).[63]

In this civilizational consciousness, the term *yí* was often used to refer to non-Zhōu others negatively as 'barbarians.' Like the Modern English word *barbarian*, the meaning of the Old Chinese word *yí* was not fixed once and for all but differed from context to context. McGrane (1989) describes how the concept of the 'non-European others' evolved over time. In the Renaissance it was grounded mainly in religion; non-believers were pagan "barbarians" who could become "civilized" by conversion. Later, for some eighteenth-century Enlightenment thinkers, Reason was the main criterion; "barbarians" were mired in superstitious and traditional customs. Finally, in the nineteenth century, theories of race and evolution grounded the civilizational deficiencies of the "barbarians" in their natural biological endowments. Thus, for some, the dividing line between the "civilized" and the "barbarians" was fluid and could be transcended via religious conversion or adoption of rational mores and government institutions informed by Reason. For others, the dividing line was untranscendable and immutably determined by biology. Just like the word *civilization*, the term *barbarian* meant different things to different people and at different times. Nevertheless, at a certain level of abstraction, these different uses of the word *barbarian* share a number of meaning molecules and can be paraphrased as 'peoples or groups who differ from the civilized by their lack of 'progress' in the dimensions of moral values and mores ('civility') and government institutions ('police').'

Pejorative uses of the pre-Qín word *yí* tend to possess the same core meaning that can be paraphrased in Old Chinese terms as 'peoples or groups who differ from the 'proper, elegant' (*yǎ*) 'civility/civilization' (*wén*) of the *Xià* 'the Great Xià' by their 'lack of rulers' (*wú jūn* 無君) and their adherence to 'vulgar' (*sú*) 'customs' (*sú*) rather than the universally valid 'rites' (*lǐ*).' This concept of 'civilizationally inferior others' (*yí*) shares the same core meaning as the eighteenth-century European concept of 'peoples or groups who differ from the civilized by their lack of 'progress' in the dimensions of moral values and mores ('civility') and government institutions ('police').' In this sense, it can be argued that some pre-Qín uses of the word *yí* (and *yídí*) can be translated as 'barbarian(s).' In some Warring States works, such as the *Mencius* and the *Xúnzi*, the dividing line between the "civilized" and the "barbarians" was evidently perceived as fluid; it was potentially possible for 'civilizationally inferior others' (*yí*) to become

Ethnographic vocabulary of civilizational otherness   185

"civilized" by adoption of the moral values and mores of the 'rites' (*lǐ*) and the government institution of the early Zhōu dynasty. For others, such as the authors of the *Lǐjì* passages in (3) above (and in [6] in Chapter 4), the divide between the "civilized" and the "barbarians" may have been more difficult to transcend.[64]

Notes

1 *Xúnzǐ* 20.60–92, Wáng Xiānqiān (1988: 380–81), Chinese: 使夷俗邪音不敢亂雅，大師之事也。 See also (2) below.
2 See Hall (1989); Hall (1997); Nippel (2002); and Harrison (2002).
3 Hall (1989: 17). The word *bárbaros* (Gr. βάρβαρος) is a reduplicative onomatopoeia which "originally was simply an adjective representing the sound of incomprehensible speech" (Hall 1989: 4); *bar-bar* was the equivalent of *blah-blah* in Modern English, see Weidner (1913: 303–4) and Pokorny (1959: 91–2).
4 Hall (1989: 5). For criticism of Hall (1989), see Gruen (2011) and Vlassopoulos (2013: 34–41; 161–225).
5 I am not assuming a simple causal relationship between the emergence of civilizational consciousness and the coining of a vocabulary of ethnographic comparison. The coining of terms such as 'elegant/proper' (*yǎ* 雅), 'civilizationally inferior others' (*yí*), 'customs' (*sú* 俗), 'vulgar' (*sú* 俗), was triggered by a complex set of factors. However, emergence of these terms was clearly informed by (and in turn informed) the strengthening of civilizational consciousness that took place during the period from the end of the Spring and Autumn period to the late Warring States period.
6 Other pre-Qín meanings of the term *xià* 夏 include: (i) 'summer' and (ii) 'variegated.' As observed by Mair (2013: 7–8), the use of the graph <夏> to write the word *summer* can probably be explained as a phonetic loan graph. As for the use of the word *xià* 夏 in the meaning 'variegated,' Mair proposes that it may be due to the connection to the word *huá* 華 ("flowery"), which is also used as an autonym epithet for the Zhōu elite: "From the Warring States period on, Xià has been intimately linked with Huá ('flowery') as ubiquitous epithets for the people of the Central Plains. This tight linkage would seem to speak for the 'variegated' signification as being operative in the bisyllabic expression Huáxià because it matches the meaning of Huá quite well, hence 'florescent [and] variegated.' Indeed, native philologists speak of Huá and Xià in this semantic context as being in a *jiǎjiè* ('phonetic loan') or *tōng* ('phonologically interchangeable') relationship with each other" (Mair 2013: 27). The idea that *Huá* and *Xià* in the meanings 'flowery' and 'variegated' are in a *jiǎjiè* ("phonetic loan") or *tōng* ("interchangeable") relationship is problematic. According to Baxter and Sagart (2014: 7; 83), 'flowery' (華 *N-qʷʰˤra → *huá*) is derived from the noun 'flower' (華 *qʷʰˤra → *huā*) by adding the stative-intransitivizing prefix *N-. The noun meaning 'flower' (*huā*) which is now written <花> was written with the same graph <華> as the derived word meaning 'flowery' (*huá*) in the pre-Qín period. Since the words 'Great/Grand Ones' 夏 (*ɢˤraʔ → *xià*) and 'flowery' (華 *N-qʷʰˤra → *hwae* → *huá*) have different consonantal onsets (*ɢˤr- vs. *N-qʷʰˤr-) and rhymes (*-aʔ vs. *-a), the likelihood of them being phonetically *jiǎjiè* graphs is low. In the reconstructions of Baxter and Sagart (2014), the relationship between adjectival 'flowery' (華 *N-qʷʰˤra) and the noun 'flower' (華 *qʷʰˤra → *huā*) is parallel to the relationship between adjectival 'elegant/proper, Xià-like' (*N-ɢˤraʔ → *yǎ*) and the noun 'Great/Grand Ones' 夏 (*ɢˤraʔ → *xià*). Both adjectival forms are derived by adding the stative-intransitivizing prefix *N-. In spite of their different pronunciations in OC, 華 and 夏 overlap in distribution in the expressions 諸華 *zhū-huá* 'the Huá (flowery) states' and 諸夏 *zhū-Xià* 'the Xià (Great) states' in a few passages in the *Zuǒzhuàn*. See, for example, *Zuǒ*, Xiāng 11 (Legge 1960a: 453), which mentions the 'Flowery states' (*zhū huá* 諸華) and *Zuǒ*, Xiāng 13 (Legge 1960a: 458),

186 *Ethnographic vocabulary of civilizational otherness*

which has 'Great States' (*zhū xià* 諸夏). In these passages, *zhū huá* 'the Huá (Flowery) states' and *zhū xià* 'the Xià (Great) states' appear to be interchangeable. They also occur in close proximity in the same section of the *Zuǒzhuàn*. Both expressions contrast or juxtapose the Zhōu states with 'non-Zhōu others' referred to by the ethnonym compounds *Róng-dí* and *Mán-yí*. In sum, while not phonetically interchangeable, the words *huá* 'flowery' and *xià* 'great' seem to be used interchangeably in certain contexts due to their semantic similarity; both were positive autonyms for the Zhōu elite.

7 Baxter and Sagart (2014: 121) list 'great' as the meaning of the word 夏 *ɢˤraʔ → *xià*. For discussion of other hypotheses about possible early meaning(s) of the term, see Behr (2007).

8 Unless otherwise indicated, I follow the reconstructions of Baxter and Sagart (2014). The arrow → indicates phonological change and shows how Old Chinese reconstructions (indicated by the asterisk *) develop into Mandarin (indicated by italics), as in *ɢˤraʔ → *xià*.

9 Schuessler (2007) and Mair (2013). Based on phonological and semantic similarities, Mair (2013: 9) suggests that the Old Sinitic reconstruction of Xià ("great, large") as *ɢˤraʔ [Mair uses Li Fang-kuei's reconstruction *gragh] is cognate to the Written Tibetan word *rgya* meaning 'great, wide, broad.' See also Yu Min (1989), which is cited by Mair (2013: 9). As further support for this hypothesis, Mair (2013: 13) also mentions that both terms "were used as epithetic descriptors of extensive lands, *Xià* for the Central Plains of the [East Asian Heartland] and *rgya* for the Indus Valley (i.e., India) and the Yellow River Valley (i.e., China)."

10 The *Ěryǎ*, a Warring States collection of word glosses, states: "*xià* means 'large' (夏, 大也)" (*Ěryǎ* 1.3). The *Fāngyán*, a Hàn dynasty dialect dictionary, states that "In the areas of the states of Qín and Jin, whenever a thing is mightily large then people call it 嘏 (*kˤraʔ → *jiǎ*), or 夏 (*ɢˤraʔ → *xià*) 秦晉之間, 凡物狀大者谓之嘏, 或曰夏" (*Fāngyán* 3b12: 4), see also Behr (2007: 737).

11 According to Wang Li (1982: 144), 'large building' 廈 (*[g]ˤraʔ) belongs to the same word family, i.e., derives from the same root, as 嘏 (*kˤraʔ → *jiǎ*) and 夏 (*[ɢ]ˤraʔ → *xià*), see also Mair (2013: 7).

12 Schuessler (1987: 663).

13 *SSJZS* (1980: 522), tr. adapted from Karlgren (1974: 196), Chinese: 不長夏以革. Qū Wànlǐ (1983: 334) tentatively suggests that Máo 241 may date from the early Western Zhōu. As observed by Schuessler (1987: 287, 2007: 301), the word(s) 假~嘏 (*kˤraʔ → *jiǎ*) 'great' are also used to describe the 'greatness' of rulers. In Máo 272, 嘏 (*kˤraʔ → *jiǎ*) is used as an adjective in the meaning 'great, magnificent': "The **great** King Wén (伊嘏文王)." In Máo 240.4 *jiǎ* 假 is probably the same word as *jiǎ* 嘏: "His brilliance and **greatness** had no flaw (烈假不瑕)."

14 Schuessler (1987: 663). Chinese: 夏屋渠渠、今也每食無餘, *SSJZS* (1980: 374), tr. adapted from Karlgren (1974: 87). Qū Wànlǐ (1983: 334) suggests that Máo 241 may date from the period from the reign of Duke Xiang of Qin (r. 777–766 BCE) to the middle of the Spring and Autumn period.

15 Mair (2013: 8).

16 Legge (1960b: 429–30). Chinese: 我不可不監于有夏 ... 有夏服天命惟有歷年.

17 For the authenticity and date of composition of the different subparts of the *Shàngshū*, see also Jiǎng Shànguó 蒋善国 (1988), Shaughnessy (1993), Meyer (2014), and Meyer (forthcoming). For discussion of the date and authenticity of the "Gao" chapters, see Vogelsang (2002).

18 Li (2006: 286–7, fn. 14) argues that references to the *Xià* dynasty in the "Duo fang" and "Proclamation of Shao (召誥)" chapters of the *Shàngshū* show that this use of the word *xià* "certainly" date back to the Western Zhōu. He finds additional support for this hypothesis in the discovery of a late Western Zhōu bronze "cast to commemorate

Ethnographic vocabulary of civilizational otherness 187

the virtue of Great Yu, the attributed founder of the Xia dynasty." For discussion of this bronze inscription, see Lǐ Xuéqín (2002).

19 Victor Mair and Bruce Brooks do not believe the *Xià* dynasty is mentioned in pre-Warring States texts and argue the *Xià* dynasty and the mythological narratives surrounding it are Warring States inventions aimed at magnifying the glory of the Zhōu elite by anchoring its dynastic history in remote antiquity. As observed by Mair (2013: 8), *Xià* is not used as a dynastic title in pre-Warring States bronze inscriptions. In contrast, the term Shāng does occur as the name of the conquered dynasty in Western inscriptions. Furthermore, the term Zhōu also "occurs scores of times as the name of the capital (or as Zhōuyuán ['Plains of Zhōu']). Shāng and Zhōu as dynastic titles are thus fundamentally different from Xià in that the graphs to write them are preserved in contemporaneous sources" (Mair 2013: 8).

20 *JC* 8.4325.

21 The use of *Xià* as an autonym referring to the Zhōu elite appears to be attested in a bronze inscription from the Western Zhōu. However, the evidence remains controversial. Behr (2007: 733) and Schuessler (1987: 663) suggest that the following bronze inscription (*JC*: 10175) from the reign of King Gòng of Zhōu (r. 917/15–900 BCE) may contain an early version of the graph <夏> used to write the autonym *Xià*: 上 帝司▓ (夏?) "The Lord on High *ttek-s watches over *Xià*(?)" (Eng. tr. of the Germ. original in Behr 2007). However, Shaughnessy (1991: 3) translates the same passage as "The Lord on High, Hou Ji." Clearly, opinions differ on the exact meaning of the graph ▓ in this context. Given the scarcity of evidence, hypotheses about the origin of the autonym *Xià* and the dynastic title *Xià* therefore remain tentative. For an overview of various hypotheses, see Behr (2007).

22 In Sanskrit texts from the first millennium BCE, the word *aryā* 'noble' was used as a self-identifying term. See Behr (2007) for other examples.

23 As observed by Wáng Zhòngfú 王仲孚 (1989: 363–76), Ogura (1967), and Poo (2005: 47–8), among others.

24 See also the discussion of the 'flowery' or 'flower-like' (華 *N-qʷʰˤra → *huá*) in note 6 above.

25 Baxter and Sagart (2014: 121). For specific examples in excavated texts, see Bái Yúlán 白於藍 (2008: 115), Wáng Huī 王輝 (2008: 84). For interchangeable uses of <夏> or <雅> in received texts, see Féng Qíyōng 馮其庸 and Zhèng Anshēng 鄭安生 (2006: 268; 986).

26 A handful of attestations of the use of *yǎ* as an adjective meaning 'elegant, proper' are found in the *Analects*. The graph <雅> occurs twice in *Analects* 7.18 (tr. Slingerland (2003: 70)) in the phrase 'elegant, proper language/pronunciation' (*yǎ yán* 雅言). As argued by Brooks and Brooks (1998: 167), while chapter 7 in the *Analects* may have been composed in the fifth century BCE, 7.18 may be a later interpolation. For a discussion of the role of 'elegant language' (*yǎ yán* 雅言) in the formation of pre-Qín identity, see Behr (2010: 572–76), Chén Zhì 陳致 (2007: 108–13), and Zhū Zhèngyì 朱正義 (1994: 15–25). The word 'elegant, proper' (*yǎ*) appears in *Analects* 17.18: "I hate that the tunes of Zheng have are bringing disorder to 'elegant' (*yǎ*) music" (惡鄭聲之亂雅樂也). However, if Brooks and Brooks (1998: 39) are correct, then chapter 17 was composed in the early third century BCE. In *Analects* 9.15 (tr. Slingerland 2003: 91), which may have been composed in the late fifth century BCE (Brooks and Brooks 1998: 51), *yǎ* refers to the "Yǎ 雅" sections of the *Book of Songs*. The word 'elegant' (*N-Gˤraʔ → *yǎ*) is not attested in adjectival uses in received texts composed before Warring States period BCE. The graph <雅> occurs once in the *Book of Songs* (Máo 208), but only as a reference to the "Yǎ 雅" sections of the *Book of Songs*. In the *Zuǒzhuàn*, the graph <雅> is only used in the name Zǐyǎ and in references to the "Yǎ 雅" sections of the *Book of Songs*. In the *Mòzǐ*, the adjective 'elegant' (*N-Gˤraʔ → *yǎ*) likewise is not attested and the graph <雅> is only used in references to the "Yǎ 雅" sections of the *Book of Songs*. In the *Mencius*, the graph <雅> is not attested and

188 *Ethnographic vocabulary of civilizational otherness*

the word 'elegant' (*N-Gˤraʔ → *yǎ*) is not used. As mentioned above, in the *Analects*, the graph <雅> occurs in three passages. Even if we read the use of the graph <雅> in *Analects* 9.15 to refer to the "Yǎ 雅" sections of the *Book of Songs* as an adjective meaning 'the elegant [songs],' then the earliest occurrence still does not predate Máo 208, which may have been composed as late as the sixth century BCE. According to Gāo Míng and Tú Báikuí (2008: 1268) the earliest attestation of the graph <雅> is found in the *Shuìhǔdì* Qín manuscripts, where it is written as 雅. Although the *Shuìhǔdì* manuscripts were likely entombed during the Qín dynasty, Gāo Míng and Tú Báikuí (2008: 1268) dates this occurrence of the graph <雅> to the Warring States period. The occurrences of the graph <雅> in received pre-Qín texts were probably originally written with [different forms of the] graph <夏> and then changed to <雅> by later scribes.

Warring States bamboo manuscripts use a range of graphs to write the words *N-Gˤraʔ → *yǎ* and *N-Gˤraʔ → *xià*. In the *Guōdiàn* manuscripts the graphs <顕> and <夓> are used to write the word that is later written as <夏>; see Wèi Yíhuī (2000: 74–7). See, for example: "The Yu employed might and the Xia employed warfare – this was to subdue (/rectify) the unsubmissive. To cherish them and rectify them was the rule of Yu and Xia" (Guōdiàn, "Way of Tang and Yu," tr. Cook (2012: 555)). As observed by Cook (2012: 554, fn. 55), the graph <夓> "is an abbreviated form of the graph elsewhere written 顕, equivalent to 夏. On how the form, with its 出 element, derived from a gradual process of graphic corruption, see [Wèi Yíhuī (2000: 74–7)]." In the Qīnghuá manuscripts, the graph <顕> is also frequently used to write the word that is later written as <夏> to refer to the Xià dynasty; see, for example "Duke Cai 蔡公," strip 14, vol. 1, p. 174; "Yǐn gào 尹誥," strip 2, vol. 1, p. 133; "Jī nián 繫年," strip 17, vol. 2, p. 144, etc. The same graph <顕> is also used to write the word 'summer' (*xià* 夏); see "Shì fǎ 筮法," 31, vol. 4, p. 98, etc. In the *Shàngbó* manuscripts, the graphs <顕> and <夓> are used also interchangeably for <夏> in the phrases "Dà yǎ" 大雅 (and "Xiǎo yǎ" 小雅), which function as titles of sections of the *Book of Songs*; see "Kǒngzi shī lùn," strip 2, Mǎ Chéngyuán (2007: vol. 1: 127) vol. 1: 127. The graph <顕> is also used twice in the "Human Nature Comes Via Mandate" in the *Guōdiàn* manuscripts to refer to a musical dance of the Xià dynasty; see Cook (2012: 719–20). The graphs <顕> and <夓> are used interchangeably for <夏> in the phrases "Dà yǎ" 大雅 and "Xiǎo yǎ" 小雅, which function as titles of sections of the *Book of Songs*; see Cook (2012: 382; 408).

27 As indicated by the *Lǚshì Chūnqiū* passage in (7) in chapter 3, not having rulers was considered to be characteristic of both the primitive ancestors of the Zhōu themselves (before the intervention of the sage–kings) and contemporary civilizationally inferior non-Zhōu groups.

28 *Analects* 3.5, Chéng Shùdé (1997: 147), tr. adapted from Slingerland (2003: 18).

29 *Xúnzǐ* 20.60–92, Wáng Xiānqiān (1988: 380–81), tr. adapted from Hutton (2014: 219–20).

30 As observed by Knoblock (1988–1994: 106, n. 88), "an important part of the model of the Later Kings was the notion of *yǎ* 'elegant standards.' The term *yǎ* is etymologically related to the idea of the 'standards of Xià,' or those of the Chinese proper, from the vantage of the inhabitants of the old Central States."

31 Earlier versions of the analysis of *sú* 俗 in this subsection were presented as a conference paper at the 224th meeting of the American Oriental Society (AOS), March 15, 2014, at the European Association for Chinese Studies (EACS) 2014 Meeting in Coimbra and Braga, Portugal, July 22–27, 2014, and as an invited lecture at Academia Sinica, Taipei, Taiwan, December 12, 2017. I am grateful to the audiences at these events for valuable feedback and suggestions.

32 Lewis (2003: 308–22).

33 The graph <俗> does not occur in the *Annals* or the *Book of Songs*. It occurs once in the received *Changes* and four times in the received *Shàngshū*, but only in parts identified

Ethnographic vocabulary of civilizational otherness 189

as dating to the Warring States period or later by Nylan (2001: 120–67) and Shaughnessy (1993: 376–89).

34 For uses of the graph <俗> in names, see Wú Zhènfēng (2004: 234). The graph <俗> is most frequently used to write the verb 'to want, wish desire' (Schuessler 1987: 787); see, for example, Máogōng *dǐng* (*JC*: 2841): "We wish/hope that the former kings will not worry about us" 俗我弗乍先王憂 (Fāng Shùxīn 方述鑫 et al. 1993: 586).

35 The inscription on the lid of the so-called Jū Fǔ *xǔ* vessel (*JC*: 4464) from the ninth century BCE features the graph <俗/🔲>. For the Jū Fǔ *xǔgài* inscription, see also Huáng Shèngzhāng 黃盛璋 (1983: 53). According to Chén Chūshēng 陳初生 (2004: 778), in this inscription <俗> writes the word 'customs' (*sú*). Wáng Huī 王輝 (1982: 58) suggests that the phrase 堇(謹)夷(尸)俗 in this inscription means 'to respect the customs of the *yí*.' In contrast, the CHANT database transcribes <俗> in this inscription as 'desire, want' (*yù* 欲). Wú Dàyàn and Luó Yīngjié (1976) provide a punctuation of the same inscription in which 夷 and 俗 belong to different phrases separated by a comma (堇夷，俗). This punctuation is incompatible with analyzing 夷 and 俗 as forming a noun phrase meaning 'customs/habits of the *yí*' (夷俗). Finally, neither Schuessler (1987) nor Fāng Shùxīn et al. (1993: 586) lists 'customs' as one of the meanings of <俗> in Shāng and Western Zhōu inscriptions. A recent translation by Maria Khayutina in Cook and Goldin (2016: 195–96) renders the first part of the Jū Fǔ *xǔgài* inscription as follows: "Nanzhong Ban Fu commanded Ju Fu: "Attain [the cooperation of] the regional rulers of the south. Lead Gao Fu to visit the *yí* peoples of Huai River and to see what they collect, what they contribute. Be cautious with regard to the *yí* people's customs (夷(尸)俗). May nobody then even dare not to respect and fear the King's command." It is not clear why Nanzhong Ban Fu would admonish Ju Fu, an emissary of the Zhōu ruler, to be cautious of the *yí* people's customs. Since he is sent to the south to secure the cooperation and submission of the *yí* people of the Huai river region, it seems more plausible that he would be told to pay close attention to 'what the *yí* peoples want or desire.' That is, the graph <俗> is used here to write the word 'want/desire' *yù* (now written with the graph <欲>). In other words, the passage should be rendered as follows: "Attain [the cooperation of] the regional rulers of the south. Lead Gao Fu to visit the Yi-peoples of Huai River and to see what they collect, what they contribute. Be cautious with regard to 'what the Yi people want' (夷(尸)俗). May nobody then even dare not to respect and fear the King's command." To be sure, the context in this inscription appears to allow for both interpretations. However, there are no other instances of the graph <俗> which have been read as meaning 'customs' in Western Zhōu bronzes (and oracle bone inscriptions). Furthermore, when it does not occur in names, the graph <俗> always means 'want/desire' (now written with the graph <欲>) in other bronze inscriptions from the pre-Warring States period; see Schuessler (1987: 787). Based on this, the default assumption should be that it also means 'want/desire' *yù* (now written with the graph <欲>) in the Jū Fǔ *xǔgài* inscription. Finally, as I argue in this chapter, the word 'customs' (*sú*) is a specialized term coined by a group of thinkers and masters of statecraft that emerged around the middle of the first millennium BCE. In contrast, in the ninth century BCE no such group of thinkers and masters of statecraft was around. That is, there was no economy of cultural capital which would allow such thinkers to articulate and circulate ideas about the role of conventionalized behavior (or 'customs') in theories of governance. Hence, it is unlikely that anyone would feel the need to coin the word 'customs' (*sú*).

36 Fourth-century BCE archaeological texts appear to contain the word 'customs' (*sú* 俗). The *Guōdiàn*, *Shàngbó* (vol. 1–9), and *Qīnghuá* (vols 1–4) bamboo manuscripts do not contain the graph <俗>. However, in the fluid writing system of the bamboo manuscripts, several different (often [partially] homophonous) graphs were often used to write the same word; see Baxter and Sagart (2014) and Park (2016). Alleged attestations of the word 'customs' (*sú* 俗), written with various graphs, in these manuscripts are

190 *Ethnographic vocabulary of civilizational otherness*

surrounded by varying degrees of uncertainty and scholarly disagreement. According to the editors of the *Shàngbó* manuscripts, the "Kǒngzǐ shī lùn" (strip 3, vol. 1, p. 129) evidently uses the graph <谷> to write the word 'customs' (*sú* 俗) in the phrase 'to observed customs of people' (觀人俗). As support they adduce the parallelism with the sentence "observe the customs of the people" (觀民風) in the "Wáng Zhì" chapter in the *Lǐjì*, SSJZS (1980: 1328). The Shàngbó editors also suggest that the graph <谷> writes the word 'customs' (*sú* 俗) in strip 4 of the "Black Robes (Zī yī 緇衣)" (Shàngbó vol. 2, p. 178). However, as observed by Cook (2012: 381, fn. 39), 谷 is also used in the Shàngbó manuscripts to write 'to want' (*yù* 欲), e.g., "Wáng jū 王居" (strip 6, vol. 8, p. 211), which he suggests is the correct reading of <谷> in the Guōdiàn version of this passage from the "Black Robes." According to the Shàngbó editors, the graph <欲> writes the word 'customs' (*sú* 俗) in Shàngbó vol. 8, p. 180. However, in numerous other cases in the Shàngbó manuscripts the graph <欲> is clearly used to write the word 'desire, want' (*yù* 欲). Finally, the Shàngbó editors suggest that the word *sú* 俗 is written as <浴> in vol. 5, page 268. Although they do not mention it, support for this reading can be found in the *Shuìhǔdì* 睡虎地 manuscripts dating to the Qín dynasty. According to Féng Qíyōng and Zhèng Anshēng (2006: 457–8), *yù* 浴 is used to write *sú* 俗 in the "The Way of Serving as Government Clerk (*Wéi lì zhī dào* 為吏之道)" chapter of the *Shuìhǔdì* manuscripts: "to change the practices and customs of the people" 變民習浴. In sum, although the graph <俗> is not attested in Warring States bamboo manuscripts, it is very likely that other graphs were used to write the word 'customs' (*sú* 俗). This does not, however, change the fact that the word 'customs' (*sú* 俗) is not attested in pre-Warring States texts. Since the manuscripts studied here were entombed in the late fourth or early third century BCE, they do not provide conclusive evidence for dating the emergence of the word 'customs' (*sú* 俗) much earlier than the fourth century BCE.

37 E.g., *Lǐjì*, "*Qū lǐ*," SSJZS (1980: 1251).

38 See also Lewis (2003: 308–22).

39 The 'five regions' (*wǔ-fāng*) include the four cardinal directions plus the 'Central States' (*Zhōng guó*) as the fifth region.

40 *Lǐjì* "Wáng zhì" 3.13, *SSJZS* (1980: 1338), tr. adapted from Legge (1967: 229–30).

41 The received version of the *Lǐjì* was edited during the Hàn dynasty. However, parts of the *Lǐjì* have now been confirmed by archaeological texts from the Warring States period to contain material that was composed in pre-Qín times. Whether this applies to the passage in (3) is not clear. However, it remains a possibility. Even if the passage in (3) was composed during the early Western Hàn dynasty, it still largely reflects late Warring States period views on the geography of otherness.

42 *Lǔshì Chūnqiū* 19.6.2, tr adapted from Knoblock and Riegel (2000: 497–98).

43 See also discussion of (6) in chapter 4, as well as the subsections titled "Pre-Qín concept of 'progress'" and "Contrasting the Xià elites of the Zhōu realm and 'non-Zhōu others'" in chapter 3.

44 *Xúnzǐ* 2.41–44, Wáng Xiānqiān (1988: 23), tr. adapted from Hutton (2014: 10).

45 *Analects* 12.1. Chéng Shùdé (1997: 821), (非禮勿視，非禮勿聽，非禮勿言，非禮勿動).

46 *Xúnzǐ* 8, Wáng Xiānqiān (1988: 120), tr. adapted from Hutton (2014: 54).

47 See *Mencius* 4B:9: "Following the practices of the present day, unless there is a changes in the customs of the people, a man could not hold the Empire for the duration of one morning, even if it were given to him" 由今之道，無變今之俗，雖與之天下，不能一朝居也 (tr. adapted from Lau (2004: 141)). 'Customs' (*sú*) need to be 'changed' (*biàn* 變) by beautification (*měi* 美). *Mencius* 4B:9 thus provide an illustration of the pre-Qín concept of 'progress' as 'change for the better,' discussed in chapter 3.

48 The parentheses () in *ɢ(r)ok indicates that the word may have had an *r. That is, while there is no independent reason to believe that there was an *r, the resulting derived forms would be the same with or without it. However, in *s-[ɢ]ok there could not have been an *r since this would have resulted in a retroflex initial in Middle Chinese, which

Ethnographic vocabulary of civilizational otherness 191

is not the case. If *ɢ(r)ok → *yù* 'desire' and *s-[ɢ]ok → *sú* 'customs' derive from the same root, then this root must have been *ɢok.

49 Another possibility is that the *s- prefix derives from a reduced version of the word *suǒ* 所 'that which.' According to this hypothesis, the derived word *s-[ɢ]ok → *sú* thus means 'that which (people) want' (Baxter, p.c.).

50 *Shìmíng*, Wáng Xiānqiān (2008). Based on a different parse (7) can also be translated as follows: "*Sú* is defined as 'desiring.' *Sú* is defined as 'that which people desire' (俗，欲也。俗，人所欲也)." However, even in this alternative reading *sú* is still clearly linked to *yù*. The "Treatise on Geography (地理志)" chapter in the *Hànshū* 漢書 also provides support for a connection between 'wants' (*yù*) and 'customs' (*sú*): "[The people's] likes and dislikes, taking or leaving [things], moving or remaining calm, all these follow the 'inner state' (*qíng* 情) and 'wants' (*yù*) of the rulers on high, hence they are called 'customs' (*sú*)" 好惡取舍，動靜亡常，隨君上之情欲，故謂之俗 (Bān Gù 班固 1962: 1640).

51 According to *Xúnzǐ* 20.135–39, "the gentleman takes joy in attaining the Way. The petty man takes joy in attaining the object of his 'desires' (*yù*). If one takes the Way to regulate one's 'desires' (*yù*), then one will be happy and not disordered. If one forgets the Way for the dake of one's 'desires' (*yù*), then one will be confused and unhappy" (Wáng Xiānqiān (1988: 382), tr. Hutton (2014: 221)).

52 *Xúnzǐ* 8.386–432, Wáng Xiānqiān (1988: 138), tr. adapted fr. Hutton (2014: 63–4), Chinese: 故有俗人者，有俗儒者，有雅儒者，有大儒者.

53 Adjectival use of *sú* is also attested in the received *Lǎozǐ*, chapter 20 (ca. 400 BCE), the *Xúnzǐ* (ca. 250 BCE), and the *Lǚshì Chūnqiū* (239 BCE). As observed by Lewis (2003: 308–22), *sú rén* 俗人 in the received *Lǎozǐ* refers to the 'the people of (local) customs.' Since *Lǎozǐ* 80 celebrates 'local customs' (*sú*), being a 'common man' of 'local customs' is not considered negatively. The fact that the passages in the received *Lǎozǐ* containing the expressions 'common man' (*sú rén* 俗人) are not found in the Guōdiàn *Lǎozǐ*, lends further support to the hypothesis that these were late fourth or early third century BCE innovations.

54 In the third century BCE, the terms 'elegant, proper' (*yǎ*) and 'morally refined' (*wén*) began to be juxtaposed in descriptions of 'noble men' (*jūnzǐ*): "The person whom [the virtuous ruler] sends to persuade another lord will surely be a 'noble man' (*jūnzǐ*) who is 'elegant, proper' (*yǎ*) and 'morally refined' (*wén*) and who has skill in arguing and great intelligence 所以説之者，必將雅文辯慧之君子也" (*Xúnzǐ* 10.539–540, Wáng Xiānqiān (1988: 198), tr. adapted from Hutton 2014: 97).

55 See (15) in chapter 4. See also *Analects* 9.16: "The master wanted to live among the nine-*Yí*. Someone said: '[They] are vulgar, how can you tolerate [living among them]?' The master said: 'If a noble man lived among them, what vulgarity would they have?' 子欲居九夷。或曰陋如之何。子曰君子居之何陋之有 (Chéng Shùdé (1997: 604–6), tr. Slingerland (2003: 91)).

56 See Lewis (2003: 308–22).

57 Other anti-*wén* works also use the term *sú* in neutral ways to refer to conventionalized behaviors. The authors of the *Hánfēizǐ*, for example, were explicit in their condemnation of *rú* insistence on the timeless superiority of Zhōu ritual. Refraining from using the term 'rites' (*lǐ*), they point out that the 'customs' (*sú*) of ancient times differ from those of the present: "As a rule, ancient times and the present times differ with respect to 'customs' (*sú*)" 夫古今異俗 (*Hánfēizǐ* 49, Wáng Xiānshèn (2006: 445).).

58 *Mòzǐ* 49.7, tr. adapted from Johnston (2010: 705–07). Johnston translates the expression *yí rén* 夷人 as 'barbarians.' As argued below, such a translation is infelicitous.

59 See the discussion of the concepts of 'non-Zhōu others' and 'all under Heaven' (*tiānxià*) in the *Mòzǐ* in note 40 in chapter 4. The *Mòzǐ* also never uses the autonym 'Great ones' (*Xià*) to contrast Zhōu and non-Zhōu and has no use for the term 'elegant, proper, *Xià*-like' (*yǎ*). In the *Mòzǐ*, <夏> only means 'summer' or the '*Xià* dynasty' and <雅> only refers to a section in the *Book of Songs*.

192 *Ethnographic vocabulary of civilizational otherness*

60 *Zuǒ*, Xī 27.1 (Legge 1960a: 201) contains the phrase *Yí lǐ* 夷禮. However, it most likely does not refer to the "*lǐ* of the *Yí*" (i.e., the *Yí*'s own practices), but rather to the [Zhōu] rituals (*lǐ*) prescribed by the Zhōu tradition to regulate how the *Yí* peoples should behave when attending a royal audience. Durrant, Li, and Schaberg (2016: 400–401) translate 夷禮 as "*lǐ* of the *Yí*." In a footnote they explain that the "designation of 'Yi' is sometimes understood vaguely as 'barbarian'; here it seems to indicate deviance from Zhou rituals."

61 It is not entirely clear what "killing the father and rewarding" refers to. It may be an allusion to the many cases where rulers of the state of Chǔ came to power through patricide (Eric Henry, p.c.).

62 The term *sú* could also be used without negative connotations to describe conventionalized practices of different Central States. In the *Lǚshì Chūnqiū* the great minister Wǔ Zǐxū tries to persuade King Fūchāi (r. 495–473 BCE) of Wú to attack Yuè rather than Qí: "The 'customs and practices' (*xí sú* 習俗) of Qí are not the same as those of Wú . . . If we obtained their land, we would not be able to dwell there, nor would we be able to govern those of its people we conquered. But with Yuè . . . we have the same 'customs and practices' (*xí sú*) . . . We can dwell on the land we win and govern the people we conquer" (*Lǚshì Chūnqiū* 23/3.2, tr. adapted from Knoblock and Riegel 2000: 594–5). The use of *sú* as a neutral term referring to common practices specific to a certain region is not unique to the *Lǚshì Chūnqiū* but is found widely in Warring States texts.

63 I use the phrase 'Confucian' classics in the sense of Nylan (2001).

64 For theories of the relationship between 'customs' (*sú*) and 'human nature' (*xìng*) in Warring States texts, see Lewis (2003: 308–22).

References

Bái Yúlán 白於藍. 2008. *Jiǎn dú bó shū tōng jiǎ zì zì diǎn* 簡牘帛書通假字字典 (Fujian remin chubanshe: Fuzhou).

Bān Gù 班固. 1962. *Hàn shū* 漢書 (Zhōnghuá shūjú: Běijīng).

Baxter, William Hubbard, and Laurent Sagart. 2014. *Old Chinese: A New Reconstruction* (Oxford University Press: Oxford).

Behr, Wolfgang. 2007. 'Xia: Etymologisches zur Herkunft des ältesten chinesischen Staatsnamens', *Asiatische Studien*, 41: 727–54.

———. 2010. 'Role of Language in Early Chinese Constructions of Ethnic Identity', *Journal of Chinese Philosophy*, 37: 567–87.

Brooks, Bruce, and Taeko Brooks. 1998. *The Original Analects: Sayings of Confucius and His Successors* (Columbia University Press: New York).

Chén Chūshēng 陳初生. 2004. *Jīnwén chángyòng zìdiǎn* 金文常用子典 (Shanxi ren min chu ban she: Xi'an).

Chén Zhì 陳致. 2007. *The Shaping of the Book of Songs: From Ritualization to Secularization* (Steyler: Nettetal).

Chéng Shùdé 程樹德. 1997. *Lúnyǔ jíshì* 論語集釋 (Zhōnghuá shūjú: Běijīng).

Cook, Constance A., and Paul R. Goldin. 2016. *A Source Book of Ancient Chinese Bronze Inscriptions* (Society for the Study of Early China: Berkeley, CA).

Cook, Scott Bradley. 2012. *The Bamboo Texts of Guodian: A Study & Complete Translation* (East Asia Program & Cornell University: Ithaca).

Durrant, Stephen W., Wai-yee Li, and David Schaberg. 2016. *Zuo Tradition: Zuozhuan* (University of Washington Press: Seattle).

Fāng Shùxīn 方述鑫, Lín Xiǎo'ān 林小安, Cháng Zhèngguāng 常正光, and Péng Yùshāng 彭裕商. 1993. *Jiǎgǔ jīnwén zìdiǎn* 甲骨金文字典 (Bashu shushe: Chengdu).

Ethnographic vocabulary of civilizational otherness   193

Féng Qíyōng 馮其庸, and Zhèng Anshēng 鄭安生. 2006. *Tōngjiǎ zìhuì shì* 通假字彙釋 (Beijing daxue chubanshe: Beijing).

Gāo Míng 高明, and Tú Báikuí 涂白奎. 2008. *Gǔ wén zì lèi biān* 古文字類編 (Shanghai guji chubanshe: Beijing).

Gruen, Erich S. 2011. *Rethinking the Other in Antiquity* (Princeton University Press: Princeton).

Hall, Edith. 1989. *Inventing the Barbarian: Greek Self-Definition Through Tragedy* (Clarendon Press: Oxford).

Hall, Jonathan M. 1997. *Ethnic Identity in Greek Antiquity* (Cambridge University Press: Cambridge).

Harrison, Thomas. 2002. *Greeks and Barbarians* (Edinburgh University Press: Edinburgh).

Huáng Shèngzhāng 黃盛璋. 1983. 'Jū Fǔ xǔgài míngwén yánjiū 駒父盨蓋銘文研究', *Kaogu yu wenwu*, 4: 53.

Hutton, Eric L. 2014. *Xunzi* (Princeton University Press: Princeton).

Jiǎng Shànguó 蔣善国. 1988. *Shàngshū zōng shù* 尚书综述 (Shanghai guji chubanshe: Shanghai).

Johnston, Ian. 2010. *The Mozi: A Complete Translation* (Columbia University Press: New York).

Karlgren, Bernhard. 1974. *The Book of Odes* (Museum of Far Eastern Antiquities: Stockholm).

Knoblock, John. 1988–1994. *Xunzi: A Translation and Study of the Complete Works* (Stanford University Press: Stanford, CA).

Knoblock, John, and Jeffrey Riegel. 2000. *The Annals of Lü Buwei* (Stanford University Press: Stanford, CA).

Lau, D. C. 2004. *Mencius* (Penguin: London).

Legge, James. 1960a. *The Chinese Classics. Vol. 5: The Ch'un Ts'ew with the Tso Chuen. London, Trübner, 1862, rpt.* (Hong Kong University Press: Hong Kong).

———. 1960b. *The Shoo King or the Book of Historical Documents* (Hong Kong University Press: Hong Kong).

———. 1967. *Li chi: Book of Rites: An Encyclopedia of Ancient Ceremonial Usages, Religious Creeds, and Social Institutions*. Translated by James Legge. Edited with an introduction and study guide by Ch'u Chai and Winberg Chai (University Books: New York).

Lewis, Mark Edward. 2003. 'Custom and Human Nature in Early China', *Philosophy East and West*, 53: 308–22.

Li, Feng. 2006. *Landscape and Power in Early China: The Crisis and Fall of the Western Zhou, 1045–771 BC* (Cambridge University Press: Cambridge).

Lǐ Xuéqín 李學勤. 2002. "Lùn Suì gōng xǔ jí qí zhòngyào yìyì 論遂公盨及其重要意義," reprinted in Lǐ Xuéqín, *Zhōngguó gǔdài wénmíng yánjiū* 中國古代文明研究 (Shanghai: Huadong shifan daxue, 2005), 126–36.

Mǎ Chéngyuán 馬承源. 2007. *Shànghǎi bówùguǎn cáng zhànguó Chǔ zhúshū* 上海博物館藏戰國楚竹書, Vol. 6 (Shànghǎi gǔjí chūbǎnshè: Shànghǎi).

Mair, Victor H. 2013. 'Was There a Xià Dynasty?' *Sino-Platonic Papers*, 238.

McGrane, Bernard. 1989. *Beyond Anthropology: Society and the Other* (Columbia University Press: New York).

Meyer, Dirk. 2014. 'The Art of Narrative and the Rhetoric of Persuasion in the "Jīnténg" (Metal Bound Casket) from the Tsinghua Collection of Manuscripts', *Asiatische Studien/Études asiatiques*, 68: 937–68.

———. forthcoming. *Traditions of Documents* 書 *and Political Argument in Early China*. (Walter de Gruyter: Berlin).

194 *Ethnographic vocabulary of civilizational otherness*

Nippel, Wilfred. 2002. 'The Construction of the "Other"', in Thomas Harrison (ed.), *Greeks and Barbarians* (Edinburgh University Press: Edinburgh), pp. 278–310.

Nylan, Michael. 2001. *The Five "Confucian" Classics* (Yale University Press: New Haven).

Ogura Yoshihiko 小倉芳彦. 1967. 'I i no toriko: Saden no Ka I kannen 裔夷の俘 – 左傳の華夷觀念', in Chūgoku kodai shi kenkyūkai 中國古代史研究會 (ed.), *Chūgoku kodai shi kenkyū* 中國古代史研究 (Yoshikawa: Tokyo).

Park, Haeree. 2016. *The Writing System of Scribe Zhou: Evidence from Late Pre-imperial Chinese Manuscripts and Inscriptions (5th–3rd Centuries BCE)* (Walter de Gruyter: Berlin).

Pokorny, Julius. 1959. *Indogermanisches etymologisches Wörterbuch* (Francke: Bern).

Poo, Mu-chou. 2005. *Enemies of Civilization: Attitudes Toward Foreigners in Ancient Mesopotamia, Egypt, and China* (SUNY Press: Albany).

Qū Wànlǐ 屈萬里. 1983. *Xiān-Qín wénshǐ zīliào kǎobiàn* 先秦文史資料考辨 (Lianjing chuban shiye gongsi: Taibei).

———. 1984. *Gǔjí dǎodú* 古籍導讀 (Liánjīng chūbǎn shìyè gōngsī 聯經出版事業公司: Taipei).

Schuessler, Axel. 1987. *A Dictionary of Early Zhou Chinese* (University of Hawaii Press: Honolulu).

———. 2007. *ABC Etymological Dictionary of Old Chinese* (University of Hawaii Press: Honolulu).

Shaughnessy, Edward L. 1991. *Sources of Western Zhou History* (University of California Press: Berkeley, CA).

———. 1993. 'Shang shu 尚書 (Shu ching 書經)', in Michael Loewe (ed.), *Early Chinese Texts: A bibliographical guide* (Society for the Study of Early China: Berkeley, CA), pp. 376–89.

Slingerland, Edward G. 2003. *Analects: With Selections from Traditional Commentaries* (Hackett: Indianapolis).

SSJZS. 1980. *Shísān jīng zhù shū* 十三經注疏 (Zhōnghuá shūjú: Běijīng).

Vlassopoulos, Kostas. 2013. *Greeks and Barbarians* (Cambridge University Press: Cambridge).

Vogelsang, Kai. 2002. 'Inscriptions and Proclamations: A Study of the "Gao" Chapters in the *Book of Documents*', *Bulletin of the Museum of Far Eastern Antiquities*, 74: 138–209.

Wáng Huī 王輝. 1982. 'Ju fu xu gai ming shi wen 駒父盨盖铭试释', *Kaogu*, 5: 56–9.

———. 2008. *Gǔ wén zì tōng jiǎ zì diǎn* 古文字通假字典 (Zhonghua shuju: Beijing).

Wáng Xiānqiān 王先謙. 1988. *Xúnzǐ jíjiě* 荀子集解 (Běijīng Zhōnghuá shūjú: Běijīng).

———. 2008. *Shìmíng shūzhèng bǔ* 釋名疏證補 (Zhonghua shuju: Beijing).

Wáng Xiānshèn 王先慎. 2006. *Hánfēizǐ jíjiě* 韓非子集解 (Běijīng Zhōnghuá shūjú: Běijīng).

Wáng Zhòngfú 王仲孚. 1989. 'Shilun chunqiu shidai de zhuxia yishi 試論春秋時代的諸夏意識', *Di er jie guoji Hanxue lunwenji* 第二屆國際漢學會議論文集, 1: 363–76.

Wèi Yíhuī 魏宜輝. 2000. 'Shìxī chǔjiǎn wén zì zhōng de "xià," "xià" zì. 試析楚簡文字中的『曰虫頿』,『曰虫』字', *Jiāng-Hàn kǎogǔ* 江漢考古, 83: 74–7.

Weidner, E. 1913. 'Βάρβαρος', *Glotta*, 4: 303–4.

Wú Dàyàn 吳大焱, and Luó Yīngjié 罗英杰. 1976. 'Shaanxi wugong xian chu tu ju fu xu gai 陕西武功县出土驹父盖', *Wénwù* 文物, 1976.5: 94.

Wú Zhènfēng 吳鎮烽. 2004. *jīnwén rénmíng huìbiān* 金文人名彙編 (Zhonghua shuju: Beijing).

Yu Min. 1989. 'Han-Zang tongyuan zipu gao (A Draft of Cognate Words of Chinese and Tibetan)', *Languages and Scripts of Nationalities* (*Minzu Yuwen*), 1: 56–77.

Zhū Zhèngyì 朱正義. 1994. 'Zhōu dài "yǎ yán"—《Guān zhōng fāng yán gǔ cí lùn gǎo》jié xuǎn周代"雅言"—《关中方言古词论稿》节选', *Wèinán shī zhuān xuébào* 渭南师专学报, 1994.1: 15–24.

Conclusion

The word (as Civilization for example) . . . conveys scarcely to any two minds the same idea. No two persons agree in the things they predicate of it; and when it is itself predicated of anything, no other person knows, nor does the speaker himself know with precision, what he means to assert.

—John Stuart Mill 1843, *A System of Logic*[1]

Widespread teaching of "Chinese civilization" began with the introduction of Western Civilization courses at American colleges in the 1920s. In such courses, other "civilizations" (Indian, Egyptian, Chinese) served mainly as a foil for "the West."[2] For example, where the supposedly holistic Chinese tradition was said to focus more on ineffable intuition, the "Western" mind was described as empirically and analytically oriented. In other words, China was portrayed as the Yin to the Yang of "the West." The myth of the irreducible alterity of an allegedly 5,000-year-old "Chinese civilization" introduced in many "Western Civ" courses still informs Western perceptions of China.[3] Existing textbooks on "Chinese civilization" tend to cover everything from the Neolithic to the present day, or from the mythological King Yáo, traditionally said to have reigned during the third millennium BCE, to Máo Zédōng (1893–1976), the founding father of the People's Republic of China.[4] The term *civilization* as it is used in the phrase *Chinese civilization* has thus played an important role in perpetuating the modern Western idea of China as an antipodal civilizational *other* that has existed for millennia. This has prompted Westerners to see China not as it is but instead how they imagine it to be from their own epistemic vantage point.

When it comes to the range of meanings of the phrase *Chinese civilization*, Anaïs Nin is right: we do not see things as they are; we see them as *we* are.[5] We see what we imagine to be "Chinese civilization" through the kaleidoscopic lens of the different concepts of 'civilization' (universal, ethnographic, racialized, archaeological) that the Anglophone word *civilization* has been given since it was coined in the 1760s.[6] In this sense, Western perceptions of "Chinese civilization" are, to use the title of one of Wierzbicka's books, "imprisoned in English."[7] Since English is the global language of science and scholarship, Anglophone concepts are often assumed to be universal.[8] If researchers in the humanities and

Conclusion 197

social sciences do not question the language-specific history and meanings of the English term *civilization*—as well as the other key words through which we formulate and communicate our study of civilizational consciousness in early China—then we are, in a very real and problematic sense, imprisoned in English.

The word *civilization* has different meanings when archaeologists ask how old "Chinese civilization" is versus when we ask how old civilizational consciousness is in China. The first question posits how far back in time we can find evidence of a state formation that satisfies a list of criteria (cities, monumental, architecture, writing, etc.). Answers tend to vary from 5,000 to 3,000 years ago. The second question focuses on when people in what we now call China began to think of themselves as belonging to a 'civilization.' As argued in Chapters 2–5, this happened around 600–400 BCE. These two questions use the term *civilization* in very different meanings. Hence, they do not necessarily have bearing on each other. But since the word *civilization* is used in both, the two questions are often mixed up in confusing ways, creating the mistaken impression that both questions involve the same concept of 'civilization.'

It may be better to abandon scholarly use of the term *civilization* as an analytical category altogether, along with attempts to date the origin of "Chinese civilization."[9] Instead, it may be more interesting to explore how the semantic changes in the language-specific pre-Qín concept of 'civility/civilization' and its coining in the word *wén* have informed the nature of civilizational consciousness in early China. Civilizational consciousness constantly changes in response to epistemic and sociopolitical changes. It would therefore be wrong to assume that the particular form of pre-Qín civilizational consciousness studied in Chapters 2–5 has somehow moved unscathed through time to the present day. Indeed, the history-word-by-word approach predicts that concepts of 'civility/civilization' (*wén*) (as well as the meanings of the lexicalized molecules of these concepts) would continue to change in response to sociopolitical contexts and epistemic changes after it was first coined in the Warring States period. Calling pre-Qín civilizational consciousness "Chinese civilization" would potentially perpetuate the misleading and essentializing idea of a millennia-old "Chinese civilization."

This book has traced the emergence of an indigenous form of civilizational consciousness in pre-Qín China. Around 600–400 BCE, people began to coin new terms to formulate the idea of belonging to 'civilization' explicitly. That is, people began to consciously hear themselves formulating (in their inner stream of consciousness or actually uttering or writing down) the idea of belonging to 'a social formation that has undergone a universal process of progress (change for the better) operating on individuals and social formations along the dimensions of 'civility' (refinement of manners, behavior) and 'police' (laws, government institutions) resulting in the establishment of value-laden distinctions between self (the civilized) and the civilizationally inferior others (the barbarians), and between a primitive past and an advanced 'Golden Age."

As summarized in Figure 6.1, at around 600–400 BCE tradition-specific pre-Qín concepts that at some level of abstraction can be viewed as corresponding to the semantic molecules of the eighteenth-century European universal concept

198 *Conclusion*

Pre-Qín 'wén'

1 'change (*biàn* 變) for the better'
2 'moral refinement'/'civility' (*wén* 文), 'rites' (*lǐ* 禮)
3 'promulgated regulations' (*fǎ* 法), 'rites' (*lǐ* 禮)
4 'not the same' (*bù tóng* 不同), 'distinguish' (*biàn* 辨)
  a 'the barbarians' (*yí* 夷) vs. 'the Great ones' (*Xià* 夏)
    '(local) customs' (*sú* 俗) vs. '(universal) rites' (*lǐ* 禮)
  b 'living in nature' (*yě chǔ* 野處) vs. Golden Age

5 'all under Heaven' (*tiānxià* 天下)

Anglophone 'civilization'

1 Progress
2 Civility
3 Police
4 Distinctions
  a Barbarian vs. civilized
    Superstition vs. Reason
  b Primitive past vs. civilized present

5 Universality

Figure 6.1 Pre-Qín 'wén' and the eighteenth-century European universal concept 'civilization.'

of 'civilization' had been lexicalized in language-specific pre-Qín Old Chinese words. And, around the same time, the word *wén*, which had already been lexicalized in the meaning 'civility,' came to be used in extended meanings to refer to a language-specific pre-Qín concept of 'civility/civilization' comprising all the semantic molecules in lines 1–5 in Figure 6.1.

My proposed dating of the coining of the word *wén* in the meaning 'civility/ civilization' to around 600–400 BCE is not based solely on the absence of attestations of *wén* in this meaning in texts from before 600 BCE. Since the corpus of extant pre-Warring States texts is relatively small and biased in nature, we must avoid automatically construing the absence of evidence as evidence of absence.[10] To mitigate this problem, the genealogy of a number of other terms that played a role in the emergence of civilizational consciousness were studied in Chapters 2–5 in order to make the dating of the emergence of civilizational consciousness in pre-Qín China more robust. I have showed that semantic changes in a number of terms related to the emergence of civilizational consciousness took place more or less at the same as the coining of *wén* in the meaning 'civility/civilization' around 600–400 BCE. These terms and their semantic changes (indicated by the arrow →) include: (i) 'rites' (*lǐ*) ['aristocratic code of conduct' → 'morally refined conduct (regardless of birth)'], (ii) 'all under Heaven' (*tiānxià*) ['domain under direct control of the Zhōu king' → 'universal realm of value'], (iii) 'non-Zhōu others' (*yí*) ['specific peoples of the *yí* group (e.g., *Huái-yí*, *Dōng-yí*, etc.)' → 'civilizationally inferior others/barbarians'], (iv) 'nobleman/noble man' (*jūnzǐ*) ['aristocratic nobleman' → 'morally refined noble man (regardless of birth)'], and (v) 'charismatic power/virtue' (*dé*) ['aesthetically interpreted charismatic power' → 'ethically interpreted charismatic virtue'].

The lexicalization of yet other terms in new meanings was also shown to be related to the emergence of civilizational consciousness. As argued in Chapter 5, the word 'customs' (*sú*), for example, was coined only in the fourth century BCE in response to the growing need for an abstract concept to refer to the different conventionalized behaviors of people who did not live according to the 'rites' (*lǐ*). The emergence of the use of the word *sú* in the meaning 'vulgar' in the late

Conclusion 199

Warring States period made it possible to contrast the 'vulgarity' (*sú*) of the 'local customs' (*sú*) of the 'civilizationally inferior others'/'barbarians' (*yí*) with the universality of the 'elegant and proper' (*yǎ*) 'civility/civilization' (*wén*) and 'rites' (*lǐ*) of the 'Great ones' (*Xià*). The dating of the coining of civilizational consciousness therefore does not rely on the chronological changes in the word *wén* alone, but rather on dating to the Warring States period of a large number of interconnected semantic changes in a large set of terms through which civilizational consciousness was explicitly articulated. The combined result of these parallel historical studies is more fruitful and reliable than studies of any of these terms would have been individually.

That being said, the dating of the emergence of civilizational consciousness to the middle of the first millennium BCE proposed here is not intended as the final word in the matter. Several factors limit our ability to date semantic changes in Old Chinese terms with a high degree of precision and certainty. First, the relatively small body of authentic pre-Warring States texts often do not always contain enough occurrences of these terms to enable us to make definite conclusions about the exact chronology of semantic changes. Second, there is often considerably scholarly disagreement on the authenticity and date of composition of specific texts.[11] Third, paleographical issues also often lead to disagreement on the interpretation of specific words.

This does not mean that we should refrain from articulating hypotheses about the date of the emergence of civilizational consciousness. On the contrary, this amplifies the need for explicit hypotheses. Many existing English translations and studies of early Chinese texts are based on hypotheses about pre-Qín civilizational consciousness that are not explicitly articulated. Few would probably disagree that late Warring States texts such as the *Xúnzǐ* bear witness to a constructed division between the 'civilized/refined' (*yǎ*) 'rites' (*lǐ*) of the 'Great ones' (*Xià*) and the 'vulgar' (*sú*) 'customs' (*sú*) of the 'civilizationally inferior others' (*yí*). But how far does this civilizational consciousness extend into the past? Existing renderings of King Wén as the 'Cultured King' in English translations of Western Zhōu texts seem to presuppose that the authors of these inscriptions had a concept of 'culture.' That is, implicit in the translation "Cultured King" lies an unarticulated hypothesis that civilizational consciousness emerged around 1000 BCE or earlier. According to the analysis of civilizational consciousness proposed here, this seems unlikely.

The history-word-by-word approach to the study of epistemic changes in collective consciousness through lexical change provides a framework that allows us to formulate specific hypotheses about the emergence of civilizational consciousness in early China. The dating of the emergence of civilizational consciousness to around 600–400 BCE proposed here is an explicitly formulated and therefore potentially falsifiable hypothesis. If, for example, we were to discover an authentic inscription from the tenth century BCE which clearly articulates a division between the 'civilized/refined' (*yǎ*), 'rites' (*lǐ*) of the 'great ones' (*Xià*), and the 'vulgar' (*sú*) 'customs' (*sú*) of the 'civilizationally inferior others' (*yí*), then this hypothesis would have to be revised.

200　*Conclusion*

Someone might object that the hypothesis about the emergence of civilizational consciousness in pre-Qín China proposed here still relies on the word *civilization* (in the phrase *civilizational consciousness*) and therefore is also in danger of being "imprisoned in English." In order to free our understanding of pre-Qín civilizational consciousness from the hegemony of Anglophone terms, it would therefore be better (and more accurate) to call it a *wén*-consciousness, using the pre-Qín term *wén* ('civility/civilization') instead of the Anglophone adjective *civilizational*. At a certain level of abstraction, the concepts of 'wén' and 'civilization' consist of similar semantic molecules. While this facilitates cross-linguistic comparison, we should not forget that the specific terms for these molecules also can have quite different meanings in each language.[12] The hermeneutical violence done to the pre-Qín concept of '*wén*' when we translate it as *civilization* or *culture*, or when we say that a pre-Qín *civilizational consciousness* was coined in it, cannot be ignored.[13] To illustrate this hermeneutical violence, let us turn the tables and use the pre-Qín vocabulary of the molecules of the concept of 'wén' in Figure 6.1 to ask to what extent a *wén*-consciousness was coined in sixteenth- to eighteenth-century English texts.

To determine whether a *wén*-consciousness was present in early modern Europe, we need to identify indigenous language-specific terms for the semantic molecules of the concept of *wén* 'civility/civilization.' That is, when did people in Europe begin to formulate the idea of belonging to a social formation that has undergone a process of 'change' (*biàn* 變) for the better, extending to 'all under Heaven' (*tiānxià*) and operating on 'individuals' (*rén* 人) and 'states' (*guó* 國), or 'dynasties' (*dài* 代), along the dimensions of 'moral refinement'/'civility' (*wén*)/'rites' (*lǐ*) and 'promulgated models' (*fǎ*)/'institutionalized rites' (*lǐ*)'? Does this idea result in value-laden 'distinctions' (*biàn* 辨) between the 'elegant' (*yǎ*) 'Great ones' (*Xià*) and the 'vulgar' (*sú*) 'others' (*yí*), and between 'living in nature' (*yě chǔ*) as 'birds and beasts' (*qín shòu*) and the pinnacle of 'civility/civilization' (*wén*) during a Golden Age? With a bit of abstraction, it seems possible to give affirmative answers to these questions.

The core idea of 'change' (*biàn*) for the better is certainly part of the meaning of the English word *progress*. Evidence of a notion of 'change for the better' taking place in the dimension of 'rites' (*lǐ*) and 'promulgated models' (*fǎ*) can also be argued to be found in sixteenth- to eighteenth-century European discussions of the concepts of 'civility' and 'police.' The core elements of the pre-Qín notion of 'personal moral edification' (*xiū shēn* 修身) through patterns of 'civility/civilization' (*wén*) and 'rites' (*lǐ*) are present in the Anglophone term *civility*. That is, like the pre-Qín terms 'civility' (*wén*) and 'rites' (*lǐ*), the English word *civility* also refers to a decorum of refined manners and conventionalized behavior. Similarly, the early European concept of 'police' expressed by the words *police* and *policed* (among others) does overlap semantically with the pre-Qín concepts of institutionalized 'rites' (*lǐ*) and 'promulgated models' or 'laws' (*fǎ*) used to rule a state. Both the Anglophone term *police* and the pre-Qín terms 'rites' (*lǐ*) and 'promulgated models' (*fǎ*) refer to government regulations and institutions.

Conclusion   201

Did the European thinkers in the sixteenth to eighteenth centuries articulate an idea of a development of humankind from a savage state of 'living in nature' (*yě chǔ* 野處) to a pinnacle of human 'wén' during a Golden Age in the past? Yes and no. At a certain level of abstraction, the European concept of a Hobbesian primordial state of nature is similar to the pre-Qín idea of humans living like 'birds and beasts' (*qín shòu*) before the intervention of the sage–kings. But eighteenth-century European thinkers do not seem to have had much use for the idea that it was 'sages' (*shèng rén* 聖人) who brought humankind from a state of living 'in nature' to a perfect state of 'civility/civilization' (*wén*) during a Golden Age in antiquity. Rather, optimistic European notions of 'progress' tend to attribute the liberation from an original chaotic state of nature to the collective workings of human Reason. However, abstracting away from these language-specific connotations of Anglophone terms such as *progress*, *civility*, *police*, and *civilization*, it seems possible to argue that a form of *wén*-consciousness emerged in Europe in the sixteenth- to the eighteenth century.

It may seem odd to talk about the emergence of a *wén*-consciousness in early modern Europe. However, the Warring States authors of texts such as the *Analects* and the *Xúnzǐ* would likely have been similarly struck by the oddity of hearing their notion of 'wén' analyzed as a concept of 'civilization' comprising Anglophone concepts 'progress,' 'civility,' 'police,' and so forth. This exercise of studying modern European intellectual history using the pre-Qín metalanguage of *wén*-consciousness illustrates the dangers of being imprisoned in English. As pointed out by Wierzbicka, we need to pay more attention to variations in how different languages pre-package reality through historically contingent lexicalization.[14]

The history-word-by-word approach allows us to bridge hermeneutical gaps between different languages and time periods. The similarities and differences of complex abstract concepts—such as those referred to by the pre-Qín word *wén* and the Enlightenment word *civilization*—can be better understood when we decompose them into independently lexicalized (or paraphrasable) semantic molecules in their respective languages and traditions. This allows us to use these molecules, as they are lexicalized in both languages/traditions being compared, as our metalanguage in which we articulate cross-linguistic conceptual comparisons. The lexicalized molecules (Eng. *civility*, *police*, etc.; pre-Qín Chin. 'civility/civilization' (*wén*), 'rites' (*lǐ*), 'promulgated models'/'laws' (*fǎ*), etc.) carry their own language-specific "prejudices," to use a Gadamerian term. If need be, they can be broken down further into even smaller molecules and atoms, which in turn can then be used as metalanguage for our cross-linguistic and cross-cultural study of the emergence of civilizational consciousness.

While this book focuses on determining when civilizational consciousness first emerged in ancient China, I explore this question as a hermeneutic dialogue between Old Chinese and modern European concepts. Imagine Confucius and Adam Smith engaging in a dialogue about the concepts of 'wén' and 'civilization' (Figure 6.2).[15] As promoters of the concepts and terms *wén* and *civilization* in pre-Qin China and eighteenth-century Europe respectively, their differences in terms of language,

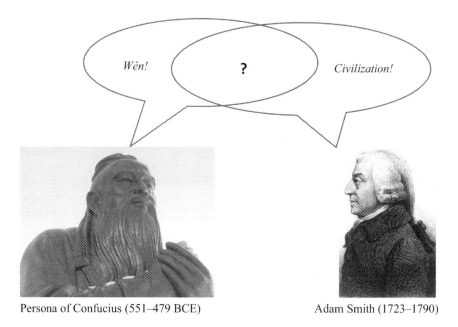

Figure 6.2 Is dialogue between the coiners of *wén* and *civilization* possible?[16]

historical context, and basic epistemic assumptions are so vast and seemingly unbridgeable that it is difficult to imagine any common ground.

While some mediation will be needed, the compositional analysis of complex concepts in cross-linguistic and cross-cultural comparison adopted here does make it possible for Confucius and Adam Smith to agree that, with a certain amount of abstraction, their respective concepts of 'wén' and 'civilization' do share a common core of semantic molecules. While the Warring States coiners of *wén* 'civility/civilization' may not share Smith's optimistic faith in human Reason to produce endless 'progress,' Adam Smith would agree that the efforts of the sages and sage–kings of old led to a 'change (*biàn*) for the better.' Similarly, Smith could probably be persuaded to accept a broad definition of 'progress' as 'change for the better.' The two would probably also agree that what they assumed to be the deplorable Hobbesian 'state of nature' in which their own ancestors lived as 'birds and beasts' was remarkably similar to the ways of living that characterized many of the contemporary peoples they considered to be *barbarians* or 'civilizationally (inferior) others' (*yí*). Similarly, they would likely agree that their respective concepts of 'wén' and 'civilization' are grounded in what they each take to be universally valid values. The scope of 'wén' and 'civilization' are both extended to the 'civilized world' or 'all under Heaven' (*tiānxià* 天下), understood as a "regime of value," although the particular values are grounded in two very different ethnocentric traditions.

Conclusion 203

However, the significant differences between Confucius' concept of 'wén' (as portrayed in the *Analects*) and Adam Smith's concept of 'civilization' should not be minimized. As shown by the quotes in (1) and (2) below, these concepts led them to entertain diametrically opposed policies on the use of military force in the distribution of material wealth:

(1) I have heard that those who have a state or household do not worry that people are scarce but that they are content; they do not worry about being poor but that wealth is evenly distributed. Because with equitable distribution there is no real poverty, with harmony, no real scarcity, with contentment, no real peril. When such a situation exists, if distant peoples do not submit [to your ruler], then enhance your 'morally refined' (*wén*) 'charismatic power' (*dé*) and make them come to you, and once you have made them come to you, offer them stability. (丘也聞有國有家者，不患寡而患不均，不患貧而患不安。蓋均無貧，和無寡，安無傾。夫如是，故遠人不服，則修文德以來之。既來之，則安之)[17]

(2) The great expence [sic] of fire-arms gives an evident advantage to the nation which can best afford that expence, and consequently to an opulent and *civilized* over a poor and barbarous nation. In ancient times the opulent and *civilized* found it difficult to defend themselves against the poor and barbarous nations. In modern times the poor and barbarous find it difficult to defend themselves against the opulent and *civilized*. The invention of fire-arms, an invention which at first sight appears to be so pernicious, is certainly favorable both to the permanency and to the extension of *civilization*.[18]

According to the passage in (1), for Confucius the accumulation of wealth was less important than its equal distribution. It is possible to be poor and 'civilized' (*wén*) at the same time, as long as resources are equally distributed. Similarly, material wealth does not necessarily lead to 'civility/civilization' (*wén*). As discussed in Chapter 3, Confucius' emphasis is on moral edification of the individual and the elaboration of government institutions conducive to instilling a sense of right and wrong. In contrast, for Smith, who considered laws protecting private property and free commerce to be the cornerstones of his concept of 'civilization,' there is a strong connection between material wealth and stage of civilization.[19] The wealthy nations in his *Wealth of Nations* (1776) are the civilized ones. Uncivilized nations/peoples are, almost per definition, also materially poor.[20] The emphasis is on maximizing production and extraction of wealth by creating a legal system that is conducive to industry and trade and protects accumulated wealth regardless of how unevenly it is distributed.

According to the *Analects*, Confucius is said to have refused to discuss military affairs,[21] proposing instead ways to avoid armed conflict by cultivating and displaying the magnificent 'civility/civilization' (*wén*) of the ruler and the institutions of his state in such a way that restive states and peoples would want to submit of their own free will.[22] In contrast, Adam Smith extolled the invention of fire-arms because they enabled rich, "civilized" nations to militarily defeat and

204   *Conclusion*

control "poor and barbarous nations." Clearly, a discussion on warfare and the distribution of wealth between the authors of the *Analects* and Adam Smith would be characterized by their very different takes on the role of the use of armed force in their respective concepts of 'wén' and 'civilization.'

This imagined dialogue between the Warring States thinkers who composed the *Analects* and Adam Smith is not a frivolous exercise. Rather, it is undertaken by hermeneutic necessity. As observed by Gadamer, meaning is always produced in the meeting of horizons. Breaking down the early modern European concept of 'civilization' and the pre-Qín concept of 'wén' into their constitutive semantic molecules and atoms enables us not only to make sense of the pre-Qín concept of 'wén' in terms of the modern concept of 'civilization,' but also to use the semantic molecules of the pre-Qín concept of 'wén' to make sense of the European universal concept of 'civilization.' The history-word-by-word approach can help us facilitate a fusion of the horizons of Warring States thinkers and European Enlightenment thinkers such as Adam Smith in a way that elucidates and illuminates both of these language-specific concepts of 'civilization.'

In the word-by-word approach to the history of ideas, lexicalization is the umbilical link between semantic changes in words and historical changes in sociopolitical infrastructure and epistemic assumptions. The sociolinguistic theory of lexicalization that is part of the history-word-by-word approach allows us to turn the otherwise purely linguistic exercise of tracing diachronic changes in word meanings into—in the words of the French historian Lucien Febvre (1878–1956)—"food for the historian."[23] That is, we can now use words and historical changes in word meanings as source material in historical studies of changes in thought and sociopolitical structures. Put simply, the lexicon can be used as a historical source.

Linking the coining of civilizational consciousness to specific hypotheses about developments in the sociopolitical infrastructure of the society in which the coiners lived also makes the dating of these changes more robust. At a relatively high level of abstraction it can be argued that structurally similar sociopolitical changes enabled the coining of civilizational consciousness in modern Western Europe and in pre-Qín China. In both contexts, a certain shift took place—from aesthetically interpreted charismatic power in a system where royal and aristocratic primogeniture determined rank in society and position in government, to (the idea of)[24] a more meritocratic system of government in which acquired, ethically interpreted charismatic virtue played a bigger role in determining a person's standing in society and position in government. As was discussed, this shift occurred in tandem with an increasing bureaucratization of government and professionalization of official positions, which in turn created a market of cultural capital where specialists of statecraft and moral philosophy could exchange and communicate their theories of the relationship between the individual and the state. In both early modern Europe and pre-Qín China, this rethinking of the role of the individual vis-à-vis the state motivated masters of statecraft and political philosophers to coin words for 'civility'/'rites' (*lǐ*) [the moral refinement of the individual] and 'police'/'promulgated models' (*fǎ*) [the structuring of institutions of the state]. It was the ideas of 'progress' or 'change for the better' along the dimensions of

Conclusion 205

'police' and 'civility' conceived by moralizing political thinkers in both traditions that created the need for a single word for this complex concept. Hence, the words *civilization* and *wén* were coined.

It is therefore, as mentioned above, very unlikely that a form of civilizational consciousness (encompassing the semantic molecules of the universal concept of 'civilization') could have developed in the small nomadic or hunter–gatherer (or foraging) groups that preceded the earliest state formations.[25] Lacking elaborate state bureaucracies which could support markets of cultural capital needed for the exchange of theories of statecraft, people in such pre-state groups would presumably feel no need to coin a word for a concept of 'civilization' built on semantic molecules akin to those found in the words *civilization* and *wén*. However, members of such groups most likely had other concepts in their collective consciousness that informed the way they constructed identities. That is, they probably also had autonyms and various words for people who belonged to other groups than their own. As in pre-Warring States texts, they probably used an autonym with flattering connotations for themselves and may have referred to other groups using specific toponymic terms or phrases such as 'those living on the other side of the mountain.' But since there likely were no professional salaried specialists whose job it was to produce theories of statecraft, it seems improbable that words for concepts such as 'wén' and 'civilization' would have been coined. No one would have felt they needed to lexicalize such terms at the time.[26,27]

The theoretical framework outlined in Chapter 1 is designed to facilitate a cross-linguistic dialogue between the different horizons of the modern European concept of 'civilization' and the pre-Qín concept of 'wén.' However, it can also be used to trace the emergence of kindred forms of civilizational (or *wén*-) consciousness in other traditions—such as, for example, India and the Arab world—both in their pre-modern traditions and texts and in their modern and post-colonial responses to their encounters with "Western civilization" and Western concepts of 'civilization.'[28] The reason this book began with a study of the English word *civilization* is that it is written for an Anglophone audience. It begins that way by hermeneutical necessity in order to make sense of pre-Qín words, such as *wén*, through a Gadamerian fusion of epistemic horizons. If this book had been written in Arabic, then a study of the language-specific "prejudices" of the Arabic word 'civilization' *ḥaḍāra* (حضارة) would have had to be undertaken.[29]

Writing about pre-Qín civilizational consciousness in Arabic can be used to illustrate the need to escape the hegemony of Anglophone terms and concepts. In principle, Swahili, Tagalog, or other language could have been used instead. However, Arabic is a good example because it has a word (i.e., *ḥaḍāra*) that was used in pre-modern times to refer to an indigenous concept that bears some resemblance to the modern Anglophone concept 'civilization.' In this respect, *ḥaḍāra* is comparable to the Old Chinese term *wén*. Furthermore, *ḥaḍāra* is also used to refer to 'civilization' in modern Arabic.

As observed by Morewedge (2001: 218), Ibn Khaldun (1332–1406) used the word *ḥaḍāra* in ways "similar in some respects to the European concept of civilization." Some contemporary scholars use the word *civilization* to translate the word

206 *Conclusion*

ḥaḍāra in Ibn Khaldun's works into English.[30] From the late nineteenth century onward, the word *ḥaḍāra* has been informed by the modern Anglophone universal concept of 'civilization.' Guizot's lectures on European history were translated into Arabic in 1877 and inspired influential thinkers such as Sayyid Jamāl al-Dīn al-Afghānī (1838/9–1897) to incorporate elements of Guizot's notion of civilizational progress into a new concept of *ḥaḍāra* informed by a fusion of Arabic and European ideas.[31] The fact that the meaning of the word *ḥaḍāra* in Modern Arabic is informed by the European universal concept of 'civilization' may contribute to the tendency among modern Arab-speaking scholars to translate Ibn-Khaldun's use of *ḥaḍāra* as *civilization*.

This raises the question of what kind of hermeneutical violence is done to Ibn Khaldun's fourteenth-century use of *ḥaḍāra* by translating it into English as *civilization*. Scholars have noted several important differences between the modern European universal concept of 'civilization' and the fifteenth-century Arabic concept of 'ḥaḍāra.' First, as observed by Morewedge, Ibn Khaldun does not appear to have used the word *ḥaḍāra* "as a concept with which to view human development, or in reference by which to judge it."[32] That is, unlike the modern European concept of 'civilization,' the pre-modern concept of 'ḥaḍāra' does not emphasize a molecule of 'progress' to the same extent. Second, Ibn Khaldun often used the term *ḥaḍāra* to refer to the concept of "living in the city as opposed to living in the desert."[33] That is, the pre-modern Arabic concept of 'civilization' (*ḥaḍāra*) includes the concept of 'city/urbanism,' also referred to by the term *madaniyya* (مدنية), as a key semantic sub-component or molecule. Third, an element of religion—that is, Islam—also plays a prominent role in Ibn Khaldun's pre-modern concepts of 'ḥaḍāra.'[34] It is questionable whether these three aspects of Ibn Khaldun's pre-modern concept of 'ḥaḍāra' are captured by translating it as *civilization*.[35]

Like the Modern Arabic word *ḥaḍāra*, some of the meanings of the Modern Chinese term *wénmíng* 文明 'civilization' derive from European concepts of 'civilization.'[36] In the late nineteenth century, *wénmíng* was introduced into Japanese (where it is pronounced *bunmei*) as a calque loan word from English and French intended to express the universal concept of 'civilization' in Guizot's definition.[37] From Japanese into it was borrowed into Chinese. By the turn of the twentieth century this Western-inspired definition of *wénmíng* imported from Japan had become dominant in Chinese usage.[38] This concept of *wénmíng* was further developed by Chinese intellectuals to construct a new national identity.[39] Eventually, the use of the term *wénmíng* to refer to various universal, ethnographic, and archaeological concepts of civilization came to play a pivotal role in Chinese archaeologists' debates on the origin of "Chinese civilization."[40]

The widespread process of "translating the West" and appropriating Western terms and concepts from the humanities and social sciences, which took place in the nineteenth and early twentieth centuries in the Arab world, Japan, China, and elsewhere, contributed greatly to the current global imprisonment in English.[41] Not only is English the global lingua franca of scientific and academic research,

Conclusion 207

but even when scholars writing in Arabic, Chinese or Japanese use the modern terms *ḥaḍāra*, *wénmíng*, and *bunmei*, they are, to a certain extent, imprisoned in Eurocentric concepts of 'civilization.'[42] This epistemic hegemony and global dominance of Anglophone terminology (and Eurocentric concepts "translated into" terms in other languages and traditions) is perhaps one of the most insidious legacies of colonialism and Orientalism.

Pondering the implications of using a pre-modern language as our metalanguage helps illustrate the current global dominance of Anglophone categories. As a thought experiment, imagine a dialogue between Ibn Khaldun and the persona of Confucius as portrayed in the *Analects* on their respective concepts of 'ḥaḍāra' and 'wén.' Confucius and Ibn Khaldun both formulated their theories of *wén* and *ḥaḍāra* long before the coining of the English word *civilization* and were completely unaffected by modern European concepts of 'civilization,' which only date back to the early sixteenth century at the earliest. Using *wén* as well as the Old Chinese terms for the semantic molecules of this concept of civility/civilization' as metalanguage to study Ibn Khaldun's concept of *ḥaḍāra*, and vice versa, can allow us to free ourselves from the contemporary epistemic hegemony of Eurocentric English terms and concepts and would surely reveal other facets of meaning of both terms than existing Anglophone studies of each concept. Meaning is always the outcome of an interpretive process consisting of a fusion of epistemic horizons. Hence, different choices of metalanguage—that is, which language-specific tradition we use as our vantage point from which we study other traditions—will result in different interpretations of the concepts of the tradition being studied.

Key differences between pre-Qín 'wén,' fifteenth-century 'ḥaḍāra,' and eighteenth-century 'civilization' can be summarized as in Table 6.1. Confucius' pre-Qín concept of 'wén' emphasizes 'civility'; Ibn Khaldun's 'ḥaḍāra' emphasizes monotheistic religion and the contrast between the nomadic way of life and 'urbanism'; and Adam Smith's 'civilization' emphasizes 'progress' and the rule of law to protect free commerce and private property.

Using Ibn Khaldun's concept of 'ḥaḍāra' to analyze pre-Qín *wén* would lead us to ask whether the concept of 'wén' embodies an element of 'urbanism' and whether the concept of a monotheistic religion (akin to Islam) plays a role in its internal semantic molecular structure. Clearly, those questions differ from the analytical task of identifying the counterparts to the elements of 'progress,' 'civility,' and 'police' in the pre-Qín concept of 'wén' that we set for ourselves in earlier chapters. Thus, using either one of the first two concepts in Table 6.1 as metalanguage to study the other two would bring to light new facets of these

Table 6.1 Language-specific concepts of 'civilization' in three different traditions/horizons.

Early proponents	Concept	Term
Confucius (551–479 BCE)	'civility/civilization'	*wén* (文)
Ibn Khaldun (1332–1406)	'urbanism/civilization'	*ḥaḍāra* (حضارة)
Adam Smith (1723–1790)	'laws/civilization'	*civilization*

208   *Conclusion*

traditions. Employing pre-modern Arabic or Chinese as the metalanguage in which we engage in cross-linguistic conceptual comparisons would also enable us to step outside the hegemony of Anglophone concepts that dominates much of the current global academic discourse on 'civilization' and 'Chinese civilization.' The repercussions of doing so are not just epistemological but also political.[43] Hence, I hope that it may contribute to a deconstruction of the essentializing and highly problematic dichotomies between the "West and the Rest" and "China and the West."

Notes

1 Mill (1843: vol. 2: 239, italics added).
2 Segal (2000: 798). For the "Western Civ" course, see also Allardyce (1982).
3 The French philosopher François Jullien (b. 1951) exemplifies the long tradition of portraying China as an essentialized and exoticized other diametrically different from the "West." Jullien (1995) contrasts a presumed logical, analytical tradition of "Western" thinking (e.g., Plato) with a supposedly holistic, intuition-based thinking of Chinese philosophers. As pointed out by Billeter (2006), this myth of China as an antipodal other has roots in the writings on China by Jesuits and Enlightenment thinkers. The phrase "irreducible alterity" is from Billeter (2006).
4 Books with the phrase *Chinese civilization* in the title date back to shortly after the emergence of the ethnographic concept of 'civilization' in the nineteenth century. See for example: Laffitte (1861) *La civilisation chinoise et les relations de l'Occident avec la Chine*, which appeared in English as Laffitte (1887) *A General View of Chinese Civilization and of the Relations of the West with China*; and Lacouperie (1880) *Early History of the Chinese Civilisation*. The emergence of the "Western Civ" course triggered a burst of textbooks on "Chinese civilization" in the 1920s and 1930s. See, for example, Wilhelm (1929) *A Short History of Chinese Civilization*; Goodrich and Fenn (1929) *A Syllabus of the History of Chinese Civilization and Culture*; Granet (1930) *Chinese Civilization*; Gale (1934) *Basics of the Chinese Civilization*; Kiang (1935) *Chinese Civilization: An Introduction to Sinology*; Creel (1937) *The Birth of China, a Study of the Formative Period of Chinese Civilization*. The publication of books on "Chinese civilization" has continued into the twenty-first century; see, for example, Chang et al. (2005) *The Formation of Chinese Civilization*; and Yuan et al. (2012) *The History of Chinese Civilization*.
5 The saying "We don't see things as they are; we see them as we are" is often attributed to Anaïs Nin.
6 See the study of the different meanings and use of the phrase *Chinese civilization* the subsection titled "Invention and transformations of 'Chinese civilization'" in chapter 1.
7 Wierzbicka (2014).
8 See the discussion of Wierzbicka's criticism of the overreliance on English in the subsection titled "Comparing concepts across languages and historical contexts" in chapter 1.
9 Gideon Shelach's *The Archaeology of Early China* (2015) explicitly avoids the term *civilization*. The result is refreshing.
10 For the problem of making inferences based on absence of evidence, see Sober (2009).
11 Existing evidence is often insufficient to allow us to definitively determine the date of composition of specific texts. Disagreement will therefore continue to exist. However, that does not diminish the usefulness of framework for studying civilizational consciousness proposed here. Scholars with different assumptions about the dating of

Conclusion 209

certain texts may use it to date the emergence of civilizational consciousness to different periods. Thus, for example, scholars who assume that the *Zuŏzhuàn* reflects fifth-century BCE thought and vocabulary, as I do here, may use the history-word-by-word approach to place the emergence of civilizational consciousness a century or so later than scholars who assume the *Zuŏzhuàn* to reflect Spring and Autumn period language and thought.

12 As discussed in the subsection titled "Comparing concepts across languages and historical contexts" in chapter 1, the language-specific meanings of semantic molecules can be bridged by breaking down these molecules into linguistic atoms which have similar or identical meanings in all languages.

13 The English word *culture* is a widespread translation of Old Chinese *wén*. For a historical study of translations of *wén* as *culture* in the *Analects*, see Bergeton (forthcoming) "Found (and Lost?) in Translation: 'Culture' in the *Analects*," *Harvard Journal of Asiatic Studies*.

14 Wierzbicka (2008, 2014); see the subsection titled "Comparing concepts across languages and historical contexts" in chapter 1.

15 It is important to distinguish between the historical Confucius and the persona(s) of Confucius presented in the *Analects* and other early Chinese texts. As is often noted, the words reportedly uttered by Confucius according to the *Analects* may or may not in fact have been his actual words. Due to the lack of sources, it is impossible to know. The figure of Confucius engaged in the imagined dialogue with Adam Smith in figure 6.2 should therefore be seen as a visual representation of the persona of Confucius as he is portrayed by the Warring States authors of the *Analects*, rather than the historical Confucius. For different personas of Confucius, see Nylan and Wilson (2010).

16 The image of Adam Smith is from https://commons.wikimedia.org/w/index. php?curid=497250.

17 *Analects* 16.1, Chéng Shùdé (1997: 1137), tr. adapted from Slingerland (2003: 192). The words *wén* and *dé* can also be translated as two nouns: 'civility/civilization' (*wén*) and 'charismatic power' (*dé*).

18 Smith (1776: 21, italics added).

19 As mentioned in endnote 70 in chapter 3, the Old Chinese term 'promulgated models/regulations' (*fǎ*) and the modern English term *laws* refer to two very different concepts. Thus, while Adam Smith's concept of 'civilization' was informed by a notion of the *rule of law* protecting the rights of the individual, the Old Chinese concept of 'civility/civilization' (*wén*) was informed by 'promulgated models' issued by rulers to regulate the population.

20 Elsewhere in *The Wealth of Nations* Adam Smith elaborates the idea that wealth and poverty are correlated with "civilization" and "barbarity": "Among the *savage* nations of hunters and fishers, every individual . . . provide[s] . . . the necessaries and conveniencies [sic] of life, for himself . . . Such nations, however, are . . . miserably poor . . . Among *civilized* and thriving nations, on the contrary, . . . produce of the whole labor of the society is so great, that all are often abundantly supplied; and a workman, even of the lowest and poorest order, . . . may enjoy a greater share of the necessaries and conveniencies of life than it is possible for any savage to acquire" (Smith 1814 [1776]: 2–3, italics added).

21 *Analects* 15.1, Chéng Shùdé (1997: 1049), tr. Slingerland (2003: 174).

22 *Analects* 16.1, Chéng Shùdé (1997: 1137). According to the *Xúnzĭ*, the ideal ruler perfects " 'civility/civilization' (*wén*) [in his own person and in the institutions of his state] in order to display it to 'all under Heaven' (*tiānxià*) so that aggressive states will be at peace and transform themselves" (*Xúnzĭ* 7.1, Wáng Xiānqiān (1988: 108)). See the discussion of this passage in chapter 3.

23 Febvre (1973: 219). See the full quotation of this passage from Febvre (1973: 219), in endnote 23 to chapter 1.

210 Conclusion

24 While the idea of meritocracy can be found in the *Analects*, the *Mòzǐ*, and other Warring States texts, it is also clear that the actual systems of promotion practiced in the various states were far from meritocratic during the period when civilizational consciousness was coined in the sixth to fourth centuries BCE. The reforms of Shāng Yāng (390–338 BCE) in the state of Qín in the mid-fourth century BCE was likely one of the first times meritocratic ideas began to be institutionalized on a significant scale.

25 I am using the definition of early state formations proposed by Trigger (2003).

26 Using the lexicon as a historical source thus allows us to formulate hypotheses about the evolution of ideas in periods from which we have few or no texts directly devoted to discussing these ideas. The lexicon has been used as a source to reconstruct the world in which speakers of proto–Indo-European lived in pre-historic times; see Martinet (1986).

27 The approach to civilizational consciousness developed here does not imply a value difference between those social formations that have various forms of civilizational consciousness and those that do not. To be sure, both the sixteenth- to eighteenth-century European concept of 'civilization' and the pre-Qín concept of 'wén' are based on notions of 'progress' or 'change for the better.' However, we as scholars studying these traditions are not the ones making evolutionary assumptions. We are merely describing and comparing the ideas of 'progress' and 'change for the better' that are inherent in the terms for the universal concepts of 'wén' and 'civilization' as they are used by the people in the traditions who coined them.

28 See Duara (2001) and Duara (2004b).

29 Other Arabic terms, such as 'city/urbanism' *madaniyya* (مدنية), which are part of the Arabic vocabulary of concepts related to notions of 'civilizations,' would also have to be studied. For simplicity, I have limited the present discussion to the term *ḥaḍāra*.

30 See, for example, Khaldun, *The Muqaddimah*: "Social organization, is necessary to the human species. Without it, the existence of human beings would be incomplete. God's desire to settle the world with human beings and to leave them as His representatives on earth would not materialize. This is the meaning of civilization [*ḥaḍāra*]" (tr. Rosenthal (1969: 46)).

31 Kohn (2009).

32 Morewedge (2001: 218).

33 Morewedge (2001: 218). For discussion of Ibn Khaldun's concept of '*ḥaḍāra*,' see also Ahmed (2002); Al-Azmeh (1992); Baali (1988); Costi (1949); and Kohn (2009).

34 As observed by Kohn (2009: 411), "Ibn Khaldun identifies religion as the one factor that can create a more stable basis of civilization. Although Ibn Khaldun recognizes that religion is not the only possible source of order and stability, he notes that it is a particularly effective one."

35 According to Morewedge (2001: 218), part of the confusion about what *ḥaḍāra* means in Ibn Khaldun's work stems from "the writings of later Arab researchers [who] . . . simply want to justify the European meaning they already have in mind."

36 *Wénmíng* is composed of the morphemes *wén* 文 'writing; language; culture; civil; refined; tattoo' and *míng* 明 'bright; explicit; clear-sighted; understand.' These are modern Mandarin meanings of *wén* and *míng*. Some current meanings of the word *wén* (e.g., 'writing, literary') did not exist in the pre-Warring States period. Conversely, some old meanings of the word *wén* (e.g., 'awe-inspiringly beautiful') have now become obsolete. The first morpheme of the Modern Chinese word *wénmíng* appears to be identical to the Old Chinese word *wén* 文. But this is an illusion. As shown in chapters 2–3, the Old Chinese word *wén* 文 meant something very different from Modern Chinese *wénmíng*.

37 Yukichi Fukuzawa (1835–1901) was one of the most influential promoters of Western 'civilization' in Meiji Japan. Inspired by Guizot's (1911 [1828]) *General History of Civilization in Europe* and the English historian Thomas Buckle's (1872–3 [1857: vol.1; 1861: vol. 2]) *History of Civilization in England*, he came to the conclusion that Japan suffered under an anemic and outdated 'Chinese civilization' and that it needed

Conclusion 211

to invigorate its national spirit with a new 'civilization' based on that of 'the West.' The word he used to express the idea of 'civilization' in his influential *An Outline of a Theory of Civilization* (1875) was *bunmei* (Chin. *wénmíng*), which had only been coined in this sense a few years earlier.

38 For this process of translating Western concepts of 'civilization' into Japanese and Chinese, see Howland (2002, 1996).

39 Because this concept of 'civilization' was non-Sinocentric (since it originated from Europe), it was the ideal conceptual tool for the group of Chinese intellectuals who wanted to make a clean break from what they perceived to be the stagnant worldview of the Qīng dynasty in order to allow the fledgling Chinese nation-state to join the community of other 'civilized' nation-states. For studies on the role played by Western concepts of 'civilization' on the use of the term *wénmíng* by late nineteenth- and early twentieth-century Chinese scholars to construct a Chinese national identity, see also Duara (2001; 2004a: 96–7), Wang (1991), and Jenco (2015).

40 The idea that China has 5,000 years of history is a widely accepted popular perception in China. This notion that "Chinese civilization" is 5,000 years old is also politically attractive since it allows contemporary politicians to root Chinese national identity in remote antiquity. As observed by Anderson (1983: 5), while historians are aware of the "objective modernity" of modern nations as imagined communities, "their subjective antiquity in the eyes of nationalists" has often been used to legitimize the nation and construct national identities. The modern Chinese term *wénmíng* has played, and continues to play, an important role in these processes. Hence, the word *wénmíng* is very popular among Chinese archaeologists. As observed by Shelach (2015: 159), "A recent survey identified more than eight hundred publications on the origins of 'Chinese civilization' by members of the Chinese Academy of Social Sciences alone (Chén Yōng 陈雍 2009)."

41 The phrase "translating the West" is from the title of Howland (2002).

42 To be sure, the word *wénmíng* has taken on a life of its own following its (re-) introduction into Modern Chinese around the turn of the twentieth century. It has thus developed meanings and uses that differ from those of the English word *civilization*. However, this does not make uncritical use of the word *wénmíng* to study the onset of civilizational consciousness in the pre-Qín period any less problematic than the use of the English word *civilization*. Although *wénmíng* is part of the collectively shared lexicon of speakers of Mandarin, it is a modern word informed to a large extent by the universal concept of 'civilization' in Guizot Eurocentric definition and by its subsequent redefinitions in the ethnographic and archaeological senses by Western-educated archaeologists.

43 Jenco (2015: 92–120).

References

Ahmed, Akbar. 2002. 'Ibn Khaldun's Understanding of Civilizations and the Dilemmas of Islam and the West Today', *Middle East Journal*, 56: 20–45.

Al-Azmeh, Aziz. 1992. 'Barbarians in Arab Eyes', *Past & Present*: 3–18.

Allardyce, Gilbert. 1982. 'The Rise and Fall of the Western Civilization Course', *The American Historical Review*, 87: 695–725.

Anderson, Benedict. 1983. *Imagined Communities: Reflections on the Origin and Spread of Nationalism* (Verso: London).

Baali, Fuad. 1988. *Society, State, and Urbanism: Ibn Khaldun's Sociological Thought* (SUNY Press: Albany).

Bergeton, Uffe. forthcoming. 'Found (and Lost) in Translation: The Emergence of "Culture" in the Analects', *Harvard Journal of Asiatic Studies*.

Billeter, Jean-François. 2006. 'Contre François Jullien', Annales. Histoire, *Sciences Sociales*, 61: 1481–82.

212 Conclusion

Buckle, Henry Thomas. 1872–3 [1857, Vol. 1; 1861, Vol. 2]. *History of Civilization in England* (Appleton and Company: New York).

Chang, Kwang-chih, Sarah Allan, Liancheng Lu, and Pingfang Xu (eds.). 2005. *The Formation of Chinese Civilization: An Archaeological Perspective* (Yale University Press: New Haven).

Chén Yōng 陈雍. 2009. 'Yīgè cóng "Lǐ" tànsuǒ Zhōngguó wénmíng qǐyuán de móshì 一个从"礼"探索中国文明起源的模式 (A Model for Exploring the Origins of Chinese Civilization from the Concept of "Lǐ")', *Wenwu*: 90–3.

Chéng Shùdé 程樹德. 1997. *Lúnyǔ jíshì* 論語集釋 (Zhōnghuá shūjú: Běijīng).

Costi, K. Zurayk. 1949. 'The Essence of Arab Civilization', *Middle East Journal*, 3: 125–39.

Creel, Herrlee Glessner. 1937. *The Birth of China, a Study of the Formative Period of Chinese Civilization* (Reynal & Hitchcock: New York).

Duara, Prasenjit. 2001. 'The Discourse of Civilization and Pan-Asianism', *Journal of World History*, 12: 99–130.

———. 2004a. *Sovereignty and Authenticity: Manchukuo and the East Asian Modern* (Rowman & Littlefield: Lanham, Boulder, New York, Toronto, Oxford).

———. 2004b. 'The Discourse of Civilization and Decolonization', *Journal of World History*, 15: 1–5.

Febvre, Lucien. 1973. *A New Kind of History: From the Writings of Febvre* (Harper & Row: New York).

Gale, Esson M. 1934. *Basics of the Chinese Civilization* (Kelly & Walsh: Shanghai).

Goodrich, L. C., and H. C. Fenn. 1929. *A Syllabus of the History of Chinese Civilization and Culture* (China Society: New York).

Granet, Marcel. 1930. *Chinese Civilization* (Kegan Paul & Trench, Trubner & Co., Ltd: London).

Guizot, François. 1911 [1828]. *The History of Civilization in* Europe [Eng. tr. of *Histoire de la civilisation en Europe*] (Cassell and Company: London, New York, Toronto & Melbourne).

Howland, Douglas. 1996. *Borders of Chinese Civilization: Geography and History at Empire's End* (Duke University Press: Durham).

———. 2002. *Translating the West: Language and Political Reason in Nineteenth-Century Japan* (University of Hawaii Press: Honolulu).

Jenco, Leigh. 2015. *Changing Referents: Learning Across Apace and Time in China and the West* (Oxford University Press: Oxford).

Jullien, François. 1995. *The Propensity of Things: Toward a History of Efficacy in China* (Zone Books & Distributed by MIT Press: New York).

Kiang, Kanghu. 1935. *Chinese Civilization: An Introduction to Sinology* (Chung Hwa Book Co: Shanghai).

Kohn, Margaret. 2009. 'Afghani on Empire, Islam, and Civilization', *Political Theory*, 37: 398–422.

Lacouperie, Terrien de. 1880. *Early History of the Chinese Civilisation* (Vaton: London).

Laffitte, Pierre M. 1861. *La Civilisation chinoise et les relations de l'Occident avec la Chine* (Dunod: Paris).

———. 1887. *A General View of Chinese Civilization and of the Relations of the West with China*. Translated by John Carey Hall (Trübner: London).

Martinet, André. 1986. *Des steppes aux océans: l'indo-européen et les "indo-européens"* (Payot: Paris).

Conclusion 213

Mill, John Stuart. 1843. *A System of Logic, Ratiocinative and Inductive: Being a Connected View of the Principles of Evidence and the Methods of Scientific Investigation* (Parker: London).

Morewedge, P. 2001. *The Scholar Between Thought and Experience: A Biographical Festschrift in Honor of Ali A. Mazrui* (Institute of Global Cultural Studies Global Publications Binghamton University: Binghamton, NY).

Rosenthal, Franz. 1969. *The Muqaddimah: An Introduction to History* (Princeton University Press: Princeton).

Segal, Daniel A. 2000. ' "Western Civ" and the Staging of History in American Higher Education', *The American Historical Review*, 105: 770–805.

Shelach, Gideon. 2015. *The Archaeology of Early China: From Prehistory to the Han Dynasty* (Cambridge University Press: Cambridge).

Slingerland, Edward G. 2003. *Analects: With Selections from Traditional Commentaries* (Hackett: Indianapolis).

Smith, Adam. 1776. *In Inquiry into the Nature and Causes of the Wealth of Nations* (Methuen: London).

———. 1814 [1776]. *An Inquiry Into the Nature and Causes of the Wealth of Nations: In Three Volumes. With Notes, and an Additional Volume by David Buchanan* (Oliphant, Waugh & Innes and John Murray: Edinburgh & London).

Sober, Elliott. 2009. 'Absence of Evidence and Evidence of Absence: Evidential Transitivity in Connection with Fossils, Fishing, Fine-tuning, and Firing Squads', *Philosophical Studies*, 143: 63–90.

Trigger, Bruce G. 2003. *Understanding Early Civilizations: A Comparative Study* (Cambridge University Press: Cambridge).

Wang, Gungwu. 1991. *The Chineseness of China* (Oxford University Press: Hong Kong).

Wáng Xiānqiān 王先謙. 1988. *Xúnzǐ jíjiě* 荀子集解 (Běijīng Zhōnghuá shūjú: Běijīng).

Wierzbicka, Anna. 2008. 'Why There Are No "Colour Universals" in Language and Thought', *Journal of the Royal Anthropological Institute*, 14: 407–25.

———. 2014. *Imprisoned in English: The Hazards of English as a Default Language* (Oxford University Press: New York).

Wilhelm, Richard. 1929. *A Short History of Chinese Civilization* (Viking Press: New York).

Yuan, Xingpei, Xiaonan Deng, David R. Knechtges, Yulie Lou, Wenming Yan, and Chuanxi Zhang. 2012. *The History of Chinese Civilization* (Cambridge University Press: Cambridge).

Index

Note: Page numbers in *italic* indicate a figure and page numbers in **bold** indicate a table on the corresponding page.

aesthetic *wén* ('awe-inspiringly beautiful') 4, 49–50, 51–52, 53–5, 56, 57, 58, 61, 63, 64, 65, 66, 67, 68, 69, 74, *75*, 76, 77n6, 77n14, 80n42, 80n44, 86n108, 87n126, 87n133, 96, 99, 108, 114, 124n21, 174, 210n36; transition from aesthetical to ethical understanding of *wén* 64–8

agriculture metaphors for self-cultivation 119, 130

Allan, Sarah 43n112, 157n5

'all the *Xià* (states)' (*zhū-Xià* 諸夏) 151, 152, 153, 177, 185n6

'all under Heaven' (*tiānxià* 天下) 4, 7n9, 71, 81n59, 98, 100–2, 104, 109, *110*, 117, 123, 125n24, 125n29, 125n35, 125n36, 126n37, 126n38, 126n39, 126n40, 126n42, 127n52, 129n84, 143, 144, 151, 161n40, 182, 191n59, *198*, 200, 202, 209n22; 'civility'/'civilization' (*wén*) 100–2, 109, 115; *Mòzǐ* 115, 143, 144, 161n40

Analects 49, 53, 55–6, 62, 68, 79n28, 82n85, 95, 100, 104, 114, 122–23, 128n68, 155, 163n64, 181, 182, 184; 'civility/civilization' (*wén*) 96, 111, 115, 116, 118–19, 120, 127n51, 179; Confucius 59, 68, 69, 80n54, 82n75, 85n102, 85n107, 87n126, 95, 99, 105, 106, 123n5, 123n7, 129n79, 130n98, 203, 204, 207, 209n15; craft metaphors 49, 70–4, 75, 86n112, 119, 120; edification 68, 70, 71, 73, 106, 114, 120, 203; 'elegant, proper' (*yǎ* 雅) 187n26; human nature is moral 'blank slate' 120; (institutionalized) 'patterns'

(*wén*) 68, 70, 74, 86n112, 96, 114, 119; *jūnzǐ* 53, 64, 68, 69, 70, 73, 77n16, 86n114, 87n126, 99, 112, 181, 191n55; meritocracy 210n24; metaphorical interpretation of the line 'as if cut, as if carved' in the *Songs* 70, 73; moral education 73; 'moral refinement' 53, 68–69, 70, 71, 73, 87n126, 96, 97, 102, 112, 119, 130n103; 'noble men' (*jūnzǐ*) 53, 64, 68, 69, 70, 73, 77n16, 86n114, 87n126, 99, 112, 181, 191n55; 'rites' 70, 100, 86n116, 99, 102, 106, 115, 116, 119–120, 176, 179, 181; self-cultivation 64, 74, 75, 86n112, 96, 106, 122–123; *Songs* 49, 55, 70, 73, 111; virtue ethics 64, 75, 95, 96, 99, 112, 115, 116, 122, 123, 181; Warring States 69, 79n28, 79n33, 178, 201, 204; *wén* 53, 55, 56, 61, 68–9, 70, 71, 73, 74, 75, 85n103, 86n112, 86n114, 86n115, 86n116, 87n126, 95, 96, 97, 99, 100, 114, 116, 119, 120, 203, 204, 207, 201–4, 207–8, 209n13; *yídí* 166n84, 176–7

Annals 78n17, 83n85, 104, 137, 140, 145, 155, 158n14, **160**, 161n43, 162n52, 164n69, 164n70, 165n77, 175, 188n33

Arabic 3, 205, 206, 207, 208

archaeological concept of 'civilization' 1, 2, 5, 11, 26, 27, 29–31, *30*, *31*, 33, **35**, 36, 42n96, 43n112, 207

'armed opponents' 137–8; *see also* 'belligerent others'

'awe-inspiring' (*wēi* 威) 54, 55, 65, 66, 67, 69, 84–5n92, 124n9

'awe-inspiringly beautiful' (*wén* 文) 4, 49–50, 51–52, 53–5, 56, 57, 58, 61, 63,

Index 215

64, 65, 66, 67, 68, 69, 74, *75*, 76, 77n14, 80n42, 80n44, 87n126, 87n133, 96, 99, 108, 114, 124n21, 174, 210n36; 'awe -inspiring beauty' as marker of inherited status and rank 52–5; charismatic authority 50–8; compared to 'beautiful' (*kalós*) heroes of pre-Classical Greece 51–2, 77n14, 82n80; semantic change from 'pattern' to 'beautiful' 50–8

bà 霸 ('lord–protector'/'overlord'/ hegemon') 80n47, 82n85, 101
barbarians (English word and concept) 18, 19, 20, 25, 26, *27*, 32, 34, 34n5, 39n44, 106, 108, 135, 138, 154, 166n82, 182, 183, 184, 198, 202
'barbarians' (Greek word *bárbaroi*) 39n44, 125n36, 141, 166n82, 172, 185n2, 185n3, 185n4
'barbarians' (*yí* 夷) 5, 7n8, 7n9, 103, 106, 108, 109, 110, 123, 126n38, 135–57, 157n3, 157n4, 158n13, 159n30, 159n31, **160**, 161n40, 162n53, 162n56, 162n57, 163n60, 164n75, 165n80, 166n83, 173, 174, 175, 176, 177, 182, 183, 184, 185, 192n60, 197, 198, 199; 'belligerent others' (*róng*) 136–40, 155, 159n22, 176, 177; Classical Greece 158n20; combinatorial potential of *yí* as default term 144–7; 'civilizationally inferior others' 5, 7n8, 106, 107, 109, 135, 136, 137, 139, 140, 141, 142, 143, 144, 145, 147, 149, 150, 152, 154, 155, *156*, *157*, **160**, 161n40, 163n57, 164n69, 167n93, 172, 173, 176, 177, 179, 181, 182, 183, 184, 185n5, 197, 198, 199; ethnonym compounds 139, 140, 147, 150–5, 162n53, **164**, 164n70, 165n78, 185n6; 'four (civilizationally inferior) non-Zhōu others' (*sì yí*) 82n85, 143–4, 146, 147, 150, 151, 159n26, **160**, 161n40, 161n41, 162n53; Hàn dynasty 166n90; *mányí* (*mán-yí*) 66, 82n85, 84n90, 140, 141, 150, 151, 152, 153, 154, 155, *156*, 159, 163n65, **164**, 164n70, 166n81, 167n93, 179, 185n6; *mányíróngdí* (*mányí-róngdí*) 141, 150, 151, 153, 154, 155, *156*, **164**, 164n70, 165n80; *Mencius* 147–50; Poo 7n8, 138, 157n4; post-Hàn 166n90; pre-Warring States vocabulary of identity 136–40; *róngdí* (*róng-dí*) 140, 141, 151, 152, 153, 154, 155, *156*, 159n30, **160**, 162n53, 163n66, 163n69, **164**, 164n70, 165n76, 165n77, 166n81,

185n6; toponym compounds 137, 138–40, 146, 155; *yí* as default term for 'civilizationally inferior non-Zhōu others' or 'barbarians' 141–50; *yídí (yí-dí)* 140, 141, 150, 151, 154, 155, *156*, *157*, 159n30, 162n53, 163n60, 163n64, 164n70, 166n83, 166n84, 166n86, 166n90, 176, 177, 184
Baxter, William Hubbard 80n41, 84n92, 123n7, 166n93, 176, 180, 185n6, 186n7, 186n8, 187n25, 189n36, 191n49
'beautiful' (Greek word *kalós*) heroes of pre-Classical Greece 51–2, 77n14, 82n80
běi-dí 北狄 140, 142, 143, 146, 147, 150, 161n36, 162n53
běi-róng 北戎 144, 145, 146, **160**, 161n44, 162n50, 162n52
'belligerent others' (*róng* 戎) 135, 136–38, 145, 146, 155, 158n19, 159n22, 176, 177
Bergeton, Uffe 77n6, 130n99, 130n102, 159n30
Bodin, Jean 20
(Book of) Changes (*Yìjīng/Yì*) 78n17, 80n47, 126n46, 137, 140, 161n43, 175
(Book of) Documents (*Shàngshū/Shū*) 73, 78n17, 80n47, 83n85, 102, 104, 113, 137, 140, 159n25, **160**, 161n41, 161n43, 163n65, 175, 186n17, 186n18, 186n33
(Book of) Songs (*Shījīng/Shī*) 53, 56, 57, 61, 69, 70, 73, 78n16, 78n17, 78n18, 80n47, 80n44, 80n47, 82n85, 83n85, 84n85, 86n117, 87n125, 87n127, 111, 113, 115, 130n102, 137, 140, 145, 149, **160**, 161n43, 162n53, **164**, 164n70, 165n77, 175, 187n26, 188n33, 191n59; and the *Analects* 49, 70, 73, 111; date of composition of "Canon of Yao" chapter 163n65
Boswell, James 23
Bourdieu, Pierre 19, 39n48
Brindley, Erica 124n22, 125n24, 125n34, 157n4, 159n31, 165n75
Brooks, Bruce 79n28, 187n19, 187n26
Brooks, Taeko 79n28, 82n85
bunmei ('civilization') 206–7, 211n37
Burnouf, Eugène 28, 41n90
Bury, J. B. 105, 127n54

'Central States' (*Zhōng guó* 中國) 6n2, 60, 101, 103, 106, 115, 123, 126n37, 129n84, 136, 137, 138, 139, 140, 141, 142, 143, 144, 149, 151, 152, 155,

216 *Index*

158n7, 161n40, 163n60, 166n84, 178, 179, 182, 183, 188n30, 190n39, 192n62
Chāng (name of King Wén) 9, 76n4, *see* King Wén
Chang, K. C. 33, 43n112, 77n7, 127n50, 158n13
charismatic authority/power 4, 19, 20, 34, 36, 49, 50, aesthetically grounded 50–6, 61, 63, 69, 76, 204; Weber 39n45, 39n46, 51, 52, 53, 77n9
'charismatic power'/'moral virtue' (*dé* 德) 66–7, 69, 76, 85n95, 85n105, 99, 102, 112, 117, 118, 198, 203, 209n17
Chinese civilization: archaeological concept of 'civilization' 1, 5, 28, 29–30, 33, 43n106, 43n110, 43n111, 43n113, 121, 157n5, 197, 206, 208, 208n4, 208n6, 211n40; ethnographic concept of 'civilization' 29, 32, 33, 41n90, 196; invention and transformation of the English phrase 'Chinese civilization' 31–4; universal concept of 'civilization' 8–9, 31, 32 196, 197, 208
civility (English and French words and concepts) 7n11, 17, 18, 20, 21, 22, 23, 24, 25, 26, 30, 34, **35**, 36, 38n39, 40n54, 40n60, 40n61, 40n62, 70, 75, 76, 109, 110, 121, 125n28, 154, 184, *198*, 200, 201, 205; coined to mean 'civilization' 20, 21, 22, 34, **35**, 109; combined with *police* to mean 'civilization' 20, 21, 23, 34, **35**, 40n59; semantic molecule of universal concept of 'civilization' 16, 17, 18, 21, 22, 23–6, *24*, 62, 95, 96, 97, 105, 108, 109, 110, 121, 122, 197, *198*, 200, 201, 202, 204, 205, 207, 209n12
'civility' and 'police' 18, 21, 23, 34, 96, 154, 184, 197, 205; 'rites' embodies both 'civility' and 'police' 98–100; *wén* 96–9, 101, 106, 108, 109, 176, 205, 207
'civility/civilization' (*wén* 文) 4, 5, 7n11, 11, 14, 22, 39n40, 53, 56, 62, 63, 64, 73, *75*, 95–123; *Analects* 49, 53, 55–6, 62, 68, 79n28, 82n85, 85n107, 95, 96, 100, 104, 111, 114, 115, 116, 118–19, 122–23, 127n51, 128n68, 155, 163n64, 179, 181, 182, 184; 'civil' versus 'military' contrast of principles of government 97–8, 124n9, 124n11, 124n12; 'civility' in pre-Qín period 63–76; 'as if carved, as if polished' 70–4; coining of *75*, 95–111; compared to Arabic *ḥaḍāra* ('urbanism/ civilization') 205–7; compared to

English *civilization 110, 198*; critics of 111–18; ethical reinterpretation of aesthetic *wén* 63–74; *Hánfēizǐ* 112–14, 116; history of meaning changes 49–88, 95–130, *108*; "Mending Nature" (Shàn xìng 繕性) chapter in the *Zhuāngzǐ* 117–18; *Mencius* 118–21; 'moral refinement' of 'dynasties' and states' 96–7; *Mòzǐ* 114–17; professionalization of the arts of peace and war 97–8; 'progress' 102–6; 'rites' embodies both 'civility' and 'police' 98–100; semantic change from 'beautiful' (*wén*) 'nobleman' (*jūnzǐ*) to 'morally refined'(*wén*) 'noble man'(*jūnzǐ*) 63–74; 'universality' and 'all under Heaven' (*tiānxià*) 100–2; *wén* as acquired cultural capital 70–4; *wén* referring to 'moral refinement' or 'civility' of an individual 68–9; Xià elites in Zhōu realm and 'non-Zhōu others' 106–8
civilization (the English and French word) 1, 10, 11, 34, **35**, 36, 196, 208; archaeological concept of 'civilization' 29–31, **35**, 36, 42n96, 42n97, 43n112, 197, 208n9; *civilizational* in the phrase *civilizational consciousness* 200; coining or lexicalization of the universal concept of 'civilization' 12, 14, 18–26, 40n69, 41n84, 41n91, 41n92, 42n93, 109, 205, 207; compared to Arabic *ḥaḍāra* ('urbanism/civilization') 3, 205–7, 210n29, 210n30, 210n33, 210n35; compared to Modern Chinese *wénmíng* ('civilization') 2, 206–7, 211n39, 211n42; compared to Old Chinese *wén* ('civility/civilization') *110, 198*; critics of the universal concept of 'civilization' 26–8, 34, **35**, 36; ethnographic concept of 'civilization' 27–9, *29*, **35**, 36, 41n88; French word *civilisation* 18, 20, 23, 26, 29, 30, 31, 39n42; in the phrase *Chinese civilization* 31–3, 42n99, 42n103, 43n106, 43n111, 196, 197, 208, 208n4; problems related to using the word *civilization* to study pre-Qín civilizational consciousness 2–5, 6n4, 6n5, 6n6, 6n7, 9, 15–17, 75, 121, 122, 197; racialized concepts of 'civilization' 33, 43n110, 196; universal concept of 'civilization' 23–6, *24*, 36n2, 40n52, 40n62, 110, 111, 197, 201, *202*, 204, **207**, 209n20; *wén*-consciousness 201

Index 217

'civilization' (Modern Chinese *wénmíng* 文明) 2, 206–7, 210n36, 211n39, 211n40, 211n42

civilizational consciousness 1, 3, 5, 9, 10, 12, 16, 18, 20, 22, 25, 26, 28, 31, 34, **35**, 36, 42n96, 50, 58, 62, 73, 74, 76, 95, 96, 102, 106, 109, 112, 121, 122, 135, 136, 139, 141, 143, 155, 157n5, 172, 173, 175, 176, 177, 178, *183*, 184, 185n5, 197, 198, 199, 200, 201, 204, 205, 208n11, 210n24, 210n27, 211n42; *ḥaḍāra*-consciousness 3, 205–7; modern Europe 3, 4, 9, 16, 18, 20, 22, 25, 26, 28, 34, **35**, 36, 135, 175, 176, 200, 210n27; pre-Qín period 1–6, 6n7, 7n9, 12, 16, 31, 36, 50, 58, 62, 73, 74, 76, 95, 96, 102, 106, 109, 112, 121, 122, 135, 136, 139, 141, 143, 155, 157n5, 172, 173, 175, 176, 177, 178, *183*, 184, 185n5, 197, 198, 199, 200, 201, 205, 208n11, 210n24, 210n27, 211n42; *wén*-consciousness 200–207

'civilizationally inferior others' 5, 7n8, 25, 39n44, 136, 137, 139, 140, 141, 150, 154, 155, *156*, 161n40, 163n57, 165n77, 167n93, 172, 173, 176, 177, 182, 183, 184, 185n5, 199; *see also* barbarians (English word and concept); 'barbarians' (Greek word *bárbaroi*), and 'barbarians' (*yí* 夷)

civilized world 6n6, 8, 36n5, 101, 102, 109, 137, 151n40, 181, 182, 202

coining of words *see* lexicalization

collective consciousness 2, 4, 6, 9, 10, 12, 13, 14, 16, 26, 50, 121, 199, 205; definition 10–16

Confucius 6n5, 73, 76, 101, 102, 104, 164n75, 180, 181; *Analects* 49, 55, 59, 68, 69, 79n28, 80n54, 82n75, 85n102, 85n107, 87n126, 95, 96–7, 99, 105, 106, 123n5, 123n7, 129n79, 130n98, 203, 204, 207, 209n15; 'civilizationally inferior others' 135, 202; *wén* 68, 70, 71, 82n77, 85n107, 87n126, 96, 97, 105, 106, 114, 116, 119, 122, 124n21, 130n103, 135, 201, 202–3, 204, 207, **207**

consciousness: definition 13, 37n19; *ḥaḍāra* 3; historically-effected 16, 38n34; self-consciousness of the West 9; *wén* 200, 201, 205; *see also* civilizational consciousness; collective consciousness; cultural consciousness

conventions for talking about different aspects of words *10*, 10–11

craft metaphors 49, 70–74, 75, 86n112, 86n118, 87n124, 87n133, 106, 119, 120, 121, 130n98, 130n106

cultural capital 19, 20, 25, 34, 36, 39n48, 58, 62–9, 70–4, 76, 81n55, 81n77, 189n35, 130n98, 130n106, 205; acquired 19, 20, 34, 36, 70–4, 130n98, 130n106; economy/market of 58, 62–9, 76, 81n55, 81n77, 189n35, 205

cultural consciousness 2, 6n7, 7n8

cultural hegemony 43n112, 157n5

culture 2, 5, 6n6, 15, 16, 29, 30, 39n42, 41n92, 124n22, 172, 199; 210n36

cultured as translation of *wén* 4, 50, 56, 57, 58, 75, 76n4, 79n34, 111, 122, 128n64, 199, 200, 209n13

'customs' (*sú* 俗) 5, 62, 73, 82n85, 115, 125n24, 127n52, 136, 142, 157, 172, 173, 176, 177, 178–9, 180, 181, 182, *183*, 184, 185n5, 189n35, 189n36, 190n47, 191n48, 191n50, 191n57, 192n62, 192n64, 198, 199; absence from pre-Warring States and early Warring States texts 82n85, 178, 189n35; adjectival meaning 'vulgar' 5, 139, 173, 176, 177–83, 184, 185n5, 191n53, 198–9, 200; coining of the word 'customs' (*sú*) 73, 178, *180*, 181, 183, 185n5, 191n48, 190n49; local customs anchored in time and place 102 105, 106, *110*, 115, 126n38, 173, 177, 178, 179, 180, 181, 182; in recently discovered bamboo manuscripts 189n36

Cuvier, Georges 43n110

dé 德 ('charismatic power'; 'moral virtue') 66–7, 69, 76, 85n95, 85n105, 99, 102, 112, 117, 118, 198, 203, 209n17

'decorate' (*shì* 飾) 65, 116

'decorated accouterments' (*wén wù* 文物) 67

'decorated'/'decoration'/'decorative pattern' (*wén* 文) 4, 11, 53, 55, 57, 58, 63, 66, 67, 70, 74, *75*, 77n6, 77n8, 80n42, 86n112, 87n121, 87n133, 88n135, *108*, 114, 115, 116; 119, 128n64, 130n102; 'decorated chariots' (*wénxuān* 文軒) 115; moral decoration (metaphor) 68, 70, 119, 130n108

'decorated body'/'tattooed body' (*wén shēn* 紋身) 53, 57, 58, 79n38, 80n42, 142, 179

de Guignes, Chrétien-Louis-Joseph 24, 32, 43nn101–2

218 Index

'desire(s)' (*yù* 欲) 177, 178, *180*, 181, *183*, 184, 191n51; *Analects*: 'perfected man' (*chéng rén* 成人) does not man (*yù*) 70; same root as the word customs' (*sú*) 181, *183*, 191n48, 191n49, 191n50; written with the graph (俗) 178, 189n34, 189n35, 190n36; *Xúnzǐ*: regulating 191n51

d'Holbach, Baron 39n42

dí 狄 139; 140, *141*, 142, 143, 144, 146, 147, 150, 151, 156; *běi-dí* 北狄 140, 142, 143, 146, 147, 150, 161n36, 162n53; *chì-dí* 赤狄 'the Red *Dí* 159n27; *dí rén* (狄人) 152; see also *yídí* (*yí-dí*) 夷狄

diachronic semantics 12, 37n13, 38n37, 74, 88n135, 204

Di Cosmo, Nicola 6n4, 163n60, 165n75, 165n81, 166n83, 166n84

directional associations of *mán*, *yí*, *róng*, and *dí* 140, *141*, 142, 143, 144–147, 150, 152, 154, 155, *156*, 157, 161n36; see also *dí*; *mán*; *róng*; *yí*

directional compounds 139, 140, 142, 143, 144–5, 146, 147, 148, 150, 159n26, **160**, 161n36, 162n53

"distant reading" 12, 37n14

Dobson, W. A. C. H. 82n85

dōng-yí 東夷 140, 142, 143, 144, 145, 146, 147, 148, 150, 151, **160**, 161n36, 162n47, 162n53, 198

Donlan, Walter 77n13

Duke of Zhōu *see also* Zhōu Gōng 104

Eastern Zhōu period 126n47, 159n21, 176

'elegant/proper, *Xià*-like' (*yǎ* 雅) 5, 106, 103n108, 139, 157, 172, 173, 174, *174*, 176, 177, 179, 180, 181, 182, 183–4, 185n5, 187n26, 188n30, 191n54, 191n59, 199, 200

Elias, Norbert 9, 14–15, 25

Ěryǎ 186n10

ethnographic concept of 'civilization' 26, definition 28–9, 31, 32–3, **35**, 36, 41n88, 41n90, 42n103, 43n110, 43n111, 196, 206, 208n4; lexicalizing the ethnographic concept of 'civilization' 29

ethnonym compounds 139, 140, 147, 150–5, **164**, 164n70, 165n78, 185n6; *Mencius* 162n53; *see also mányí*; *mányí-róngdí*; *róngdí*; and *yídí*

European concept of 'civilization' *see civilization* (the English and French word)

externalist philosophy 119, 121, 122, 129n97

fǎ 法 ('laws/promulgated models') 66, *110*, 122, 123, 128n70, 128n75, 200, 201; versus 'civility'/'civilization' (*wén*) 112–14, 122, 123, 128n75

Falkenhausen, Lothar von 55, 77n6, 79n24, 79n25, 79n27

Fāngyán 方言 186n10

'fear'/'hold in awe' (*wèi* 畏) 66, 125n27

Febvre, Lucien 15, 23, 37n23, 40n55, 41n88, 74, 204, 209n23

'filial piety' (*xiào* 孝) 39n40, 99, 119, 120, 129n79

Foucault, Michel 7n10

'four non-Zhōu others' (*sì yí* 四夷) 82n85, 143–4, 146, 147, 150, 151, 159n26, **160**, 161n40, 161n41, 162n53

Fukuzawa, Yukichi 210n37

Furetière, Antoine: *Dictionnaire Universel* 21, 49

fusion of horizons 15, 16, 18, 36; *see also* horizons

Gadamer, Hans-Georg 15–16, 18, 36; horizon 15, 16, 18, 36, 38n31, 201, 204, 205–6; "historically-effected consciousness" 16, 38n34

Gawlikowski, Krzysztof 77n6

Geeraerts, Dirk 37n13, 88n134

Gerson, Michael 8

Golden Age 108, 127n52, 197, 200, 201; 'ancient period' 127n55, 201; early Zhōu 87n126, 105, 180; King Wén 104, 110; Yellow Emperor 1; Western Zhōu 104

Gōngyáng 公羊 commentary to the *Spring and Autumn Annals* 145, 154, 155, 163n64, 163n66, 164n69, 166n84

'Goodness' (*rén* 仁) 112, 113, 114, 119, 121, 125n31, 148, 180; 'Goodness and duty' (*rén yì* 仁義) 112, 113, 114, 121

Guǎn Zhòng 管仲 82n85, 101, 102

Guǎnzǐ 管子 82n85, 124n9, 142, 161n35, 161n41, 163n65, 163n66

Guizot, François 24, 206, 207; *The History of Civilization in Europe* 23, 40n71, 41n73, 210n37, 211n42

Gǔliáng 穀梁 commentary to the *Spring and Autumn Annals* 82n85, 145, 154, 155, 163n64, 164n69

Guōdiàn 郭店 (manuscripts) 140, 163n66, 188n26, 189n36, 191n53

guó rén 國人 126n47, 138, 159n21
Guóyǔ 國語 163n64, 163n65, 163n66, 165n80, 166n84

ḥaḍāra ('urbanism/civilization') 3, 206, 207, 210n29, 210n30, 210n33, 210n35; -consciousness 3, 205–7
Hàn dynasty 5, 6, 56, 98, 123, 154–55, 184; collapse 6; concept of 'civility/civilization' 184; projection of concepts from the Hàn and post-Hàn periods into the pre-Qín and pre-Warring States periods 56; ideology of empire 5, 123; 'military' vs. civil 'officials' (*guān* 官) 98; study of 'Classics' 123; *yídí* 夷狄 as default term for 'civilizationally inferior others' 154, 155
Hán Fēi 82n75, 112, 128n69
Hánfēizǐ 62, 82n77, 95, 111, 112–14, 116128n75, 131n115; 'civility'/'civilization' (*wén*) versus 'laws' (*fǎ*) 112–14, 116; contemporary problems need contemporary solutions 87n126; critique of *rú* notion of *wén* 112–14, 116, 128n71, 191n57; date of composition 62, 82n76, 82n85, 128n69; 'law'-based state machineries 112, 123, 128n70; professionalization of 'war' 124n9
hegemon see *bà* 霸 ('lord–protector'/'overlord')
Herder, Johann Gottfried 28, 41n91
history-word-by-word approach 1, 3, 4, 9, 10–18, 25, 34, 155, 197, 199, 201, 204, 209n11; comparing concepts across languages and historical contexts 16–18; conventions for talking about different aspects of words *10*; lexicon as historical source 11–16
Homer 49, 172; *Odyssey* 52
Horace: *Ars Poetica* 8
horizons (in Gadamer's philosophical hermeneutics) 15, 16, 18, 36, 38n31, 201, 204, 205–6, **207**, 208
Huá 華 6n2, 107, 128n66, 148, 159n25, 163n57, 165n77, 176, 185n6, 187n24
Huái-yí 淮夷 ('the *Yí* of Huái') 7n8, 137, 139, 145, 155, **160**, 162n46, 189n35, 198
'human nature' (*xìng* 性) 75, 87n133, 96, 100, 106, 117, 118, 119, 120, 121, 122, 129n97, 130n108, 178, 179, 192n64; "Mending Nature" (Shàn xìng 繕性) chapter in the *Zhuāngzǐ* 117–18

Humboldt, W. 23
Huppert, George 21, 39n49, 40n52, 40n56, 40n62, 40n63

Ibn Khaldun 127n56, 206, 207, 210nn33–4, 210n35
internalist philosophy 118, 119, 121, 122, 129n97

Jackendoff, Ray 13
jade carvings 33, 53, 55, 65, 72, 115; *bì* disc *72*; metaphor 54, 70–74, 71, *72*, 75, 86n118, 87n133, 100, 106, 120, 130n110, 130n112
Jì Xùshēng 57, 166n93
Johnson, Samuel 71, 86n118; *Dictionary of the English Language* 23
Jullien, François 208n3
jūnzǐ 君子 (nobleman'/'noble man'/'lord'/'ruler') 4, 53, 54, 61–2, 63–4, 65, 66, 67, 68, 69, 70, 73, 75, 76, 77n16, 82n84, 85n93, 85n95, 86n108, 86n114, 86n117, 87n126, 95, 98, 99, 100, 109, 111, 112, 114, 116, 130n103, 130n108, 181, 191n54, 191n55, 198

kalós ('beautiful') heroes of pre-Classical Greece 51–2, 77n14, 82n80
Karlgren, Bernhard 56, 82n85
Kern, Martin 77n6, 86n121
Khaldun, Ibn 127n56, 206, 207, 210nn33–4, 210n35
Khayutina, Maria 78, 80n41, 80n50
King Wén (Wén Wáng 文王) 50, 51, 52, 66, 74, 75, 76n3, 76n4, 97, 104, 110, 119, 124n10, 130n100, 135, 148, 149, 174, 186n13; 'awe-inspiringly beautiful' 50, 52, 66, 74, 87n126; 'barbarian' 135, 148, 149, **160**, 162n56; Chāng (name of King Wén) 9, 76n4; 'civility/civilization' 97, 98, 110, 122, 124n10, 135; 'Cultured King' or 'Civil King' 50, 75, 76n4, 122, 199;'greatness' 174, 186n13; 'magnificent' 174
Knox, Robert: *Races of Men* 33
Kǒng Yǔ 68, 85n102
Koselleck, Reinhart 81n74, 126n44; *Geschichtliche Grundbegriffe* 15
Kultur (German word and concept) 29, 41n91, 41n92, 42n93, 43n106

Lacouperie, Albert Terrien de 43n110, 43n111, 208n4
Lakoff, George 71, 86n118

220 Index

language-specific concepts of 'civilization' in three different traditions/horizons **207**

Lassen, Christian: *Essai sur le Pali* 28, 41n90

'laws'/'models' (*fǎ* 法) 66, *110*, 122, 123, 128n70, 128n75, 200, 201; versus 'civility'/'civilization' (*wén*) 112–14, 122, 123, 128n75

Legge, James 55–6, 86n121

Le Roy, Loys 20

Lewis, Mark E. 60, 81n65, 127n50, 191n53

lexicalization (coining of words) 14, 15, 16, 17, 18, 26, *29*, 34, **35**, 36, 40n52, 50, 58, 62, 87n133, 109, 173, 181, 198, 201, 204, 210n27; civilizational consciousness in modern Western Europe 4, 9, 18–28, 34, **35**, 127, 196, *198*, 200, *202*, 204, 205, 206, 207; civilizational consciousness in pre-Qín China 2–3, 9, 36, 50, 62, 63, 73, 74, *75*, 76, 82n77, 95–111, *110*, 122, 135, 136, 141, 155, 172, 173, 175, 176, 178, 183, 185n5, 189n35, 197, *198*, 199, 200, *202*, 204, 205, 206, 207; definition 12, lexicon as historical source 11–16, 204, 210n26

lexicon 17, 64, 109, 151, 181, 211n42; definition 11–12; historical source 11–16, 204, 210n26

lǐ 禮 ('rites') 4, 5, 56, 62, 70, 71, 85n99, 98, 101, 102, 103, 106, 107, 110, 111, 113, 115, 116, 119, 120, 121, 124n13, 124n15, 125n24, 125n34, 126n38, 130n108, 136, 147, 148, 157, 173, 176, 177, 178, 179, 180, 181, 182, 183, 184, 185, 191n57, 198, 199, 200, 201, 204; 'rites' embodies both 'civility' and 'police' 98–100; '(universal) rites' vs. '(local) customs' (*sú* 俗) 102, 106, 110, 125n34, 126n38, 136, 157, 173, 176, 177, 178, 180, 181, 182, *183*, 184, 191n57, 199, 200

Lǐjì 98, 139, 142, 151, 155, 161n33, 163n64, 163n66, 163n69, 165n80, 178, 179, 185, 190n41; date of composition 161n33, 190n41; *Róng-dí*, 163n66; *sì-yí* 161n41

'lord–protector'/'overlord' *see bà* 霸 ('lord–protector'/'overlord')

Lǚshì Chūnqiū 82n85, 98, 103, 124n12, 125n34, 140, 159n28, 160 (Table 4.1), 161n41, 163n65, 163n69, 164n70 (Table 4.2), 179, 188n27, 191n53, 192n62

Maisels, C. K. 30, 42n95

mán 蠻 137, 139, 142, 143, 147, 151, 152, *156*, 160 (table 4.1), 164n69; as (part of) specific ethnonym referring to a particular group 137, 139, 145; in directional compounds *see nán-mán* 南蠻; in ethnonym compounds *see mányí* (*mán-yí*); *mányí-róngdí*; non-Zhōu others to the south 142, 143, 144, 147, 150, 151, 152, *156*

Mán-Jīng 137, 139

mányí (*mán-yí*) 66, 82n85, 83, 84n90, 140, 141, 150, 151, 152, 153, 154, 155, 156, 159n30, 163n65, **164**, 166n81, 167n93, 179, 185n6

mányíróngdí (*mányí-róngdí*) 141, 150, 151, 153, 154, 155, 156, **164**, 165n80

material culture 49, 57, 136, 157n5, 163n60, 165n75, 179

Mencius 82n75, 85n102, 85n105, 96, 104, 112, 116, 119, 121, 122, 130n102, 135, 148, 149, 150, 184, 187n26

Mencius 85n85, 85n102, 96, 99, 113, 125n34, 129n80; 'civilizationally inferior non-Zhōu others' (*yí* 夷) 135, 147–50, 182, 184; 'customs' (*sú*) 127n52, 178, 190n47; date of composition 82n85, 130n99; ethnonyms 135, 140, 147–50, 155, **160**, 161n41, 163n53, 163n64, 163n66, **164**, 182; internalist philosophy 119, 121, 122, 129n97, 120n110; King Wén 130n100, 135, 148–50, 162n56; progress 104, 126n49, 127n51, 127n52; *róng*, 148–50; *Róng-dí* 149, 162n53, 163n66, **164**; *sì-yí* 150, 161n41, 162n53; *wén* ('civility/civilization') 118–21, 122, 127n51, 130n100, 130n102, 130n103, *yídí* 155, 163n64

"Mending Nature" (Shàn xìng 繕性) chapter in the *Zhuāngzǐ* 75, 111, 117–18, 122, 123n2, 129n95

Metalanguage 9, 16, 17–18, 39n41, 201, 207, 208; Natural Semantic Metalanguage 16, 38n35

Meyer, Dirk 77n16, 81n74

'military'/'martial[ity]' (*wǔ* 武) 83n85, 98, 124n9, 158n16; 'warrior-like/martial' 54, 55; 'war/military force/military prowess' 98, 112, 123, 124n11, 124n12, 158n16

Mill, John Stuart 196

Millar, John 27

modern European civilizational consciousness 3, 4, 9, 16, 18, 20, 22, 25,

26, 28, 34, **35**, 36, 135, 175, 176, 200, 210n27
Montaigne, Michel de 26, 183
moral edification 55, 68, 70, 71, 86n118, 120, 121, 200, 203, *see also* moral education; self-cultivation
moral education 24, 56, 71, 73, 96, 111, 120, 121; *see also* moral edification; self-cultivation
'morally refined'/'moral refinement' (*wén*) 4, 50, 53, 55–6, 62, 63, 64, 65, 68–9, 70, 71, 74, 76, 87n126, 86n108, 87n126, 95, 98, 99, 101, 102, 112, 116, 124n9, 124n11, 124n21, 174, 177, 181, 191n54, 203; or 'civilized' 96–7, 99, 100, 107, 108, 109, 200; 'conduct' 198; of 'dynasties' and states' 96–7; 'gentleman' 86n117; 'noble man' 111, 198; 'patterns' 100; 'person' 82n84; 'power/virtue' 97; 'tradition of values and institutions' 97; 'virtue' 79n33
Moras, Joachim 40n69
Moretti, Franco 37n14
Mòzǐ 114, 116, 129n78, 129n80, 129n84, 129n88, 144, 182, 183
Mòzǐ 95, 111, 129n80, 129n82, 163n65, 178, 187n26, 210n24; 'all under Heaven' (*tiānxià*) 161n40, 191n59; 'civility/civilization' (*wén*) 114–17, 122, 129n83, 129n88; 'customs' (*sú*) 178, 182, 183; date of composition 114, 129n80; progress 126n49; *sì-yí* ('four non-Zhōu others') 143, 144, 161n40, 161n41, *yí* 夷 ('non-Zhōu people') 182, 183, 191n58

nán-mán 南蠻 142, 143, 146, 147, 149, 150, 151, 161n36, 162n53
Natural Semantic Metalanguage 16, 38n35, *see also* metalanguage
Niceforo, Alfredo 28, *29*, 41n89
'nobleman'/'noble man'/'lord'/'ruler' (*jūnzǐ* 君子) 4, 53, 54, 61–2, 63–4, 65, 66, 67, 68, 69, 70, 73, 75, 76, 77n16, 82n84, 85n93, 85n95, 86n108, 86n114, 86n117, 87n126, 95, 98, 99, 100, 109, 111, 112, 114, 116, 130n103, 130n108, 181, 191n54, 191n55, 198

Obama, Barack 8
OED see *Oxford English Dictionary*
otherness 5, 137, 155, 177, 190n41; ethnography vocabulary of civilizational otherness 172–185, *183*

Oxford English Dictionary (*OED*) 21, 22, 39n43, 40n58, 40n60, 40n61, 40n64, 40n65

'pattern'/'patterns' (*wén* 文) 57, 67, 75, 77n8, 87n133, 88n134, 102, 107, 108, 122, 177, 200; ideal patterns of conventionalized behavior 64, 68, 70, 71, 72, 73, 96, 111, 114; ideal patterns of government institutions 101; institutionalized patterns 99, 100, 101, 116, 119; intercrossing 57; moral refinement/civility 99; *wén* 文 decorative 53, 55, 58, 63, 70, 74, 116
Patterson, Thomas C. 19, 36n2, 39n44, 41n83, 41n84
'people of the field' (*yě rén* 野人) 126n47, 138, 159n21
Persian Wars 39n44, 172
Plato 20, 82n80, 127n54, 208n3
'police' (semantic molecule of the pre-Qín concept 'civilization') 26, 36, 95, 96, 100, 101, 108, 109, 110, 111, 121, 176, 197, 198, 201, 204, 205, 207; 'civil' (*wén*) vs. 'military' (*wǔ* 武) contrast 97–98; pre-Qín concept of 'progress' 103, 105, 106; 'rites' (*lǐ*) embodying both 'civility' and 'police' 98–100, 200, 204; *wén* ('moral refinement) of 'dynasties' and 'states' embodying an element of 'police' 96–97, 174
police (the word and concept in English and French) 18, 19, 20, 21, 22, 23, 25, 26, 27, 28, 32, 34, 40n54, 200 coined in the meaning 'civilization' 21, 22, 23, 25, **35**, 39n43, 40n58, 40n59; combined with *civility* to mean 'civilization' 18, *21*, 22, 32, 34, **35**, 40n55; referring to laws and government institutions 18, 19, 20, 21, 23, 40n57, 41n90, 154, 200, 201; semantic molecule of the Anglophone concept 'civilization' 18, 20, 21, 22, 23, *24*, 25, 26, 27, 28, 32, 34, 36, 184, 197, 198, 201
'police' and 'civility' 18, 21, 23, 34, 154, 184, 197, 205; 'rites' (*lǐ* 禮) embodies both 'civility' and 'police' 98–100; *wén* 96–9, 101, 106, 108, 109, 176, 205, 207
'polite studies' (*wénxué* 文學) ('imitation of the ideal patterns of conventionalized behavior'/'pattern imitation'/'polite studies') 71, 86n118, 86n121, 113–14, 115, 128n75
Poo, Mu-chou 187n23; barbarian 7n8, 138, 157n4; cultural consciousness 2,

222 Index

6n6, 6n7, 7n8; Eastern Zhōu period of consciousness 176; *Enemies of Civilization* 2; foreigners as enemies 158n8; *róng* 138, 158n18, 158n19; Shāng civilization 161n37; *Xiǎnyǔn* 158n17, 158n18; *yi* 159n31
posthumous names/naming 55, 79n24, 85n99
posthumous titles 55, 58, 68, 74, 76n4, 79n27, 85n101, 85n102, 85n103
Powers, Martin Joseph 77n6, 77n8, 84n88
prejudices (in Gadamer's philosophical hermeneutics) 15, 16, 18, 36, 75, 201, 205
pre-Qín civilizational consciousness 1–6, 6n7, 7n9, 12, 16, 31, 36, 50, 58, 62, 73, 74, 76, 95, 96, 102, 106, 109, 112, 121, 122, 135, 136, 139, 141, 143, 155, 157n5, 172, 173, 175, 176, 177, 178, *183*, 184, 185n5, 197, 198, 199, 200, 201, 205, 208n11, 210n24, 210n27, 211n42
'progress'18, 20, 24, 25–6, 31, 32, 102–6, 108, 110, 121, 127n52, 127n54, 190n47, 201, 202, 204, 206, 207, 210n27; 'civility' and 'police' 23; lack of 184
Puett, Michael 79n34
Pulleyblank, Edwin G. 162n56

Qín dynasty 3, 6n2, 60, 187n26, 190n36
Qīnghuá (manuscripts) 140, 163n64, 163n65, 163n66, 167n93, 187n26, 189n36; race 6n4, 32, 33; racialized concept of 'civilization' 33, 43n107, 43n110, 196; yellow race 33, 43n107, 43n110

race 6n4, 32, 33; racialized concept of 'civilization' 33, 43n107, 43n110, 196; yellow race 33, 43n107, 43n110
Renfrew, Colin 30
'retainer-officials'/'men of service' (*shì* 士) 59, 61, 63, 71, 72, 77n10, 81n66, 86n119, 101, 104, 105, 114, 129n75
'rites' (*lǐ* 禮) 4, 5, 56, 62, 70, 71, 85n99, 98, 101, 102, 103, 106, 107, 110, 111, 113, 115, 116, 119, 120, 121, 124n13, 124n15, 125n24, 125n34, 126n38, 130n108, 136, 147, 148, 157, 173, 176, 177, 178, 179, 180, 181, 182, 183, 184, 185, 191n57, 198, 199, 200, 201, 204; 'rites' embodies both 'civility' and 'police' 98–100; '(universal) rites'

vs. '(local) customs' (*sú* 俗) 102, 106, 110, 125n34, 126n38, 136, 157, 173, 176, 177, 178, 180, 181, 182, *183*, 184, 191n57, 199, 200
róng 戎 (particular groups) 49, 125n36, 135, 136, 138, 139, 144, 148 149, 151, 155, 159n22, **160**, 162n56, 163n65, 165n76, 165n78; 'belligerent others' 135, 136–8, 145, 146, 155, 158n19, 159n22, 176, 177; expression for 'non-Zhōu others to the West'; 139, 140, *141*, 142, 143; 144, 144, 147, 148, 150, 151, 152, 155, *156*, 157, 161n36, 165n78, 165n80, 179; 'military, war' 158n15, 158n16
róngdí (*róng-dí*) 戎狄 140, 141, 151, 152, 153, 154, 155, 156, 159n30, **160**, 162n53, 163n66, 163n69, **164**, 165n77, 165n76, 165n77, 166n81, 185n6
róng-mán 150, 151, 164n69
Rousseau, Jean Jacques 23, 27, 41n83, 41n84, 118, 183
rú 儒 ('masters of the rites') 106, 112, 113, 114, 115, 116, 122, 180, 181, 182
Rubin, Vitali 77n16
rú notion of *wén* 87n126, 106, 112–13, 122, 125n35, 127n55, 128n71, 129n83, 176, 180, 181, 182, 183, 191n57

Sapir–Whorf hypothesis 39n40
savage (English word) 20, 21, 25, 26, 154, 166n82, 209n20; noble 26, 41n81
Schaberg, David 77n6, 79n28, 87n127, 128n64, 152, 164n74, 165n80, 192n60
Schlegel, Karl Wilhelm Friedrich: *Philosophy of History* 43n106
Schleiermacher, Friedrich 38n30
self-cultivation 20, 64, 73, 74, 75, 82n83, 86n112, 87n133, 96, 106, 123, 130n112, 148, *see also* moral edification; moral education
September 11 and 'civilization', 2001 36n5
Shāng 30, 59, 104, 157n5; 'civility/civilization' 95, 96; civilization 161n37; 'customs' 189n35; elite 57, 157n5; 'four sides/regions' (*sì fāng*) 143; inscriptions 55, 56, 57, *57*, 58, 74, 77n6, 78n16, 78n17, 79n27, 80n44, 80n51, 83–4, 102, 126n39, 102n47, 137, 140, 145, 158n19, 159n21, **160**, 161n43, 162n46, *164*, 166n93, 167n93, 175, 178, 186n18, 187n19, 187n21, 189n35; *jūnzǐ* 77n16; king 61, 76n3; late 87n133,

174; military 49–50, 76n3; patterns 7n8; people 6n7, 128n61, 161n37; posthumous naming 79n24; rank-based system of promotion 63; ruling lineage 51, 61, 69, 104; 'Shāng center'/'central Shāng' (Zhōng Shāng) 6n7, 61, 141, 143; visual displays of social rank and wealth 50, 115; *wén* 53, 57, 74, 76, 77n8, 87n133, 96; *Xià* 174, 175, 177, 187n19; Zhōu conquest 59, 80n46, 144
shàng 上 ('those above') 125n27, 125n28
Shàngbó 上博 (manuscripts) 140, 163n64, 163n66, 178, 187n26, 189n36
(Shàng)shū (尚)書 *see* (*Book of*) *Documents*
Shāng Yāng 60, 210n24
Shàn xìng 繕性 ("Mending Nature") chapter in the *Zhuāngzǐ* 117–18, 129n92
Shaughnessy, Edward J. 76n3, 76n4, 80n46, 126n46, 126n46, 158n19, 159n25, 162n46, 187n21
Shelach, Gideon 43n113, 211n40; *The Archaeology of Early China* 208n9
shì 士 ('men of service'/'retainer-officials') 59, 61, 63, 71, 72, 77n10, 81n66, 86n119, 101, 104, 105, 114, 129n75
shì 飾 ('decorating') 65, 116
Shǐjì 史記 73n3, 84n85
Shī(jīng) 詩(經) *see* (*Book of*) *Songs*
Shìmíng 釋名 date of composition 53, 181; definition of *sú* 俗 181, 191n50
Shirakawa Shizuka 77n6, 158n18
sì-mán 四蠻 ('four Mán') 144, 161n42
sì yí 四夷 ('four non-Zhōu others') 82n85, 143–4, 146, 147, 150, 151, 159n26, **160**, 161n40, 161n41, 162n53
Slingerland, Edward G. 86n112, 87n124, 121, 129n97
Smith, Adam 25, 39n42, 111, 201, 202–3, 204, 207, 209n15, 209n19, 209n20
sociopolitical changes from Western Zhōu to Warring States period 58–63; economy of cultural capital 62–3; ritualized lineage-based government 59–62
Spring and Autumn period 186n14; *bà* 80n47; city-state model 81n65; elite 136; end 81n61; government 59; *jūnzǐ* 61, 77n16; linguistic usage patterns 82n85; *róng* 137, 159n22; 'Rongdi' 165n77; rulers 59; *Shījīng* 78n18; sociopolitical system 63, 77n16; *tiānxià*

126n39; *wén* 61; *Xià* 174, 175, 176; *Xià–yí* dichotomy 144; *yǎ* 185n5; *Zuǒzhuàn* 82n85, 209n11
Stocking, George W. 39n42, 41n92
Sterckx, Roel 2, 128n62, 130n108
sú 俗 ('customs') 5, 62, 73, 82n85, 115, 125n24, 127n52, 136, 142, 157, 172, 173, 176, 177, 178–9, 180, 181, 182, *183*, 184, 185n5, 189n35, 189n36, 190n47, 191n48, 191n50, 191n57, 192n62, 192n64, 198, 199; absence from pre-Warring States and early Warring States texts 82n85, 178, 189n35; adjectival meaning 'vulgar' 5, 139, 173, 176, 177–83, 184, 185n5, 191n53, 198–9, 200; coining of the word 'customs' (*sú*) 73, 178, *180*, 181, 183, 185n5, 191n48, 191n49; local customs anchored in time and place 102 105, 106, *110*, 115, 126n38, 173, 177, 178, 179, 180, 181, 182; in recently discovered bamboo manuscripts 189n36
'substance' (*zhì* 質) 70, 86n112, 86n114, 88n133, 95, 117, 118, 123n2, 130n98

Tarasov, Pavel 42n97
Taylor, A. E. 82n80
'those above' (*shàng* 上) 125n27, 125n28
'those below' (*xià* 下) 68, 101, 125n27
tiānxià 天下 ('all under Heaven') 4, 7n9, 71, 81n59, 98, 100–2, 104, 109, *110*, 117, 123, 125n24, 125n29, 125n35, 125n36, 126n37, 126n38, 126n39, 126n40, 126n42, 127n52, 129n84, 143, 144, 151, 161n40, 182, 191n59, *198*, 200, 202, 209n22; 'civility'/'civilization' (*wén*) 100–2, 109, 115; *Mòzǐ* 115, 143, 144, 161n40
toponym compounds 137, 138–40, 146, 155
Trigger, Bruce G. 42n95, 210n25
Turgot, Baron 39n42

universal concept of 'civilization' 8–9, 17, 18–27, *24*, 28, 30, 31, 32, 34, 36, 38n39, 39n42, 76, 95, 96, 105, 109, 110, *110*, 122, 135, 197–8, *198*, 204, 206, 207, 210n27, 211n42; semantic molecules of universal concept 23–26
universality 9, 17, 23, *24*, 121, 199; 'all under Heaven' (*tiānxià*) and the molecule of 'universality' 100–2, 109; semantic molecule of European

224 Index

universal concept of 'civilization' 23, 24, 95, 109, *110*, 121, *198*; semantic molecule of Old Chinese universal concept of 'civility/civilization' (*wén*) 100–2, 109, 110, 121, *198*

'urbanism/civilization' (*ḥaḍāra*) 3, 206, 207, 210n29, 210n30, 210n33, 210n35

virtue ethics: *Analects* 64, 75, 95, 96, 99, 112, 115, 116, 122, 123, 181; 'civility/civilization' (*wén*) 64, 69, 75, 95, 96, 99, 112, 115, 116, 122, 123, 181; craft metaphors for self-cultivation 86n118; definition 82n83; 'customs' (*sú*) 181, *Mencius* 96, 99, 112, 122; *Xúnzǐ* 69, 75, 95, 96, 99, 112, 116, 122, 123, 181

Volney, Constantin-François 32, 42n100

Voltaire: *Philosophie de l'Histoire* 21

'vulgar' (*sú* 俗) 5, 139, 173, 176, 177–83, 184, 185n5, 191n53, 198–9, 200

Waley, Arthur 79n36, 164n72

Wang Aihe 61

Wáng Guówéi 79n24

Warlpiri 38n37

Warring States (period) 2, 6n2, 20, *72*, 80n51, 81nn59–60, 81n74, 82n79, 82n85, 103–4, 123n5, 125n30, 126n44, 126n49, 128n70, 146, 158n16, 159nn24–5, 159n28, 159n30, 179, 185n5, 187n26; 'all under Heaven' 100, 109; *Analects* 69, 79n28, 79n33, 104, 178, 201, 204, 209n15, 210n24; bamboo manuscripts 189n36; 'barbarians' 5, 137–8, 149, 153, 165n77, 184; 'belligerent others' 137–8, 176; 'charismatic power' 69, 85n95; 'civility/civilization' 98, 100, 109, 113, 114, 117, 122, 123, 135, 136, 139, 140, 155, 197, 203; civilizational consciousness 6, 26, 121; cultural consciousness 7n8; cultural capital 81n55; *culture* 111; 'customs' 73, 82n85, 178, 189n35, 192n64; *dé* 69, 85n95; *dí* 142–3, 144, 150, 151, 152; elites 141, 172; 'empire' 166n91; *fǎ* 123; 'four non-Zhōu others' 144; *fúfú* 84n88; 'Great ones' 173, 176; *Hánfēizǐ* 82n76, 122; *jūnzǐ* 64, 86n117; 'laws' 123; *lǐ* 98–9; *Lǐjì* 190n41; *mán* 142–3, 144, 150, 151, 152; *mányí* 155, 163n65; *Mencius* 147, 148, 184; *Mòzǐ* 114, 122, 210n24; otherness 5, 7n8, 136, 137–8; political power 53; posthumous names 79n24; 'progress' 102; 'rites' 98–9;

róng 137–8, 139, 142–3, 144, 148, 150, 151, 152, 159n22, 165n77; *róngdí* 155, 163n66; *rú* 181; *Shàngshū* 137, 140, 187n33; "Shao Gao" 126n41; *sì yí* 144; sociopolitical changes from Western Zhōu period to the Warring States period 58–63, 80n45; *sú* 192n62, 198–9; *tiānxià* 100, 102, 109, 126nn39–40; toponym compounds 140; *Wèi Liáozǐ* 124n9; *wén* 4, 50, 52, 53, 54, 58, 63, 70, 73–5, 76, 77n8, 77n10, 78n21, 85n99, 95, 98, 100, 108–9, 111, 113, 114, 116, 117, 122, 123, 135, 136, 139, 155, 183, 197, 203, 210n36; *Xià* 173–5, 176, 183, 185n6, 187n19; *Xúnzǐ* 104, 153, 181, 184, 199, 201; *yí* 142, 150, 151, 152, 153, 161n36; *yídí* 154; *Zuǒzhuàn* 165n77, 178

Weber, Max 19; authority 39n46; bureaucratization 39n45; charismatic authority 39n45, 39n46, 51, 52–3, 77n10; rational–legal or bureaucratic authority 39n46; traditional authority 39n46

wēi 威 ('awe-inspiring') 54, 55, 65, 66, 67, 69, 84–85n92, 124n9

wèi 畏 ('fear'/'held in awe') 66, 125n27

Wèi Liáozǐ 尉繚子 81n62, 124n9; date of composition 124n9

wén 文: aesthetic 52–8; 63–74, 75–6, 86n108, 109; 'decorated'/'decoration'/'decorative pattern' 11, 53, 55, 58, 63, 66, 67, 70, 74, 87n133, 88n134, 108, 114, 116; history of word *108*; 'moral refinement' or 'civility' of an individual 68–9; oracle bone and bronze inscriptions *57*; pre-Warring States texts 55–8, *57*; transition from aesthetical to ethical understanding 63–8; *see also* 'civility'/'civilization'; 'pattern'/'patterns'

wén 文 ('awe-inspiringly beautiful') 4, 49–50, 51–52, 53–5, 56, 57, 58, 61, 63, 64, 65, 66, 67, 68, 69, 74, *75*, 76, 77n14, 80n42, 80n44, 87n126, 87n133, 96, 99, 108, 114, 124n21, 174, 210n36; 'awe-inspiring beauty' as marker of inherited status and rank 52–5; charismatic authority 50–8; compared to 'beautiful' (*kalós*) heroes of pre-Classical Greece 51–2, 77n14, 82n80; semantic change from 'pattern' to 'beautiful' 50–8

wén 文 ('civility/civilization') 4, 5, 7n11, 11, 14, 22, 39n40, 53, 56, 62, 63,

64, 73, *75*, 95–123; *Analects* 49, 53, 55–6, 62, 68, 79n28, 82n85, 85n107, 95, 96, 100, 104, 111, 114, 115, 116, 118–119, 122–23, 127n51, 128n68, 155, 163n64, 179, 181, 182, 184; 'civil' versus 'military' contrast of principles of government 97–8, 124n9, 124n11, 124n12; 'civility' in pre-Qín period 63–76; coining of *75*, 95–111; compared to Arabic *ḥaḍāra* ('urbanism/ civilization') 206, 205–7; compared to English *civilization 110, 198*; critics of 111–18; ethical reinterpretation of aesthetic *wén* 63–74; *Hánfēizǐ* 112–14, 116; history of meaning changes 49–88, 95–130, *108*; "Mending Nature" (Shàn xìng 繕性) chapter in the *Zhuāngzǐ* 117–18; *Mencius* 118–21; 'moral refinement' of 'dynasties' and states' 96–7; *Mòzǐ* 114–17; professionalization of the arts of peace and war 97–8; 'progress' 102–6; 'rites' embodies both 'civility' and 'police' 98–100; semantic change from 'beautiful' (*wén*) 'nobleman' (*jūnzǐ*) to 'morally refined'(*wén*) 'noble man'(*jūnzǐ*) 63–74; 'universality' and 'all under Heaven' (*tiānxià*) 100–2; *wén* as acquired cultural capital 70–4; *wén* referring to 'moral refinement' or 'civility' of an individual 68–9; Xià elites in Zhōu realm vs. 'non-Zhōu others' 106–8

Wén Wáng 文王 ('King Wén') 50, 51, 52, 66, 74, 75, 76n3, 76n4, 97, 104, 110, 119, 124n10, 130n100, 135, 148, 149, 174, 186n13; 'awe-inspiringly beautiful' 50, 52, 66, 74, 87n126; 'barbarian' 135, 148, 149, **160**, 162n56; Chāng (name of King Wén) 9, 76n4; 'civility/ civilization' 97, 98, 110, 122, 124n10, 135; 'Cultured King' or 'Civil King' 50, 75, 76n4, 122, 199;'greatness' 174, 186n13; 'magnificent' 174

wén-consciousness 200–207

wén dé 文德 ('awe-inspiring charismatic power'/ 'fine virtue'/'morally refined virtue') 56, 69, 79n33, 97

Wén of Jìn, Duke 67, 130n103

wénmíng 文明 (Modern Chinese word for 'civilization') 2, 206–7, 210n36, 211n39, 211n40, 211n42

wén shēn 紋身 ('decorated body'/'tattooed body'/'tattoo') 53, 57, 58, 79n38, 80n42, 142, 179

wénxué 文學 ('imitation of the ideal patterns of conventionalized behavior'/'pattern imitation'/'polite studies') 71, 75, 86n118, 86n121, 112, 113–14, 115, 128n74–5

wénzhāng 文章 (emblems and insignia') 65, 78n21, 116; textual composition 77n6

Western Zhōu (period): 7n8, 50–58, 76, 77n6, 81n55, 97, 104, 106, 107, 123, 53, 136, 158n6; authority of ruler 50, 51; 'awe-inspiring beauty' 52, 76; bureaucratization 81n55; cities 159n21; 'customs' 189n35; *Dōng-yí* 145; elite 77n16, 136; founding rulers 104–5; 'four non-Zhōu others'(*sì yí*) 143; Golden Age 104, 105, 106, *110*, 123, 127n55; history 80n46; *jūn* 77n16; lineage-based social hierarchy 58, 59, 63, 76; moral and institutional development 104, 123; non-Zhōu as 'belligerent others' 136–140; posthumous names 79n24; ritual system of offices and ranks 80n51, 97; sociopolitical changes from the Western Zhōu to the Warring States period 58–63, 80n45, 136; visual displays of social rank and wealth 50–1, 56, 68; warfare 60; *wén* 53, 56–7, 76, 77n6, 97, 105, 123; *Xià* 175, 186n19, 187n20; *Xià–yí* dichotomy144

Wierzbicka, Anna 16–17, 38n37, 38n39, 39n40, 39n41, 196, 201; Natural Semantics Metalanguage theory 38n35; overreliance on English 16–18, 208n8

word-by-word approach to intellectual history 1, 3, 4, 9, 10–18, 25, 34, 155, 197, 199, 201, 204, 209n11; comparing concepts across languages and historical contexts 16–18; conventions for talking about different aspects of words *10*; lexicon as historical source 11–16; *see also* history-word-by-word

wǔ 武 ('military'/'martial[ity]') military 83n85, 98, 124n9, 158n16; 'warrior-like/martial' 54, 55; 'war/military force/ military prowess' 98, 112, 123, 124n11, 124n12, 158n16

Xenophanes 127n54

Xià 夏 (dynasty) 173, 174, 175, 177, 186n18, 187n19, 187n21, 187n21, 187n26, 191n59

Xià 夏 ('great, large') 174, 186n9, 186n10

226 Index

Xià 夏 ('Great ones') 5, 6n2, 96, 115, 139, 149, 156, 157, 159n25, 162n57, 172, 182, 184, 185, 187n21, 187n26, 188n30, 191n59, 199, 200; 'all the *Xià* (states)' (*zhū-Xià*) 151, 152, 153, 177, 185n6; 'elegant/proper, *Xià*-like' (*yǎ* 雅); 5, 174, 176, 177, 179–80, 181, 183; *Mencius* 149; rise of 173–7

xià 下 ('those below') 68, 101, 125n27

Xià–yí (夏–夷) dichotomy *110*, 135–6, 144, 157, 175, 177, 183, *198*, *see also* Zhōu–barbarian dichotomy

Xiǎnyǔn 獫狁 7n8, 138, 145, 158n17, 158n18

xìng 性 'human nature' 75, 87n133, 96, 100, 106, 117, 118, 119, 120, 121, 122, 129n97, 130n108, 178, 179, 192n64; "Mending Nature" (Shàn xing 繕性) chapter in the *Zhuāngzǐ* 117–18

xī-róng 西戎 135, 140, 142, 143, 144, 145, 146, 147, 148, 149, 150, **160**, 161n36, 161n44

xī-yí 西夷 (Western barbarian') 135, 146, 147, 148, 149, 150, **160**, 162n53, 162n56

Xúnzǐ 荀子 69, *72*, 76, 82n75, 85n102, 96, 104, 105, 106, 112, 119, 127n55, 129n88, 181

Xúnzi 荀子 62, 64, 82n85, 84n87, 85n102, 140, 161n41, 177, 179, 180, 181, 199, 201, 209n22; 'civility'/'civilization' (*wén*) 95, 96, 99, 100, 101, 103, 112, 113, 114, 115, 116–17, 118, 119, 120, 122–3, 124n13, 126n49, 127n51; craft metaphors 86n112, 119, 120; "Discourse on Heaven" 85n107; externalism 129n97; *jūnzi* 56, 65; *Mán-yí* 154, 163n65; 'morally refined' 68–9, 71, 72, 73, 74, 75, 87n124; 'music' 100, 125n24; 'progress' 104; 'rites' 99, 111, 125n24, 130n108; *Róng-dí*, 154, 163n66; *wén* 65, 86n112, 99, 111, 129n89; *wénxué* 86n121

Xú Zhōngshū: *Dictionary of Oracle Bone Inscriptions* 58

yǎ 雅 ('elegant/proper, *Xià*-like') 5, 106, 103n108, 139, 157, 172, 173, 174, *174*, 176, 177, 179, 180, 181, 182, 183–4, 185n5, 187n26, 188n30, 191n54, 191n59, 199, 200

Yates, Robin D. S. 81n65

Yellow Emperor 1, 117

yě rén 野人 ('people of the field') 126n47, 138, 159n21

yí 夷 ('barbarians') 5, 7n8, 7n9103, 106, 108, 109, 110, 123, 126n38, 135–57, 157n3, 157n4, 158n13, 159n30, 159n31, **160**, 161n40, 162n53, 162n56, 162n57, 163n60, 164n75, 165n80, 166n84, 173, 174, 175, 176, 177, 182, 183, 184, 185, 192n60, 197, 198, 199; 'belligerent others' (*róng*) 136–40, 155, 159n22, 176, 177; Classical Greece 158n20; combinatorial potential of *yí* as default term 144–7; 'civilizationally inferior others' 5, 7n8, 106, 107, 109, 135, 136, 137, 139, 140, 141, 142, 143, 144, 145, 147, 149, 150, 152, 154, 155, *156*, *157*, **160**, 161n40, 163n57, 164n69, 167n93, 172, 173, 176, 177, 179, 181, 182, 183, 184, 185n5, 197, 198, 199; ethnonym compounds 139, 140, 147, 150–5, 162n53, **164**, 164n70, 165n78, 185n6; 'four (civilizationally inferior) non-Zhōu others' (*sì yí*) 82n85, 143–4, 146, 147, 150, 151, 159n26, **160**, 161n40, 161n41, 162n53; Hàn dynasty 166n90; *mányí* (*mán-yí*) 66, 82n85, 84n90, 140, 141, 150, 151, 152, 153, 154, 155, *156*, 159, 163n65, **164**, 164n70, 166n81, 167n93, 179, 185n6; *mányíróngdí* (*mányíróngdí*) 141, 150, 151, 153, 154, 155, *156*, **164**, 164n70, 165n80; *Mencius* 147–50; Poo 7n8, 138, 157n4; post-Hàn 166n90; pre-Warring States vocabulary of identity 136–40; *róngdí* (*róng-dí*) 140, 141, 151, 152, 153, 154, 155, *156*, 159n30, **160**, 162n53, 163n66, 163n69, **164**, 164n70, 165n76, 165n77, 165n81, 185n6; toponym compounds 137, 138–40, 146, 155; *yí* as default term for 'civilizationally inferior non-Zhōu others' or 'barbarians' 141–50; *yídí* (*yí-dí*) 140, 141, 150, 151, 154, 155, *156*, *157*, 159n30, 162n53, 163n60, 163n64, 164n70, 166n83, 166n84, 166n86, 166n90, 176, 177, 184

yídí (*yí-dí*) 夷狄 ('civilizationally inferior others'/'barbarians') 140, 141, 150, 151, 154, 155, 156, 159n30, 162n53, 163n60, 163n64, 164n70, 166n83, 166n84, 166n86, 166n90, 176, 177, 184

Yìjīng 易經 see *(Book of) Changes*

Yì Zhōu shū 逸周書 85n99

Yoffee, Norman 42n96, 43n112

yù 欲 ('desires') 177–83, 177, 178, *180*, 181, *183*, 184, 191n51; *Analects*: 'perfected man' (*chéng rén* 成人) does 'not desire' (*yù* 不欲) 70; in bamboo manuscripts 190n36; same root as the word customs' (*sú*) 181, *183*, 191n48, 191n49, 191n50; written with the graph (俗) 178, 189n35; *Xúnzǐ*, regulating 191n51

zhāng 章 (insignia) 78n21, 116
Zhànguócè 戰國策 163nn65–6
Zhèng Xuán 鄭玄 78n20
zhì 質 ('substance') 118, 130n98
Zhōng guó 中國 ('Central States') 6n2, 60, 101, 103, 106, 115, 123, 126n37, 129n84, 136, 137, 138, 139, 140, 141, 142, 143, 144, 149, 151, 152, 155, 158n7, 161n40, 163n60, 166n84, 178, 179, 182, 183, 188n30, 190n39, 192n62
Zhòu 紂 (last king of the Shāng) 76n3, 104; aka Dì Xīn 49, 76n3
Zhōu–barbarian dichotomy 5, 7n9, 137, 147, 149, 157n4, 172, 174, 177
Zhōu elite 4, 5, 57, 64, 101, 102, 106, 107, 108, 109, 112, 114, 121, 124n23, 125n28, 125n34, 125n35, 126n38, 136, 138, 140, 141, 142, 147, 149, 155, 156, 157n5, 158n7, 172, 173, 178, 179, 181, 182, 183, 184, 185n6, 187n19, 187n21; self-identity 173–7

Zhōu Gōng 周公 ('Duke of Zhōu') 79n34, 85n99, 104, 149
Zhōulǐ 周禮 80n51, 161n41, 163n65, 161n66
Zhuāngzǐ 莊子 95, 111, 117, 129n92, 161n41
zhū-Xià 諸夏 ('all the *Xià* [states]') 151, 152, 153, 177, 185n6
Zuǒzhuàn 左傳 53, 77n16, 140, 155, 159n28, **160**, 161n41, 162n52, 162n57, 164n69, 178, 165n77, 185n6, 185n26, 209n11; 'awe-inspiringly beautiful' 66, 68, 69; 'barbarians 161n40, 162n56; *běi-róng* 144–6, **160**, 162n50, 162n52; 'Central States' (*zhōng guó*) 161n40; 'civilized world' 102, 125nn35–6, 161n40; 'customs' (*sú*) 178; date of composition 82n85, 155, 159n28; 'four non-Zhōu others' 143; *Huá-Yí* 163n57; *jūnzǐ* 64, 69, 78; language 82n85; *mán-yí* 151, 155, 163n65; morally refined 68, 69, 97, 107–8; 'moral virtue' 67; music 124n22; physical appearance 67; ritual ceremonies 59; *Róng-dí*, 151, 163n66, 165n77; *sì-yí* 143, 161nn40–1, 161n41; *sú* ('customs')178; 'those above' (*shàng*) 125nn27–8; 'those below' (*xià*) 125n27; *tiānxià* 102, 125nn35–6, 161n40; *wén* 64, 65, 66, 67–8, 69, 77n6, 107–8, 111, 115, 116, 125n27, 128n64, 128n65; *Xià–yí* 175; *yí* 161n40, 162n57; *zhū-Xià* 185n6